Multimobile Development

Building Applications for the iPhone and Android Platforms

Matthew Baxter-Reynolds

Apress®

Multimobile Development: Building Applications for the iPhone and Android Platforms

Copyright © 2010 by Matthew Baxter-Reynolds

ISBN-13 (pbk): 978-1-4302-3198-1

ISBN-13 (electronic): 978-1-4302-3199-8

Printed and bound in the United States of America (POD)

President and Publisher: Paul Manning
Lead Editor: Jonathan Hassell
Technical Reviewer: Matthew Fitchett
Editorial Board: Clay Andres, Steve Anglin, Mark Beckner, Ewan Buckingham, Gary
    Cornell, Jonathan Gennick, Jonathan Hassell, Michelle Lowman, Matthew Moodie,
    Duncan Parkes, Jeffrey Pepper, Frank Pohlmann, Douglas Pundick, Ben Renow-Clarke,
    Dominic Shakeshaft, Matt Wade, Tom Welsh
Coordinating Editor: Anita Castro
Copy Editor: Mary Ann Fugate
Compositor: Lynn L'Heureux
Indexer: Potomac Indexing, LLC
Artist: April Milne
Cover Designer: Anna Ishchenko

Distributed to the book trade worldwide by Springer Science+Business Media, LLC., 233 Spring Street, 6th Floor, New York, NY 10013. Phone 1-800-SPRINGER, fax (201) 348-4505, e-mail orders-ny@springer-sbm.com, or visit www.springeronline.com.

For information on translations, please e-mail rights@apress.com, or visit www.apress.com.

Apress and friends of ED books may be purchased in bulk for academic, corporate, or promotional use. eBook versions and licenses are also available for most titles. For more information, reference our Special Bulk Sales–eBook Licensing web page at www.apress.com/info/bulksales.

Contents at a Glance

Contents

About the Author

Matthew Baxter-Reynolds is an independent software development consultant, trainer, and author based in the UK, specializing in mobile technology solutions. He can be contacted via LinkedIn at www.linkedin.com/in/mbrit.

About the Technical Reviewer

In 2004, Matthew, with experience in VB.Net, joined a small e-commerce team to trial C# within a (then) small DVD and CD–focused e-commerce company.

Play.com went on to become one of Europe's largest e-commerce companies, with Matthew playing a major role as one of a handful of senior software developers. After six and a half enjoyable years, Matthew decided to move on to specialize in mobile technology, which he sees as a significant growth area for software developers and enterprises.

Working alongside Matthew Baxter-Reynolds, Matthew produced prototypes on a variety of technology platforms (Android, iPhone, Windows Phone 7, to name three) for a leading company in the mobile survey software market.

Matthew and his beautiful wife, Sarah, have a young boy, Isaac, and live in the beautiful town of Bury St. Edmunds. He enjoys films, games, music, and eating good food while drinking good beer, and he regularly practices muay thai.

His blog at `www.mattfitchett.com` covers all of the above, along with more mobile technology discussion.

Acknowledgments

With much thanks and appreciation to my wife, Andy, for the patience and support she has shown during writing and development of this book, Matt Fitchett for his excellent suggestions and review work, and Jonathan Hassell, Anita Castro, and the others at the Apress team for their sterling work in turning this book into reality.

CHAPTER 1

■ ■ ■

Introduction

For me, this book has become all about change. In the time that I have been watching the mobile computing marketplace and developing software solutions for it, there has never been a time when there has been a more rapid series of shifts and changes. A good friend of mine tells me that this is because of market consolidation. As of the time of writing (August 2010), we're looking at the time when the people who will be leaders in this space for the next 20 years jostle for position. There is a ton of money out there being spent, which is fantastic news for the typical reader of this book. Position yourself correctly and you could earn a seriously good living out of it all. .

To illustrate this point about change, I proposed this book to Apress in February 2010, and in just half a year between then and August 2010, here are just some of the changes that have happened. In a normal year, in a normal market, just a few of these things would be big news.

- Microsoft was still developing and building Windows Mobile 6.5. Windows Phone 7 had not been announced. No one really knew what sort of impact Windows Phone 7 will have.

- The iPad had not been announced, let alone sold over three million units (to date). (For me, this is perhaps the biggest change of all—the world will never be the same now that this class of device has been introduced.)

- The Pre was included in the original proposal. HP has now bought Pre, but the platform is now more or less obsolete.

- Just today, a research firm (Canalys) announced that Android's market share has grown 886 percent year-on-year.

- Canalys has also recently announced that 50 percent of BlackBerry users are looking to defect to iOS or Android.

- The image of Flash hadn't been damaged by Apple's insistence that it had no place on their platform.

- iPhone 4 had not been announced or released, and "Antennagate" had not happened.

- You couldn't multitask on an iPhone.

- iOS was still a trademark owned by Cisco.

- Gartner had not come out and likened Symbian to "re-arranging the deck chairs on the Titanic" in the face of the Android threat.

- The industry is starting to describe iPad-class devices as "slates" as opposed to "tablets."

- Even today, BlackBerry still hasn't given any formal details of version 6 of its platform, plus the BlackPad has been given as the name of its new slate only in the past few days. (Personally, I'm very excited about RIM's slate—it could be a real "game changer.")

- Steve Ballmer hadn't said that Apple had "sold more iPads than he would have liked and that "Microsoft-powered tablets are 'job one' urgency."

- We didn't know that Google could remote uninstall applications from any Android phone using a "kill switch."

- The UAE had not turned off BlackBerry Enterprise Services within the country.

- Motorola was looking very sick indeed, but is now looking much healthier thanks to the Droid and Droid X.

- MeeGo had not been announced (and as of the time of writing is not substantial enough to include in this book). My prediction, for what it's worth, is that this will get traction in spaces like automotive as opposed to slate or phone factors.

- Microsoft announced, launched, and killed a device called "Kin." To give you some idea of how much money is being thrown around, Microsoft attributes US $240 million of written-off monies to Kin. That's not small change.

In fact, this book has been difficult to write because of the velocity of all of this change. I'll be forever grateful to the team at Apress for managing to corral it into the place where, I hope, it's helpful and relevant to you, in spite of this almost constant upheaval in the market.

What's the Purpose of This Book?

In 2001, I set up a web site called .NET 247 (www.dotnet247.com/) that at the time achieved some success in the community that had sprung up around Microsoft's new software development toolset. The premise of the site was to help me as a developer migrate my knowledge from pre-.NET technologies (Win32, MFC, classic ASP, etc.) over to .NET. I found it frustrating that spinning up a thread or opening a file would be a few seconds' work prior to .NET, but in .NET it took hours of research.

With this book, I've looked to do a similar thing—answer the common questions and give you a leg up into understanding the platform so that you can get on and do the clever thing that only you've thought of. The idea of this book is not to go into masses of detail on every little thing; however, if you work through all of the different platforms in this book and its companion, you'll know enough to be proficient on any platform that you turn your hand to.

Specifically, what I've tried to concentrate on is the following:

- Getting to a point where you can compile and run an application on the emulator or device

- Showing how to build a user interface—specifically move between forms, handle events, get data on the screen, and capture input

- Showing how to connect to HTTP-based resources so that you can talk to services in the cloud

- Showing how to store and cache data locally for performance and for offline support

- Showing how to build a simple, but real, application that works end to end

How Is This Book Structured?

This book is split into three sections. There's an introduction section, which takes you through the background of the two applications that we're going to build. There is then a section on Android and another section on iOS. There is also a bonus chapter on using MonoTouch with iOS. (As of the time of writing, MonoDroid for Android had not been released; hence there's no MonoDroid chapter, but it will obviously operate in a similar fashion to MonoTouch.)

In addition, this book has a sister book, which is structured similarly and takes you through building the same application that we're going to build in this book. The book's title—"Multimobile Development: Building native applications for Windows Phone, BlackBerry and generic applications using HTML5"—should tell you what you need to know.

■NOTE The sister book also includes a chapter on Windows Mobile 6.5. Those of you looking to move an application away from Windows Mobile 6.5 to any platform, including iOS and Android, will want to read this. This chapter is available free of charge from the book's web site—see the following.

Each section starts with instructions on how to install the toolset that you are supposed to use with the platform. Some toolsets are very easy to install, while some have gotchas; thus the aim of the toolset installation chapter is mainly to cover the gotchas.

The next three chapters in each section take you through building what's called the "Six Bookmarks" application. This is a very simple application that is designed to show six buttons on the screen, and each button can be configured with a URL that invokes the device's default browser. The purpose of the application is not to be a fantastic piece of UI—it's designed to be a "carrier" to help you understand how to build all of the backend bits and pieces that you need to make an application functional. Figure 1-1 shows an example.

Figure 1-1. *The Six Bookmarks application running on an iPhone*

Each volume contains two chapters that are *essential* to following the work in the book, and I strongly recommend that you read them first.

To reduce the amount of work required to build the application, Six Bookmarks works on the assumption that there is a cloud-based service that holds the user's bookmarks. In order to use the software on a device, the user needs an account on this service. (This model will seem familiar to all readers of this book, I hope.) Chapter 2 discusses the structure of this service and familiarizes you with the service calls that make the application work.

The second important chapter is Chapter 3, which discusses the functional specification of the Six Bookmarks application and the technical architecture. Again, it's important that you read this in order to understand what it is that you are trying to build.

Where Can You Get Help and Support?

This book has a companion web site, located at www.multimobiledevelopment.com/, which hosts important resources that will support you in getting the most out of this book. Specifically, you will find the following:

- Downloads of all of the code for all of the platforms

- The Six Bookmarks cloud service implementation that you need to use to make the applications work

- A hosted version of the Six Bookmark HTML application (discussed in detail in Volume 2)

- Support forums (I'll be monitoring and contributing to these, so if you have a question or a problem, this is the best place to try.)

Finally, going back to my earlier point about the amount of flux in the market at the moment, I'll be updating the Web site to keep it up-to-date with changes in the toolsets and other movements within the industry.

Conclusion

Thanks for purchasing this book. Remember that if you do need help or support, then please visit the web site's discussion forums; but if you would like to contact me personally, you can find me at www.linkedin.com/in/mbrit/.

Matthew Baxter-Reynolds, August 2010

CHAPTER 2

■ ■ ■

The Six Bookmarks Server Service

We're going to talk more about the architecture and specification of the Six Bookmarks application in Chapter 3. In this chapter, we're going to look at the Six Bookmarks service. To support this book, I have set up a server with REST-based (aka "RESTful") services that allow the application to log on, retrieve bookmarks over the OData protocol, and post updates back, again using the OData protocol. (We'll talk more about OData later on.)

As discussed previously, Six Bookmarks is a commercial product provided in two ways—once as a commercial product and once as an open-source product. In this book, we're going to be accessing a service based on the open-source version of the code. Both applications communicate with a publically accessible server. The open-source server operates a sandbox, and in order to complete the work in this book, you'll need your own account.

■**NOTE** It's currently very popular to talk about the "cloud" and storing things "in the cloud." The Six Bookmarks server service is one of these "cloud" services—I've provided a server hosted on the public Internet that allows you to store bookmarks "in the cloud" and retrieve bookmarks "from the cloud."

We will not be covering how to build this service in the book; however, the source code for the service be downloaded from the source repository at http://code.multimobiledevelopment.com/. This code and all of the other code downloads are distributed under the Mozilla Public License 1.1. More information on this can be found here: www.mozilla.org/MPL/MPL-1.1-annotated.html.

Creating an API Account

To create an API account, visit the services web site at http://services.multimobiledevelopment. com/. You will find a link on that page entitled **Register a new API account**. Click this to access a standard registration form as shown in Figure 2-1:

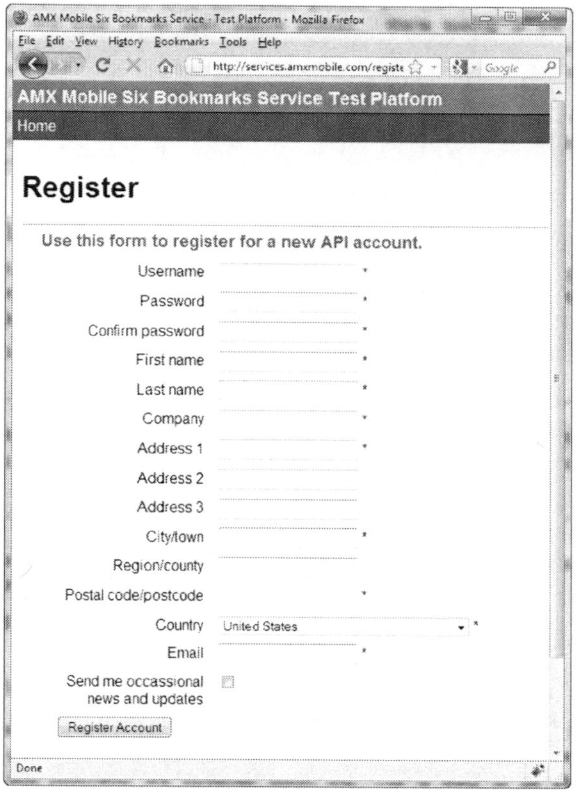

Figure 2-1. *The service registration form*

■**NOTE** The site at http://services.multimobiledevelopment.com is a live work-in-progress. Some of the screenshots presented here may differ from the current reality of the site as you see it today. Also, the site you are using is not secured when accessed over HTTPS, as this is a test site not intended for production use. Were you to build a similar thing for production applications, it would be essential that you secure the site using HTTPS.

Go ahead and create your account. Please provide a valid email address, as you will need this should you need to reset your password in the future. (You will not get spammed.)

Registering your account will automatically log you on.

Creating a User

The purpose of registering for an account is to partition off a private section of the database for you to keep your own data in. A single SQL Server database exists on the server, and everyone's users and bookmarks are contained within this. This is likely to be slightly different for your own applications. For this book, we need to provide you with a sandbox service that makes it easier for you to work with the chapters on the actual application creation on the devices; however, in production applications, you typically do not need this. I have to hive off individual readers' data into separate "virtual databases" to prevent corruption of data and weird behavior, and with potentially tens of thousands of you out there doing this, it's impractical to create physically separate databases.

Under the covers, you're going to be working with three tables: **ApiKeys**, **Users**, and **Bookmarks**. This entity-relationship diagram (ERD) shown in Figure 2-2 illustrates:

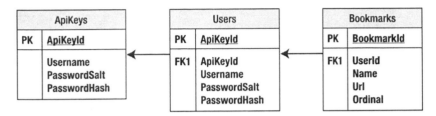

Figure 2-2. *ERD showing relationship between the ApiKeys, Users and Bookmarks tables*

When you register for an API account, you do not get any users created for you. A user in this context relates to someone who would use an instance of the mobile Six Bookmarks applications. To create a user, click on the **Manage Users** link. You will be presented with a message that indicates no users are available as per Figure 2-3.

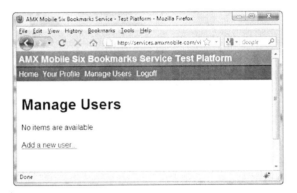

Figure 2-3. *The "Manage Users" page showing no available users*

Click on the **Add a new user** link to enter a new user. Figure 2-4 illustrates.

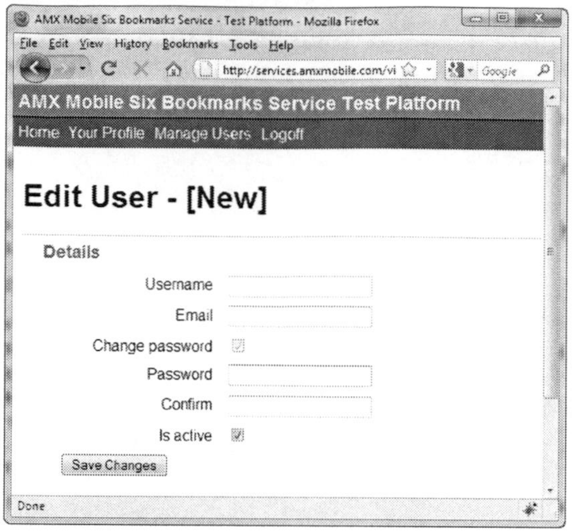

Figure 2-4. *The "Edit User" page*

You'll need to create at least one user in order to proceed to the next section.

The Users Service

The "users" service is a RESTful web service that provides a capability to log on a user. (This book deals only with logging users on; however, the service is capable of other functions, including registering users.)

It's important to familiarize yourself with how the service works, as it will aid in understanding the flow of the applications that we will build in later sections.

RESTful Web Services

A "RESTful" web service is a service that is based on the principle of REST, which stands for "Representational State Transfer." It is not a formal, standardized protocol, but rather a set of principles or constraints that describes the shape and operational usage of a service that you can get data from or provide data to. It is a very natural way of working with remote services, which is why they are so popular and prevalent. That naturalness translates into being very easy to build, and equally very easy to consume.

One common and straightforward way of structuring a RESTful web service is to request data using an HTTP GET request and retrieving results back as XML. The HTTP request can be a GET request, including parameters specified in the query string. Alternatively, the parameters can be made via a POST request that works by passing up XML.

Let's continue this by looking in more detail at the logon operation on the Users service.

Testing the Calls

The API relies on sending up custom HTTP headers, and as such we can't test it using a regular web browser. Rather than asking you to build some custom code to call the service, you can download a test harness for trying the service. You can download this from the source repository at http://code.multimobiledevelopment.com/. Look for a file in the **Downloads** section of the form Amx.Services-<Version>-TestClient.zip. This is a .NET application.

If you download the utility and run it, you'll see you have an area to enter a URL and an area to enter two values: API username header and Token header. We'll talk about these values later, but essentially they provide additional information to the service to help guide the response.

Examining Logon Operations

The first thing we can try and do with our Users service is log on a user. Ultimately, a successful logon will return a token that we can use in subsequent requests.

If you open the test harness, the URL will be given as follows:

```
http://services.multimobiledevelopment.com/services/apirest.aspx?operation=↵
logon&password=APIPASSWORD
```

Click the **Send Request** button and you'll see a result like Figure 2-5.

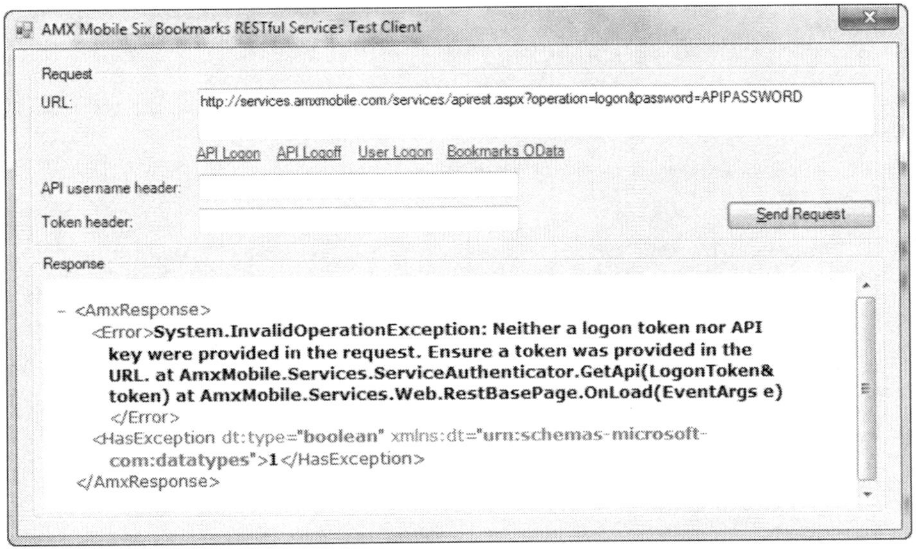

Figure 2-5. *An example of a failed request to the API service*

You can see in the response that an error has been returned.

The protocol for the REST services exposed by the service is that exceptions are returned back in the Error element, and the HasException element is set to true if an error has been returned. (The value shown in the XML is 1, but the datatypes schema is used to indicate that this is a Boolean value.)

■**NOTE** This error notification and transmission is just how I have designed the service—it doesn't follow that all RESTful web services will use this approach. It's down to the owner of the service to design a protocol that is sensible and logical to use within the loose construct of what a RESTful service typically looks like.

Referring back to Figure 2-5, the error indicates that "Neither a logon token nor API key were provided in this request." What this is telling us is that the headers have not been provided to the server.

To call the operations on the server, we need a token. In order to get a token, we need to call the server, so we have a chicken and egg situation! However, one operation on the server does not need a token—this is the Logon operation on the API service, which is used solely to obtain a token for use with the other methods.

Obtaining a Token

By default, when you start the harness, it will be set to connect to the API service and to call the Logon method. First, into the API username header text box, enter the username of the account you created in the first part of the chapter. Second, modify the password value in the URL to be the username on your account.

If you click Send Request now and the details are correct, you'll see something similar to the image shown in Figure 2-6.

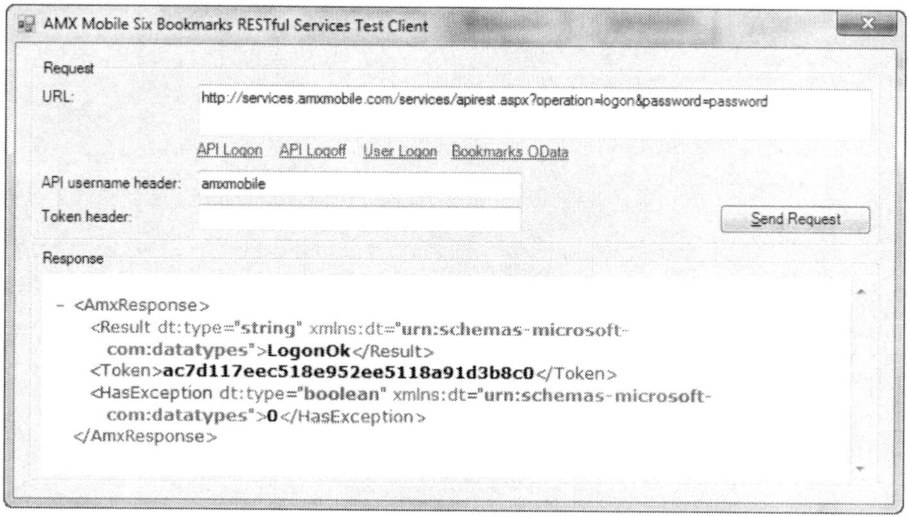

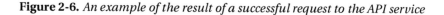

Figure 2-6. *An example of the result of a successful request to the API service*

You'll see in this case an error has not been returned. The Result element will be set to LogonOk or InvalidPassword. (Any other errors will result in an exception being returned.)

The most important element here is the Token value. This is the token that we'll use in all other requests. Copy the token into the clipboard, and then paste it into the Token header field. We'll use this later.

Logging On the User

Now that we have obtained a token to use and authenticated the API, we can actually log on the user. We've used the API service so far—we're now going to use the Users service.

If you click the User Logon link on the test harness, the URL will be rewritten to the following:

```
http://services.multimobiledevelopment.com/services/usersrest.aspx?operation=↵
logon&username=USERNAME&password=PASSWORD
```

This URL is configured to call the Users REST service. If you replace the USERNAME and PASSWORD placeholders in that string, and assuming you have copied the token into the Token header field, and click **Send Request**, you'll get a response like Figure 2-7, which, apart from the URL, looks identical to Figure 2-6.

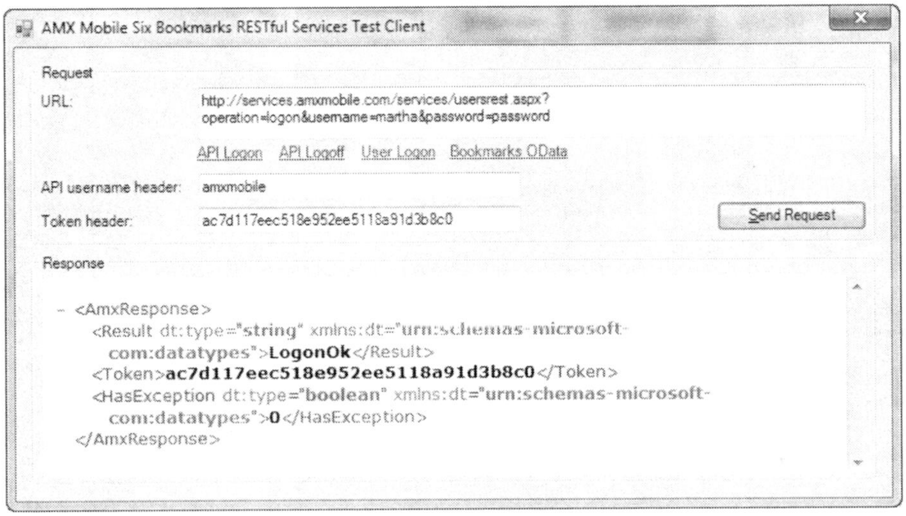

Figure 2-7. *An example of a response from a successful request to the Users service*

Assuming this works, you'll see another LogonOk response. What a LogonOk tells you here is that the token is now bound to the user you authenticated. (This is important—this means that you cannot use the same token with different users. This will never be a problem on a mobile device as you are not multiuser, but in a web application, it is worth considering.) Other results you can get back from the service are InvalidUsername, InvalidPassword, or AccountInactive.

Cleaning Up

To clean up the service, we have to log off of the API. This is done via the Logoff operation. Click the **API logoff** link on the harness, and the URL will be rewritten once again. Click the **Send Request** button, and you'll see a response much like in Figure 2-8.

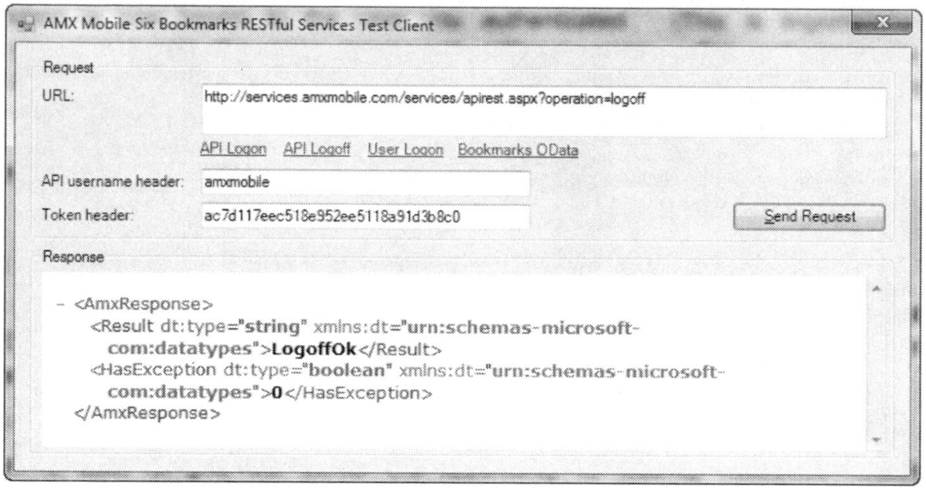

Figure 2-8. *An example of a successul "Logoff" call to the API service*

This operation is used to give the server the opportunity to clean up resources related to the token. (Specifically, it deletes a row in the database.) We'll look at token cleanup in more detail when we build the native device applications.

The Bookmarks Service

The final service exposed from the server is the Bookmarks OData service. OData is an up-and-coming data format that is currently being pitched as the proposed *de facto* standard for data interchange in a Web 2.0 world. My opinion is that it is a decent standard with a good, practical working method, and hence I've chosen to use it in this book to bridge the gap between relational data stored in the cloud and data stored on the device.

■**TIP** You can find out more about OData at the official site: `http://www.odata.org/`.

Adding Some Test Data

In order to see how the OData service works, you're going to need some test data. There's an interface on the service that lets you maintain the bookmarks against a user.

Log on to `services.multimobiledevelopment.com` and find a user that you want to work with. Click on the **Manage this user's bookmarks** link at the bottom of the page. You will see an interface that allows you to define bookmarks. Figure 2-9 illustrates.

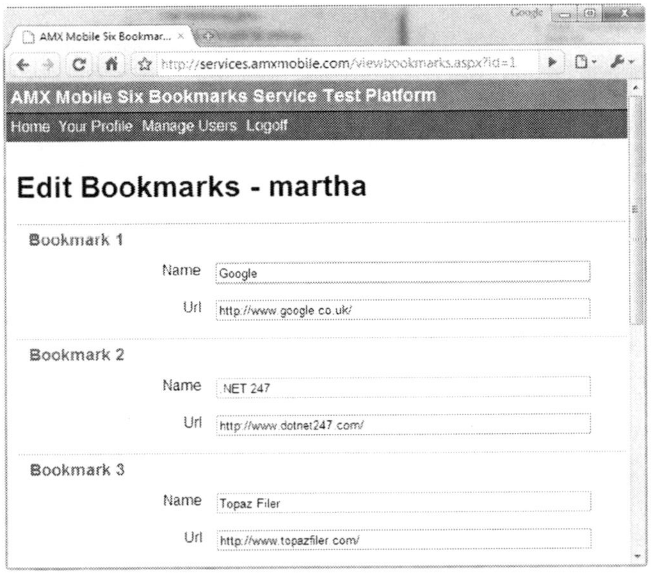

Figure 2-9. *The "Edit Bookmarks" screen showing three bookmarks*

Add a number of bookmarks and click **Save Changes**.

Working with OData

Now that we have some bookmark data, we can look at using the Bookmarks service. We're going to be using the test harness again, and you will need a token—so if you do not currently have a token, go through the steps described previously to obtain one.

On the harness, if you click the **Bookmarks OData** link, you'll get a rewritten URL, like this one:

```
http://services.multimobiledevelopment.com/services/bookmarks.svc/
```

Click **Send Request** and you'll get a response like Figure 2-10. You should note that the test harness continues to send up the special headers. The service call would be rejected should these headers be missing or incorrect.

■NOTE The OData standard allows for data to be returned either in Atom or JSON format. Atom format is the most relevant here—JSON is typically used when working with Ajax calls from a web page. The actual format of the data is not important—what is important is that OData is built on open standards. (Notably, Microsoft sees OData as a core data protocol going forward, starting with a full implementation in .NET 3.5 SP1 and support on the Azure platform.)

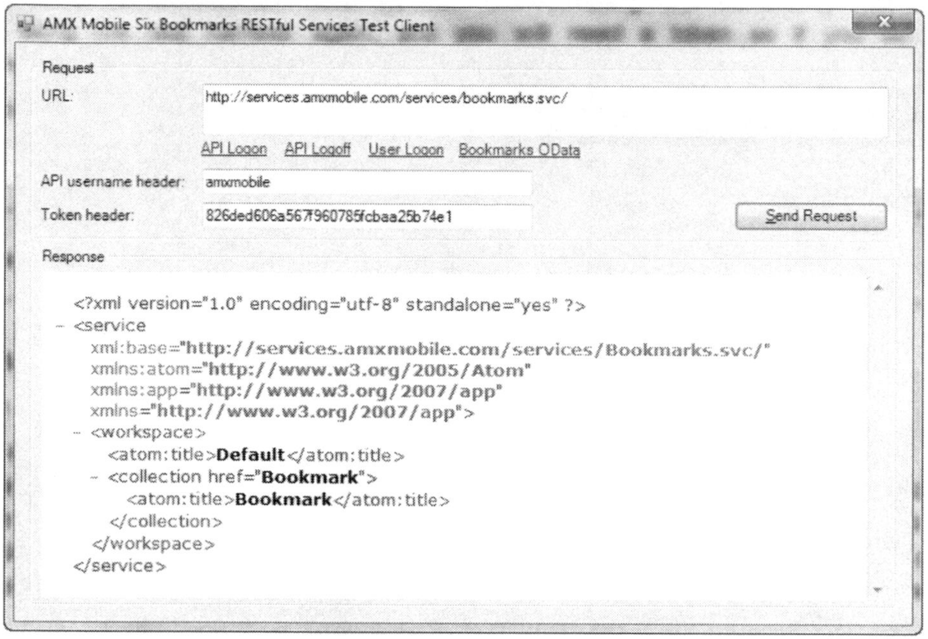

Figure 2-10. *An example of a successful call to the Bookmarks OData service*

The preceding output is telling us that the Bookmarks service is about to return data of type
Bookmark (look for the //collection/atom:title element in the XML). Thus, if we issue this URL, again
using the test harness, we'll get back some bookmarks. Here's the URL:

```
http://services. multimobiledevelopment.com/services/ bookmarks.svc/Bookmark
```

From this point, I'm going to show you the XML output as a listing, rather than screenshots. This
will make it easier to follow the discussion.

In the following example, three bookmarks are returned from this call, and these are shown in the
following listing. (Your output will vary depending on the bookmarks you've set up against the user that
you've logged in as, obviously.) Here's the listing:

```
<?xml version="1.0" encoding="iso-8859-1" standalone="yes"?>
<feed xml:base="http://services. multimobiledevelopment.com/services/Bookmarks.svc/"↵
 xmlns:d="http://schemas.microsoft.com/ado/2007/08/dataservices"↵
 xmlns:m="http://schemas.microsoft.com/ado/2007/08/dataservices/metadata"↵
 xmlns="http://www.w3.org/2005/Atom">
  <title type="text">Bookmark</title>
  <id>http://services. multimobiledevelopment.com/services/bookmarks.svc/Bookmark</id>
  <updated>2010-04-18T10:54:32Z</updated>
  <link rel="self" title="Bookmark" href="Bookmark" />
```

```xml
<entry>
    <id>http://services. multimobiledevelopment.com/services/Bookmarks.svc/Bookmark(1002)</id>
    <title type="text"></title>
    <updated>2010-04-18T10:54:32Z</updated>
    <author>
      <name />
    </author>
    <link rel="edit" title="Bookmark" href="Bookmark(1002)" />
    <category term="AmxMobile.Services.Bookmark" scheme="http://schemas.microsoft.com/↵
ado/2007/08/dataservices/scheme" />
    <content type="application/xml">
      <m:properties>
        <d:BookmarkId m:type="Edm.Int32">1002</d:BookmarkId>
        <d:UserId m:type="Edm.Int32">1001</d:UserId>
        <d:Name>.NET 247</d:Name>
        <d:Url>http://www.dotnet247.com/</d:Url>
        <d:Ordinal m:type="Edm.Int32">1</d:Ordinal>
      </m:properties>
    </content>
  </entry>
  <entry>
    <id>http://services. multimobiledevelopment.com/services/Bookmarks.svc/Bookmark(1001)</id>
    <title type="text"></title>
    <updated>2010-04-18T10:54:32Z</updated>
    <author>
      <name />
    </author>
    <link rel="edit" title="Bookmark" href="Bookmark(1001)" />
    <category term="AmxMobile.Services.Bookmark" scheme=↵
"http://schemas.microsoft.com/ado/2007/08/dataservices/scheme" />
    <content type="application/xml">
      <m:properties>
        <d:BookmarkId m:type="Edm.Int32">1001</d:BookmarkId>
        <d:UserId m:type="Edm.Int32">1001</d:UserId>
        <d:Name>Google</d:Name>
        <d:Url>http://www.google.co.uk/</d:Url>
        <d:Ordinal m:type="Edm.Int32">0</d:Ordinal>
      </m:properties>
    </content>
  </entry>
```

```
<entry>
  <id>http://services.multimobiledevelopment.com/services/Bookmarks.svc/Bookmark(1003)</id>
  <title type="text"></title>
  <updated>2010-04-18T10:54:32Z</updated>
  <author>
    <name />
  </author>
  <link rel="edit" title="Bookmark" href="Bookmark(1003)" />
  <category term="AmxMobile.Services.Bookmark" scheme=↩
"http://schemas.microsoft.com/ado/2007/08/dataservices/scheme" />
  <content type="application/xml">
    <m:properties>
      <d:BookmarkId m:type="Edm.Int32">1003</d:BookmarkId>
      <d:UserId m:type="Edm.Int32">1001</d:UserId>
      <d:Name>Topaz Filer</d:Name>
      <d:Url>http://www.topazfiler.com/</d:Url>
      <d:Ordinal m:type="Edm.Int32">2</d:Ordinal>
    </m:properties>
  </content>
</entry>
</feed>
```

Thanks to the clarity of the Atom format, it's very easy to understand the format of the data, even though the dataset is an unfamiliar one. Each of the feed/entry elements contains a single data item (which we'll be calling an "entity" throughout to keep in line with nomenclature on the object relational mapping structures that we're going to be using). The m:properties element within them contains the data. (For information, this maps 1:1 to the structure of the table used to store the bookmarks.)

An interesting element here is the ID element against each entry. These provide a URL that can be used to access an individual item. (Although, remember that you need to pass up the special headers in order for the service to return the data.)

Pick the ID of an item in your set of bookmarks and issue a request for it, passing in the token, e.g.:

http://services.multimobiledevelopment.com/services/bookmarks.svc/Bookmark(1003)

This time you will just see that item, as per the following listing:

```
<?xml version="1.0" encoding="iso-8859-1" standalone="yes"?>
<entry xml:base="http://services.multimobiledevelopment.com/services/Bookmarks.svc/"↩
xmlns:d="http://schemas.microsoft.com/ado/2007/08/dataservices"↩
xmlns:m="http://schemas.microsoft.com/ado/2007/08/dataservices/metadata"↩
xmlns="http://www.w3.org/2005/Atom">

  <id>http://services.multimobiledevelopment.com/services/Bookmarks.svc/Bookmark(1003)</id>
  <title type="text"></title>
  <updated>2010-04-18T10:55:13Z</updated>
  <author>
    <name />
  </author>
```

```
<link rel="edit" title="Bookmark" href="Bookmark(1003)" />
<category term="AmxMobile.Services.Bookmark" scheme=↵
"http://schemas.microsoft.com/ado/2007/08/dataservices/scheme" />
<content type="application/xml">
  <m:properties>
    <d:BookmarkId m:type="Edm.Int32">1003</d:BookmarkId>
    <d:UserId m:type="Edm.Int32">1001</d:UserId>
    <d:Name>Topaz Filer</d:Name>
    <d:Url>http://www.topazfiler.com/</d:Url>
    <d:Ordinal m:type="Edm.Int32">2</d:Ordinal>
  </m:properties>
</content>
</entry>
```

OData Queries

The OData standard provides for a number of operations that should be available on providers.

One of these is the $metadata directive. This is a neat way of determining the format of data returned by the service. For example, if you issue the following request, you'll see the structure of the data, as per the following listing.

```
http://services.multimobiledevelopment.com/services/ bookmarks.svc/$metadata
<edmx:Edmx Version="1.0" xmlns:edmx="http://schemas.microsoft.com/ado/2007/06/edmx">
  <edmx:DataServices xmlns:m="http://schemas.microsoft.com/ado/2007/↵
08/dataservices/metadata" m:DataServiceVersion="1.0">
    <Schema Namespace="AmxMobile.Services" xmlns:d=↵
"http://schemas.microsoft.com/ado/2007/08/dataservices" xmlns:m=↵
"http://schemas.microsoft.com/ado/2007/08/dataservices/metadata" xmlns=↵
"http://schemas.microsoft.com/ado/2007/05/edm">
      <EntityType Name="Bookmark">
        <Key>
          <PropertyRef Name="BookmarkId" />
        </Key>
        <Property Name="BookmarkId" Type="Edm.Int32" Nullable="false" />
        <Property Name="UserId" Type="Edm.Int32" Nullable="false" />
        <Property Name="Name" Type="Edm.String" Nullable="true" />
        <Property Name="Url" Type="Edm.String" Nullable="true" />
        <Property Name="Ordinal" Type="Edm.Int32" Nullable="false" />
      </EntityType>
      <EntityContainer Name="BookmarkCollection" m:IsDefaultEntityContainer="true">
        <EntitySet Name="Bookmark" EntityType="AmxMobile.Services.Bookmark" />
      </EntityContainer>
    </Schema>
  </edmx:DataServices>
</edmx:Edmx>
```

Another useful method is the ability to issue queries to constrain the data. For example, if you wanted to return all of the bookmarks where the name was equal to Google, you can issue the following:

```
http://services.multimobiledevelopment.com/services/ bookmarks.svc/↵
Bookmark?$filter=Name eq 'google'
```

■**NOTE** You should note here is where the additional constraints are being added to the query so that the set of bookmarks the service is working with contains only the bookmarks of the logged in user. There's more information on the mechanics of this later.

In this book, we're using this service only to retrieve all of the bookmarks for a user and to send back changes, although feel free to experiment with the ODataError! Hyperlink reference not valid.. The web site at www.odata.org/ contains plenty of information on the protocol and also includes references to sample datasets that are more interesting and more fully featured than the Six Bookmarks service. See www.odata.org/producers for some live OData services.

Issuing Updates over OData

As mentioned previously, we are looking to use OData to update our server-side data; however, this is difficult to demonstrate using a web browser, and therefore we'll cover updating the data in later chapters.

Constraining Data to the Logged-On User

Internally to the service, when a request is received by IIS, ASP.NET, ADO.NET, and the Windows Communication Foundation (WCF) work together to process the request. This ultimately results in a SQL statement being formed and passed to SQL server. Just before this SQL statement is executed, an additional constraint is added so that only bookmarks where the user ID equals the logged-on user are returned. Therefore, if WCF wants to issue the statement `select * from bookmarks`, an additional constraint is added behind the scenes that makes it read `select * from bookmarks where userid=27`, or whatever the user ID happens to be. This is done by using URL rewriting to extract the token from the URL, storing the token in the `HttpContext.Current.Items` collection, and then dereferencing that at the appropriate time and attaching the additional constraint to the SQL query.

You'll see this code if you download the server source code package, but, as I've mentioned before, it would be unusual if your own server needed this functionality.

Conclusion

In this chapter, we've taken our first look at the cloud services that we're going to use to provide data and functionality to our client applications going forward. We have looked at how to call the API and Users RESTful services, and also how to request data over the Bookmarks OData service. In the next section, we'll look at the architecture and specification of the Six Bookmarks application.

■ ■ ■

CHAPTER 3

Application Architecture
and Functional Specification

In this book, we're going to build the same application natively on five mobile phone platforms—Android, iPhone, Windows Phone, Windows Mobile, and BlackBerry. So that we know what we're going to build, we're going to spend the first half of this chapter defining the functional specification of the Six Bookmarks application. In the second half, we're going to have a quick look at the application architecture as a sort of quasi-technical specification.

As mentioned in the introduction, this book covers Android and iOS development. This book's sister book covers Windows Phone, Windows Mobile, BlackBerry, and HTML development. This chapter (which incidentally exists in both books) covers all of the platforms to give you a good overview of each platform regardless of whether you have one book, the other book, or both.

A Word About Slates

The examples used in this book and its sister book are all applications that run on smartphones, such as the iPhone and the crop of Android phones on the market. This is largely due to the time at which this book was proposed and developed—when it was started the iPad had not been announced and there was little industry interest in iPad-class devices, or what I like to call "slates."

At the time of writing (August 2010), there is *considerable* interest in slates. Although iPad is the only one that's really made inroads into the market, everyone is waiting for Android slates to come out, and there are strong rumors that BlackBerry will release the "BlackPad" before the year's end. In fact, it's the potential disruption that RIM could make to the market with the BlackPad that made me want to include the BlackBerry OS at all in this book's sister book.

Although we don't look specifically at building applications for slate-factor devices, what you learn in this book will be valuable. The underlying libraries remain the same—all that you need to do to port an application from, for example, iPhone to iPad is to build a new user interface.

Functional Specification

To illustrate the functional specification, I'm going to use the screenshots from the iOS application. To write this book, I've already written the five native applications, and so I can use these as a basis for the functional specification. Obviously, in the real world, this wouldn't happen, although you may have a prototype to work from.

We'll break the functional specification down into screens, and we'll state what the user will be able to do on each of the screens.

Logging On

The logon screen looks like Figure 3-1.

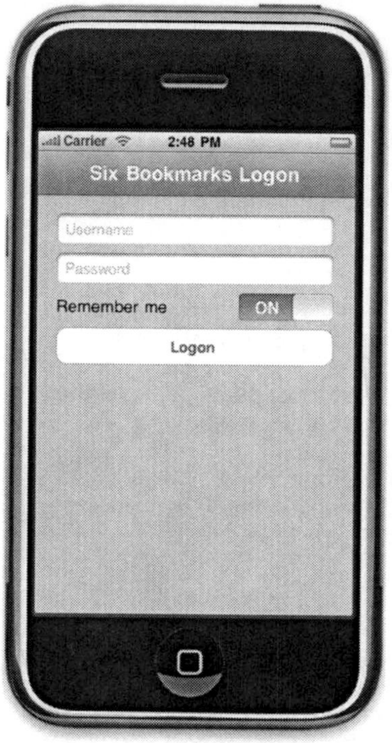

Figure 3-1. *The logon screen*

The required functions are the following:

- The user must be able to key in his or her username and password.

- If logon is successful, the local database is synchronized (see later) and the navigator screen displayed (also see later).

- The user must be able to indicate that his or her credentials should be remembered for next use.

- Where credentials have been remembered, the application should attempt to use these.

Synchronizing

The synchronize operation does not have a user interface. The required functions are the following:

- If no local database exists, a new one must be created.

- If no bookmarks table exists, a new one must be created.

- If the local database contains changes to send to the server, they must be sent to the server.
- Regardless of whether changes were sent to the server, the up-to-date list of bookmarks from the server must be downloaded, the local bookmarks table created, and the local bookmarks table updated from the server set.

Navigator

The navigator screen looks like Figure 3-2.

Figure 3-2. *The navigator screen*

The required functions are the following:

- If a bookmark exists at a given ordinal, the text of the corresponding button must be set to the name of the bookmark.
- If a bookmark does not exist at a given ordinal, the text of the corresponding button must be set to ellipsis ("…").
- If the user presses a configured button, the device's default browser must be invoked to show the URL related to the bookmark/button.
- If the user presses an unconfigured button, the configuration function (see the following) must be invoked.

- The user must have a way of accessing the configuration function directly.

- The user must be able to invoke a logoff function, which will clear the current user, reset any remembered credentials, and return the user to the logon form.

- The user must be able to invoke an "about" function, which will take the user to the www.multimobiledevelopment.com/ site.

Configuring Bookmarks

The configuration screen looks like Figure 3-3.

Figure 3-3. *The configuration screen*

The required functions are the following:

- The user must be presented with a list of the defined bookmarks.

- If the user selects a bookmark, he or she must be taken to the "configure singleton" form (see the following).

- The user must be able to add a bookmark, up to a maximum of six.

- The user must be able to delete existing bookmarks.

Configuring a Single Bookmark ("Configure Singleton")

The singleton configuration screen looks like Figure 3-4.

Figure 3-4. *The "configure singleton" screen*

The required functions are the following:

- The user must be able to change the bookmark's name.

- The user must be able to change the bookmark's URL.

- If the user tried to save a bookmark without entering both a name and a URL, an error must be displayed.

Missing Functionality

The Six Bookmarks applications are intended to be as close to real-world applications as is possible within the limitations of writing a book. There are some things that I have left out, and in each case when I've left something out, it's with the express intention of making the central thrust of the discussion easier to understand. The areas are the following:

- *New user registration.* Users will not be able to register for an account on the device. This would typically be a requirement if you were rolling an application like this out for real.

- *Offline support.* The applications will all run without having to have an active TCP/IP connection; however, code has been omitted to gracefully handle a lack of such a connection. I made this decision primarily to make the code more straightforward.

- *Defensive coding.* The code listings do not demonstrate a level of defensive coding, again to make the central thrust of things clear. (This is particularly true of the iOS chapters.)

Application Architecture and Technical Specification

Now that what we're going to build, let's have a look at how we're going to build it.

The interesting bit of this book is about how you solve the same problem on each of the platforms. Although we're building five applications, since Microsoft has deprecated Windows Mobile, in this section we're going to discuss Android, iOS, Windows Phone, and BlackBerry.

Approach

What I wanted to demonstrate with this book was that there are common things that all of the applications have to be able to do regardless of vendor. Moreover, the application has to assume that the master version of the data is held in the cloud and that each device holds a locally cached copy of the server-side master set. (But, with regards to this last point, a number of device ISVs just don't get this, particularly on iOS, and they think the device holds the master data. This is a fundamentally wrong approach.) We saw in Chapter 2 how we have a cloud-based, always-on service that holds our master data set. What I'm also keen to do as an approach is make this as "real-world" as possible.

Given that, each application has to be able to do the following:

- *Issue an HTTP request to the server to access a proprietary RESTful service.* Although I own/designed the Six Bookmarks service, it is likely that you will need to access cloud-based services that operate on protocols not of user design but based on RESTful principles.

- *Read XML documents.* The RESTful services and OData services return XML, and we need to be able to read it!

- *Read data over the OData protocol.* OData will very probably become the prevalent data transfer mechanism over HTTP. Building our applications on OData a) future-proofs it but b) gives you experience with an alternative and more complex RESTful service protocol.

- *Maintain a local store of its own data.* Ideally this would be as a SQL-compliant relational database management system.

- *Store preference data locally.* The devices each have an API for storing preference data locally, and this should always be used to reduce support problems and prevent problems with being accepted into the vendor's applications store (see the following).

- *Present a user interface using the native device framework.* In the world of mobile software, each user has a phone that he uses, and he wants all of his applications to look and feel the same. You cannot do this with a shared framework; hence each application has to use the native framework directly.

- *Write an XML document.* To push changes over OData, we need to be able to write an XML document.

- *Submit changes over OData.* If we know we can make an HTTP request and build an XML document, we should be able to push changes up.

- *Be acceptable to the vendor's applications store policy.* This varies on a case-by-case basis for each vendor, and we're not specifically going to "disassemble" each vendor's policy in this book. However, by using open standards and using each vendor's recommended tools, frameworks, and standards, the applications should go through into the applications stores without a hitch.

One requirement I have not included is a single stack of source code for each of the platforms. My personal view on this is that it is simply not possible. The recent-to-the-time-this-book-was-written press about Steve Jobs wanting to keep intermediate frameworks (like Java and Flash) off of iOS I think is entirely justified—these platforms and tools are just all too different to create a single thing that does not compromise. The answer will probably end up being HTML5, but that's going to take many years (2015 onwards) to become viable.

Another important principle was that all of this could be done using the standard downloads for the platform—e.g., if you downloaded the iPhone SDK, you did not then have to download another SDK to get some part of the application built. Everything we do will use the standard toolset.

Let's look now at how we solve these problems on each platform.

Object-Relational Mapping

The key architectural premise that I wanted to discuss in this chapter is the way that we're going to store data locally on the device. This will be done using an approach called "object-relational mapping," or ORM. Since I started my career, I have been a huge fan of ORM, and my keenness on it and familiarly with it have obviously informed my decisions with regards to using it in this book.

For your information, I am the maintainer of an open-source project called BootFX (www.bootfx.com/). The project is an application framework for .NET that has been under development since 2002. The ORM design that we're going to use in this book is based on BootFX, although it will be a heavily cut-down version.

Metadata

I want to start by talking about "metadata." In my opinion, the quality of any ORM tool, or any data access layer, (DAL) lives or dies by its metadata. I would go so far as to say it's better to have an ORM implementation with excellent metadata that's quite slow than it is to have an ORM implementation with poor metadata that's quite fast.

The reason for this is that my approach is to optimize the development process and minimize the hassle of maintenance as opposed to build an application that's blazingly fast in production. Most people work on small projects with a small set of users that's easily served by run-of-the-mill hardware, but our community tends to encourage people to design applications that are ultra-high-performance and ultra-scalable. Most of the time, "you ain't gonna need it."

What good quality metadata does for you is that it allows for code that is flexible and adapts to changes within the application. For example, you may have a need to create a database table when an application starts. With good metadata, you can dynamically build the SQL statement to create the table. Thus, if you change that table's structure over time, you can reuse the code that builds the SQL statement to build the new table, all without you having to do too much work.

The metadata system that I'm going to present is modeled on the excellent type metadata system in .NET. In .NET you have a System.Type object that represents—for example—a class in your application. That Type instance can be used to reflect against the methods, properties, events, fields, etc. of that type.

In our projects, we're going to create a class called EntityType, which holds a collection of fields on a table. EntityType will map one-to-one with a database table. (In the more fully-featured BootFX, EntityType holds information on relationships, indexes, constraints, etc.) Thus, EntityType will contain a collection of EntityField instances.

EntityType will extend a class called EntityItem. EntityItem will do something quite important for us—it will hold two names for each item. The reason for this is that oftentimes in ORM you are inheriting someone else's database schema, and you may want to abstract out naming conventions that are hard to work with (for example, TBL_CUST vs. Customer). Thus EntityItem will include a "native name" (via the NativeName property) and a "programmatic name" (via the Name property).

EntityField will also extend EntityItem, but will include extra information about the field—specifically the data type, size, and an indication as to whether it's a key field. Figure 3-5 shows a UML static structure sketch that shows these fields in play.

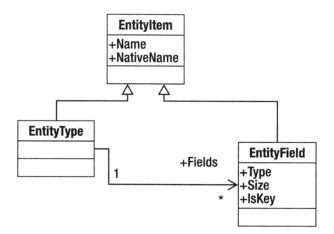

Figure 3-5. *UML static structure sketch of the metadata system*

Again, to reiterate the point, what this structure lets us do is very easily write code that builds dynamic SQL statements. For example, if we want to build a SELECT statement, we know the native name of the table, we know the fields on the table, and we know the name of each field, and from that we can build up our SELECT. (We can also add WHERE clauses to constrain the select, which we'll go into later.)

Now that you have an idea of how the metadata system is put together, let's look at how rows are represented in memory.

Entities

An EntityType is a one-to-one mapping with a database table. An Entity is a representation of a row on the entity. Each strongly-typed entity has fields that map to the columns on the database. This is where the "object-relational mapping" comes in—we have an object, and we're mapping it to a relational database.

For example, we might have a class called Customer that extends Entity. Customer might then have properties CustomerId, FirstName, LastName, and Email that map to the columns on the underlying table.

When an entity is hydrated from a row in the database, the various field-mapped properties will be populated. This allows you to do code like this:

```
foreach(Customer customer in Customer.GetAll())
        Console.WriteLine(customer.Email);
```

Internally within the entity, what happens is that each entity discovers its EntityType instance, looks at the number of fields and creates "slots" within it. So, if you have four fields, you will end up with a "slots" array that is four items in size. The properties then—simplistically—get or set values from the slots.

Thus if you hydrate an object from the database, all you have to do is create an entity instance to receive the data, allow it to create the slots and then read the column values from the database and store it in the appropriate slot.

Likewise, if you want to create an entity to store in the database, you can instantiate one in the normal way, use the properties to set the slot values and then ask the entity to save itself. This issue of "asking the entity to save itself" is something that we'll cover shortly.

Figure 3-6 shows a UML static structure sketch of the entity and our example Customer class.

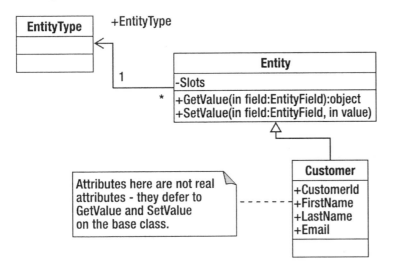

Figure 3-6. *UML static structure sketch of the* Entity *class*

Generating Entities

This sort of system makes sense only if you use a code generator to create the classes, otherwise it is a real pain keeping the entities up-to-date. Although BootFX comes with a fully-fledged code generator for just this purpose, the examples in this book do not include one, and we'll roll the entities by hand.

■**NOTE** That said, keep an eye out on the web site, as I may well end up writing an entity code generator compatible with the work in this book for Android or iOS, or perhaps an intrepid reader will.

SQL Statements

So we've discussed in theory how we can manage database records in memory, but we haven't mentioned anything about how we instruct the server to that effect.

The approach used in BootFX is to use a class called a SqlStatement. The purpose of the SqlStatement is to wrap up a command string and a collection of parameters.

A common "mistake" when building data access layers is to create methods that require the statement to be passed in as parameters, for example:

```
void Database.ExecuteNonQuery(string commandString, object[] params);
```

The problem with this approach is that it's very brittle. It's much better to wrap up the definition of a statement in a separate class because a) it makes the interface to your DAL more straightforward, but b) it allows you to issue instructions to the database that are not quite fully formed.

Let me explain that last point. If you create an interface called ISqlStatementSource and add a method to this called GetSqlStatement and make your DAL accept the interface, for example:

```
void Database.ExecuteNonQuery(ISqlStatementSource sql);
```

...it gives you more leeway about what you can pass in. One example of what you could pass in is a SqlFilter instance.

The purpose of a SqlFilter is to allow you to dynamically build a SELECT statement on the principle that you create a filter that will select everything from the table that it's mapped to, but allows you to constrain the results. For example, a filter created without constraints would return all customers. A filter with a constraint with last name starting with "C" would, obviously, return just those people whose name begins with "C."

If we make SqlFilter implement ISqlStatementSource, we can pass it directly into the DAL and let it de-reference a full statement just before it needs to run it. This makes it very easy to build the filter class, creates a DAL with a very clean and simple interface, and also allows the DAL to be extended with other types of queries going forward (for example, a full-text query).

Figure 3-7 shows a UML static structure sketch of the classes that we just discussed.

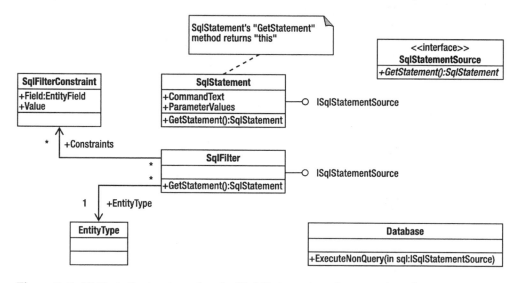

Figure 3-7. *UML static structure sketch of* SqlStatement *and companion classes*

Change Processors

The final part of our ORM tool relates to saving changes back into the database this is done through the EntityChangeProcessor.

There will be some deeper logic in our entity implementation that relates to keeping track of the internal state of the entity and the slots in order to understand what the state of the entity is. For example, an entity that's been loaded from the database without a field property being set remains in a state of "unchanged." If you set a property, it will become "modified." You may want to call a method that sets it to "deleted." Finally, you may create a new entity, in which case it needs to be flagged as "new."

Depending on the state, the ORM subsystem has to issue an INSERT ("new"), UPDATE ("modified"), or DELETE ("deleted") statement, or indeed do nothing if none of those states are active. Again, thanks to the metadata, this is easy—the ORM subsystem knows the fields that make up the entity, it knows the value in each slot, and it also knows the state. The metadata also mentions which field is the key field, and thus the UPDATE and DELETE statements can include WHERE clauses to touch just the relevant row.

That brings us to the end of our discussion on ORM. We can now look at the other major architecture component—server communication.

Server Communication

■**NOTE** This section assumes a familiarity with the discussion in Chapter 2.

In Chapter 2, I discussed how we were going to use a proprietary REST web service for some of the calls and OData for the rest of the calls. I did this primarily because I wanted to create a semi-real-world example of how you would deal with communicating with a server that you did not own.

Readers who have used SOAP web services on the Microsoft stack before will be familiar with how easy it is to code against. If you haven't, what happens is that Visual Studio creates a proxy class that looks like the service you are trying to call. Thus if you have a method exposed by a SOAP web service called HelloWorld that takes a string and returns a string, you can access it like this:

```
HelloWorldWs ws = new HelloWorldWs();
string result = ws.HelloWorld("Bob");
Console.WriteLine(result);
```

The huge "win" with this approach is that it's dead easy. The huge "loss," and why it hasn't really caught on, is that SOAP puts a ton of magic in the way that makes cross-platform communication too difficult. Over the ten or so years since SOAP was released, it's been overtaken by web services that are constructed in a "here's an XML document, can I have an XML document back?" way, with the XML going each way (we hope) as easily as possible.

What I've wanted to do with the architecture of the way we deal with these services is try to get to a point where we get some of the wins of SOAP, but still have a really easy web service in the background. Thus, when we want to call the "logon" method on the API service, we'll create an ApiService class and call the Logon method. Packaging up the request and error handling will all be dealt with by base classes.

Specifically, we'll build ServiceProxy, RestServiceProxy, and ODataServiceProxy base classes. RestServiceProxy will specialize calls to the RESTful services. ODataServiceProxy will specialize calls to the OData service. ApiService, UsersService, and BookmarksService will all provide specific implementations. Figure 3-8 illustrates.

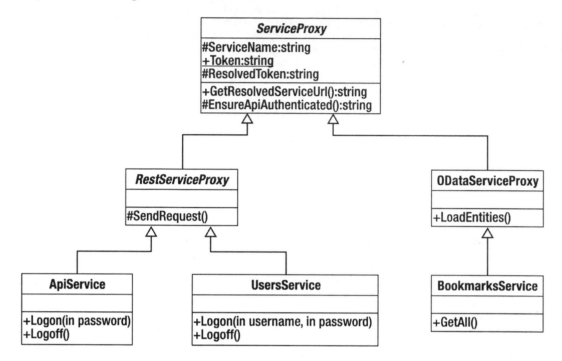

Figure 3-8. *UML static sketch of the service proxy hierarchy*

I'm not going to go into too much more detail here on this—when we build the code in the specific Android and iOS implementations, there's plenty more detail. The important fact from this chapter to take away is that we want to make calling the services as easy and as natural as possible.

Technical Approach Broken Down by Platform

In this section, we'll look at each of the major things that we wish to achieve and state the technology that we're going to use in each case.

With regards to the HTML application, in this book's sister book, where we go through this (remember you can download the code from http://code.multimobiledevelopment.com/ regardless of whether you own the book), we build an ASP.NET-based web site. Therefore the details in this section related to HTML discuss the .NET classes that you need to use. You can, of course, build mobile web applications using any platform.

Core Toolset

Table 3.1 documents the code toolset used for each platform.

Table 3-1. *Toolsets by platform.*

Platform	Approach
Android	Eclipse, available on Mac, Windows, or Linux with the "Android ADT" plugin providing extra functionality within Eclipse (http://developer.android.com/sdk/eclipse-adt.html)
iOS	Xcode, available only on Mac
Windows Phone	Visual Studio 2010, available only on Windows
Windows Mobile	Visual Studio 2008, available only on Windows
BlackBerry	Eclipse, available on Mac, Windows, or Linux with the "BlackBerry Java Plug-in for Eclipse" providing extra functionality within Eclipse (http://na.blackberry.com/eng/developers/javaappdev/javaplugin.jsp)
HTML via ASP.NET web site	ASP.NET via Visual Studio (Mono would also suffice, although in this chapter we're using Visual Studio.)

Issue HTTP Requests

This applies to calling the Six Bookmarks proprietary RESTful services, downloading OData data, and pushing changes over OData. Table 3.2 lists the technology in each case.

Table 3-2. *Technologies used for issuing HTTP requests.*

Platform	Approach
Android	Apache HTTP Client library (http://hc.apache.org/httpcomponents-client/) org.apache.http.*
iOS	Cocoa Touch NSConnection class and related types
Windows Phone	System.Net.HttpWebRequest and related classes for ad hoc requests—see the following for OData requests.
Windows Mobile	System.Net.HttpWebRequest and related classes
BlackBerry	javax.microedition.io.Connector class and related classes
HTML via ASP.NET web site	System.Net.HttpWebRequest and related classes

Read XML Document (Including Reading OData Results)

Generally speaking, there are two ways of reading an XML document—loading the entire thing into a document object model (DOM) tree and querying it as an object-hierarchy, or using a parser that is able to start at the top and read through the document, gathering data as it goes. Table 3.3 lists the technology in each case.

Table 3-3. *Technologies used for reading XML documents.*

Platform	Approach
Android	DOM-based approach using standard Java implementation `org.w3c.dom.*`
iOS	Forward-only reader/parser using `NSXMLParser`
Windows Phone	DOM-based approach using `System.X ml.Linq.XDocument` for RESTful services, Visual Studio proxy class for OData
Windows Mobile	DOM-based approach using `System.Xml.XmlDocument`
BlackBerry	DOM-based approach using standard Java implementation `org.w3c.dom.*`
HTML via ASP.NET web site	DOM-based approach using `System.Xml.XmlDocument`

Write an XML Document

Like reading an XML document, you can write an XML document either by creating a DOM tree or by writing elements in turn programmatically. Table 3.4 lists the technology in each case.

Table 3-4. *Technologies used for writing XML documents.*

Platform	Approach
Android	Writer approach using XML Pull library and `org.xmlpull.v1.XmlSerializer`
iOS	Writer approach using **Libxml2** library via native C-style API
Windows Phone	DOM-based approach using `System.X ml.Linq.XDocument` (However, we will not see this in the book, as Windows Phone creates a proxy for talking to OData services that hides this from us.)
Windows Mobile	DOM-based approach using System.Xml.XmlDocument
BlackBerry	Writer approach using XML Pull library and `org.xmlpull.v1.XmlSerializer`
HTML via ASP.NET web site	DOM-based approach using System.Xml.XmlDocument

Maintain a Local Store

SQLite is available on all of the platforms apart from Windows Phone, which gives us a great opportunity for a common implementation. A relational store makes the most sense for this book on the principle that proper, real-world applications would likely need a relational store. Our actual requirements for Six Bookmarks is that we're going to have only one table with a small number of rows in it, and practically, if that were a real-world requirement, storing the bookmarks in an XML file would likely make more sense. Table 3.5 lists the technology in each case.

Table 3-5. *Technologies used for maintaining a local store.*

Platform	Approach
Android	Managed API over SQLite via `android.database.sqlite.SQLiteOpenHelper` and related types
iOS	Direct access to SQLite via native C-style API
Windows Phone	No relational database available—will store XML files on disk
Windows Mobile	Managed API over SQLCE via `System.Data.SqlServerCe.SqlCeConnection` class and related types
BlackBerry	Managed API over SQLite via `net.rim.device.api.database.Database` and related types
HTML via ASP.NET web site	Not needed (However, if server-side storage is needed, a relational database such as SQL Server or MySQL fits the bill.)

■**NOTE** As a short rant, the fact that Windows Phone is coming to market initially without a relational database is shocking, especially as SQL Server Compact has been around for well over a decade. It would be excellent if Microsoft decided to bake SQLite into the platform like the other vendors have done.

Conclusion

In this chapter, we have taken an in-depth look at the application that we intend to build, discussed in some detail the object-relational mapping approach that we're going to take with local data storage, discussed the network communications and approach and gone through on each device how we intend to perform common activities.

■ ■ ■

CHAPTER 4

Android: Installing the Toolset

Now that we have taken an in-depth look at how to build a device-agnostic, web-based application, we can start looking at building native applications for the devices that we'll see in this book. We're going to start with Android, and in this chapter, we'll learn about how to install the toolset.

In this chapter, I won't be calling out the URLs that I used to download the bits I used when writing, as these are likely to change over time. Refer to www.multimobiledevelopment.com/ for up-to-date links.

Why Android First?

Android has the smallest market share, at the time of writing, of the platforms we're looking at in this book; however, my opinion is that it has the most promise going forward, especially with the demise of the old Windows Mobile platform. (My [current] view is that we'll be seeing Android and iPhone as the "Coke and Pepsi" of the mobile computing market for the foreseeable future.) It's also the easiest platform to write for—at least if you ignore Windows Phone 7, which has a slicker toolset but, again, at the time of writing, a market share of zero percent.

Installing the Toolset

In each of these chapters, the first thing we'll look at is the process of installing the toolset and proving that we have everything set up properly by building a simple "Hello, World" application.

Android's toolset is based on Eclipse, the open-source IDE that targets a number of different operating systems and development platforms. I had not used Eclipse before starting Android development, and, I must admit, I am now a big fan of it. It's an excellent example of what the open-source movement is capable of doing.

Anyway, here are the steps to install the toolset.

Installing Java

To run Eclipse and the Android SDK files, you'll need the Java SDK. To find the Java SDK for Windows, Google for "java sdk." The first few hits should take you to a page where you can download the **Java JDK**. The version that I have based the work in this book on is version **6u20**.

Those of you using Mac OS X will probably already have an appropriate version of the Java JDK installed. The easiest way to know for sure is to try installing and running Eclipse as per the instructions that will follow. Check out this link for more information should things not go according to plan: http://developer.apple.com/java/faq/.

Installing Eclipse

You can download Eclipse from www.eclipse.org/. In their **Downloads** section, they offer a number of what they call "packages," which target different user sets. The package (and version) that I've used in this book is the **Eclipse IDE for Java Developers**, which is based on **Eclipse 3.5 SR2**.

The installer for Eclipse is straightforward—go through and use the options that seem the most sensible to you. As this process is straightforward and obvious, I'm not going to present any screenshots or steps in this section.

Installing the Android SDK

The Android SDK can be found by Googling for "android sdk." Seeing as it's in Google's best interest that you can find the SDK, you can be fairly confident the first few hits will be relevant!

This book is based on Android 2.1, which, as of the time of writing, is the current production version, although Android 2.2 has very recently been announced. However, the installer version numbers do not match the Android platform version, mainly because all you are installing at this point is a bootstrapper for downloading the actual SDK. The version I downloaded for this book was version r05.

To continue, find and download the latest SDK download package for your platform of choice.

The installation package will contain a setup.exe file on Windows, and on the Mac, follow the instructions in the SDK Readme.txt file. Run your platform's version, and the installer will attempt to identify the latest updates from their server. It's worth downloading all of the available options rather than picking and choosing those that you feel you may need. Figure 4-1 shows a screenshot of the package installer with no packages selected. In particular, note that the SDK for Android 2.1 and older versions is listed.

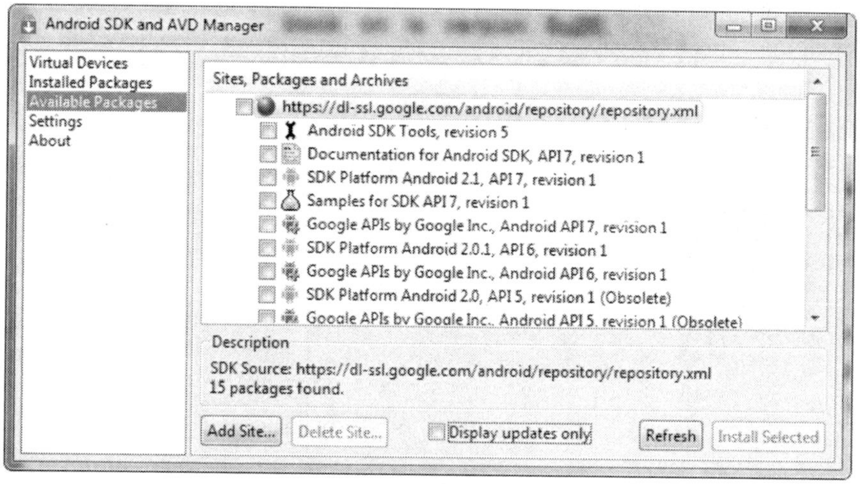

Figure 4-1. *The Android SDK and AVD Manager*

Bug in the "r05" Installer

There is a bug in the Windows version of the r05 installer, whereby it will fail to connect to an HTTPS resource containing the product catalog. You will see Figure 4-2 if you are experiencing this problem.

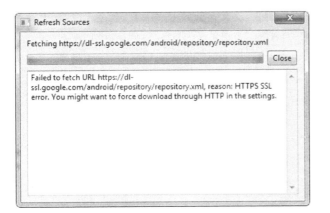

Figure 4-2. *An error that you may see when downloading the SDK repository catalog*

To resolve the problem, all you have to do is go into the **Settings** option and check on the option Force https://... sources to be fetched by http://.... Figure 4-3 illustrates.

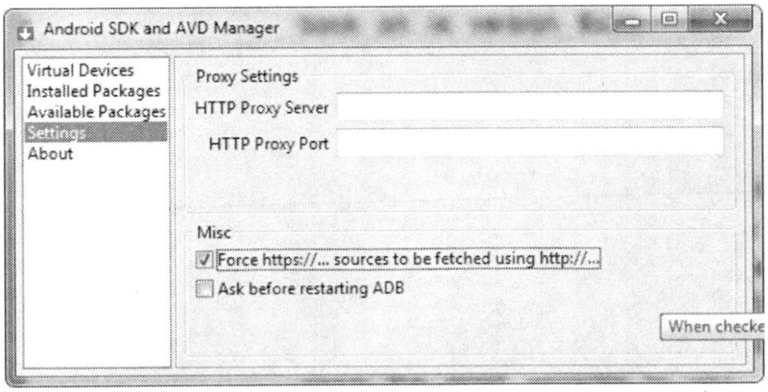

Figure 4-3. *Working around the catalog download problem*

Installing the Android Development Tools (ADT) into Eclipse

At this point you have installed Android and Eclipse; however, the next step involves installing a separate plugin that joins the two together. This is known as the Android Development Tools (ADT). You can find it as a link from the Android downloads page, or you can Google for "android sdk eclipse plugin" or "android adt."

Eclipse plugins are installed directly from within the Eclipse environment; thus to get started, we need to start Eclipse. Whenever Eclipse starts, it will prompt you for a workspace. This is simply a folder on your disk. Figure 4-4 shows an example of such a prompt dialog.

When Eclipse starts, you will see the project start page, which doesn't really have any function. (In fact, when I first ran Eclipse, I spent ages trying to work out what to do with it!) Figure 4-5 shows this screen. You can click the close button on the tab to dismiss the window.

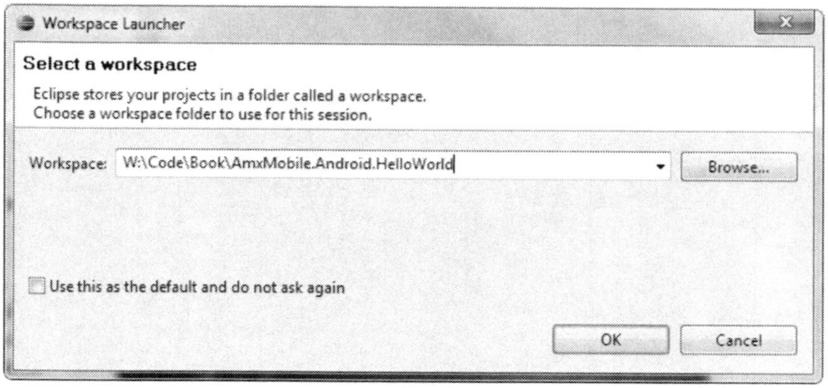

Figure 4-4. *Choosing a workspace in Eclipse*

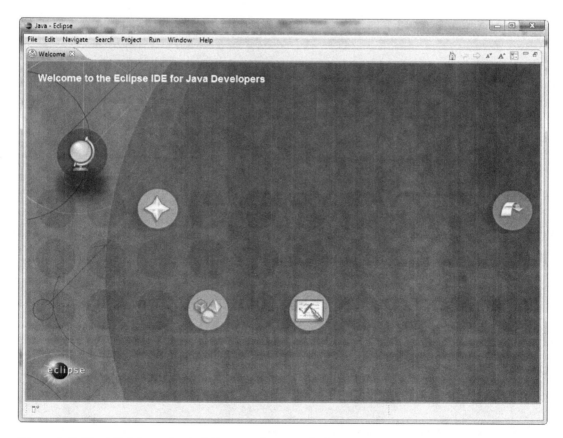

Figure 4-5. *The (slightly useless?) Eclipse workspace splashscreen*

To install the plugin, select **Help – Install New Software** from the menu. You now need to specify the location of the plugin, which is done by adding the ADT download location to Eclipse's list of plugin and update sources. On the dialog that appears when you click **Install New Software**, click the link marked **Available Software Sites**. You will see a dialog like Figure 4-6.

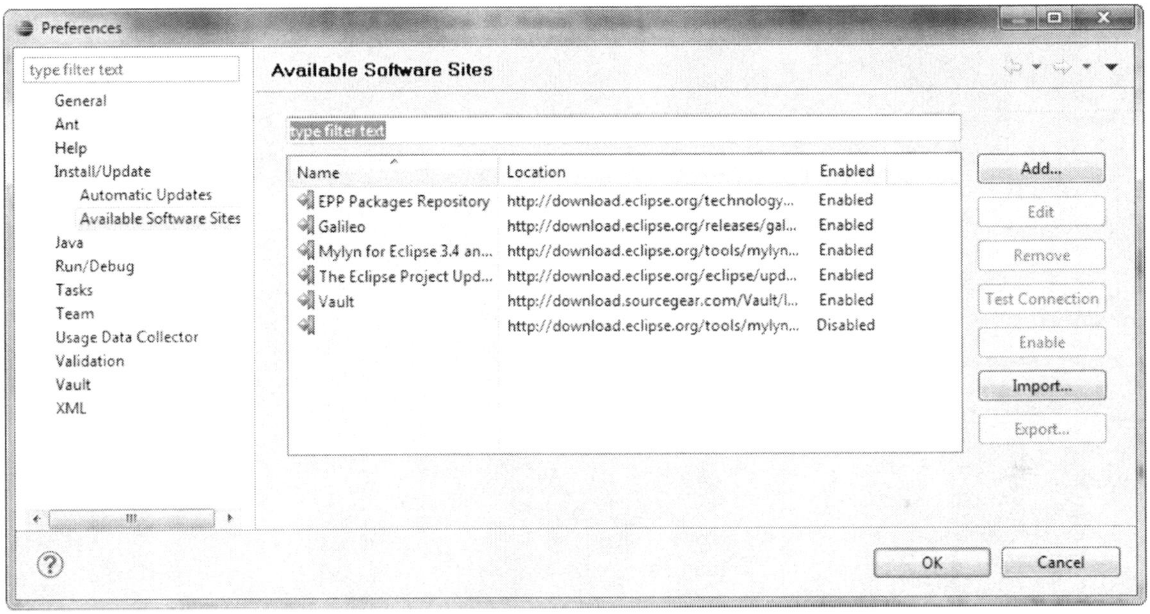

Figure 4-6. *Available software download sites in Eclipse*

Click **Add**, and you will see the dialog prompting you to specify the URL of the download site. You should take the current download site from the Android SDK site, as this is likely to change over time. However, Figure 4-7 shows the site I have used, which is `https://dl-ssl.google.com/android/eclipse/`.

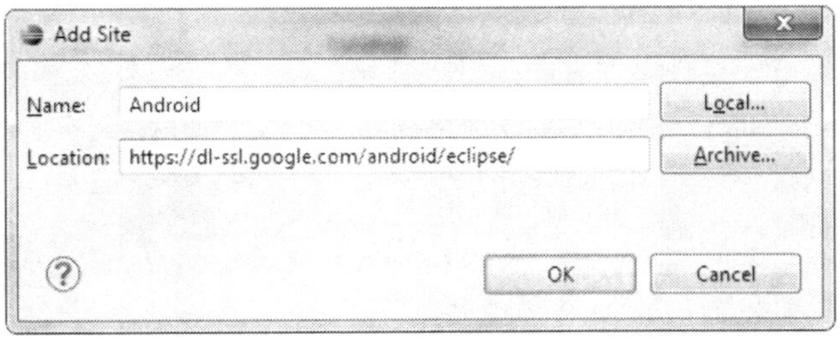

Figure 4-7. *Adding the Android SDK download site*

Click **OK,** and Android will be added to the list of sites. Click **OK** again to dismiss the **Available Software Sites** dialog.

Back in the **Available Software** dialog, select the **Android** upload location in the **Work with** list. Eclipse will download the update catalog and present new items to install. It's probably best to select everything that it offers you here, although, as you can see from Figure 4-8, I was offered **Android DDMS** and **Android Development Tools**.

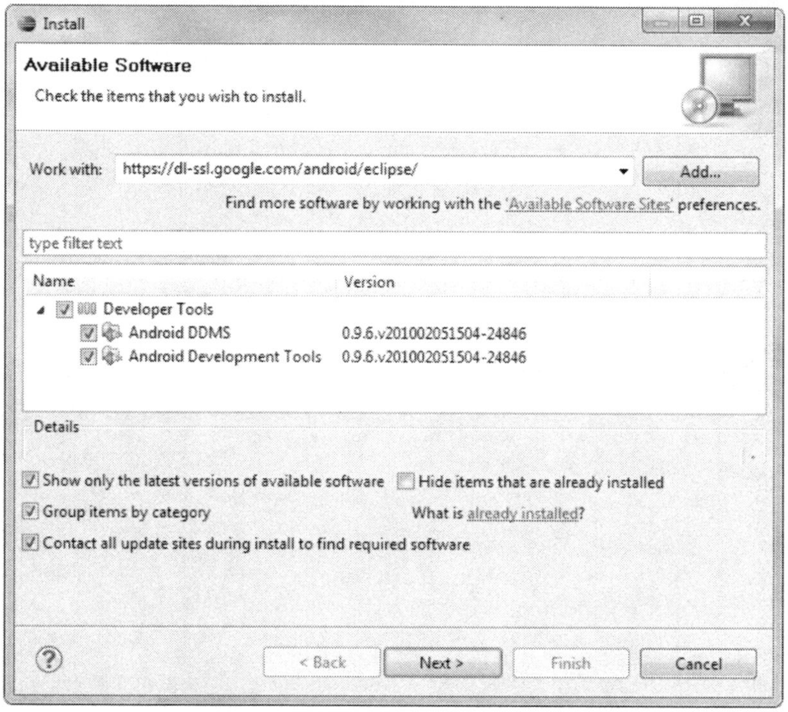

Figure 4-8. *Choosing the Android ADT components*

Click **Next** and continue through the Wizard to install the items.

■**NOTE** From personal experience of this, installation of both the Android and a selection of other Eclipse plugins into the version I used on this book takes far longer than you would imagine (particularly the "Calculating requirements and dependencies" step) and can be flaky. You may need to persevere—the steps in this book have been checked and double-checked, and if you follow them, you should have no problems.

Configuring the Emulator

Once you have downloaded and installed the SDK, it's worth starting the emulator up manually just so that you can experience the satisfaction of it working! We'll go through how to do this now.

■**NOTE** In this book I'm going to refer to software that runs a virtual version of the phone software as "emulators." Some vendors refer to them as "simulators"—thus whenever I refer to "emulator" in this book, read "emulator or simulator."

The installer bootstrapper that you have used thus far to install the packages also contains the Android Virtual Device Manager, which is the tool that you use to create and boot new emulator images. Figure 4-9 shows this tool as on its first install.

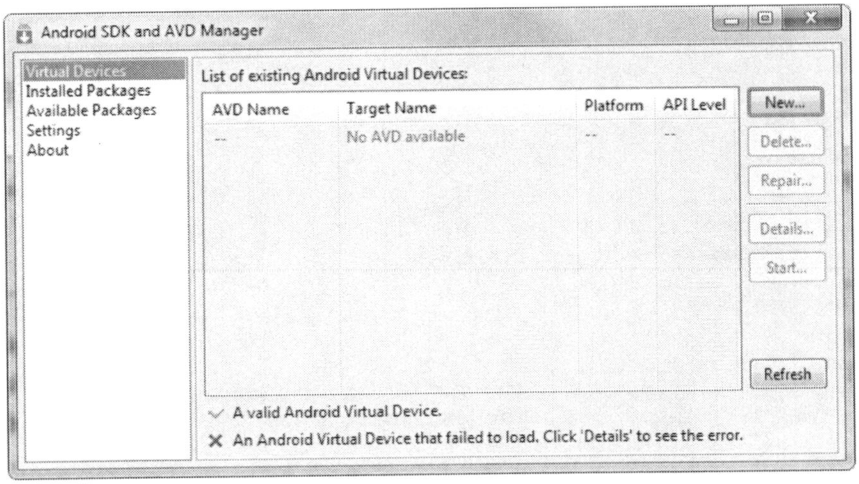

Figure 4-9. *The virtual device manager with no available devices*

To create a new Android Virtual Device (hereafter "AVD"), click the New button. The default options will generally suffice here, although you do need to provide the following information:

- For the name, you can specify anything you like, although whitespace and symbols are not allowed.

- For the target, choose the Android version that you feel is best—although note that for this chapter we have been using 2.1.

- For the size of the SD card, you need to specify something. In this book, we're not going to be using the SD card; however, I have specified 32MiB.

Figure 4-10 shows the settings that I have used.

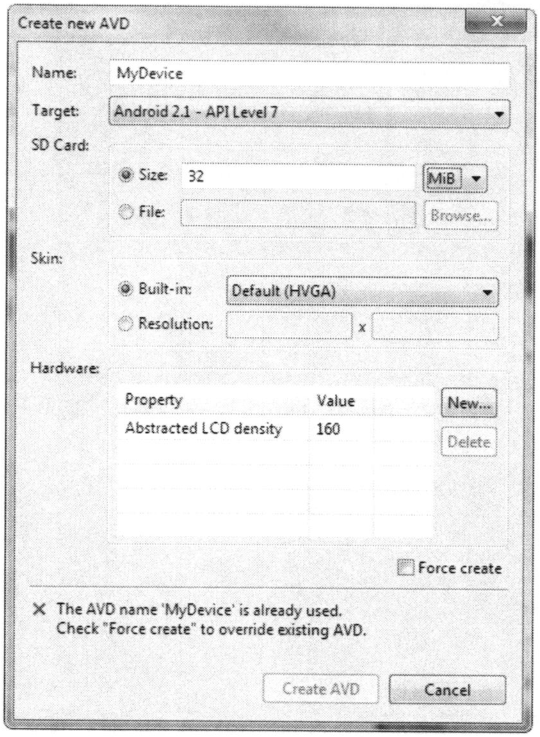

Figure 4-10. *Providing settings for a new AVD*

Click **Create AVD** to create the virtual device.

The device creation will complete in a few sections. Select the AVD and click the **Start** button. You'll see the **Launch** screen as per Figure 4-11. Click the Launch button, and you will see Figure 4-12.

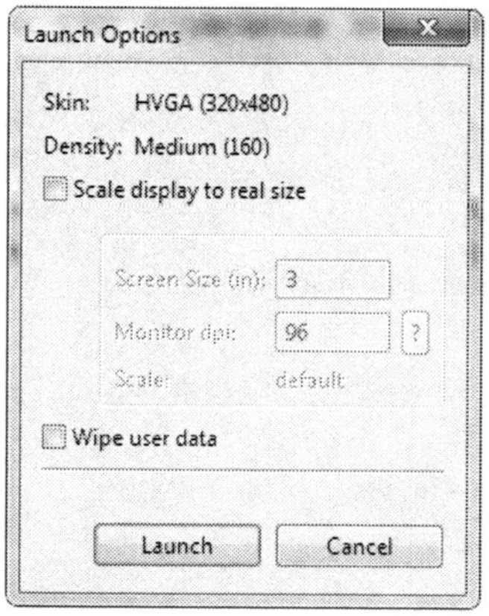

Figure 4-11. *AVD launch options*

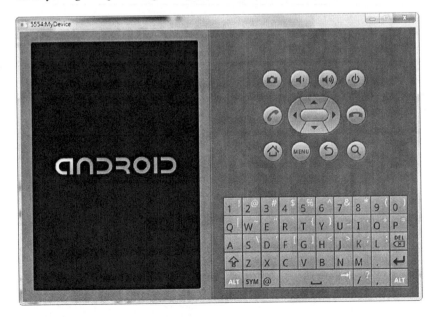

Figure 4-12. *The emulator boot screen*

The screen that appears when the emulator is booting can take a *long* time (as in several minutes) to do anything. Keep waiting, and you will see the regular Android booting screen, as per Figure 4-13.

Figure 4-13. *The emulator further through its bootstrap process*

Eventually, the emulator will start, and you can use it just like you would a regular phone. The emulator will be able to use your desktop machine's networking stack for TCP/IP traffic; thus if you start the browser, you can navigate to web resources just as if you were using a regular device's data service. Figure 4-14 shows the iWebKit-based browser application that we build in the sister book to this one. You can access this Web application at http://app.multimobiledevelopment.com/.

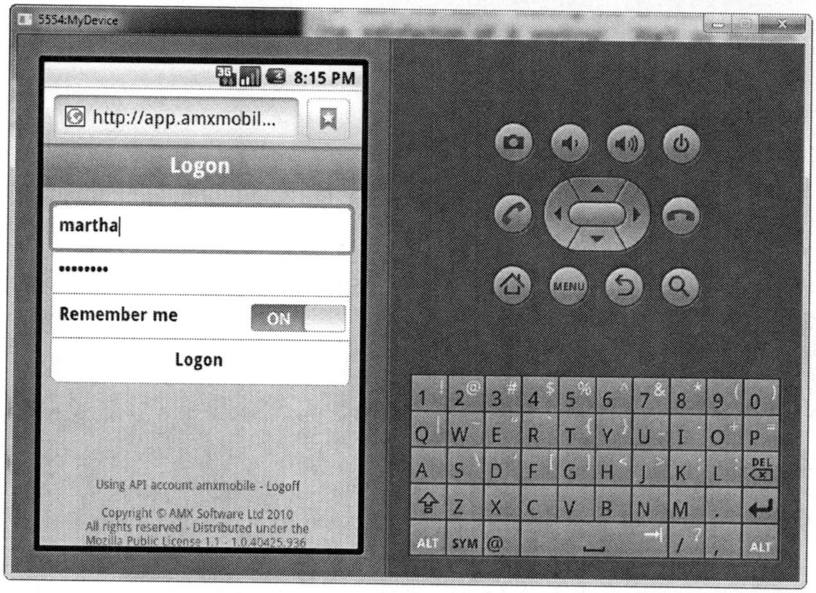

Figure 4-14. *Accessing a Web site through Android's WebKit-based browser*

■**TIP** As implied, the emulator is very slow to boot; however, when developing, you can keep the emulator running, and the Android SDK toolset will push new builds onto the running device. Thus you need to start the emulator only once per development session.

Now that we know the emulator works, we can write a short test application so that we know the toolset has been properly installed in Eclipse and that we have a fully-working test environment.

Creating Our Android "Hello, World" Application

To confirm that we know our way around the environment, whenever we introduce a new platform, we'll make sure we can build a simple "Hello, World" application.

Open Eclipse, and choose the workspace that you wish to use. (Any folder will do here—if you're new to Eclipse, it's just a folder in which to store the project files.)

The first thing we have to do is tell the plugin where you installed the Android SDK. "Installed" may be too strong a word, as all you would have done is opened the zip file downloaded from Google's site.

To continue, permanently copy the SDK files to a location on disk—for example, `C:\Program Files\Android` for Windows or `/Android` on the Mac.

From the Eclipse menu, select **Window – Preferences**, and then select the **Android** item from the list. Into the **SDK Location** field, enter the folder path you copied the files to, and click **Apply**. The plugin will confirm the location of the SDK and tell you which API target will be used. (This should be the latest one—version `2.1` in this case.) Figure 4-15 illustrates.

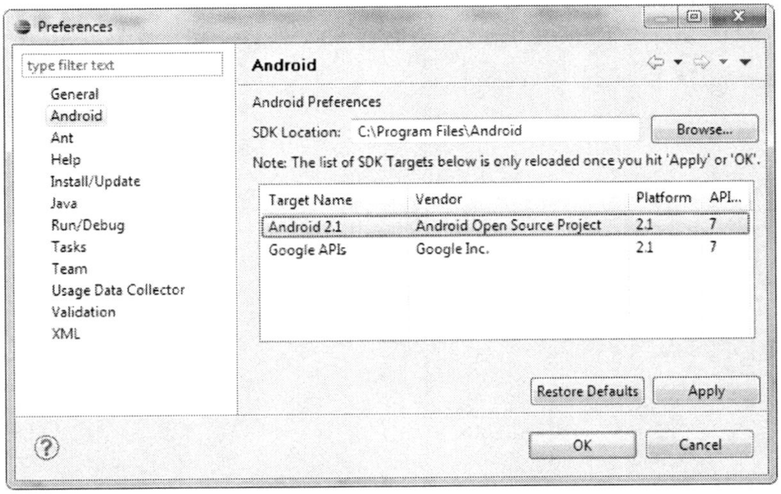

Figure 4-15. *Telling Eclipse where the Android SDK is installed*

Now that we have configured the environment, we can create the project. Select **File ➤ New ➤ Project** from the menu, and you will discover the capability to create a new **Android Project**, as per Figure 4-16.

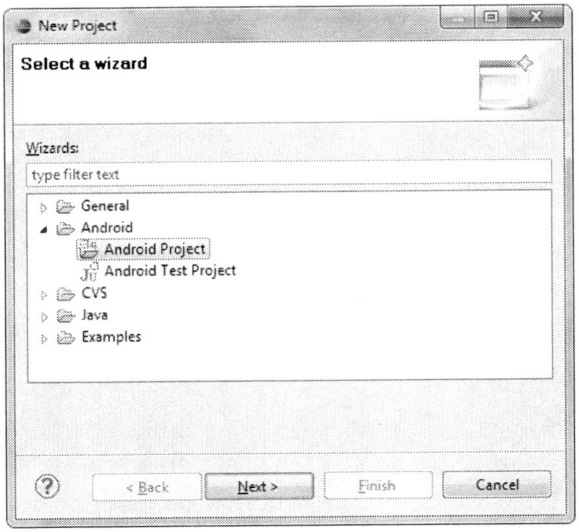

45

Figure 4-16. *Selecting the "Android Project" project type*

Click **Next** to proceed, and you'll see the **New Android Project** wizard. On this dialog, do the following:

- Enter **Project name** as AmxMobile.Android.HelloWorld

- Select Android 2.1 as the **Build Target**

- Enter **Application name** as AMX Mobile Android Hello World

- Enter **Package name** as amxMobile.Android.HelloWorld

- Check on **Create activity** and enter MyHelloWorldActivity

Figure 4-17 illustrates.

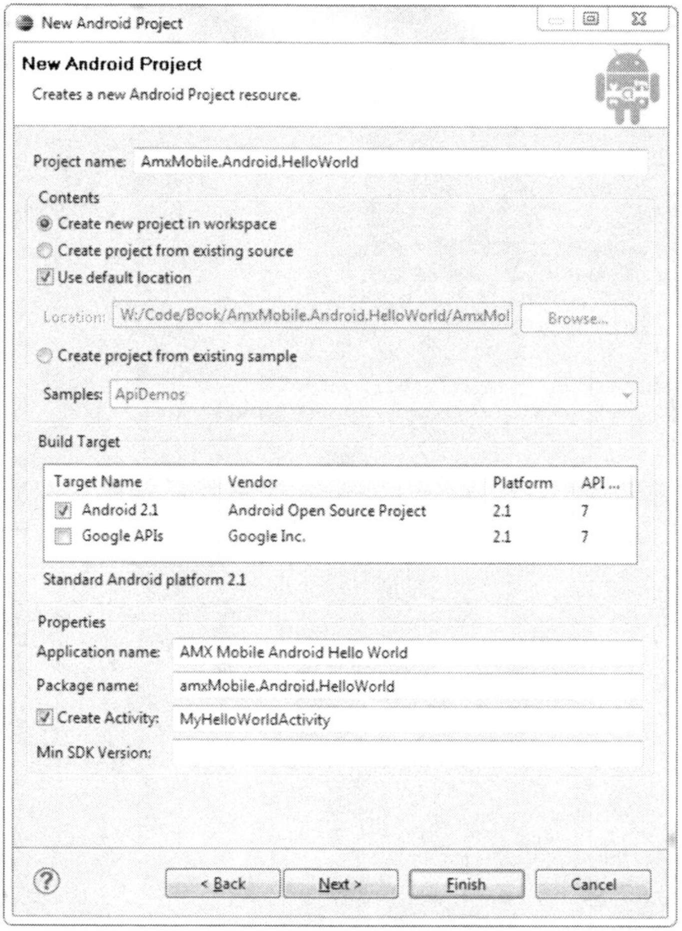

Figure 4-17. *Providing project settings to the project wizard*

Click **Finish** to create your new project.

Saying "Hello, World"

As we'll see in the next chapters, half the "fun" of Android development is wiring up all of the non-obvious bits and pieces to make the application hang together. (The actual coding of the forms and support logic is very easy, but there is a lot of fiddly "put this value here and it'll work, but get it a bit wrong and you'll be stuck.") In this chapter, I'm going to take you through very quickly how to make a "Hello, World" application work, and we'll go into far more detail on the plumbing in the next chapters.

Android applications are composed by building "activities," which are essentially chunks of user interface code, and wiring them together. When we created our default project, we got given a default activity, which we called MyHelloWorldActivity (shown in Figure 4-17). Therefore this activity is the one that we need to work with. The application is already configured to prime and run this activity when we run the project, so all we need to do is change its behavior.

Declarative Layout

The easiest way to work with Android user interface components is to compose the UI using XML. (You can compose the UI programmatically, but it's far easier to use XML.) The layout code is fairly clunky and not brilliantly sophisticated, but it is effective. (For example, when we look at the Windows Phone 7 Silverlight declarative language—XAML—you'll see that it is incredibly sophisticated by comparison. Likewise, Interface Builder for the Mac is extremely slick.)

By convention, the XML layout files used for the activities are located in the ~/res/layout folder, illustrated in Figure 4-18. You can see in the figure that we already have one layout file, called main.xml. This is the default file generated by the project wizard that is bound to our MyHelloWorldActivity activity.

Figure 4-18. *The location of the "main.xml" layout file*

If you double-click main.xml, Eclipse will open an XML editor to allow you to manipulate it. (As mentioned before, in this chapter we're not going to dwell on the details and will go through this next part quite fast.) By default, main.xml is created with a label. We'll replace that with a declaration that specifies a button, as per this listing:

```xml
<?xml version="1.0" encoding="utf-8"?>
<LinearLayout xmlns:android="http://schemas.android.com/apk/res/android"
    android:orientation="vertical"
    android:layout_width="fill_parent"
    android:layout_height="fill_parent"
    >
<Button
    android:layout_width="fill_parent"
    android:layout_height="wrap_content"
    android:text="Click me!"
    android:id="@+id/buttonGo"
    />
</LinearLayout>
```

■**NOTE** Best practice for Android applications calls for adding string resources into a central location. However, in the format of a book, such centralized string handling makes examples hard to follow, so where display text has to be added to the layout, I shall do this directly in code as opposed to referring to a string resource. In Listing 4-1, android:text="Click me!" is one such example of literal string use that would be more properly done as a string resource for a "real" application. This statement is generally true for all of the platforms.

You can run the application at this point to see the button. Select Run - Run from the menu and select Android Application from the dialog that appears. Figure 4-19 illustrates.

Figure 4-19. *Choosing the run target*

Click **OK** to run the application. You'll be prompted to start the emulator if you do not already have one up and running. But in either case, eventually your application will appear, complete with button. Figure 4-20 illustrates.

Figure 4-20. *Our form visible within the emulator*

Wiring Up the Button

If you're used to declaring markup and writing "code-behind" supporting code for it using Microsoft ASP.NET, like I was before coming to Android, you may well find Android's approach a little clunky! There is a lot of manual wiring up and fiddling around to do to make the UI work.

When we define user elements within the XML, we give it an ID value. This was done previously with this attribute in the XML: android:id="@+id/buttonGo".

The Android/Eclipse plugin maintains a special code file called ~/gen/<packageName>/R.java. This is automatically generated by looking for special references within the various files that make up the project, including the layout XML files. The @+id notation causes a value called buttonGo to be added to the R class. If you open our R class, you'll notice it looks like this:

```
public final class R {
    public static final class attr {
    }
    public static final class drawable {
        public static final int icon=0x7f020000;
    }
    public static final class id {
        public static final int buttonGo=0x7f050000;
    }
```

```
    public static final class layout {
        public static final int main=0x7f030000;
    }
    public static final class string {
        public static final int app_name=0x7f040002;
        public static final int clickMe=0x7f040001;
        public static final int hello=0x7f040000;
    }
}
```

Specifically, in there you can see our buttonGo value.

It's by referencing this value in code that we can address the button. At the moment, our MyHelloWorldActivity class looks like this:

```
package amxMobile.Android.HelloWorld;

import android.app.Activity;

public class MyHelloWorldActivity extends Activity {
    /** Called when the activity is first created. */
    @Override
    public void onCreate(Bundle savedInstanceState) {
        super.onCreate(savedInstanceState);

        // initialize the UI...
        setContentView(R.layout.main);
    }
}
```

What we want to do first is create a property getter that will retrieve our button. Although in this small application we're only going to address the button once, we'll use this getter pattern in later chapters, so it's worth familiarizing ourselves with it now. The getButton property getter will work by asking the activity to look within its internal state and discover a control with the appropriate ID. We'll cast this ID to a android.widget.Button class. Here's the code:

```
    private Button getButton()
    {
        return (Button)findViewById(R.id.buttonGo);
    }
```

For those of you new to Java, you will see an error in Eclipse indicating that there is a problem with the Button class. Eclipse shows this by putting an icon in the margin and underlining the name. Figure 4-21 illustrates.

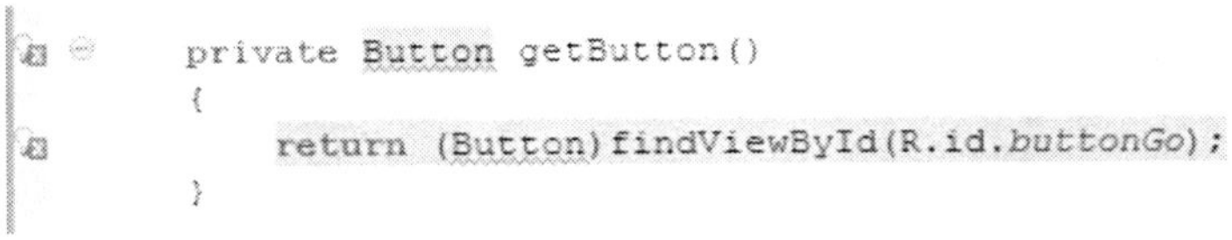

```
private Button getButton()
{
        return (Button)findViewById(R.id.buttonGo);
}
```

Figure 4-21. *Eclipse's (excellent) error highlighting*

Eclipse is typically able to offer suggestions to help resolve problems with classes. If you hover over the problem class, you'll see a popup. In this instance—shown in Figure 4-22—you have an option to Import 'Button'. Click this, and an import statement will be added to the top of the class.

```
private Button getButton()
{
        return (Button) findViewById(R.id.buttonGo);
}

public void
{
        if(v.get     Button cannot be resolved to a type
        {            7 quick fixes available:
                // t      Import 'Button' (android.widget)
                Mess      Create class 'Button'
        }             Create interface 'Button'
}                    o  Add type parameter 'Button' to 'MyHelloWorldActivity'
}                    o  Add type parameter 'Button' to 'getButton()'
                      Create enum 'Button'
                      Fix project setup...

                                           Press 'F2' for focus
```

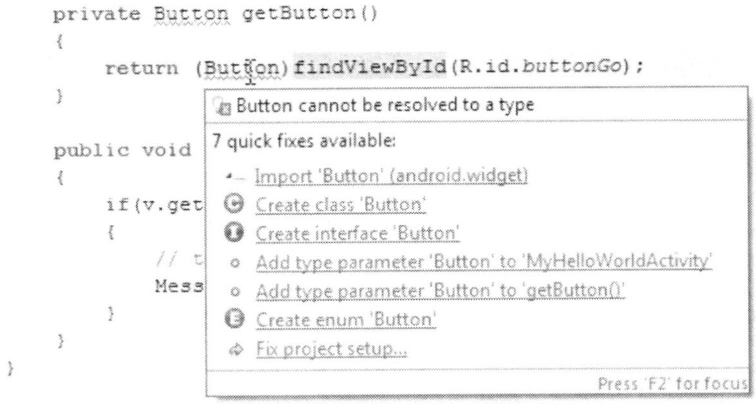

Figure 4-22. *Possible correction options for the detected error*

■**NOTE** You can bring up this window by using the Ctrl+1 key combination.

This will result in an import statement being added to the top of the class, like this:

```
package amxMobile.Android.HelloWorld;

import android.app.Activity;
import android.os.Bundle;
import android.widget.Button;

public class MyHelloWorldActivity extends Activity
```

This is a bit of a pain with Eclipse—it's helpful to have the option of doing these per-class imports, but it would be better if it were shorter. If you're unfamiliar with Java, a way to do this is to put a wildcard in, like so:

```
package amxMobile.Android.HelloWorld;

import android.app.*;
import android.os.*;
import android.widget.*;

public class MyHelloWorldActivity extends Activity
```

This will then match any class in the namespace, albeit at that level only. (For example, you can't do `import android.*` and get everything.) This makes the code much more readable.

Now that we have the getter, we can wire up the event. This is a bit of the Android SDK that I'm not particularly keen on. The event handler has to be given a reference to an interface called `android.view.View.OnClickListener`. The easiest way to do this is to make the activity implement the interface and give the button a reference to the activity. When the event needs to be raised, the sole method on the interface—onClick—will be called. In there you can de-reference the button and do whatever it is you want to do.

If you're following along, you may have to work out the `import` statements yourself—I'm not necessarily going to lead you through adding these to all of the bits of code yourself. I'll talk about this more in the next section, when I discuss the conventions for code presentation in the main Android chapters.

Here's the listing:

```
package amxMobile.Android.HelloWorld;

import android.app.Activity;
import android.os.Bundle;
import android.view.*;
import android.view.View.OnClickListener;
import android.widget.*;

public class MyHelloWorldActivity extends Activity implements OnClickListener {
    /** Called when the activity is first created. */
    @Override
    public void onCreate(Bundle savedInstanceState) {
        super.onCreate(savedInstanceState);

        // initialize the UI...
        setContentView(R.layout.main);

        // wire up a the button...
        Button button = this.getButton();
        button.setOnClickListener(this);
    }
```

```
    private Button getButton()
    {
        return (Button)findViewById(R.id.buttonGo);
    }

    public void onClick(View v)
    {
            if(v.getId() == R.id.buttonGo)
            {
                    // that's our cue...
                    MessageBox.Show(this, "Hello, world!");
            }
    }
}
```

That code won't work until we build the MessageBox class. We'll build this here, but we'll also use it in later chapters. Android has a class that will display message boxes, but there is no shorthand way to simply build and show a message box. Add this class to your project:

```
package amxMobile.Android.HelloWorld;

import android.app.*;
import android.content.*;

public class MessageBox {

        public static void Show(Activity owner, String message)
        {
                AlertDialog.Builder builder = new AlertDialog.Builder(owner);
                builder.setTitle(R.string.app_name);
                builder.setMessage(message);
        builder.setPositiveButton("OK", new DialogInterface.OnClickListener() {
            public void onClick(DialogInterface dialog, int whichButton) {
                // do something here..
            }
        });

                // show...
                AlertDialog dialog = builder.create();
                dialog.show();
        }
}
```

___

■**NOTE** You'll notice in that code the setPositiveButton takes an anonymous method. This is another way of wiring up event handlers in Android.

___

If you run the project now, you'll have a button that you can click and display a message box, as per Figure 4-23.

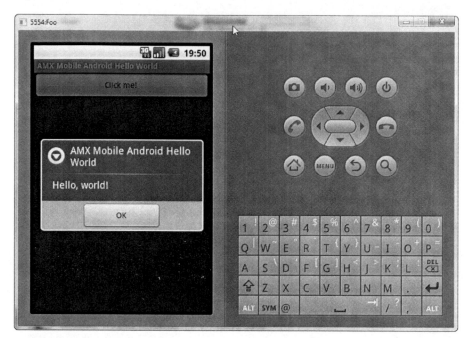

Figure 4-23. *A successful result!*

Conclusion

In this chapter, we've seen how to install the Eclipse IDE and Android SDK so that we can start developing applications for Android. In the next chapter, we'll start looking at the functionality of the Six Bookmarks application proper.

CHAPTER 5

Android: Building the Logon Form and Consuming REST Services

In this chapter, now that we have the toolset configured, we're going to start building our Six Bookmarks application for Android. This is going to involve starting a new project, creating the logon form layout, and then building the infrastructure to call up to our API and Users RESTful services at http://services.multimobiledevelopment.com/.

Creating the Project

The first place to start is creating a new Android project for the Six Bookmarks application. To do this, you need to create a new workspace in Eclipse and then add a new project. If you're not running Eclipse, when it starts and you are prompted for a workspace folder path, create a new one. If you are running Eclipse, select **File – Switch Workspace – Other**, and then specify a new workspace folder path.

In either case, add a new Android project like you did in Chapter 7. Figure 5-1 illustrates my settings. The settings you choose do not matter too much; however, for the maximum chance of following along, make sure the name of the activity specified in **Create Activity** is Logon.

In the rest of this chapter, we will be looking at calling the services, and then we'll look at building a UI to call them by presenting the logon form to the user.

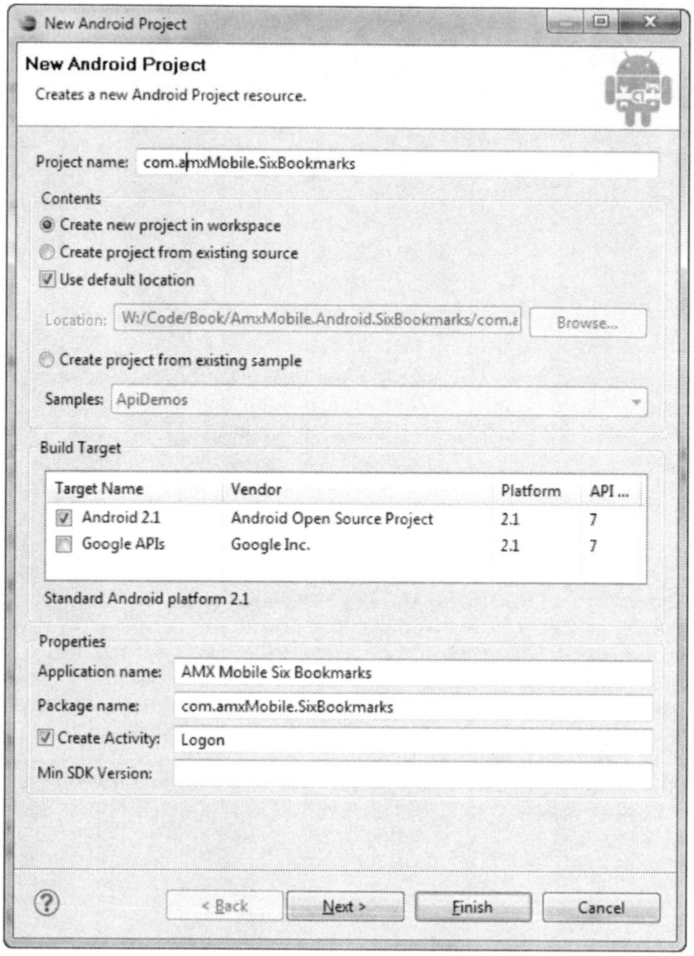

Figure 5-1. *The "New Android Project" wizard*

Conventions for Presenting Code

Each section in this book is going to have its own convention for presenting code, as each toolset presents its own challenges for presenting code in book form.

In the Android sections, in the code available on the download, I'm going to separate the code into separate packages. I won't necessarily call out the package before presenting code; therefore look for package declarations in the code listing.

Another thing that I shall do with the code in these sections is where you're adding a method to an existing class, I'll add a comment at the top of the listing telling you which class to add the code to. If the actual `class` declaration is specified, I won't do this, and you should assume the name of the file matches the name of the class.

The final point is that in Java I'm not necessarily going to follow Java's code case conventions in terms of camel case method names, but I will typically use .NET's Pascal casing. There's an argument that when trying to maintain separate code bases with the same function, it's a little easier to keep the structure and coding conventions the same. .NET and Java are sufficiently flexible to accept each other's standards, and I've arbitrarily chosen .NET's.

Calling RESTful Services

In Chapter 4, we built some classes that acted as proxy objects that could communicate with the services at `http://services.multimobiledevelopment.com/`. In this chapter and the next, we're going to build the same objects again, but this time for Android.

If you recall, in Chapter 4 we built final classes called `ApiService`, `UsersService`, and `BookmarksService`. We also built base classes of `ServiceProxy`, `RestServiceProxy`, and `ODataServiceProxy`. Figure 5-2 illustrates.

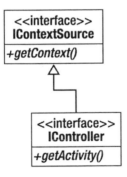

Figure 5-2. *UML static structure sketch showing proxy class relationships*

Let's now look at building these classes.

Issuing Web Requests

The first piece we need in place in order to use the API is the code that physically makes the requests to the server.

In Chapter 4, we used a class in BootFX called `HttpHelper` that internally used the .NET Framework's `System.Net.HttpWebRequest` and `System.Net.HttpWebResponse` classes to issue the requests and process the response. In this section, we're going to build a new version of `HttpHelper` for Android.

The classes available within Android to do this can be found in the `org.apache.http` namespace. (This is an implementation of the Apache HttpClient 4 implementation, which you can find out more about at `http://hc.apache.org/httpcomponents-client/`.)

We're going to create two main methods and a number of helper methods. The first of the main methods (`Download`) will return a string that represents the response from the server. The second (`DownloadXml`) will take the result of `Download` and load it into an XML document that can be processed later.

The "DownloadSettings" Class

Recall that in Chapter 4, we passed up with the request special HTTP headers that told the server the username of the API account and the token for the requests. (These headers were called x-amx-apiusername and x-amx-token.) To make this happen when the time comes, we need to provide to the Download and DownloadXml methods a list of such headers and their values. To do this, we'll create a class called DownloadSettings that's designed to hold a collection of these settings in a regular Java Hashtable.

Here's the listing:

```
package com.amxMobile.SixBookmarks.Runtime;

import java.util.*;

public class DownloadSettings
{
        private Hashtable<String, String> _extraHeaders = new Hashtable<String, String>();

        public DownloadSettings()
        {
        }

        public Hashtable<String, String> getExtraHeaders()
        {
                return _extraHeaders;
        }

        public void AddHeader(String name, String value)
        {
                if(value == null)
                        value = "";

                getExtraHeaders().put(name, value);
        }
}
```

The "Download" and "DownloadXml" Methods

The Download method is not difficult, but it is a little bit fiddly, so we'll go through it step by step. What we're looking to do is, given a particular URL, use the Apache HttpClient API to call up to the server, wait for a response, and then process it either as an error, or as success. In the case that it's successful, we want to read all of the data that the server wishes to give us and store it in a string. We'll add another method—GetHttpEntityContent—that will take the actual data from the server and turn it into a string. (We'll use this last method directly in Chapter 10.)

Before we do this, we need to create a new class to put this stuff into. Add a class HttpHelper to the project, like this:

```
package com.amxMobile.SixBookmarks.Runtime;

import java.io.*;
import java.util.*;
import org.apache.http.*;
import org.apache.http.client.*;
import org.apache.http.client.methods.*;
import org.apache.http.impl.client.*;
import org.w3c.dom.*;

public class HttpHelper {

}
```

We start off by creating a client instance and then asking it to issue an HTTP GET command to the given URL. Here's the code.

```
// Add to HttpHelper.java
        public static String Download(String url, DownloadSettings settings) throws  Exception
        {
                if(settings == null)
                        settings  = new DownloadSettings();

                // create the request...
                HttpClient client = new DefaultHttpClient();
                HttpGet request = new HttpGet(url);
```

The next bit is specific to our project as we have to pass up these special headers. We'll walk through the ExtraHeaders property of the supplied DownloadSettings instance and configure the request object appropriately. Here's the code:

```
                // additional headers...
                Hashtable<String, String> extraHeaders = settings.getExtraHeaders();
                for(String name : extraHeaders.keySet())
                        request.addHeader(name, extraHeaders.get(name));
```

We're now ready to make the requests of the server. We'll do that and wait for a response. If we don't get back HTTP 200, we'll assume an error has occurred. (This is OK for us here in this example, but relying on an HTTP 200 may not be ideal, as there are other warning codes or conditions in a more fully-featured implementation we may wish to gracefully handle.)

```
                // get the response...
                HttpResponse response = client.execute(request);

                // not a 200?
                int code = response.getStatusLine().getStatusCode();
                if(code != 200)
                        throw new Exception(String.format("Download of '%s' returned HTTP↵
'%d' (%s).", url, code, response.getStatusLine().getReasonPhrase()));
```

Once we've got this far, we know the server has returned a valid response. The Apache HttpClient API uses the paradigm of "entities" for objects that are transferred around between client and server. Thus, in this instance, we'll ask the response object to give us an entity and then use the regular Java I/O library to pump the data into a `StringBuilder` instance. It's the state of this `StringBuilder` that we'll return to the caller as the HTTP response. As mentioned before, we want to do this in a separate helper method that we can reuse, which we'll call `GetHttpEntityContent`.

Here's the code:

```
        // get...
        HttpEntity entity = response.getEntity();
        String result = GetHttpEntityContent(entity);
        return result;
}


public static String GetHttpEntityContent(HttpEntity entity) throws Exception
{
        // get...
        InputStreamReader stream = new InputStreamReader(entity.getContent());
        StringBuilder builder = new StringBuilder();
        try
        {
                BufferedReader reader = new BufferedReader(stream);
                while(true)
                {
                        String buf = reader.readLine();
                        if(buf == null)
                                break;

                        // add...
                        builder.append(buf);
                }
        }
        finally
        {
                if(stream != null)
                        stream.close();
        }

        // return...
        return builder.toString();
}
```

That's all there is to the `Download` method. As mentioned before, `DownloadXml` will take the output of `Download` and load it into an `org.w3c.dom.Document` instance. It'll do this by deferring to a class called `XmlHelper`, which we'll build shortly. Here's the code:

```
        public static Document DownloadXml(String url, DownloadSettings settings) throws↵
Exception
        {
                // get the plain content...
                String xml = Download(url, settings);

                // turn that into some XML...
                Document doc = XmlHelper.LoadXml(xml);
                return doc;
        }
```

We'll stub out LoadXml on the new XmlHelper class now, so that the application continues to compile. Here's the stub code:

```
package com.amxMobile.SixBookmarks.Runtime;

import java.io.*;
import javax.xml.parsers.*;
import org.w3c.dom.*;

public class XmlHelper
{
        public static Document LoadXml(String xml) throws Exception
        {
                throw new Exception("Not implemented.");
        }
}
```

Extra Methods on "HttpHelper"

There are two methods we will need on HttpHelper that help the caller build URLs that can be used with Download and DownloadXml.

When we come to make a request of our RESTful services, we're going to create a hashtable of name/value pairs that need to be built into the query string of the URL. We'll need methods called BuildUrl and BuildQueryString that will help us do this. Here's the code:

```
        public static String BuildQueryString(Hashtable<String, Object> values)
        {
                StringBuilder builder = new StringBuilder();
                for(Object key : values.keySet())
                {
                        if(builder.length() > 0)
                                builder.append("&");
                        builder.append(key);
                        builder.append("=");
                        builder.append(values.get(key));
                }
```

```
                // return...
                String qs = builder.toString();
                return qs;
        }

        public static String BuildUrl(String url, Hashtable<String, Object> values)
        {
                int index = url.indexOf("?");
                if(index != -1)
                        url = url.substring(0, index);

                // add...
                url = url + "?" + BuildQueryString(values);
                return url;
        }
```

Authenticating Our API Account

We've now got the pieces in place to start building the ServiceProxy, RestServiceProxy, and ApiService classes.

ServiceProxy is the base class that all of the service proxies will use. It has a number of functions:

- It will store as constant strings the username and password to your API account at http://services.multimobiledevelopment.com/. You will need to change this in order to use the project files if you download the code.

- It will store in static memory the token provided by the server that should be used with API requests. (Recall that within a session we make one request to tell the server we want a token, and then all other requests use that token.)

- It will store in instance memory the name of the service that the proxy relates to.

- It will provide a DownloadSettings instance that's configured with the special headers that we need to pass up, depending on the state of the stored token.

- It will manage the process of ensuring the API authenticated.

Here's the code that does everything apart from ensuring that the API is authenticated, which we will do later. Add this new class to the project:

```
package com.amxMobile.SixBookmarks.Services;

import com.amxMobile.SixBookmarks.Runtime.*;

public abstract class ServiceProxy
{
        private String _serviceName;
        private static String _token;

        private final String RootUrl = "http://services.multimobiledevelopment.com/services/";
```

```java
        // YOU MUST CHANGE THESE VALUES IN ORDER TO USE THIS SAMPLE...
        protected final String ApiUsername = "amxmobile";
        private final String ApiPassword = "password";

        protected ServiceProxy(String serviceName)
        {
                _serviceName = serviceName;
        }

        public String getServiceName()
        {
                return _serviceName;
        }

        public String getResolvedServiceUrl()
        {
                return RootUrl + getServiceName();
        }

        protected static String getToken()
        {
                return _token;
        }

        protected void setToken(String token)
        {
                _token = token;
        }

    protected DownloadSettings GetDownloadSettings()
    {
        DownloadSettings settings = new DownloadSettings();
        settings.AddHeader("x-amx-apiusername", ApiUsername);
        settings.AddHeader("x-amx-token", getToken());

        // return...
        return settings;
    }
}
```

Here's something else we need to add to ServiceProxy—the EnsureApiAuthenticated method. We'll build this out later.

```java
// Add to ServiceProxy.java
    protected void EnsureApiAuthenticated() throws Exception
    {
            throw new Exception("Not implemented.");
    }
```

The "LogonResponse"

Whether we're authenticating the API or authenticating the user, we'll need an object that describes the result of the call. We'll create a class called LogonResponse that holds this data and an enumeration called LogonResult that represents the ultimate result. Here they are:

```
package com.amxMobile.SixBookmarks.Services;

public enum LogonResult
{
    LogonOk,
    InvalidUsername,
    InvalidPassword,
    UserInactive
}
```

```
package com.amxMobile.SixBookmarks.Services;

public class LogonResponse
{
        private String _token;
        private String _message;
        private LogonResult _result;

        public LogonResponse(LogonResult result, String message, String token)
        {
                _result = result;
                _message = message;
                _token = token;
        }

        public String getMessage()
        {
                return _message;
        }

        public String getToken()
        {
                return _token;
        }

        public LogonResult getResult()
        {
                return _result;
        }
```

```
public static LogonResult ParseLogonResult(String asString) throws Exception
{
        return LogonResult.valueOf(asString);
}
}
```

Building the "XmlHelper" Class

In Chapter 4, we used the BootFX HttpHelper class to smooth over the intricacies of making HTTP requests. We also used the BootFX class XmlHelper to make working with XML data easier.

Android uses the regular XML DOM manipulation API found in the com.w3c.dom namespace. Although extremely fiddly, this API provides a very powerful set of functions to reading, changing XML documents in a safe and ultimately maintainable fashion. (The full version of the API also allows you to create documents, but this creation functionality is not available on Android.)

■**NOTE** For those who have not used it before but have used the .NET System.Xml namespace, it's essentially the same.

For those who are coming at this completely cold, the principle is that a document is made up of "nodes." A node represents anything and everything in the document, e.g., elements, attributes, text values, type declarations, etc. If reading the document, you walk the nodes. If building or changing the document, you create nodes and insert them as children of other nodes—although on Android, you can't create or change the document.

The first two methods we'll add to XmlHelper will load a document from a string or from a stream. (Both use the regular Java I/O library.) Here's the code:

```
// Add to XmlHelper.java

// Replace the stub method created before with this one...
        public static Document LoadXml(String xml) throws Exception
        {
                // create...
                ByteArrayInputStream stream = new ByteArrayInputStream(xml.getBytes());
                try
                {
                        return LoadXml(stream);
                }
                finally
                {
                        if(stream != null)
                                stream.close();
                }
        }

        private static Document LoadXml(InputStream stream) throws Exception
```

```
        {
                DocumentBuilderFactory factory = DocumentBuilderFactory.newInstance();
                factory.setNamespaceAware(true);

                // builder...
                DocumentBuilder builder = factory.newDocumentBuilder();
                Document doc = builder.parse(stream);

                // return...
                return doc;
        }
```

Personally, I'm a big fan of these object-model-style libraries for manipulating XML documents; however, the compromise that one has to make is that they're very fiddly to use. I tend to build helper libraries—like the one we're about to see—to make working with the documents easier.

■**NOTE** We're going to add the minimum number of functions here. Practically, you need a library that has far more variations of the types of data and the formats that can be returned. However, as always, review the version of the class in the project files at `http://code.multimobiledevelopment.com/`, as these will be developed further and have more functions.

It's worth mentioning, though, that some people do not like using these DOM-based libraries, as they are inefficient in terms of processor time and memory used. On mobile devices, this is a greater consideration than on a desktop or server; however, my personal philosophy is to follow a pragmatic, "balancing ease of building and ease of maintenance" approach, and using parsers (as we will do on the iPhone) is much harder to build and maintain.

Back to the subject of building helper libraries for reading XML, one common requirement of such a library is to extract element values from a parent element given the name of a child. For example, consider the following XML. It would be very helpful to be able to issue a single request against the Customer element to get FirstName and LastName values back:

```
<Customer>
        <FirstName>Andy</FirstName>
        <LastName>Williams</LastName>
</Customer>
```

If we have a Customer element and we want to get values back from the child values, a good approach is to have one method that returns the child element and another that extracts from the value from it. In this implementation, we're going to support three data types: string, Boolean, and 32-bit integer. The XmlDataType enumeration defines these for our use:

```
package com.amxMobile.SixBookmarks.Runtime;

public enum XmlDataType
{
        String, Boolean, Int32
}
```

Within XmlHelper, we'll go ahead and create methods that return back strongly-typed data and use a generic method that can fetch any type of data. Here's the code:

```
// Add to XmlHelper.java
        public static String GetElementString(Element element, String name, boolean↵
throwIfNotFound) throws Exception
        {
                return (String)GetElementValue(element, name, XmlDataType.String,↵
throwIfNotFound);
        }

        public static boolean GetElementBoolean(Element element, String name, boolean↵
throwIfNotFound) throws Exception
        {
                return ((Boolean)GetElementValue(element, name, XmlDataType.Boolean,↵
throwIfNotFound)).booleanValue();
        }

        public static int GetElementInt32(Element element, String name, boolean↵
throwIfNotFound) throws Exception
        {
                return ((Number)GetElementValue(element, name, XmlDataType.Int32,↵
throwIfNotFound)).intValue();
        }

        private static Object GetElementValue(Element element, String name, XmlDataType↵
dt, boolean throwIfNotFound) throws Exception
        {
                // find it...
                NodeList nodes = element.getElementsByTagName(name);
                if(nodes.getLength() == 1)
                {
                        if(dt == XmlDataType.String)
                                return GetStringValue(nodes.item(0));
                        else if(dt == XmlDataType.Boolean)
                                return (Boolean)GetBooleanValue(nodes.item(0));
                        else if(dt == XmlDataType.Int32)
                                return (Number)GetInt32Value(nodes.item(0));
                        else
                                throw new Exception(String.format("Cannot handle '%s'.", dt));
                }
                else if(nodes.getLength() == 0)
                {
                        if(throwIfNotFound)
                                throw new Exception(String.format("An element with name↵
'%s' was not found within an element with name '%s'.", name, element.getNodeName()));
```

```
                        else
                                return null;
                }
                else
                        throw new Exception(String.format("Too many (%d) child elements↵
were found.", nodes.getLength()));
        }
```

Note that in the generic GetElementValue method, we're deferring to methods called GetStringValue, GetBooleanValue, and GetInt32Value. These methods will do the actual conversion for us. As the data in the XML file is formatted as text, the GetStringValue will be the "master" method, and the others will defer to that and convert the values. Here's the code:

```
// Add to XmlHelper.java
        public static String GetStringValue(Node item) throws Exception
        {
                if(item instanceof Element)
                {
                        Node node = item.getFirstChild();
                        if(node != null)
                                return node.getNodeValue();
                        else
                                return "";
                }
                else
                        throw new Exception(String.format("Cannot handle '%s'.",↵
item.getClass()));
        }

        public static int GetInt32Value(Node item) throws Exception
        {
                String asString = GetStringValue(item);
                return Integer.parseInt(asString);
        }

        public static boolean GetBooleanValue(Node item) throws Exception
        {
                String asString = GetStringValue(item);
                if(asString.compareTo("0") == 0 || asString.compareToIgnoreCase("false")↵
== 0)
                        return false;
                else if(asString.compareTo("1") == 0 || asString.compareToIgnoreCase↵
("true") == 0)
                        return true;
                else
                        throw new Exception(String.format("The value '%s' could not be↵
recognised as valid Boolean value.", asString));
        }
```

We can now go ahead and build the ApiService class and implement the Logon method.

Creating the "Logon" Method on the API Service

In Chapter 2, we looked at the protocol exposed by the service at
http://services.multimobiledevelopment.com/. By way of a reminder, here's what the XML from a
successful call to the Logon operation looks like on the service:

```
<AmxResponse>
  <Result dt:type="string" xmlns:dt="urn:schemas-microsoft-com:datatypes">LogonOk</Result>
  <Token>d8313229998afe2de52698934a51dfb6</Token>
  <HasException dt:type="boolean" xmlns:dt="urn:schemas-microsoft-com:datatypes">↵
0</HasException>
</AmxResponse>
```

And here's what a call that exposes an error looks like:

```
<AmxResponse>
  <Error>System.InvalidOperationException: Neither a logon token nor API key were↵
provided in the request.  Ensure a token was provided in the URL.
   at AmxMobile.Services.ServiceAuthenticator.GetApi(LogonToken&amp; token)
   at AmxMobile.Services.Web.RestBasePage.OnLoad(EventArgs e)</Error>
  <HasException dt:type="boolean" xmlns:dt="urn:schemas-microsoft-com:datatypes">↵
1</HasException>
</AmxResponse>
```

The reason I wanted to present these here is that we will need to write code that can detect when the
server returned an exception and, if so, throw a Java new exception based on the data in the XML.

Recall that in Chapter 4, we created a class called RestRequestArgs that would package up the values
that we needed to send to the server. We'll do the same thing here by extending Hashtable and also
forcing a value to be set representing the operation in the constructor. Here's the code:

```
package com.amxMobile.SixBookmarks.Services;

import java.util.Hashtable;

public class RestRequestArgs extends Hashtable<String, Object>
{
        public RestRequestArgs(String operation)
        {
                this.put("operation", operation);
        }
}
```

That's all we need to do with RestRequestArgs—the standard operation of Java's Hashtable class does the rest.

The job of RestServiceProxy will be to take a RestRequestArgs instance and combine it with the root URL and the service name to make the request. It will also detect whether an exception occurred on the server and throw a Java exception if it did. The method will also return the root AmxResponse element back to the caller. Here's the code for new class RestServiceProxy:

```
package com.amxMobile.SixBookmarks.Services;

import org.w3c.dom.*;
import com.amxMobile.SixBookmarks.Runtime.*;

public class RestServiceProxy extends ServiceProxy
{
    protected RestServiceProxy(String serviceName)
    {
            super(serviceName);
    }

    protected Element SendRequest(RestRequestArgs args) throws Exception
    {
    // ensure that we have an authenticated API...
    this.EnsureApiAuthenticated();

    // get the URL...
    String url = this.getResolvedServiceUrl();
    url = HttpHelper.BuildUrl(url, args);

    // download...
    Document doc = HttpHelper.DownloadXml(url, GetDownloadSettings());
            try
            {
                    // find the response...
                    Element root = doc.getDocumentElement();
                    if(root.getNodeName().compareTo("AmxResponse") != 0)
                            throw new Exception(String.format("The root element had↵
an invalid name of '%s'.", root.getNodeName()));

                    // get...
                    boolean hasException = XmlHelper.GetElementBoolean(root,↵
"HasException", true);
                    if(!(hasException))
                            return root;
```

```
                        else
                        {
                                // get the error...
                                String error = XmlHelper.GetElementString(root, "Error",↵
true);
                                throw new Exception(String.format("The server returned↵
an error: %s", error));
                        }
                }
                catch(Exception ex)
                {
                        throw new Exception(String.format("An error occurred when↵
processing a response returned from a REST request.\nURL: %s", url), ex);
                }
        }
}
```

Note how the first thing this method does is call EnsureApiAuthenticated. We're going to build that in the next section (recall that we added it before and forced it to throw an exception).

Building the ApiService class should now be easy, as we have everything in place. Here's the code:

```
package com.amxMobile.SixBookmarks.Services;

import org.w3c.dom.*;
import com.amxMobile.SixBookmarks.Runtime.*;

public class ApiService extends RestServiceProxy
{
        public ApiService()
        {
                super("apirest.aspx");
        }

        public LogonResponse Logon(String password) throws Exception
        {
        // create the request...
        RestRequestArgs args = new RestRequestArgs("logon");
        args.put("password", password);

        // send the request...
        Element element = SendRequest(args);

        // what happened?
        String asString = XmlHelper.GetElementString(element, "Result", true);
        LogonResult result = LogonResponse.ParseLogonResult(asString);
```

```
        // message...
        String message = XmlHelper.GetElementString(element, "Message", false);

        // then what?
        if(result == LogonResult.LogonOk)
        {
                String token = XmlHelper.GetElementString(element, "Token", true);
                return new LogonResponse(result, message, token);
        }
        else
                return new LogonResponse(result, message, "");
        }

        @Override
    protected void EnsureApiAuthenticated()
    {
        // no-op...
    }
}
```

Now that we have a method that can call the Logon operation on the live service, let's wire it up so that it actually happens!

Wiring Up "EnsureApiAuthenticated"

The flow of the protocol defined by the service is that the RESTful and OData services require a server-provided token to validate the call. The "chicken and egg" situation is that we need to call the server to get a token; hence we need a special first step to do so.

EnsureApiAuthenticated is called in RestServiceProxy as part of the method that physically directs the request to the server. The operation of this method looks to see if a token is defined in global (static) memory and, if not, it creates an instance of the ApiService proxy class and calls the Logon operation that we have just rigged up. To prevent a stack overflow situation, the ApiService class overrides the operation of EnsureApiAuthenticated to turn it into a "no-operation." Here's the implementation of EnsureApiAuthenticated that needs to be added to the base ServiceProxy class:

```
// Add to ServiceProxy.java - replace the existing stub method...
    protected void EnsureApiAuthenticated() throws Exception
    {
        // check that we've authenticated...
        String asString = getToken();
        if (asString == null || asString.length() == 0)
        {
            // call up to the API service...
            ApiService service = new ApiService();
            LogonResponse response = service.Logon(ApiPassword);
            if (response == null)
                throw new Exception("'response' is null.");
```

```
            // can we?
            if (response.getResult() == LogonResult.LogonOk)
                this.setToken(response.getToken());
            else
            {
                throw new Exception(String.format("The server request failed with the↵
error '%s'.  Ensure that you have set the values of the ApiUsername and ApiPassword↵
constants to the credentials of your Six Bookmarks service account at %s.",
                    response.getResult(), RootUrl));
            }
        }
    }
}
```

You won't see much output from this flow, but it's absolutely required in order to make the protocol work the way that it needs to in order to communicate with the server.

We won't be calling this method for a while, but first let's press on and build the UsersService class.

Authenticating the User via "UsersService"

The Logon method on UsersService is very easy to implement. We've worked sufficiently hard on our base classes and supporting code that making the call is just a few lines. Here it is:

```
package com.amxMobile.SixBookmarks.Services;

import org.w3c.dom.*;
import com.amxMobile.SixBookmarks.Runtime.*;

public class UsersService extends RestServiceProxy
{
        public UsersService()
        {
                super("usersrest.aspx");
        }

    public LogonResponse Logon(String username, String password) throws Exception
    {
        // create the request...
        RestRequestArgs args = new RestRequestArgs("logon");

        // add the username and password...
        args.put("username", username);
        args.put("password", password);

        // send the request...
        Element element = SendRequest(args);

        String asString = XmlHelper.GetElementString(element, "Result", true);
```

```
        LogonResult result = LogonResponse.ParseLogonResult(asString);

        // message...
        String message = XmlHelper.GetElementString(element, "Message", false);

        // return...
        return new LogonResponse(result, message, "");
    }
}
```

And that's it! In the next sections, we'll build the logon form user interface and actually call the method (and, of course, the whole chain of operations that makes it possible).

Setting "Allow Internet Access" Permission

In this day and age, it's not possible to build a new operating system without building in a strong security subsystem, and Android is no exception. Several functions within the Android API cause a scenario whereby the user has to explicitly allow permission for the application to use them. One such example is the ability of the application to access the Internet.

What we have to do is mark the application as needing Internet access by adding an entry to the manifest. On installation, Android will ask the user to provide said permission.

The permission is easy to add—simply open the AndroidManifest.xml file and add a uses-permission attribute. However, by default, the Android/Eclipse plugin will show a custom view on the XML that makes up the manifest. I've never had much luck in getting this view to work, so click at the **XML** tab at the bottom of the view to view the raw XML.

Here's the complete listing that shows where to add the uses-permission element:

```xml
<?xml version="1.0" encoding="utf-8"?>
<manifest xmlns:android="http://schemas.android.com/apk/res/android"
      android:versionCode="1"
      android:versionName="1.0" package="com.amxMobile.SixBookmarks">

    <application android:icon="@drawable/icon" android:label="@string/app_name">

        <activity android:name=".Logon"
                android:label="@string/app_name">
            <intent-filter>
                <action android:name="android.intent.action.MAIN" />
                <category android:name="android.intent.category.LAUNCHER" />
            </intent-filter>
        </activity>

    </application>

        <uses-permission android:name="android.permission.INTERNET"></uses-permission>

</manifest>
```

Creating the Logon Form

Now that we have a project with a default activity and layout, we can get to work.

The first thing we need to do is rename the main.xml layout file. The project wizards created an activity for us called Logon, but for some reason, when it creates the XML file for the layout, it always calls it main.xml. This is obviously going to get confusing—it would seem more logical to insist that the layout files have exactly the same name as their related activities. Figure 5-3 illustrates.

Figure 5-3. *Project tree showing the mismatched name between "Logon.java" and "main.xml"*

Rename the main.xml file as logon.xml, which can be done by right-clicking on the file in Package Explorer and selecting **Refactor – Rename**. This will prompt the global constants file (R.java) to be rebuilt. We can then change the reference to R.layout.main in the Logon class to R.layout.logon, like so:

```
public class Logon extends Activity {
    /** Called when the activity is first created. */
    @Override
    public void onCreate(Bundle savedInstanceState) {
        super.onCreate(savedInstanceState);
        setContentView(R.layout.logon);
    }
```

You should try to keep your resource files, such as the layout files, named in lowercase; otherwise things can get a little confusing.

■**NOTE** In terms of the layout, I'm going to present a simple layout here and not go through the layout stuff in masses of detail. It's entirely feasible to write a whole book on Android layouts, and it's not really the focus of the book. Google for "Android layouts" if you would like to learn more.

The `LinearLayout` we're going to use in this chapter and the next two chapters is the most simple layout format that you can use in Android. It simply orders controls in a vertical list. Figure 5-4 shows the layout that we are looking achieve (to reiterate, Android has a lot of different layout formats, some of which are quite clever, but they are not covered here).

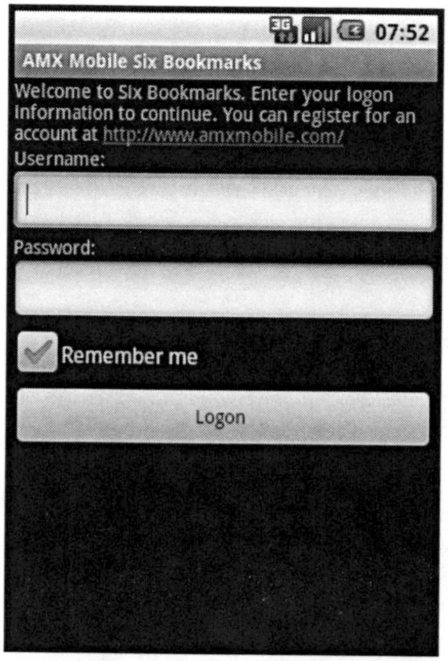

Figure 5-4. *The layout that we are looking to achieve on our logon form*

To build the layout, there's one basic rule—whenever you add a user interface element, you can choose to size it explicitly (not typical), or you can ask it to size itself to its parent or to the content that you provide. This automatic sizing, combined with the layout container, means that it's quite simple to put controls on the screen and have Android itself handle situations where the screen resolution changes or (more importantly) where orientation changes.

If you look at the `logon.xml` file that we already have, you'll find it contains something like the following XML. (When you open the file, it'll open in design mode—click the **XML** tab at the bottom of the view to show the XML.)

```xml
<?xml version="1.0" encoding="utf-8"?>
<LinearLayout xmlns:android="http://schemas.android.com/apk/res/android"
    android:orientation="vertical"
    android:layout_width="fill_parent"
    android:layout_height="fill_parent"
    >
<TextView
    android:layout_width="fill_parent"
    android:layout_height="wrap_content"
    android:text="@string/hello"
    />
</LinearLayout>
```

I want to talk initially about the namespace. We talk more about namespaces in Chapter 9, but for now, notice how all of the elements are prefixed with android: and hence refer to the Android namespace. I personally find that this adds a lot of unnecessary noise to the XML, and so I usually go through the file and rename android: to a:, like so:

```xml
<?xml version="1.0" encoding="utf-8"?>
<LinearLayout xmlns:a="http://schemas.android.com/apk/res/android"
    a:orientation="vertical"
    a:layout_width="fill_parent"
    a:layout_height="fill_parent"
    >
<TextView
    a:layout_width="fill_parent"
    a:layout_height="wrap_content"
    a:text="@string/hello"
    />
</LinearLayout>
```

The layout_width and layout_height elements are the most important attributes in this file, as these tell you how the control will be fitted to the container, and it's usually getting this right that causes the most frustration in building the layouts.

fill_parent directs the control to size the related element to the container. For LinearLayout, the container is the client area available on the screen (i.e., the physical device screen minus the status bar area). wrap_content directs the control to size the related element to the size of the content. Thus, if you have a TextView (i.e., "label") element and size the width to the parent and the height to the content, you'll end up with a label as wide as the screen and as tall as the text contained within.

If you refer back to Figure 5-4, we have one label for a blurb, one label for the username prompt, one textbox for the username, another label for the password prompt, one textbox for the password, one checkbox, and a button. All of these are configured to size their width to the parent and height to their content. Here's the XML for the logon.xml form layout:

```xml
<?xml version="1.0" encoding="utf-8"?>
<LinearLayout xmlns:a="http://schemas.android.com/apk/res/android" a:layout_width=↵
"fill_parent" a:layout_height="fill_parent"
        a:orientation="vertical">
```

```
    <TextView a:text="Welcome to Six Bookmarks. Enter your logon information to continue.↵
You can register for an account at http://www.multimobiledevelopment.com/" a:autoLink=↵
"web" a:layout_width="fill_parent" a:layout_height="wrap_content" />
    <TextView a:text="Username:" a:layout_width="wrap_content" a:layout_height=↵
"wrap_content" />
    <EditText a:id="@+id/textUsername" a:singleLine="true" a:layout_width="fill_parent"↵
a:layout_height="wrap_content" />
    <TextView a:text="Password:" a:layout_width="wrap_content" a:layout_height=↵
"wrap_content" />
    <EditText a:id="@+id/textPassword" a:singleLine="true" a:password="true" a:layout_width=↵
"fill_parent" a:layout_height="wrap_content" />
    <CheckBox a:text="Remember me" a:id="@+id/checkRememberMe" a:checked="true"↵
a:layout_width="wrap_content" a:layout_height="wrap_content" />
    <Button a:text="Logon" a:id="@+id/buttonLogon" a:layout_width="fill_parent"↵
a:layout_height="wrap_content" />

</LinearLayout>
```

Once you have the layout defined, it's easy enough to see how it works in landscape or portrait orientation by using the Layout sub-tab on the editor window. At the top of the Layout view, you'll see a drop-down list labeled Config. You can change this between portrait and landscape views. Figure 5-5 illustrates the form in landscape view. Notice how in this mode, the button is rendered off the bottom of the screen.

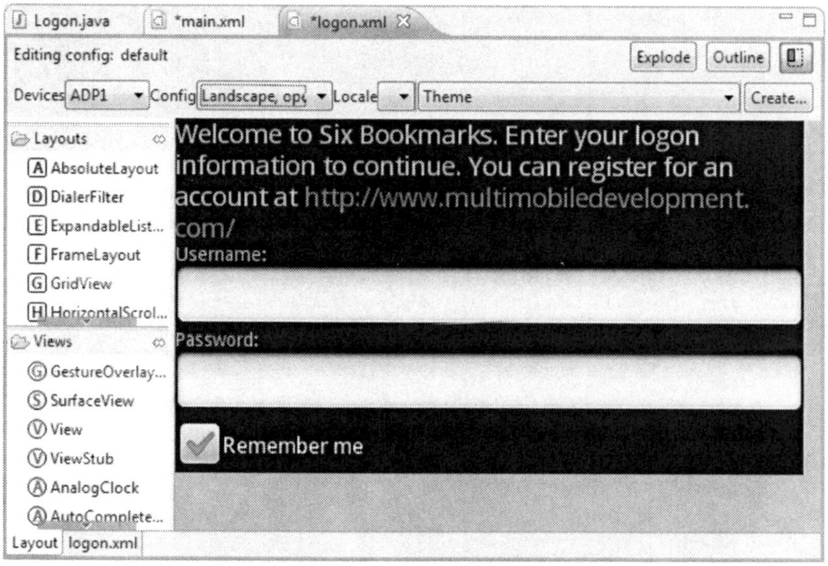

Figure 5-5. *The logon form shown in ADT's preview mode*

Model/View/Controller

When we come to do the chapters on iPhone, the recommended paradigm for building the user interface is to split the user interface and code to drive the user interface apart. There are a number of names and variations of this pattern, but a commonly known one is Model/View/Controller, or MVC. In MVC, you have separate classes for data, separate classes for views, and separate classes for code that binds the two together (the controller). Android does not mandate use of MVC, but because a) I think it's more sensible and b) the others do mandate some form of split, I'm going to recommend that we do, too.

We're going to designate our Logon class as the view and create another class called LogonController as the controller. For the logon form, there isn't really a model, but in the next chapter where we start working with bookmarks, the classes that hold the bookmark will be considered to be the model.

Contexts and Building the Controller

When our Android application is started, a "context" is created that contains global state to support the running of that application. This context is held in a class called android.content.Context, and the activities extend this class. Thus, if we have an activity, we have a context.

In the first instance, because we know that from time to time we're going to need a context, we'll create an interface called IContextSource that returns a concrete Context object. What we'll also do is create an interface called IController that extends this IContextSource interface and also adds the ability to return an activity. Figure 5-6 illustrates.

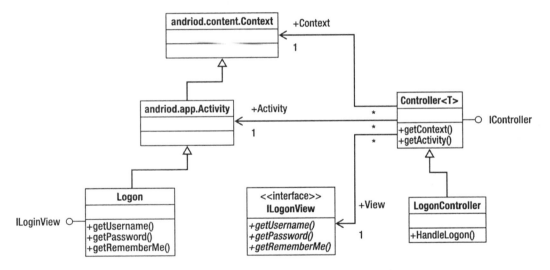

Figure 5-6. *Static structure sketch showing MVC implementation for the Logon form*

In the second instance, we need to bind the controllers and views together, which is a touch more complicated.

All MVC-like patterns call for representation of the view via an interface. This is because one of the basic tenets of MVC-like patterns is to remove dependence between the controller and view. (Practically, this is done for ease of maintenance and unit testing, although sometimes the more "academic" pitch is that you can create different views and reuse the same controllers and models.) Thus, whenever we create an activity, we're going to create a view interface for it that exposes out the data we want from the view. Specifically in this case, it's the username, password, and "remember me" values.

We're going to build our controller using generics. Therefore, if we create our view interface as ILogonView, we'll create a controller called LogonController and have this extend Controller<ILogonView>. This will give our controller a nice, strongly-typed representation of the view for internal consumption. Controller<T> will implement IController, and therefore IContextSource. Figure 5-7 illustrates.

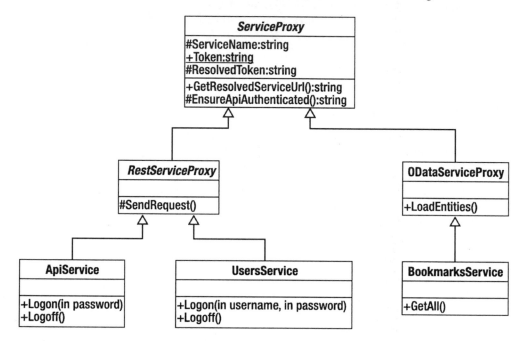

Figure 5-7. *UML static structure sketch showing the relationship between the controller and view classes*

■**NOTE** This UML diagram isn't perfectly rendered XML—I've added in some additional, non-purist bits to aid understanding.

Let's start building. Here's IContextSource:

```
package com.amxMobile.SixBookmarks.Runtime;

import android.content.*;

public interface IContextSource
{
        public Context getContext();
}
```

And here's IController:

```
package com.amxMobile.SixBookmarks.Runtime;

import android.app.*;

public interface IController extends IContextSource
{
        public Activity getActivity();
}
```

The Controller<T> implementation is straightforward—all it needs to do is expose the view, activity, and context. The name of the file should be Controller.java, and here's the code:

```
package com.amxMobile.SixBookmarks.Runtime;

import android.app.Activity;
import android.content.Context;

public abstract class Controller<T> implements IController
{
        private T _view;

        protected Controller(T view)
        {
                this._view = view;
        }

        public T getView()
        {
                return _view;
        }

        public Activity getActivity()
        {
                return (Activity)_view;
        }

        public Context getContext()
        {
                return getActivity();
        }
}
```

ILogonView needs to expose out the data values to the controller. I've chosen to do this as properties on the view. If we're building a more "purist" MVC implementation, we might choose to create a separate model class that contains these values and pass these around. However, this is perfectly serviceable for our needs. Here's the code:

```
package com.amxMobile.SixBookmarks;

public interface ILogonView
{
    public String getUsername();
    public String getPassword();
    public boolean getRememberMe();
}
```

Now we can get into the meaty bits of the problem by building the LogonController and adding functionality to Logon.

Binding the View and Controller

We'll start by building the view. As all of the magic and hard work are going to go into the controller, this should be easy.

- We'll implement ILogonView.

- We'll create a LogonController instance bound to the form when we create an instance.

- When onCreate is called, we'll set up a listener for the button's click event, and we'll tell the controller that we need to load.

- We'll create private and public properties to access the controls and expose out the controls' values.

- We'll handle the click event on the button by deferring to the controller.

Here's the code to merge into the existing Logon class:

```
package com.amxMobile.SixBookmarks;

import com.amxMobile.SixBookmarks.R;
import com.amxMobile.SixBookmarks.Runtime.*;
import com.amxMobile.SixBookmarks.Runtime.*;

import android.app.*;
import android.os.*;
import android.view.*;
import android.view.View.OnClickListener;
import android.widget.*;

public class Logon extends Activity implements OnClickListener, ILogonView
{
        private LogonController Controller;

        public Logon()
        {
                this.Controller = new LogonController(this);
        }
```

```java
/** Called when the activity is first created. */
@Override
public void onCreate(Bundle savedInstanceState) {
    super.onCreate(savedInstanceState);
    setContentView(R.layout.logon);

    // subscribe...
    getLogonButton().setOnClickListener(this);

    // load...
    try
    {
            Controller.HandleLoad();
    }
    catch(Exception ex)
    {
            MessageBox.Show(this, ex);
    }
}

private EditText getUsernameTextBox()
{
    return (EditText)this.findViewById(R.id.textUsername);
}

private EditText getPasswordTextBox()
{
    return (EditText)this.findViewById(R.id.textPassword);
}

private CheckBox getRememberMeCheckBox()
{
    return (CheckBox)this.findViewById(R.id.checkRememberMe);
}

private Button getLogonButton()
{
    return (Button)this.findViewById(R.id.buttonLogon);
}

public String getUsername()
{
    return getUsernameTextBox().getText().toString().trim();
}
```

```
public String getPassword()
{
    return getPasswordTextBox().getText().toString().trim();
}

public boolean getRememberMe()
{
    return getRememberMeCheckBox().isChecked();
}

public void onClick(View view)
{
        try
        {
                if(view.getId() == R.id.buttonLogon)
                        this.Controller.HandleLogon();
        }
        catch(Exception ex)
        {
                MessageBox.Show(this, ex);
        }
}
}
```

You'll notice on two occasions we're calling into `MessageBox.Show`. We created a stub implementation of `MessageBox` in the last chapter. We can now add a bit more detail.

`MessageBox` will either show an arbitrary message to the user through a provided string, or create a message based on an exception that's provided. This approach gives a rudimentary error handling method that we can use anywhere in our application. (Ideally, in production applications, the display and management of unhandled exceptions would need to be more sophisticated.)

Each of the overloads of `Show` will take either a `Context` directly, or an `IContextSource`. If we get given an exception, we'll defer to a method that formats this exception up for us. Here's the code:

```
package com.amxMobile.SixBookmarks.Runtime;

import android.app.*;
import android.content.*;
import android.content.*;
public class MessageBox {

        public static void Show(IContextSource context, String message)
        {
                Show(context.getContext(), message);
        }

        public static void Show(Context owner, String message)
        {
                AlertDialog.Builder builder = new AlertDialog.Builder(owner);
```

```
            builder.setTitle("Six Bookmarks");
            builder.setMessage(message);
    builder.setPositiveButton("OK", new DialogInterface.OnClickListener() {
        public void onClick(DialogInterface dialog, int whichButton) {
            // do something here..
        }
    });

            // show...
            AlertDialog dialog = builder.create();
            dialog.show();
    }

    public static void Show(IContextSource context, Exception ex)
    {
            Show(context.getContext(), ex);
    }

    public static void Show(Context owner, Exception ex)
    {
            String message = FormatException(ex);
            Show(owner, message);
    }

    private static String FormatException(Exception ex)
    {
            StringBuilder builder = new StringBuilder();
            Throwable walk = ex;
            while(walk != null)
            {
                    if(builder.length() > 0)
                            builder.append("\n");
                    builder.append(walk.getMessage());
                    walk = walk.getCause();
            }

            // return...
            return builder.toString();
    }
}
```

Before we go on, we'll need to stub out the LogonController implementation. Here's the code:

```
package com.amxMobile.SixBookmarks;

import com.amxMobile.SixBookmarks.Runtime.*;
import com.amxMobile.SixBookmarks.Services.*;
```

```
public class LogonController extends Controller<ILogonView>
{
        public LogonController(ILogonView view)
        {
                super(view);
        }

        public void HandleLoad() throws Exception
        {
                // we'll do this later…
        }

        public void HandleLogon() throws Exception
        {
                MessageBox.Show(this, "TBD");
        }
}
```

Logging On

Towards the bottom of the Logon class listing, you'll notice that the button handler called HandleLogon on the controller. What we need to do here is validate the user input—if it's valid, run a logon operation, and if it's invalid, tell the user about the problem.

Recall in Chapter 4 that when we needed to validate the logon input, we created a class called ErrorBucket that held a simple list of strings. We need a similar thing here, and so we'll add this class:

```
package com.amxMobile.SixBookmarks.Runtime;

import java.util.*;

public class ErrorBucket
{
        private ArrayList<String> _errors = new ArrayList<String>();

        public ErrorBucket()
        {
        }

        public void AddError(String error)
        {
                this._errors.add(error);
        }
        public boolean getHasErrors()
        {
                if(this._errors.size() > 0)
                        return true;
```

```
        else
                return false;
}

public String GetAllErrors()
{
        StringBuilder builder = new StringBuilder();
        for(String error : _errors)
        {
                if(builder.length() > 0)
                        builder.append("\n");
                builder.append(error);
        }

        // return...
        return builder.toString();
}
}
```

You'll see that the structure of the code is basically the same as that given in Chapter 4. This is an important point. Because you essentially cannot share code easily between the different platforms, if you do need to manage an intellectual property stack that encompasses different platforms, you can get considerable benefit by doing things the same way on each. This makes it easier to maintain the application, as developers approach problems with a "pre-loaded" expectation about how something should work.

Back on the LogonController class, here's the HandleLogon method. This defers to DoLogon, which actually calls the service proxy.

```
// Add to LogonController.java - replace existing method…
        public void HandleLogon() throws Exception
        {
                ILogonView view = getView();

                ErrorBucket bucket = new ErrorBucket();
                String username = view.getUsername();
                if(username == null || username.length() == 0)
                        bucket.AddError("Username not specified");
                String password = view.getPassword();
                if(password == null || password.length() == 0)
                        bucket.AddError("Password not specified");

                // errors?
                if(!(bucket.getHasErrors()))
                        DoLogon(username, password, view.getRememberMe());
                else
                        MessageBox.Show(this, bucket.GetAllErrors());
        }
```

```
        private boolean DoLogon(String username, String password, boolean rememberMe)↵
throws Exception
        {
                UsersService users = new UsersService();
                LogonResponse response = users.Logon(username, password);

                // now what?
                if(response.getResult() == LogonResult.LogonOk)
                {
                        // in a while we'll add code here to show the bookmarks page...
                        MessageBox.Show(this, "Logon OK!");
                        return true;
                }
                else
                {
                        MessageBox.Show(this, response.getMessage());
                        return false;
                }
        }
```

I hope you can see there the power of creating these nicely defined service proxy objects, as the actual code to manipulate the remote service is very easy.

There isn't much to show in this chapter, as most of the code is behind-the-scenes stuff. However, if you do run the project, you can at least try providing different values for the username and password and seeing the results. Figure 5-8 shows the result of a successful logon.

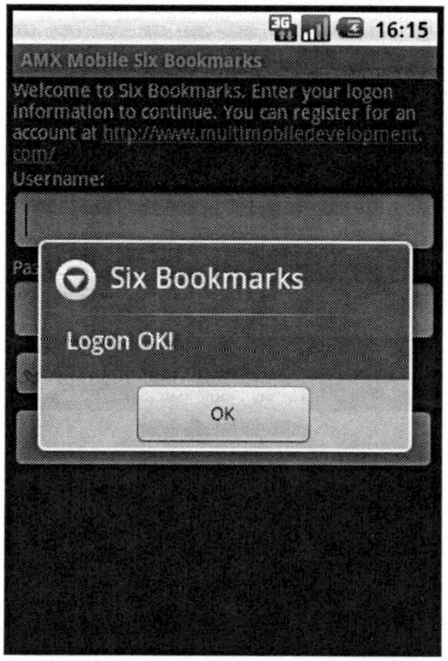

Figure 5-8. *Success! We've logged on*

"Remember Me"

The final bit of this that we'll round off is the "remember me" functionality.

There are a few ways to do this, but an easy-but-a-bit-clunky way of doing it is to store the user's username and password locally on the device. When the logon form runs, we can see if we have preset credentials and try to log them in.

Android offers a thing called "shared preferences" that can be used for this. This is basically a bucket of values indexed by name that is stored locally to the application. They cannot be accessed by other applications, but they are not super-super secure, in that they are on the device and they're not stored in an encrypted fashion. I tend to think they offer a "good enough" level of security; however, if your business mandate is to be uber-secure, you should seek to encrypt or otherwise secure those values.

Shared preferences are accessed through the context. You ask the context to provide you with an `android.context.SharedPreferences` instance. You can read directly from that, but if you want to write to it, you need to ask for an editor object. Here's the code to add to the controller:

```java
// Add to LogonController.java
        private void StoreCredentials(String username, String password)
        {
                // get the prefs...  (we'll add these constant strings later...)
                SharedPreferences prefs = getContext().getSharedPreferences⏎
(PreferencesFilename, 0);
                SharedPreferences.Editor editor = prefs.edit();
                editor.putString(UsernameKey, username);
                editor.putString(PasswordKey, password);

                // save...
                editor.commit();
        }

        private void ClearCredentials()
        {
                // store a null string...
                this.StoreCredentials(null, null);
        }
```

`PreferencesFilename` is an arbitrary string—I've defined that and the `UsernameKey` and `PasswordKey` values as constants within the class. We'll see those in a moment.

In the `DoLogon` method, we need to call `StoreCredentials` and `ClearCredentials`. Modify `DoLogon` to include the calls:

```java
        private boolean DoLogon(String username, String password, boolean rememberMe)⏎
 throws Exception
        {
                UsersService users = new UsersService();
                LogonResponse response = users.Logon(username, password);
```

89

```
                // now what?
                if(response.getResult() == LogonResult.LogonOk)
                {
                        // store the credentials?
                        if(rememberMe)
                                StoreCredentials(username, password);
                        else
                                ClearCredentials();

                        // in a while we'll add code here to show the bookmarks page...
                        MessageBox.Show(this, "Logon OK!");
                        return true;
                }
                else
                {
                        MessageBox.Show(this, response.getMessage());
                        return false;
                }
        }
```

Recall that we created a stub method for HandleLoad but provided no operation. We can now do this by loading the username and password from the shared preferences bucket and calling DoLogon. If DoLogon fails, we'll clear the credentials and allow the natural flow of the application to prompt the user for new credentials. Here's code to add to the controller, which defines the constant strings used for the methods and the new HandleLoad implementation.

```
public class LogonController extends Controller<ILogonView>
{
        private final static String PreferencesFilename = "UsernamePreferences";
        private final static String UsernameKey = "Username";
        private final static String PasswordKey = "Password";

        public LogonController(ILogonView view)
        {
                super(view);
        }

        public void HandleLoad() throws Exception
        {
                SharedPreferences prefs = getContext().getSharedPreferences↵
(PreferencesFilename, 0);
                String username = prefs.getString(UsernameKey, null);
                String password = prefs.getString(PasswordKey, null);
```

```
            // can we automate the logon?
            if(username != null && username.length() > 0)
            {
                    // try - if we fail clear the credentials and prompt the user...
                    if(!(DoLogon(username, password, true)))
                            ClearCredentials();
            }
    }

    // code omitted for brevity…
}
```

Conclusion

In this chapter, we've covered a lot of ground related to building our proper Android application and being able to call the hosted services at http://services.multimobiledevelopment.com. We built a set of support methods for working with web resources and XML, and the proxy objects needed to call up to the server. We then went on to build the user interface and ultimately called the server's Logon method to log on the user. In the next chapter, we'll see how to use the bookmarks OData service to bring back bookmarks and store them in a local SQL database.

■ ■ ■

CHAPTER 6

Android: An ORM Layer on SQLite

In the last chapter, we built the foundation of our application and built a logon screen that connected up to the Bookmarks service over the Internet. In this chapter, we're going to look at downloading the bookmarks from the OData service, storing them in a local SQLite database and displaying them in the screen. We'll look at capturing changes to the bookmarks and pushing them back up to the server in the next chapter.

SQLite on Android

This will be the first time that we meet the SQLite database engine in this book. SQLite is used and mentioned heavily in this book and this book's sister book that covers the Microsoft mobile technologies, BlackBerry and HTML5.

SQLite is an open source in-memory database engine that is long-established and is published under an unusual license in that it is placed in the public domain with no licensing restrictions. It is baked into Android, iOS, BlackBerry and HTML5 Web browsers that wish to support HTML5 local storage also use SQLite. In fact, the only place where it is not supported natively by the device vendor is on Windows Phone 7 and Windows Mobile, although community efforts exist to make the platform available there as well.

It is an ANSI-92 compatible database, thus if you already know how to develop software that uses a relational database, you already know how to use SQLite.

Entities

In Chapter 3, we went through the principle of building an object relational mapping layer that could be "repurposed" for use in the Android, iPhone, and BlackBerry applications. (This layer will work on Windows Phone 7, just as soon as it has a database management system available!) Chapter 3 discusses the theory about how you build such a thing. This chapter is going to look at how you actually do it.

As discussed in Chapter 3, the most important thing about an ORM layer is to imbue it with decent metadata. It's only through this metadata that you can code in a decent level of "magic" to make working with the ORM entities easier than working with the native data directly. Without good metadata, you'll spend half your life fighting the ORM tool.

In this section, we're going to look at building the metadata to support the entities and the entity class itself. In the next section, we'll look at physically calling the database and obtaining a list of entities.

■**NOTE** The ORM layer that we build here and in the other chapters is going to be pretty basic and missing support for various data types and other functions. This is done to make the book easier to comprehend. However, keep an eye on the documentation at www.multimobiledevelopment.com/, as it's my fervent hope that this author continues to develop and enhance such functionality for all of the platforms going forward.

"EntityType"

In Chapter 3, I discussed the idea of an EntityType class. This class does two things. In the first instance, there exists exactly one instance of an entity type for every database table in the system. In the second instance, static members of the entity type maintain a register of all of the available entity types. The upshot of this is that from anywhere in the application, you access a list of all of the tables that exist, and from there, all of the fields that exist on any table.

In more sophisticated implementations of this sort of metadata system that you might see, the entity types are loaded from attributes (C#) or annotations (Java) embedded within the code. However, in the simple implementations we'll see in this book, we're going to programmatically set up the entity types.

In Chapter 3, we discussed that we need an EntityItem class, EntityField class, and EntityType class. EntityItem is used to provide every piece of metadata in the system will with both a "programmatic name" and a "native name". The "native name" is the name of the item in the underlying store, and the "programmatic name" is the name that we would prefer to use. This abstraction is helpful for situations where you have a table called—for example—TBL_CUST and would prefer your related class to be called Customer. (In our actual implementation, both the native name and programmatic name will generally be the same.)

Without further ado, here's a listing that contains the code for EntityItem. Add this to the project in the usual way.

```
package com.amxMobile.SixBookmarks.Entities;

public abstract class EntityItem
{
        private String _name;
        private String _nativeName;

        protected EntityItem(String name, String nativeName)
        {
                _name = name;

                if(nativeName != null)
                        _nativeName = nativeName;
                else
                        _nativeName = name;
        }
```

```
        public String getName()
        {
                return _name;
        }

        public String getNativeName()
        {
                return _nativeName;
        }
}
```

Now we can look at the fields.

A single field has a number of attributes, mainly the following:

- A native name and a (programmatic) name

- A data type

- A size

- Flags indicating special functionality (In this chapter, we're going to have only one, which indicates whether the field is a key field. In a full-on implementation, another example of a flag would be indicating whether the field could be nullable.)

In this example, we're going to support just two data types—in a more full-on implementation, we'd obviously need to support all of the data types that the underlying database supports. (If we implement all of them now, half the book will be taken up with methods exposing out all of the data types.) Our server-side service used only strings and 32-bit integers, so these are the two that we will use.

■**NOTE** We will use Boolean data types on the entity, but we'll store them as integers in the SQLite database. SQLite's data type support is a little strange—you can store any value in any column in SQLite regardless of the definition, and it just tries to "work it out" when it retrieves data. For this and other reasons, we're going to handle Boolean data in our data access layer rather than natively in SQLite.

We'll add this DataType enumeration so that we can refer to these two types:

```
package com.amxMobile.SixBookmarks.Entities;

public enum DataType
{
        String, Int32
}
```

Now that we have the enumeration, we can build EntityField. As well as supporting native name (defined in the base), name (also defined in the base), data type, size, and an indication as to whether the field is a key, we'll have another property holding the ordinal of the field within the type. I'll explain more about this ordinal value later. Here's the listing:

```java
package com.amxMobile.SixBookmarks.Entities;

public class EntityField extends EntityItem
{
        private DataType _type;
        private int _size;
        private boolean _isKey;
        private int _ordinal;

        public EntityField(String name, String nativeName, DataType type, int size, int↵
 ordinal)
        {
                super(name, nativeName);

                // set...
                _type = type;
                _size = size;
                _ordinal = ordinal;
        }

        public int getOrdinal()
        {
                return _ordinal;
        }

        public DataType getDataType()
        {
                return _type;
        }

        public int getSize()
        {
                return _size;
        }

        public boolean getIsKey()
        {
                return _isKey;
        }

        public void setIsKey(boolean value)
        {
                _isKey = value;
        }
}
```

The EntityType class has a number of different functions. I won't go through them all here; rather, I will concentrate on the basics for keeping a register of the available entity types and the fields against each one.

So that we can effectively work with entities, we need EntityType to be able to instantiate instances of individual entities and collections of entities. In this example, we're going to have only one entity—Bookmark. In any real world application, you're likely to have many entitity types. We'll hold references to the relevant Java types so that we can create the object instances that we want programmatically. (A Java type is synonymous to a .NET type. Both provide runtime access to the type metadata system.) Our motivation for this arrangement is so that we can say to framework code "give me a list of bookmarks," and the framework code itself will be able to create an appropriate collection type and individual entities.

In addition, we're going to add a method to EntityType called AddField. This will be used to programmatically define the fields available on an entity type. This AddField method will look at the size of the fields collection and use this size as the ordinal for the field. Thus, when we add fields, the first will have ordinal 0, the second ordinal 1, and so on. Having field ordinals will come in handy when getting or setting in-memory values against the entity.

Here's the listing for EntityType that looks after storing the instance and collection types, and storing the list of fields. It, too, extends EntityItem—note how when we create an instance, we'll call the base class and set the programmatic name to the name of the Java class, and the native name to whatever the user specifies.

```
package com.amxMobile.SixBookmarks.Entities;

import java.lang.reflect.*;
import java.util.*;

public class EntityType extends EntityItem
{
        private ArrayList<EntityField> _fields = new ArrayList<EntityField>();
        private Class _instanceType = null;
        private Class _collectionType = null;

        public EntityType(Class instanceType, Class collectionType, String nativeName)
        {
                super(instanceType.getName(), nativeName);
                _instanceType = instanceType;
                _collectionType = collectionType;
        }

        public ArrayList<EntityField> getFields()
        {
                return _fields;
        }

        public EntityField AddField(String name, String nativeName, DataType type, int size)
        {
                EntityField field = new EntityField(name, nativeName, type, size,↵
_fields.size());
                _fields.add(field);
```

```
                // return...
                return field;
        }

        public Class getInstanceType()
        {
                return _instanceType;
        }

        public Class getCollectionType()
        {
                return _collectionType;
        }

        public Entity CreateInstance() throws Exception
        {
                return (Entity)getInstanceType().newInstance();
        }

        public ArrayList<Entity> CreateCollectionInstance() throws Exception
        {
                return (ArrayList<Entity>)getCollectionType().newInstance();
        }
}
```

We've assumed that entities will always have a base class of Entity (which we'll build shortly) and also be of type ArrayList. (Entity is going to hold an instance of a row in a table in the database.)

Also on an entity type, we're going to need to be able to find a field with a specific name, find the key fields, or determine whether a field with a specified name actually exists. (This latter one is used for populating entities from data received over XML where the XML may reference fields that we don't know about.) Here are the three methods that also need to be added to EntityType:

```
// Add to EntityType.java
        public EntityField GetField(String name, boolean throwIfNotFound) throws Exception
        {
                for(EntityField field : _fields)
                {
                        if(field.getName().compareToIgnoreCase(name) == 0)
                                return field;
                }

                // throw...
                if(throwIfNotFound)
                        throw new Exception(String.format("Failed to find a field with⏎
name '%s'.", name));
```

```
        else
                return null;
}

public EntityField GetKeyField() throws Exception
{
        for(EntityField field : _fields)
        {
                if(field.getIsKey())
                        return field;
        }

        // throw...
        throw new Exception("Failed to find a key field.");
}

public boolean IsField(String name) throws Exception
{
        EntityField field = this.GetField(name, false);
        if(field != null)
                return true;
        else
                return false;
}
```

Another method that we'll need on EntityType is one that returns the short name of a class. The getName method on a regular Java Class type returns a fully-qualified name, including the package, e.g., com.AmxMobile.SixBookmarks.Database.Bookmark. This method—which needs to be added to EntityType—returns just the last part:

```
// Add to EntityType.java
        public String getShortName()
        {
                String name = getName();
                int index = name.lastIndexOf((char)'.');
                return name.substring(index + 1);
        }
```

Next, recall that the other function EntityType needs is the ability to hold a register of the available entity types. We'll do this by creating a static hashtable on EntityType and methods called RegisterEntityType and GetEntityType.

Here's the code to hold and query the register:

```
public class EntityType extends EntityItem
{
        private static Hashtable<String, EntityType> _entityTypes =↩
 new Hashtable<String, EntityType>();
```

```
// code omitted for brevity…

public static void RegisterEntityType(EntityType entityType)
{
        _entityTypes.put(entityType.getInstanceType().getName(), entityType);
}

public static EntityType GetEntityType(Class type) throws Exception
{
        String name = type.getName();
        for(String key : _entityTypes.keySet())
        {
                if(key.compareTo(name) == 0)
                        return _entityTypes.get(key);
        }

        // throw...
        throw new Exception(String.format("Failed to get entity type for↵
'%s'.", type));
}

// code omitted for brevity…
}
```

Creating the Basic "Entity" Class

We need a way of programmatically registering the entity type for the bookmark entity. One way to do this is to create a global "runtime" class that is used to boot up and tear down the application. We'll add one of these to our project called SixBookmarksRuntime; however, we won't build this until a little later.

Before we do that, we need to create our Bookmark and BookmarkCollection objects.

BookmarkCollection is the easy one, as all we're going to do with this is create a new class that inherits from ArrayList<Bookmark>. Here's the listing:

```
package com.amxMobile.SixBookmarks.Database;

import java.util.*;

public class BookmarkCollection extends ArrayList<Bookmark>
{
}
```

Bookmark is a little more complicated, as we need to have an Entity class to inherit from. Entity is quite a lengthy class, and we're going to add to this as we go. For now we'll stub the basics.

The basic functionality of an entity is to store a dynamic list of data that represents the columns in the underlying database table. An entity will be created manually either by the developer or by framework code that retrieves the data from some source. At some point during the entity's life, the data stored within will either be read for display on a screen, or be used to issue some sort of change request to the underlying store.

In our entity, we are going to hold three sets of values. First, we're going to store a reference to our related EntityType instance. Second, we're going to store an array of values that map 1:1 with the columns defined as being in the underlying store. (The entity type is going to tell us which columns are defined.) Third and finally, we're going to store a bunch of flags and other fields that will help the entity keep track of its internal state.

Storage of data within the entity will be done in "slots." You will notice on our EntityField instance, we have a property called Ordinal and that we calculated this ordinal in the AddField method on EntityType. This ordinal value is the index of the slot in the entity. Thus, if we have five fields, we'll have five slots numbered from zero to four inclusive.

■**NOTE** Recall in Chapter 3, we spoke about the BootFX application framework and its ORM functionality. Internally within BootFX, this functionality is known as "storage."

Here's the listing for this basic "storage" functionality in Entity:

```
package com.amxMobile.SixBookmarks.Entities;

import java.util.*;
import com.amxMobile.SixBookmarks.Runtime.*;

public abstract class Entity
{
        private EntityType _entityType;

        private Object[] _values;
        private int[] _flags;

        private static final int FIELDFLAGS_NOTLOADED = 0;
        private static final int FIELDFLAGS_LOADED = 1;
        private static final int FIELDFLAGS_MODIFIED = 2;

        protected Entity() throws Exception
        {
                _entityType = EntityType.GetEntityType(this.getClass());

                // slots...
                int count = _entityType.getFields().size();
                _values = new Object[count];
                _flags = new int[count];
        }

        public EntityType getEntityType()
        {
                return _entityType;
        }
```

}

Note in that listing how within the constructor, we ask EntityType to provide an entity type instance back to us that represents the entity itself via the GetEntityType static method. Caching this within the class allows us quick access to the entity's metadata directly from within the class. Also worthy of note is the fact that we define the size of the _values and **_flags** arrays to be equal to the number of available fields.

Being able to store data isn't much use without a set of methods that can retrieve and set the values in them. We'll start by looking at the methods that set values.

Setting Values in an Entity

Whenever we set a value within an entity we'll be doing one of two things—we'll either be plugging in a value that the user has provided through some form of input, or we'll be plugging in a value that we have retrieved from a database or service. It's important that we can distinguish between these two operations—if the user has done something to invoke the change (e.g., keyed a value into a form), we may need to update the underlying store with that value. Conversely, if the user has not changed something, we do not want to be issuing unnecessary update requests back to the underlying store.

In the last section, we added constants to indicate the state of the field's storage slot, specifically FIELDFLAGS_NOTLOADED, FIELDFLAGS_LOADED, and FIELDFLAGS_MODIFIED. In addition, we need an enumeration that will be used to tell the entity what sort of set operation has occurred. Here's the SetReason enumeration that describes these two possible changes:

```
package com.amxMobile.SixBookmarks.Entities;

public enum SetReason
{
        UserSet, Load
}
```

As we add methods to the entity, we'll find that oftentimes we need to add overloads for each of the methods that take either the name of a field as a string or an actual instance of an EntityField. This is going to create additional code, but there is a substantially higher level of utility in not requiring the caller to dig out an EntityField instance every time they wish to access field data. Whenever one of the string-based "name" overloads is used, we'll defer to the entity type instance for the field name. Here's additional code for the Entity class that will allow values to be set within the slots.

```
// Add to Entity.java
        protected void SetValue(String name, Object value, SetReason reason)↵
 throws Exception
        {
                EntityField field = getEntityType().GetField(name, true);
                SetValue(field, value, reason);
        }

        public void SetValue(EntityField field, Object value, SetReason reason)↵
 throws Exception
        {
                int ordinal = field.getOrdinal();
                SetValue(ordinal, value, reason);
```

```java
        }
        private void SetValue(int ordinal, Object value, SetReason reason) throws Exception
        {
                _values[ordinal] = value;

                // if...
                SetFlag(ordinal, FIELDFLAGS_LOADED);
                if(reason == SetReason.UserSet)
                        SetFlag(ordinal, FIELDFLAGS_MODIFIED);
        }

        private void SetFlag(int ordinal, int flag)
        {
                _flags[ordinal] = _flags[ordinal] | flag;
        }
```

You'll also see there that there is a third, private overload that takes the ordinal of the field. This isn't strictly required here, but this pattern of a private overload that takes the ordinal makes for easier work when getting values out.

Also note the if statement towards the end of the third overload. This will set a flag to indicate that a value is available, and if the reason for calling the method was that the user asked us to (e.g., by keying in a new value into a text box), we'll also indicate that the field is modified.

Retrieving the values is—perhaps oddly—a little trickier, as we have to deal with the different data types. In the first instance, we need to be able to behave differently depending on the state of the data. For example, if we're trying to retrieve the value for a field, and we have not loaded it, we need to throw an error indicating that the value is not available. (Some implementations, including BootFX, will demand load data in this situation. However, for simplicity, we're not doing this here.)

Here are some helper methods to be placed into the Entity class that let us understand the state of field slots in the entity:

```java
// Add to Entity.java
        public boolean getIsLoaded(EntityField field)
        {
                return getIsLoaded(field.getOrdinal());
        }

        private boolean getIsLoaded(int index)
        {
                return IsFlagSet(index, FIELDFLAGS_LOADED);
        }

        public boolean getIsModified(EntityField field)
        {
                return getIsModified(field.getOrdinal());
        }

        private boolean getIsModified(int index)
        {
                return IsFlagSet(index, FIELDFLAGS_MODIFIED);
```

```
        }
        private boolean IsFlagSet(int index, int flag)
        {
                if((_flags[index] & flag) == flag)
                        return true;
                else
                        return false;
        }
```

These work on individual fields, and you can see how we've tried to keep it neat. The public modifier on the getIsLoaded and getIsModified overloads is required, as later on, we'll need to access these from another class.

Now that we can do that, we can add methods to tell whether the entity is new, or whether it has been modified. The rules here are the following:

- *In order to tell if the entity is **new***: If we do not have a key value defined, then it's new.

- *In order to tell if the entity is **modified***: If we walk the fields and discovered that at least one is modified, then the entity is modified..

Here's the code:

```
// Add to Entity.java
        public boolean getIsNew() throws Exception
        {
                EntityField key = getEntityType().GetKeyField();

                // state...
                if(!(getIsLoaded(key)) && !(getIsModified(key)))
                        return true;
                else
                        return false;
        }

        public boolean getIsDeleted()
        {
                return false;
        }

        public boolean getIsModified()
        {
                for(int index = 0; index < _flags.length; index++)
                {
                        if(getIsModified(index))
                                return true;
                }

                // nope...
                return false;
        }
```

Those methods lay the groundwork for the GetValue methods that we implied must exist when we created our SetValue methods earlier. The only difference in the rule is that if we ask for a value, if we're not new and we don't have it, we have to throw an error, as we can't demand-load the value. Here's the code:

```
// Add to Entity.java
        public Object GetValue(String name) throws Exception
        {
                EntityField field = getEntityType().GetField(name, true);
                return GetValue(field.getOrdinal());
        }

        public Object GetValue(EntityField field) throws Exception
        {
                return GetValue(field.getOrdinal());
        }

        private Object GetValue(int index) throws Exception
        {
                // do we need to demand load?
                if(!(getIsLoaded(index)) && !(getIsNew()))
                        throw new Exception("Demand loading is not implemented.");

                // return...
                return _values[index];
        }
```

Recall that before, I said that we were going to have limited support for data types in this implementation. Here's why: in order to give the entity a higher level of utility, we need to create versions of GetValue that are strongly-typed. These will deal with the mucking around with trying to get data out of the entity coerced into the type of data that the caller is expecting. Here's the implementation of GetValue equivalents that provide for strongly typed string and integer values:

```
// Add to Entity.java
        public String GetStringValue(String name) throws Exception
        {
                EntityField field = getEntityType().GetField(name, true);
                return GetStringValue(field);
        }

        public String GetStringValue(EntityField field) throws Exception
        {
                Object value = GetValue(field);
                if(value != null)
                        return value.toString();
                else
                        return null;
```

```java
        }
        public int GetInt32Value(String name) throws Exception
        {
                EntityField field = getEntityType().GetField(name, true);
                return GetInt32Value(field);
        }

        public int GetInt32Value(EntityField field) throws Exception
        {
                Object value = GetValue(field);
                if(value == null)
                        return 0;
                else if(value instanceof Number)
                        return ((Number)value).intValue();
                else
                        throw new Exception(String.format("Cannot handle '%s'.",
value.getClass()));
        }

        public boolean GetBooleanValue(String name) throws Exception
        {
                EntityField field = getEntityType().GetField(name, true);
                return GetBooleanValue(field);
        }

        public boolean GetBooleanValue(EntityField field) throws Exception
        {
                Object value = GetValue(field);
                if(value == null)
                        return false;
                else if(value instanceof Number)
                {
                        int asInt = ((Number)value).intValue();
                        if(asInt == 0)
                                return false;
                        else
                                return true;
                }
                else
                        throw new Exception(String.format("Cannot handle '%s'.",
value.getClass()));
        }
```

Now that we can get data into and out of our base entity, let's look at creating a strongly typed Bookmark class.

Building "Bookmark"

The point of ORM is that you're looking to get the entity layer to do most of the hard work of managing the data for you—the principle being that it is easier to call a property called Name and know you're getting a string value back than it is to request an item with name "name" out of a bucket of values returned over a SQL interface. Thus, we need to add a bunch of properties to Bookmark that abstract calls to GetValue and SetValue. (Plus, with an ORM layer, you don't have any application that's 50 percent dynamic SQL statements or stored procedure setup calls.)

The fields that we're going to store locally, as a minimum, are a local unique ID, the ordinal, the name, and the URL.

However, there's one thing to consider. In order for our database to support the synchronization functionality that we'll build in the next chapter, we also need to store flags to indicate whether the item has been modified or deleted *locally*. We'll add two additional columns called LocalModified and LocalDeleted to achieve this.

Here's the code for the new Bookmark class that extends entities and provides getters and setters for our six columns.

```
package com.amxMobile.SixBookmarks.Database;

import java.util.*
import com.amxMobile.SixBookmarks.Entities.*;

public class Bookmark extends Entity
{
        public final static String BookmarkIdKey = "BookmarkId";
        public final static String OrdinalKey = "Ordinal";
        public final static String NameKey = "Name";
        public final static String UrlKey = "Url";
        public final static String LocalModifiedKey = "LocalModified";
        public final static String LocalDeletedKey = "LocalDeleted";

        public Bookmark() throws Exception
        {
        }

        public int getBookmarkId() throws Exception
        {
                return GetInt32Value(BookmarkIdKey);
        }

        public void setBookmarkId(int value) throws Exception
        {
                SetValue(BookmarkIdKey, value, SetReason.UserSet);
        }

        public int getOrdinal() throws Exception
        {
                return GetInt32Value(OrdinalKey);
        }
```

```java
        public void setOrdinal(int value) throws Exception
        {
                SetValue(OrdinalKey, value, SetReason.UserSet);
        }

        public String getName() throws Exception
        {
                return GetStringValue(NameKey);
        }

        public void setName(String value) throws Exception
        {
                SetValue(NameKey, value, SetReason.UserSet);
        }

        public String getUrl() throws Exception
        {
                return GetStringValue(UrlKey);
        }

        public void setUrl(String value) throws Exception
        {
                SetValue(UrlKey, value, SetReason.UserSet);
        }

        public boolean getLocalModified() throws Exception
        {
                return GetBooleanValue(LocalModifiedKey);
        }

        public void setLocalModified(boolean value) throws Exception
        {
                SetValue(LocalModifiedKey, value, SetReason.UserSet);
        }

        public boolean getLocalDeleted() throws Exception
        {
                return GetBooleanValue(LocalDeletedKey);
        }

        public void setLocalDeleted(boolean b) throws Exception
        {
                SetValue(LocalDeletedKey, b, SetReason.UserSet);
        }
}
```

You can see there that I have created a set of constants at the top of the class that define the names of the fields. This approach makes working with the data much easier and stops errors resulting from typos.

■ **NOTE** ORM layers usually have code generation so that you do not have to scaffold up all of these classes manually—which is good, because, frankly, setting them up manually is a pain.

Registering the "EntityType"

Now that we have a functional Bookmark class defined, we can build the SixBookmarksRuntime class that we mentioned earlier. This class's sole function will be to boot up the application, a key aspect of which is defining the entity type for the Bookmark entity.

This operation is reasonably straightforward—we need to create an entity type that knows about Bookmark and BookmarkCollection, add fields to it (remembering to set the BookmarkId field to be the key), and then register the entity type in the static memory managed by EntityType. Here's the code:

```
package com.amxMobile.SixBookmarks.Runtime;

import com.amxMobile.SixBookmarks.Database.Bookmark;
import com.amxMobile.SixBookmarks.Database.BookmarkCollection;
import com.amxMobile.SixBookmarks.Entities.DataType;
import com.amxMobile.SixBookmarks.Entities.EntityType;

public class SixBookmarksRuntime
{
        public static void Start()
        {
                // create the entity type...
                EntityType bookmark = new EntityType(Bookmark.class,⏎
BookmarkCollection.class, "Bookmarks");
                bookmark.AddField(Bookmark.BookmarkIdKey, Bookmark.BookmarkIdKey,⏎
DataType.Int32, -1).setIsKey(true);
                bookmark.AddField(Bookmark.OrdinalKey, Bookmark.OrdinalKey,⏎
DataType.Int32, -1);
                bookmark.AddField(Bookmark.NameKey, Bookmark.NameKey, DataType.String, 128);
                bookmark.AddField(Bookmark.UrlKey, Bookmark.UrlKey, DataType.String, 256);
                bookmark.AddField(Bookmark.LocalModifiedKey, Bookmark.LocalModifiedKey,⏎
DataType.Int32, -1);
                bookmark.AddField(Bookmark.LocalDeletedKey, Bookmark.LocalDeletedKey,⏎
DataType.Int32, -1);

                // register it...
                EntityType.RegisterEntityType(bookmark);
        }
}
```

With the runtime class created, we can call the Start method. It doesn't really matter where this happens in the code, so long as it happens before we need to use the entities. An easy place to locate it in our code is within onCreate method in the Logon activity that we went through in the last chapter. Here's the modification to the Logon class (some code has been removed for brevity):

```
package com.amxMobile.SixBookmarks;

public class Logon extends Activity implements OnClickListener, ILogonView
{
// code removed for brevity…

    @Override
    public void onCreate(Bundle savedInstanceState) {
        super.onCreate(savedInstanceState);
        setContentView(R.layout.logon);

        // start the runtime...
        SixBookmarksRuntime.Start();

        // subscribe...
        getLogonButton().setOnClickListener(this);

        // load...
        try
        {
                Controller.HandleLoad();
        }
        catch(Exception ex)
        {
                MessageBox.Show(this, ex);
        }
    }

// code removed for brevity…
}
```

Displaying Some Fake Bookmarks

We've still got a long way to go until we can get some data out of the database and onto the screen, so we'll take a little diversion here and display some fake bookmarks. This will involve us creating the form that will be used to show the bookmarks, and then we'll manually create some Bookmark objects to show on them. Later, we'll replace the fake bookmarks with ones that we've loaded from the database.

Creating the Form

When we created our project, the Android project wizard created the logon activity and form layout for us. As of the time of writing, the Android/Eclipse plugin doesn't have a wizard for adding new activities, so we'll have to do this manually. (Here's hoping such a wizard comes along soon!) There are five steps to physically create a form and activity:

- Create a new activity class
- Create a new **Android XML File** of type **Layout**
- Specify the new activity in the `AndroidManifest.xml` file
- Create a new view interface
- Create a new controller

Creating the "Navigator.xml" Layout

We'll start by adding the layout to the project. Locate the `~/res/layout` folder within the project in **Package Explorer**, right-click and select **New – Other**, and from the window that appears, select **Android - Android XML File**. Specify the **File** as **navigator.xml**. (Remember that it's more helpful to name your resources entirely in lower case.) Figure 6-1 illustrates.

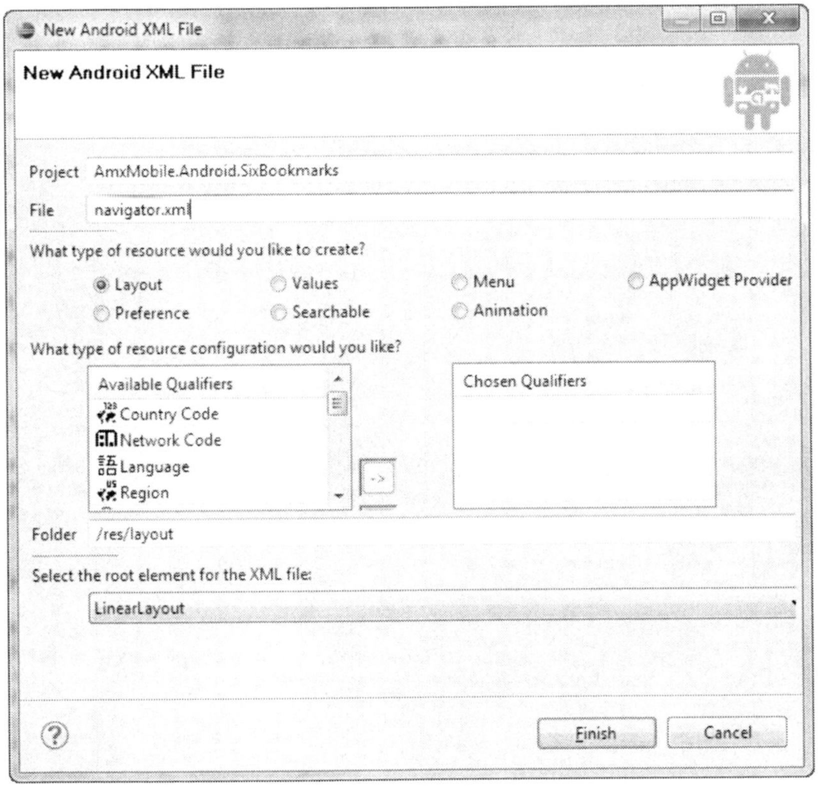

Figure 6-1. *Creating the "navigator.xml" file*

Click **Finish**, and the new layout file will be created.

Our navigator.xml layout will be quite simple—it will consist of nine buttons in a vertical list. The listing follows here. Remember that you may need to swap to the XML view using the tab at the bottom of the view to see the XML layout.

```xml
<?xml version="1.0" encoding="utf-8"?>
<LinearLayout xmlns:a="http://schemas.android.com/apk/res/android"
a:layout_width="fill_parent" a:layout_height="fill_parent"
        a:orientation="vertical">

        <Button a:text="..." a:id="@+id/buttonNavigate1" a:layout_width="fill_parent"
a:layout_height="wrap_content" />
        <Button a:text="..." a:id="@+id/buttonNavigate2" a:layout_width="fill_parent"
a:layout_height="wrap_content" />
        <Button a:text="..." a:id="@+id/buttonNavigate3" a:layout_width="fill_parent"
a:layout_height="wrap_content" />
        <Button a:text="..." a:id="@+id/buttonNavigate4" a:layout_width="fill_parent"
a:layout_height="wrap_content" />
        <Button a:text="..." a:id="@+id/buttonNavigate5" a:layout_width="fill_parent"
a:layout_height="wrap_content" />
        <Button a:text="..." a:id="@+id/buttonNavigate6" a:layout_width="fill_parent"
a:layout_height="wrap_content" />

        <Button a:text="Configure" a:id="@+id/buttonConfigure" a:layout_width=
"fill_parent" a:layout_height="wrap_content" />
        <Button a:text="Logoff" a:id="@+id/buttonLogoff" a:layout_width="fill_parent"
a:layout_height="wrap_content" />
        <Button a:text="About" a:id="@+id/buttonAbout" a:layout_width="fill_parent"
a:layout_height="wrap_content" />

</LinearLayout>
```

NOTE Recall that in Chapter 5, I mentioned that the files created by the Android SDK name the Android XML namespace with the shortname android, which leads to very wordy XML. I have again collapsed the default android shortname to a for the work in this chapter.

You can preview the layout of the form within Eclipse. Click on the **Layout** tab in the bottom left-hand corner of the view, and you'll see a layout preview. By default, this shows a landscape layout—use the **Config** drop-down at the top of the list to select a portrait view. Figure 6-2 illustrates.

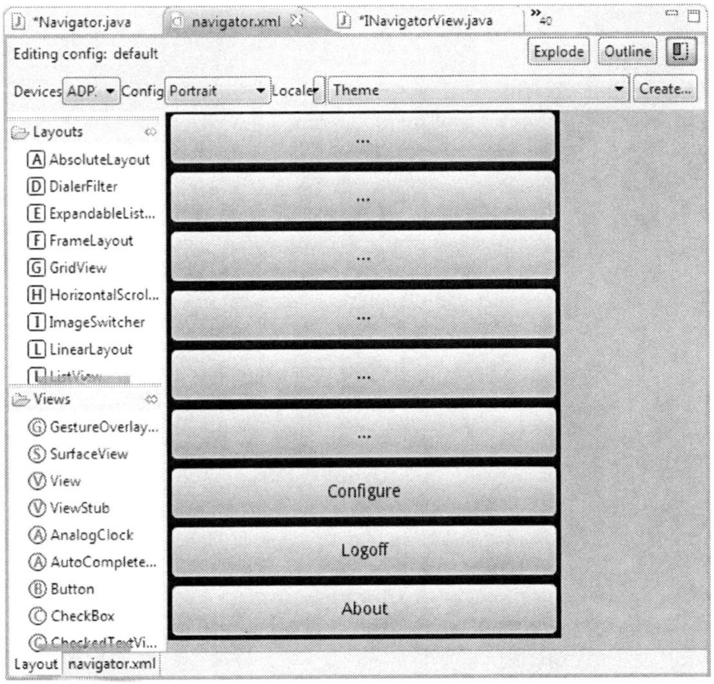

Figure 6-2. *ADT's layout preview view in portrait mode*

Creating the Controller

Next, we'll add the controller. Add this class to your project:

```
package com.amxMobile.SixBookmarks;

import android.content.*;
import android.net.*;
import com.amxMobile.SixBookmarks.Database.*;
import com.amxMobile.SixBookmarks.Runtime.*;
public class NavigatorController extends Controller<INavigatorView>
{
        public NavigatorController(INavigatorView view)
        {
                super(view);
        }

        public void HandleLoad() throws Exception
        {
                MessageBox.Show(this, "TBD");
        }
```

113

```
        public void HandleConfigure()
        {
                MessageBox.Show(this, "TBD");
        }

        public void HandleLogoff()
        {
                MessageBox.Show(this, "TBD");
        }

        public void HandleAbout()
        {
                MessageBox.Show(this, "TBD");
        }

        public void HandleNavigate(int ordinal)
        {
                MessageBox.Show(this, "TBD");
        }
}
```

As you can see from this class, the controller isn't going to do anything at present—we'll add something in later.

Creating the View Interface

Our view interface is supposed to abstract away user interface elements that we want to manipulate "at arm's length" from the controller. At this stage, we want to be able instruct the view to either reset the button text, or set the button text to be the name of the bookmark. Here's the INavigatorView implementation that we need.

```
package com.amxMobile.SixBookmarks;

import android.widget.*;

public interface INavigatorView
{
        public void ResetBookmarkButton(int ordinal) throws Exception;
        public void ConfigureBookmarkButton(int ordinal, String name) throws Exception;
}
```

When we build the Navigator activity, we'll implement those methods.

Creating the Navigator Activity

Now we have all of the pieces in place to create the navigator activity.

The activity itself (at this point) has the dual purpose of wiring up the nine buttons and deferring to the controller for processing, plus implementing the two methods on INavigatorView so that the controller can ask the view to update the buttons. In the next section, we'll make it display our mock bookmarks.

Here's the implementation of the Navigator activity:

```
package com.amxMobile.SixBookmarks;

import com.amxMobile.SixBookmarks.Runtime.*;
import android.app.Activity;
import android.os.Bundle;
import android.view.*;
import android.view.View.OnClickListener;
import android.widget.*;

public class Navigator extends Activity implements OnClickListener, INavigatorView
{
        private NavigatorController Controller;

        public Navigator()
        {
                this.Controller = new NavigatorController(this);
        }

    /** Called when the activity is first created. */
    @Override
    public void onCreate(Bundle savedInstanceState) {
        super.onCreate(savedInstanceState);
        setContentView(R.layout.navigator);

        // wire up the buttons...
        findViewById(R.id.buttonNavigate1).setOnClickListener(this);
        findViewById(R.id.buttonNavigate2).setOnClickListener(this);
        findViewById(R.id.buttonNavigate3).setOnClickListener(this);
        findViewById(R.id.buttonNavigate4).setOnClickListener(this);
        findViewById(R.id.buttonNavigate5).setOnClickListener(this);
        findViewById(R.id.buttonNavigate6).setOnClickListener(this);
        findViewById(R.id.buttonConfigure).setOnClickListener(this);
        findViewById(R.id.buttonLogoff).setOnClickListener(this);
        findViewById(R.id.buttonAbout).setOnClickListener(this);
    }
```

```java
public void onClick(View v)
{
        if(v.getId() == R.id.buttonConfigure)
                this.Controller.HandleConfigure();
        else if(v.getId() == R.id.buttonLogoff)
                this.Controller.HandleLogoff();
        else if(v.getId() == R.id.buttonAbout)
                this.Controller.HandleAbout();
        else if(v.getId() == R.id.buttonNavigate1)
                this.Controller.HandleNavigate(0);
        else if(v.getId() == R.id.buttonNavigate2)
                this.Controller.HandleNavigate(1);
        else if(v.getId() == R.id.buttonNavigate3)
                this.Controller.HandleNavigate(2);
        else if(v.getId() == R.id.buttonNavigate4)
                this.Controller.HandleNavigate(3);
        else if(v.getId() == R.id.buttonNavigate5)
                this.Controller.HandleNavigate(4);
        else if(v.getId() == R.id.buttonNavigate6)
                this.Controller.HandleNavigate(5);
}

private Button GetBookmarkButton(int ordinal) throws Exception
{
        int id = 0;
        if(ordinal == 0)
                id = R.id.buttonNavigate1;
        else if(ordinal == 1)
                id = R.id.buttonNavigate2;
        else if(ordinal == 2)
                id = R.id.buttonNavigate3;
        else if(ordinal == 3)
                id = R.id.buttonNavigate4;
        else if(ordinal == 4)
                id = R.id.buttonNavigate5;
        else if(ordinal == 5)
                id = R.id.buttonNavigate6;
        else
                throw new Exception(String.format("'%d' is an invalid ordinal.",↵
ordinal));

        // return...
        return (Button) this.findViewById(id);
}
```

```java
        public void ResetBookmarkButton(int ordinal) throws Exception
        {
                Button button = GetBookmarkButton(ordinal);
                button.setText("...");
        }

        public void ConfigureBookmarkButton(int ordinal, String name) throws Exception
        {
                Button button = GetBookmarkButton(ordinal);
                button.setText(name);
        }
}
```

That's it. Now all we have to do is create and display the mock bookmarks.

Showing the Bookmarks

The NavigatorController will be responsible for taking a set of bookmarks and instructing the view to update itself. Within its private instance state, the controller will also keep track of the URLs associated with each button ordinal. These URLs will be null in instances where no bookmark is defined for the ordinal, or the actual URL to show on click. These will be held in a private field with a private property getter; as per this listing:

```java
// Add to NavigatorController.java
public class NavigatorController extends Controller<INavigatorView>
{
        private String[] _urls = null;

        // code removed for brevity...

        private String[] getUrls()
        {
                return _urls;
        }

        // code removed for brevity...
}
```

We'll add a method called ShowBookmarks that will update the view and also keep the data within _urls valid. When we call ShowBookmarks, we'll reset the state of the six buttons, and then go through the bookmarks we were given, updating the appropriate ordinal as we go. Here's the code:

```java
// Add to NavigatorController.java
    public void ShowBookmarks(BookmarkCollection bookmarks) throws Exception
    {
        // store the bookmarks collection...
        final int maxBookmarks = 6;
        _urls = new String[maxBookmarks];
```

117

```java
        // reset the bookmarks...
        for(int index = 0; index < maxBookmarks; index++)
                ResetBookmark(index);

        // walk and set...
        for(Bookmark bookmark : bookmarks)
                ShowBookmark(bookmark);
    }

    private void ResetBookmark(int ordinal) throws Exception
    {
        // reset the view...
        getView().ResetBookmarkButton(ordinal);

        // reset the url...
        getUrls()[ordinal] = null;
    }

    private void ShowBookmark(Bookmark bookmark) throws Exception
    {
        int ordinal = bookmark.getOrdinal();

        // set the view...
        getView().ConfigureBookmarkButton(ordinal, bookmark.getName());

        // set the url...
        getUrls()[ordinal] = bookmark.getUrl();
    }
```

We're now in a position to run the process. First, we need to add code to the Navigator class to instruct the controller to load:

```java
// Add to Navigator.java - modify the onCreate method…
    /** Called when the activity is first created. */
    @Override
    public void onCreate(Bundle savedInstanceState) {
        super.onCreate(savedInstanceState);
        setContentView(R.layout.navigator);

        // wire up the buttons...
        findViewById(R.id.buttonNavigate1).setOnClickListener(this);
        findViewById(R.id.buttonNavigate2).setOnClickListener(this);
        findViewById(R.id.buttonNavigate3).setOnClickListener(this);
        findViewById(R.id.buttonNavigate4).setOnClickListener(this);
```

```
        findViewById(R.id.buttonNavigate5).setOnClickListener(this);
        findViewById(R.id.buttonNavigate6).setOnClickListener(this);
        findViewById(R.id.buttonConfigure).setOnClickListener(this);
        findViewById(R.id.buttonLogoff).setOnClickListener(this);
        findViewById(R.id.buttonAbout).setOnClickListener(this);

        // tell the controller to load...
        try
        {
                Controller.HandleLoad();
        }
        catch(Exception ex)
        {
                MessageBox.Show(this, ex);
        }
    }
```

In the Load method of the controller, we can then create and show the bookmarks. Here's the code to replace the Load method that we stubbed earlier:

```
// Add to NavigatorController.java - replace the existing Load method...
    public void HandleLoad() throws Exception
    {
    // create some fake bookmarks...
    BookmarkCollection bookmarks = new BookmarkCollection();
            AddBookmark(bookmarks, ".NET 247", "http://www.dotnet247.com/", 0);
            AddBookmark(bookmarks, "Apress", "http://www.apress.com/", 1);

            // show the bookmarks...
            this.ShowBookmarks(bookmarks);
    }

    private void AddBookmark(BookmarkCollection bookmarks, String name, String url,↵
int ordinal) throws Exception
    {
        // create...
        Bookmark bookmark = new Bookmark();
        bookmark.setName(name);
        bookmark.setUrl(url);
        bookmark.setOrdinal(ordinal);

        // add...
        bookmarks.add(bookmark);
    }
```

We're almost there! The only thing that remains is to modify the logon form so that it will start the Navigator activity when a logon has been successful.

Adding the Activity to the Manifest

Before the activity can be used, it needs to be added to the manifest file. This is easily enough done. Open the `AndroidManifest.xml` file, and add an element for the navigator.

```xml
<?xml version="1.0" encoding="utf-8"?>
<manifest xmlns:android="http://schemas.android.com/apk/res/android"
    android:versionCode="1"
    android:versionName="1.0" package="com.amxMobile.SixBookmarks">

    <application android:icon="@drawable/icon" android:label="@string/app_name">

        <activity android:name=".Logon"
                android:label="@string/app_name">
            <intent-filter>
                <action android:name="android.intent.action.MAIN" />
                <category android:name="android.intent.category.LAUNCHER" />
            </intent-filter>
        </activity>

        <activity android:name=".Navigator"
                android:label="@string/app_name">
            <intent-filter>
                <action android:name="android.intent.action.MAIN" />
                <category android:name="android.intent.category.LAUNCHER" />
            </intent-filter>
        </activity>

    </application>

        <uses-permission android:name="android.permission.INTERNET"></uses-permission>

</manifest>
```

In the next section, we'll see how to refer to the activity and launch it from the `LogonController` class.

Issuing the "Go to Navigator" "Intent"

This next bit we're going to look at is a part of Android that I'm not particularly fond of, as I personally feel it's a little complicated.

Android as a *system* is made up of activities, and activities are bundled together within applications. For example, you may have activities for showing a logon form, or showing a web page, or making a phone call. Android works on the principle that to move between activities you have to create "intents"—e.g., "I intend to show this web page" or "I intend to show this application-specific form." Thus, to move from the logon form to our new navigator form, we have to create an intent to show the navigator form and then run that intent. Android will then determine what needs to be done and then do it.

On the LogonController (note, *not* NavigatorController), in DoLogon all we need to do is create an intent, refer to the navigator, and then ask the Logon activity to start it. Here's the code that needs to be modified in LogonController:

```
// Code to modify in LogonController.java..
       private boolean DoLogon(String username, String password, boolean rememberMe)↵
  throws Exception
        {
                UsersService users = new UsersService();
                LogonResponse response = users.Logon(username, password);

                // now what?
                if(response.getResult() == LogonResult.LogonOk)
                {
                        // store the credentials?
                        if(rememberMe)
                                StoreCredentials(username, password);
                        else
                                ClearCredentials();

                        // create an intent and show the navigator...
                        Intent newIntent = new Intent(getActivity(), Navigator.class);
                        getActivity().startActivity(newIntent);

                        // return...
                        return true;
                }
                else
                {
                        MessageBox.Show(this, response.getMessage());
                        return false;
                }
        }
```

If you run the application now and log on (you'll be automatically logged in if you'd previously selected "remember me"), you'll see the two mock bookmarks, as shown in Figure 6-3.

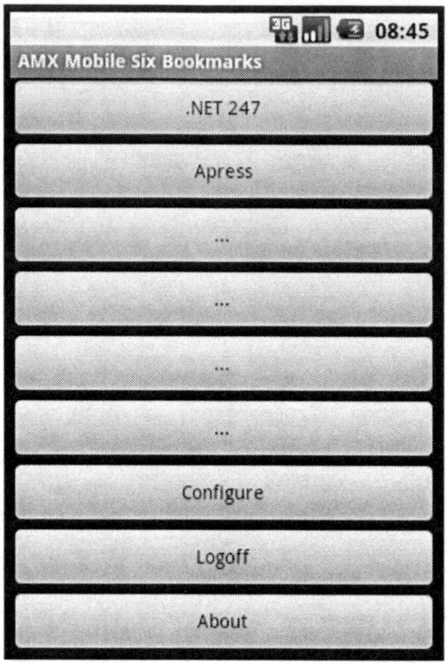

Figure 6-3. *The application showing two fake bookmarks*

Wiring Up the Bookmarks

Now that we're this far, we should at least try and make our buttons do something!

We can ask Android to open a web browser to the URL that we want by creating an intent bound to a URL.

We already have a method called `HandleNavigate` within `NavigatorController` that currently displays a message box indicating that it's pending implementation. We can change this now to look at the URL associated with the chosen ordinal. If we have a URL, we'll create an intent bound to that URL and ask Android to show it. If we do not have a URL, we'll defer to the `HandleConfigure` method. This method will ultimately show the configuration form—we'll build this in the next chapter. Here's the code to change in `NavigatorController`:

```
package com.amxMobile.SixBookmarks;

import android.content.*;
import android.net.*;
import com.amxMobile.SixBookmarks.Database.*;
import com.amxMobile.SixBookmarks.Runtime.*;

public class NavigatorController extends Controller<INavigatorView>
{
        // code removed for brevity…
```

```
// New implementation of HandleNavigate…
       public void HandleNavigate(int ordinal)
       {
              // get the url...
              String url = getUrls()[ordinal];

              // did we actually click a null button?
              if(url == null || url.length() == 0)
                     HandleConfigure();
              else
              {
                     // create an intent to show the URL...
                     Intent myIntent = new Intent(Intent.ACTION_VIEW, Uri.parse(url));
                     getActivity().startActivity(myIntent);
              }
       }
}
```

Now if you run the application, and click on one of the buttons, Android will show you the relevant URL. Figure 6-4 illustrates.

Figure 6-4. *The result of a successful navigation using Android's built-in Web browser*

If you want, now that we know how to point the browser at URLs of our choosing, we can also wire up the HandleAbout method at this point. Here's the code:

```
// Replace method in NavigatorController.java…
        public void HandleAbout()
        {
                Intent myIntent = new Intent(Intent.ACTION_VIEW, Uri.parse↵
("http://www.multimobiledevelopment.com/"));
                getActivity().startActivity(myIntent);
        }
```

Building the "Sync" Class

At this point we've covered a lot of ground. We have the foundation of an ORM system in place, we can create bookmark entities, and we can display them on the screen. In the remainder of this chapter, we're going to see how we can download bookmarks from the online service, store them in a local SQLite database, and then read them back from the SQLite database for display on the screen. In the next chapter, we're going to look at how the bookmarks can be modified and how changes can be pushed back up to the server.

Calling the Server's Bookmarks OData Service

In the last chapter, we created a few classes, including ServiceProxy, ApiService, and LogonService, to communicate with the restful services at http://services.multimobiledevelopment.com/. In this section, we're going to look at building BookmarksService, which is able to communicate with the Bookmarks OData service. We'll also build the base ODataServiceProxy class to support the operations of BookmarksService.

Although in Microsoft's toolset for targeting Windows Phone 7 and ASP.NET applications there is an library we can use for accessing OData, on Android and iOS there isn't such a library and hence we need to roll our own. A lot of this chapter will therefore be given over to this work.

■**NOTE** As of the time of writing, there isn't a dominant OData library that can be used on Android, and hence this section and the next section describe how we can do this manually. If you are reading this book in Summer 2011 or later, there is a good chance there will be a dominant library to use. The web site at www.odata.org/ will tell you if there are any Android libraries available at this point in time.

As we know, the OData service returns XML, and by default, this XML is formatted using the ATOM standard. All we have to do, then, is issue requests to the service and interpret the results. We can take the ATOM-formatted list of bookmarks and turn them into Bookmark entities for later use.

The HTTP request is the easy part—we need to issue a request to the following URL, passing up the special x-amx-apiusername and x-amx-token HTTP headers. We'll be using this URL:

http://services.multimobiledevelopment.com/services/bookmarks.svc/Bookmark

To begin, familiarize yourself with the format of data to be returned by using the test tool presented in Chapter 2. Here's a sample XML response containing a single bookmark:

```
<feed xml:base="http://services.amxmobile.com/services/Bookmarks.svc/"↵
xmlns:d="http://schemas.microsoft.com/ado/2007/08/dataservices"↵
xmlns:m="http://schemas.microsoft.com/ado/2007/08/dataservices/metadata"↵
xmlns="http://www.w3.org/2005/Atom">
  <title type="text">Bookmark</title>
  <id>http://services.amxmobile.com/services/bookmarks.svc/Bookmark</id>
  <updated>2010-05-15T06:22:09Z</updated>
  <link rel="self" title="Bookmark" href="Bookmark" />
  <entry>
    <id>http://services.amxmobile.com/services/Bookmarks.svc/Bookmark(1002)</id>
    <title type="text">
    </title>
    <updated>2010-05-15T06:22:09Z</updated>
    <author>
      <name />
    </author>
    <link rel="edit" title="Bookmark" href="Bookmark(1002)" />
    <category term="AmxMobile.Services.Bookmark" scheme=↵
"http://schemas.microsoft.com/ado/2007/08/dataservices/scheme" />
    <content type="application/xml">
      <m:properties>
        <d:BookmarkId m:type="Edm.Int32">1002</d:BookmarkId>
        <d:UserId m:type="Edm.Int32">1001</d:UserId>
        <d:Name>.NET 247</d:Name>
        <d:Url>http://www.dotnet247.com/</d:Url>
        <d:Ordinal m:type="Edm.Int32">1</d:Ordinal>
      </m:properties>
    </content>
  </entry>
</feed>
```

The thing that I like about XML is that with a bit of common sense—providing the developer has not created horrendously bad XML—it's normally easy to understand what you need to do. There, we can clearly see that the entry element contains the bookmark data and that the content/m:properties element contains the fields we want. All we have to do now is walk the document, creating new Bookmark instances for each entry that we discover.

Namespaces

If you haven't done much XML before, you may not know how to work with XML namespaces, and seeing as this document is littered with them, you're going to need to know how!

Namespaces provide a way of managing naming collisions within XML. Imagine I am trying to create a document that combines standards from two different protocols. If both standards call for me to add an element called Name, I'm going to run into a problem—for example:

```
<MyDocument>
        <Name>I'm a value from Standard XYZ</Name>
        <Name>I'm a value from Standard ABC</Name>
</MyDocument>
```

The consumer is going to struggle with this document because there is no way of knowing which Name element maps to which standard/protocol.

If the people defining the protocol insist that a namespace is used, the problem is easily solved.

Namespaces are (typically) defined within the root element of the document. They are in the form of a URI, but there is no rule that the URI has to actually point to anything that can be downloaded. (But those that define open standards often do work and redirect the caller to development information.)

Here's our previous XML file modified to include namespaces:

```
<MyDocument xmlns:a="http://www.foo.com/" xmlns:b="http://www.bar.com/">
        <a:Name>I'm a value from Standard XYZ</a:Name>
        <b:Name>I'm a value from Standard ABC</b:Name>
</MyDocument>
```

In this case, when encountering the name elements, the name prefix de-references a namespace URI, and you now know which is which.

The one final wrinkle with namespaces is that you can have a default namespace. This is defined within the document by applying an attribute to the root element with the name xmlns but without a suffix, for example:

```
<MyDocument xmlns ="http://www.foo.com/" xmlns:b="http://www.bar.com/">
        <Name>I'm a value from Standard XYZ</Name>
        <b:Name>I'm a value from Standard ABC</b:Name>
</MyDocument>
```

Where this catches newcomers out is that *both* MyDocument and Name no longer can be accessed without specifying the default namespace of http://www.foo.com/ as part of any requests to query against the XML. This is important, as our ATOM-formatted OData response has a default namespace of http://www.w3.org/2005/Atom, which you can see defined in the root feed element. As a side note, our Android layout XML files also use namespaces.

We'll go through how to query the document and handle namespaces in the next section.

Adding Functionality to "XmlHelper"

XmlHelper needs some methods added to help parse the document that we'll get back. Specifically, we need to be able to query a given element for a sub-element with a given qualified name. By qualified, I mean "we'll need to provide the namespace." Here's the method in question that needs to be added to XmlHelper:

```
// Add to XmlHelper.java
        public static Element GetElement(Element root, String namespaceUri, String name,↩
boolean throwIfNotFound) throws Exception
        {
                NodeList nodes = root.getElementsByTagNameNS(namespaceUri, name);
                if(nodes.getLength() > 0)
                        return (Element)nodes.item(0);
```

```
                else
                {
                        if(throwIfNotFound)
                                throw new Exception(String.format("A node with name '%s' ⏎
in namespace '%s' was not found.", name, namespaceUri));
                        else
                                return null;
                }
        }
}
```

Querying the Feed

Let's look now at parsing the XML we got back from the server.

First of all, let's stub our ODataServiceProxy class. This is going to extend ServiceProxy and will implement some generic support of OData-based data. Although we only work with one OData service, it's not unusual to work with several in a production application, and therefore it's worth breaking out functionality into a base class by way of illustration. Here's ODataServiceProxy:

```
package com.amxMobile.SixBookmarks.Services;

import java.util.*;
import org.w3c.dom.*;
import com.amxMobile.SixBookmarks.Database.*;
import com.amxMobile.SixBookmarks.Entities.*;
import com.amxMobile.SixBookmarks.Runtime.*;

public class ODataServiceProxy extends ServiceProxy
{
        private final String AtomNamespace = "http://www.w3.org/2005/Atom";
        private final String MsMetadataNamespace = ⏎
 "http://schemas.microsoft.com/ado/2007/08/dataservices/metadata";
        private final String MsDataNamespace = ⏎
 "http://schemas.microsoft.com/ado/2007/08/dataservices";

        public ODataServiceProxy(String serviceName)
        {
                super(serviceName);
        }
}
```

This class is going to need a couple of methods to help build URLs for the requests. We need only one now, which is the one that selects all entities for a given type. An example is http://services.multimobiledevelopment.com/services/Bookmarks.svc/Bookmark. Here's the method to add to ODataServiceProxy:

```
// Add to ODataServiceProxy.java
      public String GetServiceUrl(EntityType et)
      {
              return getResolvedServiceUrl() + "/" + et.getShortName();
      }
```

We can then add our BookmarksService class. This is going to get the URL that returns all the bookmarks, and then defer to a method called LoadEntities that we will build into the base ODataServiceProxy class in a moment. Here's the code:

```
package com.amxMobile.SixBookmarks.Services;

import org.w3c.dom.*;
import com.amxMobile.SixBookmarks.Database.*;
import com.amxMobile.SixBookmarks.Entities.*;
import com.amxMobile.SixBookmarks.Runtime.*;

public class BookmarksService extends ODataServiceProxy
{
      public BookmarksService()
      {
              super("Bookmarks.svc");
      }

      public BookmarkCollection GetAll() throws Exception
      {
              EntityType et = EntityType.GetEntityType(Bookmark.class);

              // run...
              String url = GetServiceUrl(et);
      Document doc = HttpHelper.DownloadXml(url, GetDownloadSettings());

              // load...
      return (BookmarkCollection)LoadEntities(doc, et);
      }
}
```

As you can see, the GetAll method will call up to the server and then defer to a method we'll build now, called LoadEntities, to turn the entry elements within the XML into real Bookmark instances.

I'll present this listing in chunks and comment as we go, as it's quite long.

The first job is to get back a list of feed elements, determine we have one, and then work with the first one we get.

```
// Add to ODataServiceProxy.java…
      protected ArrayList LoadEntities(Document doc, EntityType et) throws Exception
      {
      // parse...
      NodeList feedElements = doc.getElementsByTagNameNS(AtomNamespace, "feed");
```

```
if(feedElements.getLength() == 0)
        throw new Exception("A 'feed' element was not found.");

// feed...
Element feed = (Element)feedElements.item(0);
NodeList entryElements = feed.getElementsByTagNameNS(AtomNamespace, "entry");
```

Note that in the code, we're using the getElementsByTagNameNS method on the XML Document DOM class. As you can see, this method allows us to pass in a namespace name to use so that we can do this strong matching against a specific namespace.

Next, we'll ask the entity type to create a collection instance for us, and then we'll walk the elements contained within the entryElements node list.

```
// walk...
ArrayList results = et.CreateCollectionInstance();
        for(int i = 0; i < entryElements.getLength(); i++)
        {
                Element entry = (Element)entryElements.item(i);
```

The fields we want are contained within a sub-element of entry called content/m:properties. content is accessed through the default namespace, but properties require a separate namespace. This second namespace is defined in the MsMetadataNamespace constant defined at the top of the class.

```
// get the content item...
Element content = XmlHelper.GetElement(entry, AtomNamespace,↵
"content", false);
        if(content == null)
                throw new Exception(String.format("A content element↵
not found on item '%d'.", i));

// then get the properties element...
Element properties = XmlHelper.GetElement(content,↵
MsMetadataNamespace, "properties", false);
        if(properties == null)
                throw new Exception(String.format("A properties↵
element not found on item '%d'.", i));
```

The m:properties element then contains the field values we want prefixed with d:, which, in this case, maps to another namespace defined in the MsDataNamespace constant.

We need to walk each of these child elements and see whether the name maps to a field on the entity type related to the Bookmark class. In order to be less brittle, we want to allow the service (which we may not control) to pass through data that we are not interested in. Hence, for each field we encounter, we see if it is a field, and if so, we add it to a bucket of values.

Also in this code snippet, you'll see a reference to GetValue. We'll build this shortly.

```
// then get the fields...
NodeList fields = properties.getElementsByTagNameNS↵
(MsDataNamespace, "*");
        Hashtable<String, Object> values = new Hashtable<String, Object>();
```

```
                    for(int j = 0; j < fields.getLength(); j++)
                    {
                            Element field = (Element)fields.item(j);

                            // value...
                            Object value = GetValue(field);

                            // is it a field?
                            if(et.IsField(field.getLocalName()))
                                    values.put(field.getLocalName(), value);
                    }
```

We're almost there at this point. We have a collection of name/value items that we can use to populate the initial data for an entity. Here's the code that calls a constructor on Bookmark that does not exist yet but that we'll do in a moment.

```
                    // create...
                    Bookmark bookmark = new Bookmark(values);
                    results.add(bookmark);
            }
```

At this point, we're finished. We can close the loop that walks the entry element and return our collection back to the caller.

```
                    // return...
                    return results;
            }
```

Actually, though, we're not quite finished because we need to implement the GetValue method. This value will take an element instance and extract from it the value. It will use the type attribute of the element to determine the type and convert the represented-as-a-string-in-XML value back to the caller as a value of the correct type. Here's the code:

```
// Add to ODataServiceProxy.java
        private Object GetValue(Element field) throws Exception
        {
                // fields are provided with a data element, like this....
                // <d:BookmarkId m:type="Edm.Int32">1002</d:BookmarkId>
                String asString = field.getAttributeNS(MsMetadataNamespace, "type");

                // nothing?
                if(asString == null || asString.length() == 0)
                        return XmlHelper.GetStringValue(field);
                else if(asString.compareTo("Edm.Int32") == 0)
                        return XmlHelper.GetInt32Value(field);
                else
                        throw new Exception(String.format("Cannot handle '%s'.", asString));
        }
```

Creating Entities from Name/Value Collections

At the moment, we don't have a way of creating an entity from a collection of name/value items (and we've made a class within `LoadEntities` that assumes that we do), so we need to add this to `Bookmark` and to `Entity`. To `Bookmark` we need to add this additional constructor:

```
// Add to Bookmark.java…
    public Bookmark() throws Exception
    {
    }

    public Bookmark(Hashtable<String, Object> values) throws Exception
    {
        super(values);
    }
```

That method defers to a constructor on the base `Entity` class that we also need to add. Here's the listing for that:

```
// Add to Entity.java…
    protected Entity() throws Exception
    {
        _entityType = EntityType.GetEntityType(this.getClass());

        // slots...
        int count = _entityType.getFields().size();
        _values = new Object[count];
        _flags = new int[count];
    }

    protected Entity(Hashtable<String, Object> values) throws Exception
    {
        // make sure the original initialization code runs - v. important…
        this();

        // set...
        for(String key : values.keySet())
        {
            EntityField field = getEntityType().GetField(key, true);
            SetValue(field, values.get(key), SetReason.Load);
        }
    }
```

Note how when we call `SetValue`, we are specifying the `SetReason.Load`. This tells the entity that it has a value for a given field but does not update the internal state to mark the item as modified.

That's it as far as calling the service is concerned; however, we won't physically call the service until much later on in this chapter.

Managing the Database

Android's SQLite implementation is firmly welded into the Android runtime; specifically, in order to access databases, we need to use a class called `android.database.sqlite.SQLiteOpenHelper`. We're going to create a class called `DatabaseHelper` that extends `SQLiteOpenHelper`. Whenever we need to access the database, we'll create an instance of `DatabaseHelper`, passing in an `android.content.Context` instance (remember that `Activity` extends `Context` and that by passing in an activity, we're passing a context by implication). `SQLiteOpenHelper` will manage the process of creating a new or opening an existing database for us.

    `SQLiteOpenHelper` is an abstract class, and this will require us to implement two methods—`onCreate` and `onUpgrade`, which are called when the database is created or upgraded; however, we can leave these methods as "no-op" methods.

    When we call the constructor on `SQLiteOpenHelper`, we need to give it a database name. However, what we want to do with the database name is give it the same name as the logged-on user. The reason we do this is that if User A logs on and changes some bookmarks, these will be saved in the local database. If User B logs on, his bookmarks will be downloaded and overwrite User A's. This is, on a mobile device, very unlikely, but it is an obvious logic problem, and thus it's better to fix it rather than leave in what most would classify as a bug.

    To solve this problem, we'll set the database name when the user logs in. In `LogonController`, modify `DoLogon` so that it will set the database name in the shortly-to-be-built `DatabaseHelper` class:

```
// Modify method in LogonController.java
        private boolean DoLogon(String username, String password, boolean rememberMe)↵
    throws Exception
        {
                UsersService users = new UsersService();
                LogonResponse response = users.Logon(username, password);

                // now what?
                if(response.getResult() == LogonResult.LogonOk)
                {
                        // store the credentials?
                        if(rememberMe)
                                StoreCredentials(username, password);
                        else
                                ClearCredentials();

                        // set the user...
                        DatabaseHelper.setUser(username);

                        // create an intent and show the navigator...
                        Intent newIntent = new Intent(getActivity(), Navigator.class);
                        getActivity().startActivity(newIntent);

                        // return...
                        return true;
                }
```

```
                else
                {
                        MessageBox.Show(this, response.getMessage());
                        return false;
                }
        }
```

We can now build DatabaseHelper. Here's the listing:

```
package com.amxMobile.SixBookmarks.Runtime;

import java.util.*;
import com.amxMobile.SixBookmarks.Entities.*;
import com.amxMobile.SixBookmarks.Runtime.*;
import android.content.Context;
import android.database.sqlite.*;

public class DatabaseHelper extends SQLiteOpenHelper
{
        private static String DatabaseName = null;

        public DatabaseHelper(IContextSource context)
        {
                this(context.getContext());
        }

        public DatabaseHelper(Context context)
        {
                // base...
                super(context, DatabaseName, null, 1);
        }

public static void setUser(String username)
{
DatabaseName = "SixBookmarks-" + username;
}

        @Override
        public void onCreate(SQLiteDatabase db)
        {
        }

        @Override
        public void onUpgrade(SQLiteDatabase db, int oldVersion, int newVersion)
        {
        }
}
```

That doesn't get us very far through the process of writing to the database! However, now whenever we need access anywhere in the application to a database, all we have to do is create an instance of DatabaseHelper passing in either an instance of a Context object (e.g., an Activity), or an instance of an object that implements IContextSource. Recall that previously we defined our Controller class as implementing IContextSource, and hence any controllers are candidates for seeding this database helper.

The "SqlStatement" Class and "ISqlStatementSource" Interface

When building an ORM layer, the thing I have found most helpful is adding a metadata system as we've described previously in the book. A close second to this is making sure that any statements you wish to issue to the database are wrapped up in an object instance that you control. This gives you more control and flexibility as to how statements are passed over to the base data access layer within the ORM framework. (Most newcomers to the field when building data access layers pass around strings that are either dynamic SQL statements or names of stored procedures. This approach tends to be very brittle.)

To that end, we're going to create a class called SqlStatement. This will hold the command text that's to be sent to the database engine and a list of parameter values. SQLite does not support named parameters, and so we're going to just keep a simple list.

In addition to SqlStatement, we're also going to create an ISqlStatementSource interface. This adds another layer of flexibility to the data access layer (DAL) by allowing us to pass objects directly into the DAL that are not necessarily fully-formed SQL statements but do have the capability to turn into them. (We're going to see this later when we build a class called SqlFilter, which will create a SqlStatement instance immediately before the point of execution.)

Here's ISqlStatementSource—it has only a single method:

```
package com.amxMobile.SixBookmarks.Runtime;

public interface ISqlStatementSource
{
        SqlStatement GetSqlStatement();
}
```

When we implement ISqlStatementSource on SqlStatement, we're just going to return a reference to this, as we don't have to do any additional processing to build the query string once we have a SqlStatement instance.

Here's the implementation of SqlStatement:

```
package com.amxMobile.SixBookmarks.Runtime;

import java.util.*;

public class SqlStatement implements ISqlStatementSource
{
        private String _commandText;
        private ArrayList<Object> _parameterValues = new ArrayList<Object>();

        public SqlStatement()
        {
        }
```

```java
        public SqlStatement(String commandText)
        {
                _commandText = commandText;
        }

        public String getCommandText()
        {
                return _commandText;
        }

        public void setCommandText(String commandText)
        {
                _commandText = commandText;
        }

        public SqlStatement GetSqlStatement()
        {
                return this;
        }

        public void AddParameterValue(Object value)
        {
                _parameterValues.add(value);
        }

        public Object[] getParameterValues()
        {
                return _parameterValues.toArray();
        }
}
```

That's the base classes done. Let's have a look now at creating concrete instances of statements that have some function.

Creating Tables

Job one with regards to our new database is to create new tables to store data in.

We're going to do this by examining at runtime the structure of the entity that we need to create a table for, and we'll do this by walking the fields defined against the entity type. This is where the power of a good metadata system starts to shine through—this relatively complex operation of dynamically creating a SQL table is a doddle to do.

As we know, SQLite uses a regular ANSI-92 SQL syntax; therefore we want to issue a statement that looks something like this:

```
CREATE TABLE IF NOT EXISTS Bookmarks
        (BookmarkId integer primary key autoincrement,
        Ordinal integer,
        Name varchar(128),
        Url varchar(256))
```

We're going to add two methods to DatabaseHelper. One is called GetCreateScript, and this method will be responsible for returning a script like the previous one. This will defer during processing to a method called AppendCreateSnippet. This second method's job will be to write into the SQL string the snippet that defines the field, e.g., Ordinal integer or Name varchar(128). Here's the code:

```java
// Add to DatabaseHelper.java…
        private SqlStatement GetCreateScript(EntityType et) throws Exception
        {
                StringBuilder builder = new StringBuilder();
                builder.append("CREATE TABLE IF NOT EXISTS ");
                builder.append(et.getNativeName());        // now the columns...
                builder.append(" (");
                ArrayList<EntityField> fields = et.getFields();
                for(int index = 0; index < fields.size(); index++)
                {
                        if(index > 0)
                                builder.append(", ");

                        // defer...
                        AppendCreateSnippet(builder, fields.get(index));
                }
                builder.append(")");

                // return...
                return new SqlStatement(builder.toString());
        }

        private void AppendCreateSnippet(StringBuilder builder, EntityField field)↩
    throws Exception
        {
                builder.append(field.getNativeName());
                builder.append(" ");

                // switch...
                DataType type = field.getDataType();
                if(type == DataType.String)
                {
                        builder.append("varchar(");
                        builder.append(field.getSize());
                        builder.append(")");
                }
```

```
        else if(type == DataType.Int32)
        {
                builder.append("integer");

                // key?
                if(field.getIsKey())
                        builder.append(" primary key autoincrement");
        }
        else
                throw new Exception(String.format("Cannot handle '%s'.",↵
field.getDataType()));
        }
```

■**NOTE** Recall that we support only two datatypes in this implementation—strings and 32-bit integers. Here's another reason I've chosen that for this book—the `AppendCreateSnippet` method would be huge if we supported all available data types.

We obviously need to call that method somehow. One way to do this is to create a method that ensures the table for a given entity type exists prior to use. In fact, this is exactly what we'll do by adding a method called `EnsureTableExists` to the `DatabaseHelper` class.

You'll notice in our create script that we're using the special SQLite `IF TABLE EXISTS` directive to tell SQLite to ignore the create call if the table is already there. It would be acceptable, therefore, to issue a call to create the table every time we received a call into `EnsureTableExists`. However, for efficiency—especially important as we're on a low-horsepower device—we'll make `EnsureTableExists` keep track of whether a create call has been called in the running session. We'll do this by adding a static field to the `DatabaseHelper` class that keeps a list of the names of the entities that have been "ensured." If we get asked to ensure the table for an entity that we think we've already done, we'll quit the method early and save processor cycles. Here's the code:

```
public class DatabaseHelper extends SQLiteOpenHelper
{
        private static ArrayList<String> _loadMap = new ArrayList<String>();

        // code removed for brevity...

        public void EnsureTableExists(EntityType et) throws Exception
        {
                // have we already called it?
                String name = et.getName();
                if(_loadMap.contains(name))
                        return;
```

```
                // create...
                SqlStatement sql = GetCreateScript(et);
                ExecuteNonQuery(sql, true);

                // add...
                _loadMap.add(name);
        }
}
```

You'll note that EnsureTableExists calls ExecuteNonQuery. This is the first of the data access methods that execute SQL statements against the SQLite database. Note that GetCreateScript returns a SqlStatement instance, and also recall how we said that our data access methods were going to work with ISqlStatementSource instances. Our ExecuteNonQuery method is going to take an ISqlStatementSource and use the GetStatement method defined on it to de-reference an actual statement to execute. (When passing in a concrete SqlStatement instance, the call on the interface will result in a reference to the concrete SqlStatement being returned.)

Another wrinkle to using SQLite on Android is that you have to specify whether you want to read from the database or write to the database. Thus, we'll pass in a parameter to the ExecuteNonQuery method that indicates what we intend to do. (SQLite/Android does this to handle multithreading and concurrency—multiple threads reading from a database is OK, but multiple threads writing is not OK.)

Here's the implementation of ExecuteNonQuery:

```
// Add to DatabaseHelper.java
        public void ExecuteNonQuery(ISqlStatementSource sql, boolean writable)
        {
                SqlStatement statement = sql.GetSqlStatement();

                // open...
                SQLiteDatabase db = null;
                if(writable)
                        db = this.getWritableDatabase();
                else
                        db = this.getReadableDatabase();
                try
                {
                        db.execSQL(statement.getCommandText(),
statement.getParameterValues());
                }
                finally
                {
                        if(db != null)
                                db.close();
                }
        }
```

Of note in that listing is that we use a try...finally construct to close the database, regardless of whether execution succeeded or failed. This is (obviously) to keep resource usage to a minimum.

Examining the Database with Sqliteman

At this point, we can take an entity type and create a database for it. We might as well do this now, as we have quite a long way to go before we can get some real data into it!

We haven't yet built the Sync class, but we can start to do this now. We'll start it off by asking it to ensure the database exists, but we won't add the logic to do anything other than that.

The Sync class will need access to a Context object so that it can create a DatabaseHelper, which, in turn, will call the SQLiteOpenHelper class to physically create the database for us. The Sync class will also hold the database and the EntityType instance related to the bookmark entity within its instance data. Here's the code:

```
package com.amxMobile.SixBookmarks.Database;

import java.util.*;
import android.content.*;
import com.amxMobile.SixBookmarks.Entities.*;
import com.amxMobile.SixBookmarks.Runtime.*;
import com.amxMobile.SixBookmarks.Services.*;
public class Sync
{
        private IContextSource _contextSource;
        private DatabaseHelper _database;
        private EntityType _entityType;

        public void DoSync(IContextSource source) throws Exception
        {
                _contextSource = source;
                _database = new DatabaseHelper(source);

                // make sure we have a table...
                _entityType = EntityType.GetEntityType(Bookmark.class);
                _database.EnsureTableExists(_entityType);

                // we'll add more code here later...
        }

        private IContextSource getContextSource()
        {
                return _contextSource;
        }

        private EntityType getEntityType()
        {
                return _entityType;
        }
```

```
        private DatabaseHelper getDatabase()
        {
                return _database;
        }
}
```

Recall the code that we added to the LogonController to start the navigator activity. We're going to change the DoLogon method *again* to call the sync code prior to launching the navigator. Here's the listing:

```
// Modify code in LogonController.java…
        private boolean DoLogon(String username, String password, boolean rememberMe) ↵
 throws Exception
        {
                UsersService users = new UsersService();
                LogonResponse response = users.Logon(username, password);

                // now what?
                if(response.getResult() == LogonResult.LogonOk)
                {
                        // store the credentials?
                        if(rememberMe)
                                StoreCredentials(username, password);
                        else
                                ClearCredentials();

                        // set the user...
                        DatabaseHelper.setUser(username);

                        // do a sync...
                        Sync sync = new Sync();
                        sync.DoSync(this);

                        // create an intent and show the navigator...
                        Intent newIntent = new Intent(getActivity(), Navigator.class);
                        getActivity().startActivity(newIntent);

                        // return...
                        return true;
                }
                else
                {
                        MessageBox.Show(this, response.getMessage());
                        return false;
                }
        }
```

Now if you run the application and log on, a Sync instance will be created and DoSync will be called. The database and table will (one hopes) have been created. However, being engineers, we probably need to see it to believe it.

The Eclipse plugin has a number of specialized Android views available that allow you to peek inside the running emulator or connected device. One of these is called the File Explorer, and we're going to use it here to grab the database from the device and put it onto our host machine, where we can examine it with a tool. The tool I'm going to suggest using is Sqliteman. You can download Sqliteman from http://sqliteman.com/.

In Eclipse, select **Window – Show View – Other** and expand out the **Android** options. Figure 6-5 shows the **File Explorer** option available. Select it and click OK.

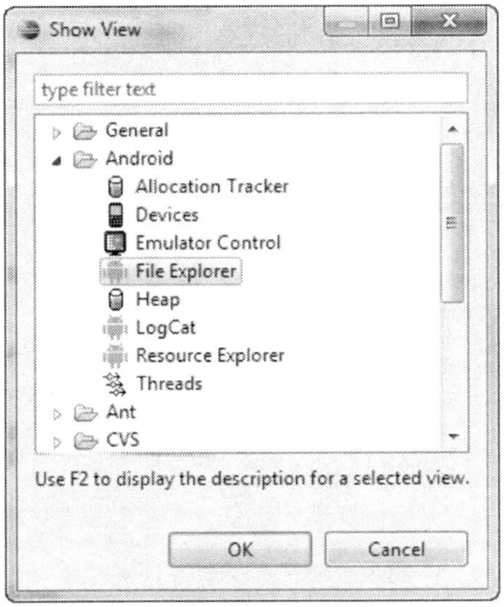

Figure 6-5. *Selecting the "File Explorer" view from the available views*

You'll then be given access to a window that allows you to explore the file system on the device. Figure 6-6 illustrates, and in this example, I've shown both the ~/data/app folder and the ~/data/data/com.amxMobile.SixBookmarks/databases folder. The ~/data/app folder I've included as a point of curiosity—this is where your application is actually installed. The databases folder is obviously the one we are interested in.

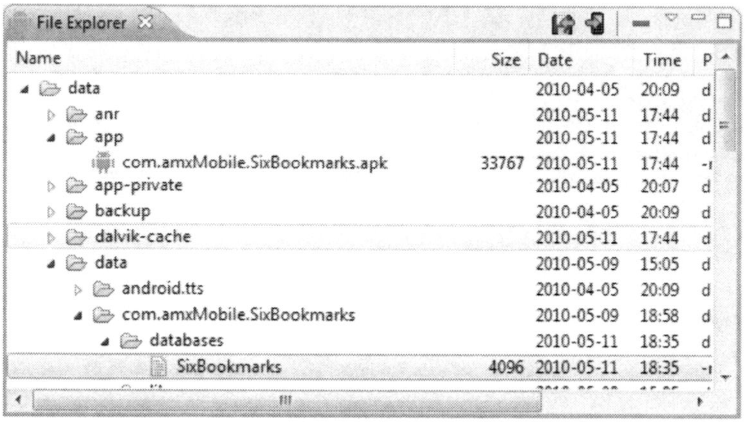

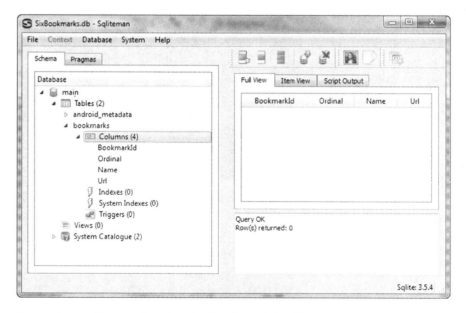

Figure 6-6. *The "SixBookmarks" database within the file tree (plus the ".apk" file that contains the Six Bookmarks applciation itself)*

If you select the SixBookmarks-<username> file, you can pull it from the device using the **Pull a file from the device** option on the view's toolbar. Save the file somewhere on disk, and open it using Sqliteman. Figure 6-7 shows the Bookmarks table in situ, although obviously we have not added any data to it yet.

Figure 6-7. *Sqliteman showing the "bookmarks" table*

Let's look in the next section as to how we can write bookmarks to the database.

Writing Bookmarks to the Database

What we'll do in this section is start developing the synchronization routine. In this chapter, we'll look at downloading the server bookmarks and storing locally. In the next chapter, we'll look at passing the changes back up to the server.

Earlier in this section, we built the BookmarksService class. We defined a method on this called GetAll, which returned a BookmarkCollection. We're going to use this to get the list of bookmarks to insert.

When using an ORM layer, what we want to be able to do is ask the entity itself to commit in-memory changes to the database. Further, we want to be able to use the metadata system to build the query that we wish to use. We're going to use a "unit of work" pattern to do this by implementing a class called EntityChangeProcessor, passing this an entity and having the processor work out whether it's to do nothing with it or whether it needs to issue an insert, update, or delete operation.

On the Entity class, we have already defined methods called IsNew, IsModified, and IsDeleted. IsNew and IsModified have been implemented to work in this chapter, whereas IsDeleted is a stub implementation that just returns false. In this chapter, we're going to make the processor understand insert operations *only* and look at update and delete in the next chapter.

Building the Change Processor

First off, let's add a SaveChanges method to Entity. This is very easy—it's going to accept in an IContextSource and create a processor based on the context and the entity type related to the entity.

```
// Add to Entity.java…
        public void SaveChanges(IContextSource context) throws Exception
        {
                EntityChangeProcessor processor = new EntityChangeProcessor(context,↵
 this.getEntityType());
                processor.SaveChanges(this);
        }
```

The basics of the EntityChangeProcessor include storing the entity type and context in instance fields and deciding whether to call an Insert, Update, or Delete method based on the change that has occurred. Here's the code:

```
package com.amxMobile.SixBookmarks.Entities;

import com.amxMobile.SixBookmarks.Runtime.*;
import android.content.*;

public class EntityChangeProcessor
{
        private IContextSource _context;
        private EntityType _entityType;

        public EntityChangeProcessor(IContextSource context, EntityType et)
        {
                _context = context;
                _entityType = et;
        }
```

```
    public IContextSource getContext()
    {
            return _context;
    }

    public EntityType getEntityType()
    {
            return _entityType;
    }

    public void SaveChanges(Entity entity) throws Exception
    {
            //  do we need to do anything?
            if(entity.getIsNew())
                    this.Insert(entity);
            else if(entity.getIsModified())
                    throw new Exception("Not implemented.");
            else if(entity.getIsDeleted())
                    throw new Exception("Not implemented.");

            // nothing to do...
    }
}
```

As mentioned previously, in this chapter, we're only going to look at inserting entities, so let's look now at the Insert method.

Inserting Entities

The Insert method simply has to build a SQL statement that can insert the entity and then execute it against the database.

The SQL statement that we wish to issue looks like the one called out here. Note how in this statement, we're not specifying a value for BookmarkId—this will be allocated for us by the database. Also, just a reminder that the ? characters in the statement are placeholders for parameters.

```
INSERT INTO Bookmarks (Ordinal, Name, Url) VALUES (?, ?, ?)
```

■**NOTE** For simplicity, the implementation here does not select back from the database the ID that was allocated as part of the statement. If you need to do this, issuing the select last_insert_rowid() statement on the same connection will return back the ID. The version of the code available from the web site does include this functionality.

The GetInsertStatement will create a SqlStatement instance that can be used to insert the provided Entity instance. Here's the code:

```java
// Add to EntityChangeProcessor.java...
    private SqlStatement GetInsertStatement(Entity entity) throws Exception
    {
        StringBuilder builder = new StringBuilder();
        SqlStatement sql = new SqlStatement();

        // et...
        EntityType et = getEntityType();

        // create...
        builder.append("INSERT INTO ");
        builder.append(et.getNativeName());
        builder.append(" (");
        boolean first = true;
        for(EntityField field : et.getFields())
        {
            if(entity.getIsModified(field))
            {
                if(first)
                        first = false;
                else
                        builder.append(", ");
                builder.append(field.getNativeName());
            }
        }
        builder.append(") VALUES (");
        first = true;
        for(EntityField field : et.getFields())
        {
            if(entity.getIsModified(field))
            {
                if(first)
                        first = false;
                else
                        builder.append(", ");
                builder.append("?");

                // add in the parameter....
                sql.AddParameterValue(entity.GetValue(field));
            }
        }
        builder.append(")");

        // return...
        sql.setCommandText(builder.toString());
        return sql;
    }
```

Once we have the statement, we can run it like so:

```
// Add to EntityChangeProcessor.java…
        protected void Insert(Entity entity) throws Exception
        {
                // get the statement...
                SqlStatement sql = this.GetInsertStatement(entity);

                // run the statement...
                DatabaseHelper db = new DatabaseHelper(getContext());
                db.EnsureTableExists(getEntityType());
                db.ExecuteNonQuery(sql, true);
        }
```

Now we just need to run it.

Our DoSync routine on the Sync class is stubbed out with some basic code, but it does not do anything yet. We need to make this call a method we'll build, called GetLatest. Here's the code:

```
// Modify DoSync method in Sync.java…
        public void DoSync(IContextSource source) throws Exception
        {
                _contextSource = source;
                _database = new DatabaseHelper(source);

                // make sure we have a table...
                _entityType = EntityType.GetEntityType(Bookmark.class);
                _database.EnsureTableExists(_entityType);

                // get the latest...
                GetLatest();
        }
```

We'll build GetLatest in the next section.

Downloading Bookmarks

The code we're about to look at is a little strange. I'll explain…

When we created the OData service proxy method to return all the bookmarks, we made this return Bookmark entities. I chose to do that because I felt it was unnecessarily complicated to have a separate set of classes representing bookmarks that go over the wire, compared to bookmarks that live in the local database. It's not unusual to have this separation, and in many cases, it is desirable.

Where this gets a little strange is that the OData service returns back the entities with the BookmarkId property populated with values that represent the internal, private IDs in the *server's* database. Our change processor is configured to treat entities that do not have a loaded ID as new, and entities that do have a loaded ID as potentially modified and deleted. Thus, if we pass our change processor an entity that we have downloaded, it will look at it and assume it has been modified because the ID value is set. It will attempt to issue an UPDATE rather than an INSERT statement, and the process will create incorrect results.

What we, therefore, have to do is walk each downloaded bookmark and create a new Bookmark instance for each. We'll walk the fields described in the metadata and patch all of the fields that are not *key* fields into the new entity. We can then pass this entity over to the change processor—it will detect an unloaded ID value and assume it is to be inserted. Thus, the operation will work properly. Here's the code to go into the Sync class:

```java
// Add to Sync.java...
        private void GetLatest() throws Exception
        {
                // clear the bookmarks table...
                getDatabase().ExecuteNonQuery(new SqlStatement("delete from bookmarks"),↵
 true);

                // get the bookmarks from the server...
                BookmarksService service = new BookmarksService();
                for(Bookmark bookmark : service.GetAll())
                {
                        // the bookmarks we get from the server have server ids populated.↵
  we need to
                        // remove the server id and save locally by creating a new item...

                        // create and copy all of the fields except the key field...
                        Bookmark newBookmark = new Bookmark();
                        for(EntityField field : getEntityType().getFields())
                        {
                                if(!(field.getIsKey()) && bookmark.getIsLoaded(field))
                                        newBookmark.SetValue(field,↵
 bookmark.GetValue(field), SetReason.UserSet);
                        }

                        // save...
                        newBookmark.SaveChanges(this.getContextSource());
                }
        }
```

■ **NOTE** This is another good example of how helpful a metadata system is. Should we add new fields to the entity, this code will automatically adapt its operation and continue to work without us having to remember to do it.

Now if we run the project, the sync routine will run and the local database will be populated. You won't see different results yet—we'll do that in the next section. However, if you pull an updated database from the device using the **File Explorer** view in Eclipse, you'll see the bookmarks downloaded from the server. Figure 6-8 illustrates.

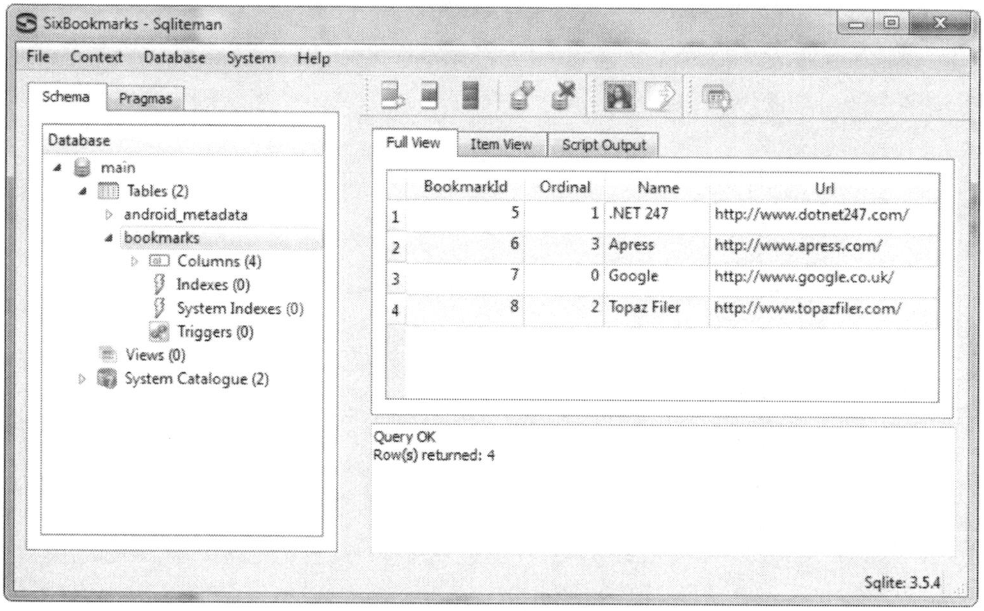

Figure 6-8. *Sqliteman showing the data within the "bookmarks" table*

Reading Bookmarks and Displaying Them on the Navigator

Now that we know we have bookmarks in our local database, we can replace the code that displays the mock bookmarks with code that retrieves the entities from the database. The code we've written to display the bookmarks on the screen remains unchanged—we need to modify only the retrieval code.

We already have a database method that will execute a query without expecting a result (ExecuteNonQuery). We now need to write a method that will return a collection of entities—ExecuteEntityCollection. To do this, we're going to create a class called SqlFilter.

The purpose of SqlFilter is to retrieve values from the database based on the principle of constraining data down from the maximum possible set (all rows in a table) to the set that you want. It could be that the set you want is the maximum possible set ("get all"), a single row represented by a key value ("get by ID"), or any other set that you fancy.

Recall that we created ISqlStatementSource earlier, and also recall that we created our ExecuteNonQuery method to accept an ISqlStatementSource and then ultimately de-reference a real SqlStatement instance to run. We'll do the same thing with our ExecuteEntityCollection, and we'll also make SqlFilter implement ISqlStatementSource.

The SQL statement that SqlFilter needs to generate is straightforward—it'll look something like this:

```
SELECT BookmarkId, Name, Value, Ordinal from Bookmarks
```

Here's the code, including a helper method also called ExecuteEntityCollection that will defer to a DatabaseHelper instance for execution:

```java
package com.amxMobile.SixBookmarks.Runtime;

import java.util.*;
import com.amxMobile.SixBookmarks.Entities.*;
import android.database.*;
import android.database.sqlite.*;

public class SqlFilter implements ISqlStatementSource
{
        private EntityType _entityType;

        public SqlFilter(Class type) throws Exception
        {
                this(EntityType.GetEntityType(type));
        }

        public SqlFilter(EntityType et)
        {
                _entityType = et;
        }

        private EntityType getEntityType()
        {
                return _entityType;
        }

        public SqlStatement GetSqlStatement()
        {
                EntityType et = getEntityType();
                SqlStatement sql = new SqlStatement();
                StringBuilder builder = new StringBuilder();

                // columns...
                builder.append("SELECT ");
                ArrayList<EntityField> fields = et.getFields();
                for(int index = 0; index < fields.size(); index++)
                {
                        if(index > 0)
                                builder.append(", ");
                        builder.append(fields.get(index).getNativeName());
                }

                // from...
                builder.append(" FROM ");
                builder.append(et.getNativeName());
```

```
            // return...
            sql.setCommandText(builder.toString());
            return sql;
    }

    public ArrayList ExecuteEntityCollection(IContextSource context) throws Exception
    {
            // shortcut method - defer to the helper...
            DatabaseHelper db = new DatabaseHelper(context);
            return db.ExecuteEntityCollection(this, getEntityType());
    }
}
```

Executing the Entity Collection

Now that we have a statement to run, we need to connect to the database and execute it. This will return back a forward-only cursor that we can iterate through creating entities as we go.

Here's the base ExecuteEntityCollection method that needs to be on DatabaseHelper:

```
// Add to DatabaseHelper.java
    public ArrayList<Entity> ExecuteEntityCollection(ISqlStatementSource sql, ↩
EntityType et) throws Exception
    {
            // get...
            SqlStatement realSql = sql.GetSqlStatement();
            SQLiteDatabase db = getReadableDatabase();
            Cursor c = null;
            try
            {
                    // execute a cursor...
                    ArrayList<Entity> results = et.CreateCollectionInstance();

                    // cursor...
                    c = db.rawQuery(realSql.getCommandText(), null);
                    while(c.moveToNext())
                    {
                            // load...
                            Entity entity = LoadEntity(c, et);
                            results.add(entity);
                    }

                    // return...
                    return results;
            }
```

```
            finally
            {
                    if(c != null)
                            c.close();
                    if(db != null)
                            db.close();
            }
    }
```

You can see there how this gets a real statement from the source object and opens a readable connection to the database. (We assume that the statement does not contain directives to change the data.) We can ask the entity type to return a collection instance, and once we have that, we can run the statement and return a cursor. Each iteration of the loop defers to LoadEntity, which we'll build now.

LoadEntity has to create an entity instance and then populate it with values from the database. There is an assumption here that the columns defined in the filter's statement include every field available on the entity type. On a more sophisticated ORM implementation, this may not be the case, but in our case it is. Thus, we need to walk the entity type fields, retrieve the value from the row, and set the value on the entity. When we do this, we need to mark the call as having SetReason.Load. This flag tells the entity that the value has been loaded but *not* modified. If we were to call SaveChanges, nothing would happen—the ID field would be loaded, and hence it would not be new, no column would be modified, and hence the whole entity would be unchanged. (The entity has obviously not been deleted either, but we have not implemented that check, yet.)

Here's the code for LoadEntity:

```
// Add to DatabaseHelper.java…
        private Entity LoadEntity(Cursor c, EntityType et) throws Exception
        {
                // create a new instance...
                Entity entity = et.CreateInstance();

                // load data...
                for(EntityField field : et.getFields())
                {
                        DataType type = field.getDataType();
                        if(type == DataType.String)
                                entity.SetValue(field, c.getString(field.getOrdinal()),↵
SetReason.Load);
                        else if(type == DataType.Int32)
                                entity.SetValue(field, c.getInt(field.getOrdinal()),↵
SetReason.Load);
                        else
                                throw new Exception(String.format("Cannot handle '%s'.",↵
field.getDataType()));
                }

                // return...
                return entity;
        }
```

Asking the Navigator Controller to Load the Real Bookmarks

All that remains now is to modify the Load method of the navigator controller so that it loads the real bookmarks from the database rather than the fake ones we've been using up until now. Here's the code:

```
// Modify method in NavigatorController.java…
        public void Load() throws Exception
        {
                // select from the database...
                SqlFilter filter = new SqlFilter(Bookmark.class);
                ShowBookmarks((BookmarkCollection)filter.ExecuteEntityCollection(this));
        }
```

If we run the project, we now go end to end, and we'll see the bookmarks get synchronized from the server and shown on the navigator. Figure 6-9 shows some sample results.

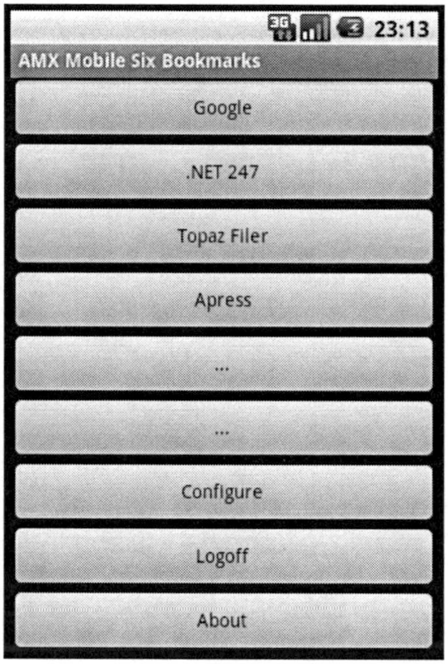

Figure 6-9. *Success! The application shows the bookmarks selected from the database after downloading from the server*

▪**NOTE** The filter created in the Load method will return all bookmarks, even ones with the LocalDeleted value set to true. In the next chapter, we'll change this method to exclude ones that have been deleted via configuration.

Conclusion

In this chapter, we have covered considerable ground in that we can now join activities together, call up to the OData service, store entities in our local database, and read them back. We also built a fully-functional (albeit slightly limited) object-relational mapping system complete with metadata subsystem. In the next chapter, we'll look to extend this by adding code to update entities locally when changed and pass the updates back to the server.

■ ■ ■

CHAPTER 7

Android: Pushing Changes to the Server

This is the last of the Android chapters where we're developing code, and it's where we pull the functionality of the application together. As of this point, we have a synchronization class that will pull the latest version of the bookmarks from the server and an ORM layer that will put them in the database. We also have forms for logging on and showing the bookmarks implemented. What we're going to do in this chapter is create two new forms—one for asking the user which bookmark needs to be edited and one that actually edits the bookmark. We'll then complete the synchronization routine by making it send inserts, updates, or deletes back to the server. This is going to include modifying the SqlFilter functionality to allow it to constrain data and doing more work with the HttpClient class and its relations.

■**NOTE** In this chapter, although we only have an entity type that relates to bookmarks, the code has been designed to be generic enough to be easily adapted to work with multiple types of entities.

Capturing Local Changes

We'll start by creating the UI to capture the changes, and in the second part of this chapter, we will look at how those changes can be streamed up to the server. First, we'll look at modifying our SqlFilter class to make it more sophisticated.

Constraining SQL Filters

When we built SqlFilter in the last chapter, we used it only to return all items. We're going to need more sophistication in this chapter, and so we'll add the ability to add constraints to the query.

In BootFX, the open-source ORM tool that the database work in this book is based on, which we discussed in Chapter 3, there are two kinds of constraints—field constraints and free constraints. A field constraint is bound to a single field and is used to say things like "I want this field to be equal to this value". A free constraint allows you to patch in a snippet of SQL if you need more sophistication. The advantage of field constraints is that they're really easy to code up, but they are limited. The disadvantage of free constraints—when working with traditional database servers that run on server hardware—is that they are SQL dialect specific, i.e., if you write one that works on SQL Server, you're not guaranteed it will run on MySQL, Oracle, etc. Here, just to illustrate the point and for consistency with

BootFX, we're going to build a base class called SqlConstraint and a field constraint implementation in SqlFieldConstraint, but we will not build SqlFreeConstraint.

When we come to build our query (recall we do this in the GetStatement method on SqlFilter), we'll walk the list of constraints that we have and call a method on the constraint called Append, which will be responsible for actually modifying the query. SqlConstraint will be an abstract class with an abstract Append method, like so:

```
package com.amxMobile.SixBookmarks.Runtime;

public abstract class SqlConstraint
{
        public SqlConstraint()
        {
        }

        public abstract void Append(SqlStatement sql, StringBuilder builder) throws⏎
 Exception;
}
```

The field constraints will need to know three things: the field that they're binding to, the value to match, and the operator to use for the matching. In this book, I've created just two operators—equal to or not equal to. In a real-world implementation, you'd likely need more operators. Here's the enumeration that holds the values:

```
package com.amxMobile.SixBookmarks.Runtime;

public enum SqlOperator
{
        EqualTo, NotEqualTo
}
```

When we're building our SQL statement, the constraint just has to add the small portion of the WHERE clause that contains the expression to match. Here's a sample statement with the constraint's area of responsibility underlined:

```
SELECT * FROM BOOKMARKS WHERE LocalDeleted=0
```

In other words, it's just a small part of the statement that the constraint cares about.

Here's the implementation of SqlFieldConstraint that holds the field, the operator, and the value:

```
package com.amxMobile.SixBookmarks.Runtime;

import com.amxMobile.SixBookmarks.Entities.EntityField;

public class SqlFieldConstraint extends SqlConstraint
{
        private EntityField _field;
        private Object _value;
        private SqlOperator _operator;
```

```java
public SqlFieldConstraint(EntityField field, Object value)
{
        this(field, SqlOperator.EqualTo, value);
}

public SqlFieldConstraint(EntityField field, SqlOperator op, Object value)
{
        _field = field;
        _value = value;
        _operator = op;
}

public EntityField getField()
{
        return _field;
}

public Object getValue()
{
        return _value;
}

public SqlOperator getOperator()
{
        return _operator;
}

@Override
public void Append(SqlStatement sql, StringBuilder builder) throws Exception
{
        // add the snippet...
        EntityField field = getField();
        builder.append(field.getNativeName());

        // what operator?
        if(_operator == SqlOperator.EqualTo)
                builder.append("=");
        else if(_operator == SqlOperator.NotEqualTo)
                builder.append(" <> ");
        else
                throw new Exception(String.format("Cannot handle '%s'.", _operator));
```

```
                    // add the parameter and its value value...
                    builder.append("?");
                    sql.AddParameterValue(getValue());
            }
    }
```

All that remains is to make SqlFilter aware of the constraints.

I've found in the past that it's more practical to design these classes by hiding the physical SqlConstraint objects away from the caller and adding methods to SqlFilter that actually add the constraints in. I've also found that it's generally a good idea that when working with items that map down to the entity metadata subsystem, creating method overload takes the item's name and a second overload that takes the related EntityField instance itself is also a good idea. Thus, we create one method that takes a field name and another that takes an EntityField instance. In addition, we also need to optionally provide the operator, assuming "equal to" in situations where an operator is not provided. Here's the code:

```
// Add field and methods to SqlFilter…
package com.amxMobile.SixBookmarks.Runtime;

public class SqlFilter implements ISqlStatementSource
{
        private EntityType _entityType;
        private ArrayList<SqlConstraint> _constraints = new ArrayList<SqlConstraint>();

        // code omitted for brevity...

        private ArrayList<SqlConstraint> getConstraints()
        {
                return _constraints;
        }

        public void AddConstraint(String name, Object value) throws Exception
        {
                EntityField field = getEntityType().GetField(name, true);
                AddConstraint(field, value);
        }

        public void AddConstraint(EntityField field, Object value)
        {
                getConstraints().add(new SqlFieldConstraint(field, value));
        }

        public void AddConstraint(String name, SqlOperator op, Object value) throws Exception
        {
                EntityField field = getEntityType().GetField(name, true);
                AddConstraint(field, op, value);
        }
```

```
        public void AddConstraint(EntityField field, SqlOperator op,Object value)
        {
                getConstraints().add(new SqlFieldConstraint(field, op, value));
        }
}
```

Now that we can create and store constraints, we just need to modify the GetSqlStatement method to detect the existence of constraints and apply them. Here's the modified version of GetSqlStatement:

```
// Modify GetSqlStatement method within SqlFilter…public SqlStatement GetSqlStatement() throws
Exception
        {
                SqlStatement sql = new SqlStatement();
                StringBuilder builder = new StringBuilder();

                // et...
                EntityType et = getEntityType();

                // columns...
                builder.append("SELECT ");
                ArrayList<EntityField> fields = et.getFields();
                for(int index = 0; index < fields.size(); index++)
                {
                        if(index > 0)
                                builder.append(", ");
                        builder.append(fields.get(index).getNativeName());
                }

                // from...
                builder.append(" FROM ");
                builder.append(et.getNativeName());

                // where...
                ArrayList<SqlConstraint> constraints = getConstraints();
                if(constraints.size() > 0)
                {
                        builder.append(" WHERE ");
                        for(int index = 0; index < constraints.size(); index++)
                        {
                                if(index > 0)
                                        builder.append(" AND ");
                                constraints.get(index).Append(sql, builder);
                        }
                }
```

```
        // return...
        sql.setCommandText(builder.toString());
        return sql;
    }
```

In the last chapter, when we created our ExecuteEntityCollection method, we didn't have any constraints; hence we did not have any parameters to pass in. What we need to do now is go back and revisit ExecuteEntityCollection, and in the part where we set up the query to run, we need to package up and pass in the variables. (Slightly sinisterly, if we forget to do this and have a query string that defines parameters, but do not pass in any parameters, SQLite quietly accepts the query and assumes the parameter values are all null.)

More oddly, when we want to use a cursor to get values back, the parameter values all need to be passed in as strings, not the native type of the parameter value. Thus, we need a method that mangles the parameter values into strings. And here it is:

```
// Add method to DatabaseHelper…
    private String[] MangleParameterValues(Object[] values)
    {
        String[] args = new String[values.length];
        for(int index = 0; index < values.length; index++)
            args[index] = values[index].toString();

        // return...
        return args;
    }
```

When we create the cursor in ExecuteEntityCollection (the db.rawQuery call), we need to pass in the result of this. Here's the modification required to ExecuteEntityCollection:

```
    public ArrayList<Entity> ExecuteEntityCollection(ISqlStatementSource sql, EntityType
et) throws Exception
    {
        // get...
        SqlStatement realSql = sql.GetSqlStatement();
        SQLiteDatabase db = getReadableDatabase();
        Cursor c = null;
        try
        {
            // execute a cursor...
            ArrayList<Entity> results = et.CreateCollectionInstance();

            // cursor...
            c = db.rawQuery(realSql.getCommandText(), ↵
MangleParameterValues(realSql.getParameterValues()));
```

```
                    while(c.moveToNext())
                    {
                            // load...
                            Entity entity = LoadEntity(c, et);
                            results.add(entity);
                    }

                    // return...
                    return results;
            }
            finally
            {
                    if(c != null)
                            c.close();
                    if(db != null)
                            db.close();
            }
    }
```

That's it! Now we can make our SQL queries more sophisticated.

Excluding Deleted Entities from the View

The reason I wanted to walk through adding the constraints to SqlFilter first was that we need to modify the code that gets the bookmarks from the local database to display in the navigator view. Specifically, we need to exclude deleted items.

We're about to start building our "Configuration" window. One of the things this will allow the user to do is delete bookmarks. However, we cannot delete bookmarks from our local database because if we do not have an item locally, we don't know that the server version is not in sync and needs to be deleted. Thus, when we delete locally, we'll "soft delete" rather than "hard delete" the item. We'll do this by setting the LocalDeleted field of the bookmark to 1.

This, then, begs the question that for our user interface, we need to not show soft deleted bookmarks—hence the need for the changes to SqlFilter.

We'll define a convention whereby we add business methods that return bookmarks back to us as static methods on the Bookmark class. We'll add GetBookmarksForDisplay now (which will bring back all bookmarks where LocalDeleted is 0), and we'll add some more methods later. Here's the listing:

```
// Add method to Bookmark...
        public static BookmarkCollection GetBookmarksForDisplay↵
(IContextSource context) throws Exception
        {
                // get those that are flagged as modified and deleted...
                SqlFilter filter = new SqlFilter(Bookmark.class);
                filter.AddConstraint("LocalDeleted", 0);

                // return...
                return (BookmarkCollection)filter.ExecuteEntityCollection(context);
        }
```

In Chapter 6, we added a method called HandleLoad to the NavigatorController, which looked like this:

```
// Existing HandleLoad method in NavigatorController...
    public void HandleLoad () throws Exception
    {
            // select from the database...
            SqlFilter filter = new SqlFilter(Bookmark.class);
            ShowBookmarks((BookmarkCollection)filter.ExecuteEntityCollection(this));
    }
```

We can now change this to defer to GetBookmarksForDisplay, rather than creating a SqlFilter directly. Here's the code:

```
// Modify HandleLoad method in NavigatorController...
    public void HandleLoad () throws Exception
    {
            // show the bookmarks...
            ShowBookmarks(Bookmark.GetBookmarksForDisplay(this));
    }
```

If you run the application now, you won't see any difference, but behind the scenes we are limiting the display items. Now that we've got that out of the way, we can build our configuration form.

Getting a Bookmark by Ordinal

Later on, we're going to need to retrieve a bookmark that has a specific audience. While we have our head into creating these filters, we'll add this now. Essentially, all we need is a filter that is configured to constrain by a specific ordinal value *and* to exclude items that have been deleted. Here's the method to add to Bookmark:

```
// Add method to Bookmark...
    public static Bookmark GetByOrdinal(IContextSource context, int ordinal)↵
throws Exception
    {
            SqlFilter filter = new SqlFilter(Bookmark.class);
            filter.AddConstraint("Ordinal", ordinal);
            filter.AddConstraint("LocalDeleted", 0);

            // return...
            return (Bookmark)filter.ExecuteEntity(context);
    }
```

This method uses ExecuteEntity on SqlFilter. We haven't built that yet, so let's add it now. Here's the code:

```
// Add method to SqlFilter...
        public Entity ExecuteEntity(IContextSource context) throws Exception
        {
                ArrayList items = ExecuteEntityCollection(context);
                if(items.size() > 0)
                        return (Entity)items.get(0);
                else
                        return null;
        }
```

Building the Configuration Form

We're going to build two forms for the configuration part of the application. One of the forms will display a list of bookmarks to configure. The second form will display the details of a single bookmark. This is different to the user interface that we build in the chapters on building the web-based Six Bookmarks applications. My choice in doing it like this is that a) it's easier for the user to work with and b) when we come to build the iPhone application, having one form with a list and another form to edit the bookmark is more in line with common practice on that device.

List Views

A standard UI pattern in all of the mobile applications that we will build is the "list and singleton" pattern. In this pattern, we have a list of items, and we can drill into detail about the item. Figure 7-1 and Figure 7-2 show a typical "list and singleton" from the iPhone's iPod application.

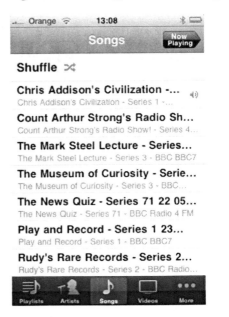

Figure 7-1. *A "list" view in the iPhone's iPod application*

Figure 7-2. *A "singleton" view of an item in the iPhone's iPod application*

The modern device platforms (Android, iOS, and Windows Phone) have support for list and singletons built in. In this section, we'll look at building a list that shows the defined bookmarks, and we'll also look at how to handle menus and how to navigate down to the singleton view.

The easiest way to build a list view in Android is to create an activity that extends ListActivity. This type of activity does not need a layout XML file—behind the scenes, Android will create a ListView control and position it on the form for us. Importantly, we can access this control and manipulate it just as if we had created it ourselves.

Although we won't be creating a custom layout, we will stick with our MVC pattern that we have been using thus far. We'll also extend it a little by creating a special view interface called IListView that we can use whenever we want to create views that extend ListActivity. Specifically, ListActivity implements a method called getListView, and we'll have our IListView implement that. Here's the listing for IListView:

```
package com.amxMobile.SixBookmarks;

import android.widget.*;

public interface IListView
{
        ListView getListView();
}
```

...and then the listing for IConfigureListView:

```
package com.amxMobile.SixBookmarks;

public interface IConfigureListView extends IListView
{
}
```

In a moment, we'll build the ConfigureListController class, but for now, we'll create a very simple implementation of the ConfigureList activity that extends ListActivity. Here's the code:

```
package com.amxMobile.SixBookmarks;

import com.amxMobile.SixBookmarks.Runtime.*;

import android.os.*;
import android.app.*;
import android.content.*;
import android.view.*;
import android.view.ContextMenu.*;
import android.view.View.*;
import android.widget.*;
import android.widget.AdapterView.*;

public class ConfigureList extends ListActivity implements IConfigureListView{
        private ConfigureListController Controller = new ConfigureListController(this);

    @Override
    public void onCreate(Bundle savedInstanceState)
    {
        super.onCreate(savedInstanceState);

        // caption...
        setTitle("Configure Bookmarks");

        // defer to the controller...
        try
        {
                Controller.HandleLoad();
        }
        catch(Exception ex)
        {
                MessageBox.Show((Context)this, ex);
        }
    }
}
```

We'll build ConfigureListController properly later on. For now, we'll add a basic stub implementation so that the project compiles. Here's the code.

```
package com.amxMobile.SixBookmarks;

import com.amxMobile.SixBookmarks.Runtime.*;

public class ConfigureListController extends Controller<IConfigureListView>
{
        protected ConfigureListController(IConfigureListView view)
        {
                super(view);
        }

        public void HandleLoad() throws Exception
        {
                // TBD...
        }
}
```

In the last chapter, we created a method called HandleConfigure on NavigatorController, which, at the time, was set to do nothing. We can now change this to start up our ConfigureList activity.

To start, we need to update the AndroidManifest.xml file and include the ConfigureList activity. This is simply a matter of copying one of the previous activity nodes and changing the name. Here's the listing with the reference to the ConfigureList activity.

```
<?xml version="1.0" encoding="utf-8"?>
<manifest xmlns:android="http://schemas.android.com/apk/res/android"
      android:versionCode="1"
      android:versionName="1.0" package="com.amxMobile.SixBookmarks">

    <application android:icon="@drawable/icon" android:label="@string/app_name">

        <activity android:name=".Logon"
                android:label="@string/app_name">
            <intent-filter>
                <action android:name="android.intent.action.MAIN" />
                <category android:name="android.intent.category.LAUNCHER" />
            </intent-filter>
        </activity>

        <activity android:name=".Navigator"
                android:label="@string/app_name">
            <intent-filter>
                <action android:name="android.intent.action.MAIN" />
                <category android:name="android.intent.category.LAUNCHER" />
            </intent-filter>
        </activity>
```

```
<activity android:name=".ConfigureList"
        android:label="@string/app_name">
    <intent-filter>
        <action android:name="android.intent.action.MAIN" />
        <category android:name="android.intent.category.LAUNCHER" />
    </intent-filter>
</activity>

</application>
    <uses-permission android:name="android.permission.INTERNET"></uses-permission>
</manifest>
```

Now we can reference the activity from `NavigatorController`. Here's the code to invoke it:

```
// Modify HandleConfigure method in NavigatorController…
    public void HandleConfigure()
    {
            Intent newIntent = new Intent(getActivity(), ConfigureList.class);
            getActivity().startActivityForResult(newIntent, 0);
    }
```

If you run the project and click the **Configure** button, the window will open; however, it's not showing any items yet. (Figure 7-3 illustrates.) We'll look at how to bind data to the list in the next section.

Figure 7-3. *The list view being shown on the screen, but without bound data*

Binding List Data

There are two principles that you need to understand in order to implement lists in Android.

The first principle is that you need to use an adapter to "mate" a datasource to a view. The adapter then allows the view to reflect over the datasource. As part of that operation, it will ask the adapter to create a view for each item.

The second principle relates to the views—views used on lists are typically defined using a layout XML file. This is analogous to how user controls work on other platforms.

The easiest adapter to use is the built-in ArrayAdapter class. This takes an array of items and the ID of the layout XML file that should be used to provide the interface for each item. However, we're going to do something a little more advanced and create our own adapter that works directly with Bookmark instances.

The first step is to create the view to use on the row. To do this, create a new Android XML layout file called bookmarkitem.xml and store it in the ~/res/layout folder. The layout we're going to use has a TextView control of the appropriate size and bounds. Here's the listing:

```xml
<?xml version="1.0" encoding="utf-8"?>

<TextView xmlns:a="http://schemas.android.com/apk/res/android"
    a:layout_width="fill_parent"
    a:layout_height="fill_parent"
    a:padding="10dp"
    a:textSize="16sp"
    a:id="@+id/textName" >
</TextView>
```

Adapters in Android extend the BaseAdapter class, and we're going to create a new BookmarkAdapter class that extends accordingly. This class will load the bookmarks, implement the methods necessary to extract data from the underlying datasource, and implement the getView method. This last method is responsible for creating a new view to show on the list.

Let's look at getting the data from the datasource first.

We know that we can reuse our GetBookmarksForDisplay business method, and we have seen that when we use this on the navigator, a process runs that goes through each bookmark and assigns each discovered bookmark item to its relevant button. It's worth nothing, though, that the GetBookmarksForDisplay method returns bookmarks in a non-deterministic order—i.e., we're going to get the bookmarks out in whatever order SQLite feels like. Therefore, we need to be able to sort the bookmarks so that they will appear in the order expected by the user, i.e., by ordinal.

To do this, we'll add a SortByOrdinal method to BookmarkCollection. This will use the standard sort routine in the standard Java library. Here's the code:

```java
// Add SortByOrdinal method and related provide class to BookmarkCollection:
package com.amxMobile.SixBookmarks.Database;

import java.util.*;
import android.util.*;
```

```
public class BookmarkCollection extends ArrayList<Bookmark>
{
        public void SortByOrdinal()
        {
                Collections.sort(this, new OrdinalComparator());
        }

        private class OrdinalComparator implements Comparator<Bookmark>
        {
                public int compare(Bookmark x, Bookmark y)
                {
                        try
                        {
                                int a = x.getOrdinal();
                                int b = y.getOrdinal();
                                if(a < b)
                                        return -1;
                                else if(a > b)
                                        return 1;
                                else
                                        return 0;
                        }
                        catch(Exception ex)
                        {
                                Log.e("Sort operation failed.", ex.toString());
                                return 0;
                        }
                }
        }
}
```

Now that we can sort the ordinals, we'll load the bookmarks and sort them in the constructor to the adapter. Here's the first part of BookmarkAdapter for you to create:

```
package com.amxMobile.SixBookmarks;

import com.amxMobile.SixBookmarks.Database.*;
import com.amxMobile.SixBookmarks.Runtime.*;
import android.app.*;
import android.util.*;
import android.view.*;
import android.widget.*;

public class BookmarkAdapter extends BaseAdapter
{
        private IContextSource _owner;
        private BookmarkCollection _bookmarks;
```

```
public BookmarkAdapter(IContextSource owner) throws Exception
{
        // save the owner...
        _owner = owner;
        // load the bookmarks and sort by ordinal...
        _bookmarks = Bookmark.GetBookmarksForDisplay(owner);
        _bookmarks.SortByOrdinal();
}

private IContextSource getOwner()
{
        return _owner;
}

BookmarkCollection getBookmarks()
{
        return _bookmarks;
}
}
```

Notice how we have made the adapter take an IContextSource instance into its constructor—at some point, we'll need that to de-reference values from the running activity and context.

BaseAdapter requires that we implement the getCount, getItem, and getItemId methods. getCount and getItem are obvious; getItemId needs a little work, as we need to choose the ID. We're going to use the ordinal of the bookmark as the ID. Although the bookmark does have an ID (the BookmarkId column in the database and associated getBookmarkId method), we've used the ordinal thus far in building the navigator, and so we'll continue for consistency. This will also help when opening the singleton view for new bookmarks—a point I'll discuss later.

The one wrinkle we have to deal with is that the value getters on the entity throw exceptions, and we cannot throw this back out through the getItemId method due to the way it has been defined. We'll also add a HandleException method that can be used to consume exceptions that occur in the adapter. These exceptions will be logged through the standard Android logging subsystem. This is a good-enough solution for an example in a book. In a real-world application, it's likely that these exceptions need to go somewhere more helpful.

```
// Add methods to BookmarkAdapter…
        public int getCount()
        {
                return getBookmarks().size();
        }

        public Object getItem(int position)
        {
                return getBookmarks().get(position);
        }

        public long getItemId(int position)
        {
```

```
        try
        {
                Bookmark bookmark = (Bookmark)getItem(position);

                // return the *ordinal* - this is the easiest thing to↵
                dereference when
                // we need to configure the singleton...
                return (long)bookmark.getOrdinal();
        }
        catch(Exception ex)
        {
                HandleException("getItemId", ex);
                return 0;
        }
    }

    private void HandleException(String method, Exception ex)
    {
            // log it...
            Log.e(String.format("Adapter operation '%s' failed.", method),↵
MessageBox.FormatException(ex));
        }
```

Thus far, when we've used layouts on the logon and navigator views, we've used the activity's setContentView method, and Android has done the magic of creating a view. Under the covers, Android is using a class called LayoutInflater to build a concrete view from the definition. We're going to use this on our adapter's getView method.

Once we have loaded the view using the inflater, we'll de-reference the TextView instance on the form and configure the text value. Here's the code:

```
// Add method to BookmarkAdapter...
        public View getView(int position, View convertView, ViewGroup parent)
        {
                try
                {
                        // what item?
                        Bookmark bookmark = (Bookmark)getItem(position);

                        // use an inflater to get the layout...
                        LayoutInflater inflater = ((Activity)getOwner().getContext())↵
                        .getLayoutInflater();
                        View itemView = inflater.inflate(R.layout.bookmarkitem, null);
```

171

```
                        // set the text...
                           TextView text = (TextView)itemView.findViewById(R.id.textName);
                        text.setText(bookmark.getName());

                        // return...
                        return itemView;
                }
                catch(Exception ex)
                {
                        HandleException("getView", ex);
                        return null;
                }
        }
}
```

Notice how that method has to handle the exception, too.

The final step at this stage is to implement the ConfigureListController class's HandleLoad method. This method will defer to a private method called RefreshView for the actual view population. (This is needed, as we're going to need to refresh the view via another path, then "load" later on.) Inside RefreshView, we'll create an adapter and hold it in a local field—we'll do this because later on, we'll need to look up a bookmark instance from a supplied ordinal, and the adapter lets us do this via its getItem method. Here's the revised version of ConfigureListController with an adapter field and read-only property and a RefreshView method:

```
package com.amxMobile.SixBookmarks;

import android.content.*;
import android.view.*;
import android.view.*;
import android.view.ContextMenu.*;
import android.widget.*;
import android.widget.AdapterView.*;

import com.amxMobile.SixBookmarks.Database.*;
import com.amxMobile.SixBookmarks.Runtime.*;

public class ConfigureListController extends Controller<IConfigureListView>
{
        private BookmarkAdapter _adapter;

        protected ConfigureListController(IConfigureListView view)
        {
                super(view);
        }

        public void HandleLoad() throws Exception
        {
                this.RefreshView();
        }
```

```
private void RefreshView() throws Exception
{
        // get the list view and set the adapter...
        ListView list = getView().getListView();
        _adapter = new BookmarkAdapter(this);
        list.setAdapter(_adapter);
}

private BookmarkAdapter getAdapter()
{
        return _adapter;
}
}
```

You can, at this stage, run the code and see real data in the configuration list. Figure 7-4 illustrates.

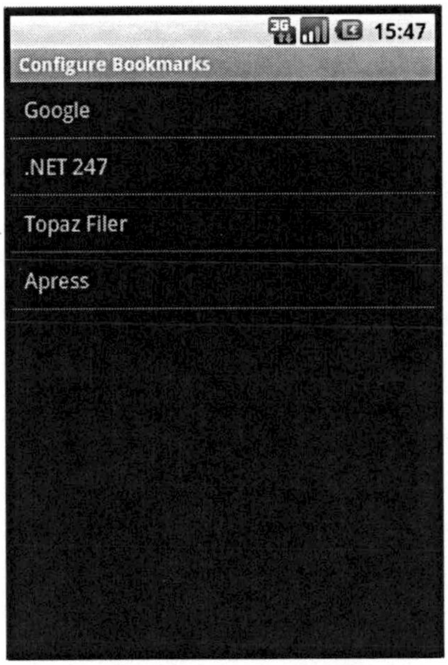

Figure 7-4. *The list view showing data delivered via the data adapter*

Selecting Items for Editing

When we click on an item, we're going to want to show the singleton view for editing that item. We're not going to build the singleton view until a bit later; however, we can now build the code for listening for selections on the list and calling a method on the controller called HandleEdit, which ultimately will run the activity tasked with editing a bookmark.

The ListView instance will raise an event called ItemClick that we can bind an OnItemClickListener to. We'll configure our ConfigureList activity as a listener for this event, and have it defer processing to the controller when the call is received.

onItemClick (the method defined on OnItemClickListener) will send through a number of arguments, one of which is the ID of the item. Recall that the ID of our bookmark item is the ordinal. This is sent through in the id parameter. Here's the listing:

```
public class ConfigureList extends ListActivity implements IConfigureListView,↵
OnItemClickListener
{
// code omitted for brevity...

    @Override
    public void onCreate(Bundle savedInstanceState)
    {
        super.onCreate(savedInstanceState);

        // caption...
        setTitle("Configure Bookmarks");

        // listen for normal clicks...
        ListView list = getListView();
        list.setOnItemClickListener(this);

        // defer to the controller...
        try
        {
                Controller.HandleLoad();
        }
        catch(Exception ex)
        {
                MessageBox.Show((Context)this, ex);
        }
    }

// code omitted for brevity...

        public void onItemClick(AdapterView<?> parent, View view, int position, long id)
        {
                Controller.HandleListItemClick(id);
        }
}
```

When we receive the click event through the HandleListItemClick method, we can defer to the HandleEdit method, which takes an ordinal. For now, we'll have this show a message box—later, we'll have this create the new view. Here's the code to add to the controller:

```
// Add methods to ConfigureListController…
        public void HandleListItemClick(long itemId)
        {
                try
                {
                        HandleEdit((int)itemId);
                }
                catch (Exception ex)
                {
                        MessageBox.Show(this, ex);
                }
        }

        public void HandleEdit(int ordinal) throws Exception
        {
                MessageBox.Show(this, String.format("Will edit '%d'.", ordinal));
        }
```

If we run the project now, we can click on items in the list and be presented with a message box. Figure 7-5 illustrates.

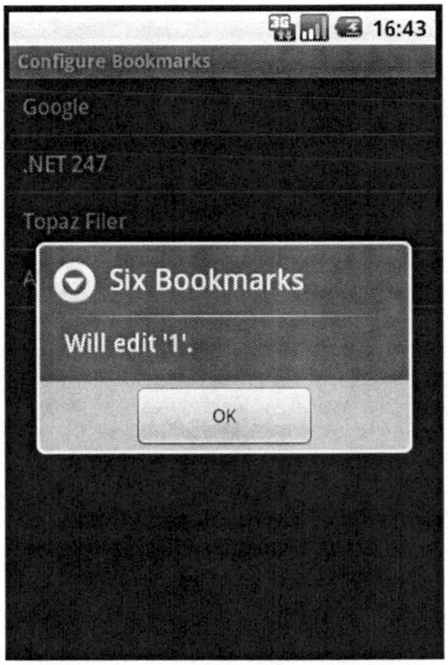

Figure 7-5. *A message box informing the user which item was clicked*

As mentioned, we'll now complete the work to implement menus and then look at the process of actually editing the bookmark item.

Implementing Menus

Another common UI element that exists on all of the platforms is the menu. Android has a special "menu" hardware button, which is designed to pop up a small menu at the bottom of the screen. In addition, if we press and hold an item in a list, we can pop up a context menu of options related to the item that we clicked on. We'll implement popup and context menus in this section.

On the popup menu, we're going to implement an option to add a new bookmark and an option to force a synchronization operation. On the context menu, we're going to present the user with an option to delete the item. We'll do the popup menu first.

Popup menus are handled directly by the activity via a virtual method called onCreateOptionsMenu on the Activity class—i.e., when the user clicks the menu button, this method will be called, and we can use the opportunity to create our menu. As we're using an MVC pattern, we'll listen for this event and defer to the controller for population. Here's the code to add to ConfigureList:

```
// Add method to ConfigureList:
    @Override
    public boolean onCreateOptionsMenu(Menu menu)
    {
        Controller.HandleCreateOptionsMenu(menu);
        return true;
    }
```

■**NOTE** This approach isn't MVC in a pure sense, as the controller will be building Android-specific UI elements. However, MVC is helpful for code separation, and for simplicity, we'll use this approach.

We get given a Menu instance to add options to by the method. We can call the add method on the menu to add items. As a minimum, items need an arbitrary item ID and some text to display.

We're also going to add some icons to the menus. You can access Android's system menus by using Android's own R class of defined constants. (Remember that we get one generated for us in our project? Android also has one.)

Android's official list is here: http://developer.android.com/reference/android/R.drawable.html. However, unhelpfully it does not have pictures next to them, so you do not know what you're getting! However, your same Google term of "android.r.drawable" will likely yield some sites that have extracted the icons for your viewing pleasure, including the one at http://androiddrawableexplorer.appspot.com/. (Your mileage may vary—as of the time of writing, this page included some icons that are not for external consumption.)

For our menu, we're going to add one button for refresh and one to trigger a sync. Each of these needs a unique menu ID. Later we're going to need a menu ID for the delete operation; hence I propose adding constants for these to the top of the controller class. Here's the code:

```
// Add constants to ConfigureListController…
public class ConfigureListController extends Controller<IConfigureListView>
{
        private static final int MENUID_ADD = 10001;
        private static final int MENUID_SYNC = 10002;
        private static final int MENUID_DELETE = 10003;
```

```
        // code omitted for brevity...
}
```

We can now implement HandleCreateOptionsMenu on the controller and configure the menu options. Here's the code:

```
// Add method to ConfigureListController…
        public void HandleCreateOptionsMenu(Menu menu)
        {
                // create an item and set the icon to be one of the android
                // standard ones...
                // http://androiddrawableexplorer.appspot.com/
                MenuItem add = menu.add(0, MENUID_ADD, 0, "Add");
                add.setIcon(android.R.drawable.ic_menu_add);

                // now do a sync method...
                MenuItem sync = menu.add(0, MENUID_SYNC, 0, "Sync Now");
                sync.setIcon(android.R.drawable.ic_menu_save);
        }
```

Now if we run the code and show the menu, we'll see something like Figure 7-6.

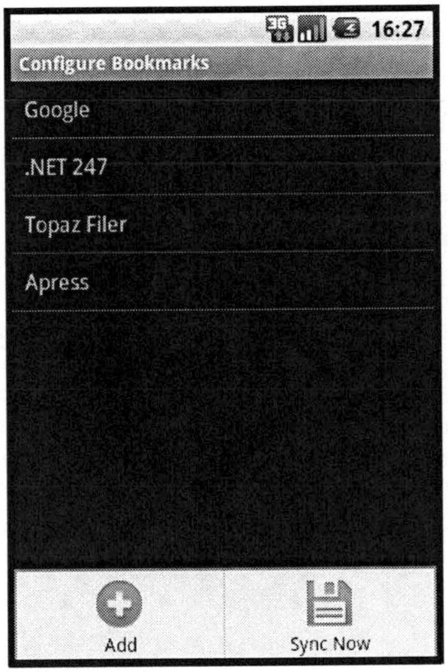

Figure 7-6. *The popup menu*

Handling Menu Actions

Now that users can click our menu, we need to handle the fact that they did! This is done by overriding another method defined on `Activity`, namely `onOptionsItemSelected`. Again, our implementation will defer to the controller for processing. Here's the code:

```
// Add method to ConfigureList…
    @Override
    public boolean onOptionsItemSelected(MenuItem item)
    {
        return Controller.HandleMenuItemClick(item);
    }
```

Our controller's method for handling button clicks is going to work on both the popup menu and context menu. In it, we'll look at the ID of the option that was clicked and defer to a private method for processing. For simplicity, we'll implement our `HandleDelete` method here, too—the other two will come later.

```
// Add methods to ConfigureListController…
public boolean HandleMenuItemClick(MenuItem item)
        {
                try
                {
                        int id = item.getItemId();
                        if(id == MENUID_ADD)
                        {
                                HandleAdd();
                                return true;
                        }
                        else if(id == MENUID_SYNC)
                        {
                                HandleSync();
                                return true;
                        }
                        else if(id == MENUID_DELETE)
                        {
                                HandleDelete();
                                return true;
                        }
                        else
                                throw new Exception(String.format("Cannot handle '%d'.", id));
                }
                catch(Exception ex)
                {
                        MessageBox.Show(this, ex);
                        return false;
                }
        }
```

```
    private void HandleDelete() throws Exception
    {
            MessageBox.Show(this, "TBD.");
}
```

We'll implement the sync method first as it's the easiest. We already have the Sync class built, but it's not fully-functional yet (and won't be until we get to the second half of this chapter). It's very easy—we'll just call DoSync and re-invoke the navigator to indicate that we've finished configuring. Here's the code:

```
// Add method to ConfigureListController…
    private void HandleSync() throws Exception
    {
            Sync sync = new Sync();
            sync.DoSync(this);

            // update...
            RefreshView();

            // show...
            Intent intent = new Intent(getContext(), Navigator.class);
            getActivity().startActivity(intent);
    }
```

The HandleAdd method has to be quite clever in that it has to find the next available ordinal given the already-defined bookmarks. It'll do this by creating a set of flags indicating which slots are available. It'll then choose the first slot and start editing that slot. (When we come to edit bookmark instances using the singleton view, this view will gracefully handle situations where a bookmark for a given ordinal does not exist by treating it as an insert.) Also, the method will detect when the maximum six bookmarks have already been defined and tell the user.

Here's the code:

```
    private void HandleAdd() throws Exception
    {
            // how many bookmarks do we have?
            if(getAdapter().getCount() < 6)
            {
                    // find the next slot...
                    Boolean[] defined = new Boolean[6];
                    for(int index = 0; index < defined.length; index++)
                            defined[index] = false;
                    for(Bookmark bookmark : getAdapter().getBookmarks())
                            defined[bookmark.getOrdinal()] = true;

                    // walk..
                    for(int index = 0; index < defined.length; index++)
                    {
                            if(!(defined[index]))
                            {
```

```
                                    // first slot found...
                                    HandleEdit(index);
                                    return;
                        }
                }
        }
        else
                MessageBox.Show(this, "The maximum number of bookmarks that↲
you can have is six.");
        }
```

Now that we can add and synchronize, we'll look at building the context menu.

Creating the Context Menu

Adding the context menu is a little weird—we have to register the ListView instance with the activity as having a context menu, and then listen for methods on the activity that tell us to create a context menu and handle any clicks. In addition, we have to tell the list that we want it to handle "long clicks," i.e., the user pressing and holding it for a short period.

This first part involves modifying the onCreate method on ConfigureList. Here's the modified listing:

```
// Modify onCreate method within ConfigureList...
    @Override
    public void onCreate(Bundle savedInstanceState)
    {
        super.onCreate(savedInstanceState);

        // caption...
        setTitle("Configure Bookmarks");

        // listen for normal clicks...
        ListView list = getListView();
        list.setOnItemClickListener(this);

        // listen for long clicks...
        list.setLongClickable(true);
        this.registerForContextMenu(list);

        // defer to the controller...
        try
        {
                Controller.HandleLoad();
        }
```

```
        catch(Exception ex)
        {
                MessageBox.Show((Context)this, ex);
        }
    }
}
```

With that done, we need to override the onCreateContextMenu and onContextItemSelected methods. As before, we'll defer to the controller for processing. Here's the code:

```
// Add methods to ConfigureList…
    @Override
    public void onCreateContextMenu(ContextMenu menu, View v, ContextMenu.ContextMenuInfo↵
menuInfo)
    {
        Controller.HandleCreateContextMenu(menu, menuInfo);
    }

    @Override
    public boolean onContextItemSelected(MenuItem item)
    {
        return Controller.HandleMenuItemClick(item);
    }
```

We're reusing the HandleMenuItemClick method on the controller—recall that this is already wired up to a HandleDelete method.

The onCreateContextMenu method passes in a View instance. In instances where we have multiple controls on a form that may have context menus, we can use this to determine which menu to show. However, as we have only one view, we'll ignore this argument, and the controller will assume that we're showing a context menu for the main list.

HandleCreateContextMenu does hold a little surprise—we have to keep track of the item that was clicked, as when we get told of a menu item being clicked, there is no straightforward way of determining the item at that point, once we receive the click notification. Being a context menu, we obviously need to know which item we are context-bound to. To handle this, we'll add a field to our class, called _lastClicked, which will keep track of the one bound to the context menu. Here's the listing:

```
// Add _lastClicked field and method to ConfigureListController…
public class ConfigureListController extends Controller<IConfigureListView>
{
        private long _lastClicked = -1;

// code omitted for brevity…

        public void HandleCreateContextMenu(ContextMenu menu, ContextMenuInfo menuInfo)
        {
                // the menu info will tell us the ID of the item that was clicked,
                // so store that for later use...
                _lastClicked = ((AdapterContextMenuInfo)menuInfo).id;
```

```
        // add...
        menu.add(0, MENUID_DELETE, 0, "Delete");
    }
}
```

The other wrinkle there is that the ContextMenuInfo instance that we get given does not contain any details of the list item. However, we can cast this to an AdapterView.AdapterContextMenuInfo instance and get the ID.

Now we can run the project and long-click on one of the items. The context menu will be displayed, as shown in Figure 7-7.

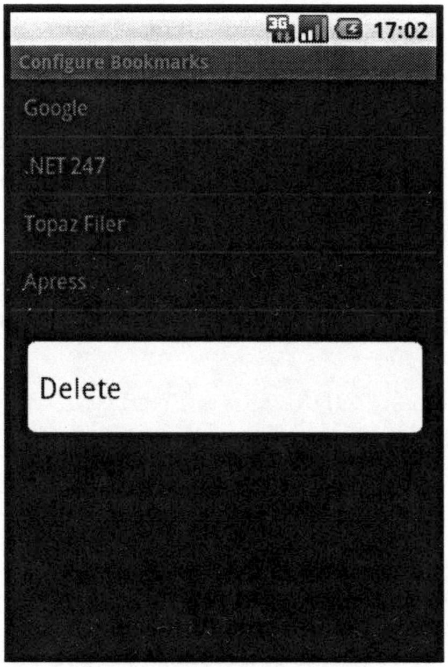

Figure 7-7. *The context menu*

For the delete operation itself, we have to find the bookmark, set its LocalDeleted value to true, and save it to the database. The GetBookmarksForDisplay method will then magically ignore any deleted bookmarks on this view and on the navigator.

Before we can build HandleDelete, though, we have to build a method to find a bookmark with the given ID from the adapter's collection. Here's a method to add to BookmarkAdapter:

```
// Add method to BookmarkAdapter...
        public Bookmark GetItemByOrdinal(int ordinal) throws Exception
        {
                return getBookmarks().GetByOrdinal(ordinal);
        }
```

And here's a method to add to BookmarkCollection:

```
// Add method to BookmarkCollection…
        public Bookmark GetByOrdinal(int ordinal) throws Exception
        {
                for(Bookmark bookmark : this)
                {
                        if(bookmark.getOrdinal() == ordinal)
                                return bookmark;
                }

                // nope...
                return null;
        }
```

Now the HandleDelete method can be added to the controller:

```
// Modify HandleDelete method within ConfigureListController…
        private void HandleDelete() throws Exception
        {
                // get the item...
                Bookmark bookmark = getAdapter().GetItemByOrdinal((int)_lastClicked);
                if(bookmark != null)
                {
                        // mark it as locally deleted...
                        bookmark.setLocalDeleted(true);
                        bookmark.SaveChanges(this);

                        // update...
                        this.RefreshView();
                }

                // reset...
                _lastClicked = -1;
        }
```

In the last chapter, when we built the EntityChangeProcessor, we gave it the ability to insert entities, but we didn't add the ability to update or delete them. Recall that when we did this, we built up an INSERT SQL statement and executed it after we detected that we had a new entity. All we have to do here is create UPDATE and DELETE statements as appropriate. Here are the methods to add to EntityChangeProcessor:

```
// Add methods to EntityChangeProcessor…
        private void Update(Entity entity) throws Exception
        {
                // get the statement...
                SqlStatement sql = this.GetUpdateStatement(entity);
```

```
        // run the statement...
        DatabaseHelper db = new DatabaseHelper(getContext());
        db.EnsureTableExists(getEntityType());
        db.ExecuteNonQuery(sql, true);
}

private SqlStatement GetUpdateStatement(Entity entity) throws Exception
{
        StringBuilder builder = new StringBuilder();
        SqlStatement sql = new SqlStatement();

        // et...
        EntityType et = getEntityType();

        // update...
        builder.append("UPDATE ");
        builder.append(et.getNativeName());
        builder.append(" SET ");

        // walk...
        boolean first = true;
        EntityField key = null;
        for(EntityField field : et.getFields())
        {
                if(field.getIsKey())
                        key = field;
                else if(entity.getIsModified(field))
                {
                        if(first)
                                first = false;
                        else
                                builder.append(", ");

                        // add the snippet...
                        builder.append(field.getNativeName());
                        builder.append("=?");

                        // add the parameter...
                        Object value = entity.GetValue(field);
                        sql.AddParameterValue(value);
                }
        }

        // append...
        AppendIdConstraint(builder, sql, key, entity);
```

```
                // return...
                sql.setCommandText(builder.toString());
                return sql;
        }

        private void AppendIdConstraint(StringBuilder builder, SqlStatement sql, EntityField
key, Entity entity) throws Exception
        {
                // constraint by ID...
                builder.append(" WHERE ");
                builder.append(key.getNativeName());
                builder.append("=?");
                sql.AddParameterValue(entity.GetValue(key));
        }

        private void Delete(Entity entity) throws Exception
        {
                // get the statement...
                SqlStatement sql = this.GetDeleteStatement(entity);

                // run the statement...
                DatabaseHelper db = new DatabaseHelper(getContext());
                db.EnsureTableExists(getEntityType());
                db.ExecuteNonQuery(sql, true);
        }

        private SqlStatement GetDeleteStatement(Entity entity) throws Exception
        {
                StringBuilder builder = new StringBuilder();
                SqlStatement sql = new SqlStatement();

                // et...
                EntityType et = getEntityType();

                // update...
                builder.append("DELETE FROM ");
                builder.append(et.getNativeName());

                // key...
                EntityField key = et.GetKeyField();
                AppendIdConstraint(builder, sql, key, entity);

                // return...
                sql.setCommandText(builder.toString());
                return sql;
        }
```

With those methods in place, we just have to change the SaveChanges method to call Update and Delete, in addition to it being able to call Insert. Here's the revised listing for SaveChanges:

```
// Modify SaveChanges method within EntityChangeRegister…
    public void SaveChanges(Entity entity) throws Exception
    {
            // do we need to do anything?
            if(entity.getIsNew())
                    this.Insert(entity);
            else if(entity.getIsModified())
                    this.Update(entity);
            else if(entity.getIsDeleted())
                    this.Delete(entity);

            // nothing to do...
    }
```

Now if you run the application, you can long-click on bookmarks and delete them from the database. However, we cannot add new ones yet! If you test the application and run out of bookmarks, remember that if you log on again or use the **Sync Now** option, your server bookmarks will be reloaded.

Configuring Singletons

The process of configuring singletons revisits a lot of the UI code that we have seen so far. One key difference is that we need to be able to pass data from one activity to another. Specifically, we need to pass over the ordinal of the bookmark that we wish to edit.

Recall that when we start our activities, we use the startActivity method. There is a variant of this method called startActivityForResult, which is used for situations where we want to pass results back to a parent activity, or when we just want to receive notification that a child activity has completed. (We want to do this because we need to update our view to reflect any changes that the user may have made rather than to actually pass data back. If we didn't use "for result," we wouldn't get told our activity had completed.)

As well as using this method, we also need to pass information over to the new activity via the "extras bag" defined on Intent. We can put anything in here that we want, but in our case, we're going to pass the ordinal of the bookmark to edit. Here's the revised version of HandleEdit that uses the "extras" and the startActivityForResult method:

```
// Modify HandleEdit method in ConfigureListController…
    public void HandleEdit(int ordinal) throws Exception
    {
            // create an intent...
            Intent newIntent = new Intent(getActivity(), ConfigureSingleton.class);

            // set...
            newIntent.putExtra("ordinal", ordinal);

            // run a sub-activity that tell us when its done...
            getActivity().startActivityForResult(newIntent, ordinal);
    }
```

We'll do this next bit backwards—now that we have started the activity using the "for result" variant, we can override a method called onActivityResult on the ConfigureList activity. As usual, we can defer processing of this back to the controller. Here's the listing for the method to add to ConfigureList:

```
// Add method to ConfigureList…
        @Override
        protected void onActivityResult(int requestCode, int resultCode, Intent data)
        {
                Controller.HandleActivityResult(requestCode, resultCode, data);
        }
```

Over in the controller, we're not going to do anything special when we're told the singleton activity completes. All we need to do is call RefreshView.

```
        public void HandleActivityResult(int requestCode, int resultCode, Intent data)
        {
                // update...
                try
                {
                        RefreshView();
                }
                catch (Exception ex)
                {
                        MessageBox.Show(this, ex);
                }
        }
```

■**NOTE** We could pass data back through the Intent instance's "extras bag" if we needed to.

To implement our singleton view, we're going to create an activity class called ConfigureSingleton, a view interface called IConfigureSingleton, a layout called configuresingleton.xml, and a controller called ConfigureSingletonController.

We'll add the configuresingleton.xml layout first. This needs to have TextView instances defined for the name and URL fields, a **Save Changes** button, and some labels. Here's the listing:

```
<?xml version="1.0" encoding="utf-8"?>
<LinearLayout xmlns:a="http://schemas.android.com/apk/res/android"↵
a:layout_width="fill_parent" a:layout_height="fill_parent"
        a:orientation="vertical">

        <TextView a:text="" a:id="@+id/labelCaption" a:layout_width="fill_parent"↵
a:layout_height="wrap_content" />
        <TextView a:text="Name:" a:layout_width="wrap_content"↵
a:layout_height="wrap_content" />
```

```
            <EditText a:id="@+id/textName" a:singleLine="true"↵
a:layout_width="fill_parent" a:layout_height="wrap_content" />
            <TextView a:text="URL:" a:layout_width="wrap_content" a:layout_height=↵
"wrap_content" />
            <EditText a:id="@+id/textUrl" a:singleLine="true"↵
a:layout_width="fill_parent" a:layout_height="wrap_content" />

            <Button a:text="Save Changes" a:id="@+id/buttonSave" ↵
a:layout_width="fill_parent" a:layout_height="wrap_content" />

</LinearLayout>
```

Figure 7-8 shows a (clipped) preview of what the layout should look like.

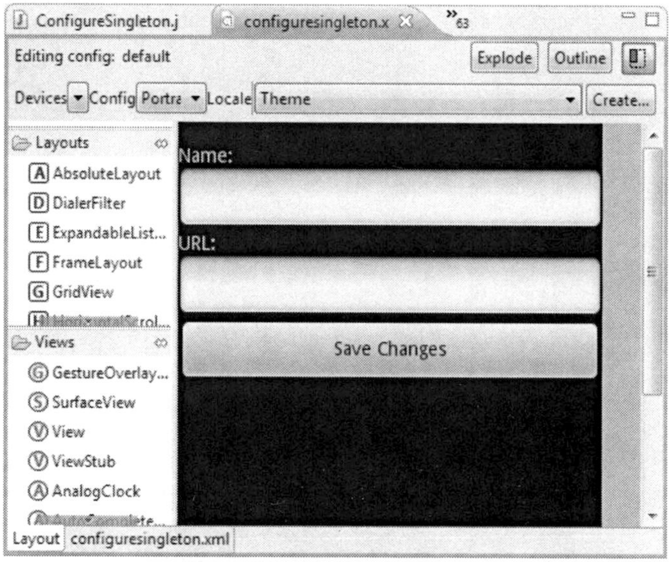

Figure 7-8. *The "configuresingleton.xml" layout shown in ADT's preview mode*

Personally, I always forget to add the activity to the manifest. Modify the AndroidManifest.xml file accordingly:

```
<!--code omitted for brevity… -->
    <activity android:name="ConfigureSingleton"
            android:label="@string/app_name">
        <intent-filter>
            <action android:name="android.intent.action.MAIN" />
        </intent-filter>
    </activity>
<!--code omitted for brevity… -->
```

The IConfigureSingletonView needs to expose out properties to set the ordinal, the name, and the URL of the bookmark. Here's the listing:

```
package com.amxMobile.SixBookmarks;

public interface IConfigureSingletonView
{
        int getOrdinal();
        void setOrdinal(int ordinal);

        String getName();
        void setName(String name);

        String getUrl();
        void setUrl(String url);
}
```

The ConfigureSingleton view class is nothing particularly special—it has to initialize the controller and implement the properties to expose the values out from the view. It also has to handle the click of the **Save Changes** button. Here's the listing:

```
package com.amxMobile.SixBookmarks;

import com.amxMobile.SixBookmarks.Runtime.*;
import android.app.*;
import android.os.*;
import android.view.*;
import android.view.View.*;
import android.widget.*;

public class ConfigureSingleton extends Activity implements OnClickListener, ↵
 IConfigureSingletonView
{
        private ConfigureSingletonController Controller;

        private int _ordinal;

        public ConfigureSingleton()
        {
                this.Controller = new ConfigureSingletonController(this);
        }

    @Override
    public void onCreate(Bundle savedInstanceState) {
        super.onCreate(savedInstanceState);
        setContentView(R.layout.configuresingleton);
```

```
        // wire up the buttons...
        findViewById(R.id.buttonSave).setOnClickListener(this);

        // tell the controller to load...
        try
        {
                Controller.HandleLoad();
        }
        catch(Exception ex)
        {
                MessageBox.Show(this, ex);
        }
}

public int getOrdinal()
{
        return _ordinal;
}

private EditText getNameTextBox()
{
        return (EditText)findViewById(R.id.textName);
}

private EditText getUrlTextBox()
{
        return (EditText)findViewById(R.id.textUrl);
}

public String getName()
{
        return getNameTextBox().getText().toString().trim();
}

public String getUrl()
{
        return getUrlTextBox().getText().toString().trim();
}

public void setOrdinal(int ordinal)
{
        _ordinal = ordinal;
}
```

```
public void setName(String name)
{
        getNameTextBox().setText(name);
}

public void setUrl(String url)
{
        getUrlTextBox().setText(url);
}

public void onClick(View v)
{
        try
        {
                int id = v.getId();
                if(id == R.id.buttonSave)
                        Controller.HandleSave();
        }
        catch(Exception ex)
        {
                MessageBox.Show(this, ex);
        }
}
}
```

Now we can look at the controller proper. This controller is quite traditional in MVC terms—it binds up the view, captures and validates results, and updates the underlying store.

We'll look at the HandleLoad method first. The first thing this does is dip into the related Intent instances extras bag to get the ordinal value out. I've written this all in one line, and we're retrieving only a single integer value, but I hope you can see how this approach can be used to store all manner of values.

After we have the ordinal, we'll use the method we built way earlier called GetBookmarkByOrdinal. (Recall that when we built this method, we ignored deleted items. This is important now, as had we not done this we would delete, say, ordinal **4**, click **Add**, be given ordinal **4** to add, and when we got here, we would resurrect that item, as technically it is still in the database until we synchronize and refresh the items.) GetBookmarkByOrdinal may return a null item—that's our cue to create a new one. In either case, we'll track the bookmark that we have locally and populate the user interface via the view interface. Here's the code:

```
package com.amxMobile.SixBookmarks;

import com.amxMobile.SixBookmarks.Database.*;
import com.amxMobile.SixBookmarks.Runtime.*;

public class ConfigureSingletonController extends Controller<IConfigureSingletonView>
{
        private Bookmark _bookmark;

        public ConfigureSingletonController(IConfigureSingletonView view)
```

```
        {
                super(view);
        }

        public void HandleLoad() throws Exception
        {
                // get the ordinal from the intent...
                int ordinal = getActivity().getIntent().getExtras().↵
getInt("ordinal");

                // load the bookmark...
                Bookmark bookmark = Bookmark.GetByOrdinal(this, ordinal);

                // if we didn't load one, create one...
                if(bookmark == null)
                {
                        // create a new one...
                        bookmark = new Bookmark();
                        bookmark.setOrdinal(ordinal);
                }

                // set...
                IConfigureSingletonView view = getView();
                view.setOrdinal(ordinal);
                view.setName(bookmark.getName());
                view.setUrl(bookmark.getUrl());

                // store...
                _bookmark = bookmark;
        }

        private Bookmark getBookmark()
        {
                return _bookmark;
        }

        public void HandleSave() throws Exception
        {
                MessageBox.Show(this, "TBD.");
        }
    }
}
```

Now we can run the project and configure a bookmark. Figure 7-9 shows a screenshot with the fields populated:

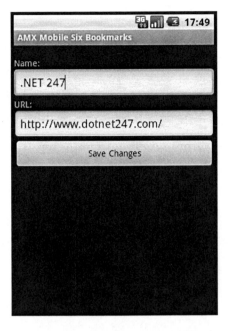

Figure 7-9. *The singleton view allowing the user to review and edit a single bookmark*

We're almost finished—all we have to do is implement HandleSave properly. All this method has to do is get the values back off of the view, validate them, populate the values in the stored bookmark instance, and save the changes to the database. Here's the code:

```
// Modify HandleSave method in ConfigureSingletonController…
      public void HandleSave() throws Exception
      {
            // get data...
            String name = getView().getName();
            String url = getView().getUrl();

            // both?
            Bookmark bookmark = getBookmark();
            if(name != null && name.length() > 0 && url != null && ↵
              url.length() > 0)
            {
                  // set...
                  bookmark.setName(name);
                  bookmark.setUrl(url);
                  bookmark.setLocalModified(true);
                  bookmark.setLocalDeleted(false);
```

```
            // save...
            bookmark.SaveChanges(this);
            getActivity().finish();
        }
        else
            MessageBox.Show(this, "Both name and URL must be↵
provided.");
    }
```

That's all we have to do! We can now change the data in our local database. All that remains is to physically pass the changes back to the server, which we'll do in the second half of this chapter.

Pushing Changes to the Server

In this section of the chapter, and the last of our work on Android, we're going to look at pushing the changes back up to the server by adding more functionality to our Sync class.

We'll split this section into two halves. The first half will look at the algorithm to detect changes between the server and local versions. The second half will look at building and sending the HTTP requests to the server.

Detecting Local Changes

The code for detecting local changes is relatively easy to understand—once we know that we have changes, we can run some code to synchronize the data. We first update the server set, and when the pre-existing GetChanges method is executed, this will delete all of the local bookmarks and replace them with server versions again. Thus, we can be confident that by the time we get through this process, not only have our changes have been merged, but also our local database contains an up-to-date set of what is on the server.

Building the "PushUpdates" Method

We'll start by building the PushUpdates method. There's going to be quite a lot of work here. In this section, we'll first look at the algorithm for detecting changes, and then we'll look at how we physically send changes up.

The algorithm for detecting changes looks like this:

- Download the latest set of bookmarks from the server.

- Walk each change detected on the client and find the matching server item based on the ordinal of the item.

- If a local change was found and that change *can* be mapped to a server item, issue an **update** to the server.

- If a local change was found and that change *cannot* be mapped to a server item, issue an **insert** to the server.

- If we delete a bookmark locally and a bookmark with that ordinal *is* in the server's set, issue a **delete** to the server.

To support this operation, we'll need a method that updates a server bookmark, a second that inserts a server bookmark, and a third that deletes a server bookmark. If none of those applies, nothing will happen. We'll add these stub methods to the ODataServiceProxy class now—recall that we built this class in the last chapter.

■**NOTE** Although this implementation is going to be used only with bookmarks in this book, this approach will work with any sort of OData entity.

Here are the stub methods that we'll add to ODataServiceProxy to help us along:

```
// Add methods to ODataServiceProxy...
        public void PushUpdate(IContextSource context, Entity entity, int serverId)↵
throws Exception
        {
                throw new Exception("TBD.");
}

        public void PushInsert(IContextSource context, Entity entity) throws  Exception
        {
                throw new Exception("TBD.");
}

        public void PushDelete(IContextSource context, Entity entity, int serverId)↵
throws Exception
        {
                throw new Exception("TBD.");
}
```

Moving back onto the PushChanges method in Sync, one thing it's going to need to be able to do is get back the changed local bookmarks and the local deleted (i.e., "soft deleted") bookmarks. I'm going to propose building these as separate methods. Although it's easy enough to build them as a single method, the discussion is easier to follow if they are separate. To do this, we'll add static methods to the Bookmark class itself.

The code for GetBookmarksForServerUpdate will return a list of the bookmarks that have been flagged as having local changes but not flagged as having been deleted. Here's the code:

```
// Add method to Bookmark...
        public static BookmarkCollection GetBookmarksForServerUpdate(IContextSource↵
context) throws Exception
        {
                // get those that are flagged as modified and deleted...
                SqlFilter filter = new SqlFilter(Bookmark.class);
                filter.AddConstraint("LocalModified", 1);
                filter.AddConstraint("LocalDeleted", 0);
```

```
        // return...
        return (BookmarkCollection)filter.ExecuteEntityCollection(context);
    }
```

Likewise, the code for GetBookmarksForServerDelete will return a list of only those bookmarks that have been specifically flagged for deletion. Here's the code:

```
// Add method to Bookmark...
    public static BookmarkCollection GetBookmarksForServerDelete(IContextSource⏎
context) throws Exception
    {
        // get those that are flagged as modified and deleted...
        SqlFilter filter = new SqlFilter(Bookmark.class);
        filter.AddConstraint("LocalDeleted", 1);

        // return...
        return (BookmarkCollection)filter.ExecuteEntityCollection(context);
    }
```

We now have everything that we need to build PushChanges. As it's quite a long method, we'll go through it in chunks.

The first thing we'll do is call our GetBookmarksForServerUpdate and GetBookmarksForServerDelete methods. If we don't get back any updates or deletes, we'll give up.

```
// Add method to Sync...
    private void PushChanges() throws Exception
    {
        BookmarkCollection updates = Bookmark.GetBookmarksForServerUpdate⏎
(getContextSource());
        BookmarkCollection deletes = Bookmark.GetBookmarksForServerDelete⏎
(this.getContextSource());
        if(updates.size() == 0 && deletes.size() == 0)
                return;
```

Next, for neatness later, we'll get and store the EntityType instance that maps to our Bookmark class. Then we'll reuse our BookmarksService class to grab a list of the bookmarks from the server.

```
        // et...
        EntityType et = EntityType.GetEntityType(Bookmark.class);

        // get the server ones...
        BookmarksService service = new BookmarksService();
        BookmarkCollection fromServer = service.GetAll();
```

Now we can get into the change detection code proper. We'll set up one loop that walks each local change, and for each local change, we'll first find a matching server change:

```
// walk the locally updated items...
for(Bookmark local : updates)
{
        // find it in our server set...
        Bookmark toUpdate = null;
        for(Bookmark server : fromServer)
        {
                if(local.getOrdinal() == server.getOrdinal())
                {
                        toUpdate = server;
                        break;
                }
        }
```

If we do detect a change (i.e., toUpdate is not null), we need to create a new Bookmark instance and populate every field on it, bar the key. When we encounter the key, we'll set the ID to be the ID of the server's copy instead of the local copy. This doesn't matter too much, as when we issue the update request we won't send up the ID, but it feels appropriate. If we do not detect a change (i.e., toUpdate is null), we'll call insert as opposed to update. Here's the code that makes that choice and also closes off the local bookmark loop.

```
        // did we have one to change?
        if(toUpdate != null)
        {
                // walk the fields...
                int serverId = 0;
                for(EntityField field : et.getFields())
                {
                        if(!(field.getIsKey()))
                                toUpdate.SetValue(field, ↩
local.GetValue (field), SetReason.UserSet);
                        else
                                serverId = toUpdate.getBookmarkId();
                }

                // send that up...
                service.PushUpdate(this.getContextSource(), ↩
toUpdate, serverId);
        }
        else
        {
                // we need to insert it...
                service.PushInsert(this.getContextSource(), local);
        }
}
```

Once we've done that work, we can look at the deletes, which is the last thing we need to do on the method. The rule here is that if we have marked a bookmark as deleted and we can find a bookmark with a matching ordinal on the server, we'll delete it from the server. This code could be improved by only deleting it if no changes were detected; however, I've chosen to keep it simple. Here's the code.

```
// what about ones to delete?
for(Bookmark local : deletes)
{
        // find a matching ordinal on the server...
        for(Bookmark server : fromServer)
        {
                if(local.getOrdinal() ==  server.getOrdinal())
                        service.PushDelete(this.getContextSource(),↩
server, server.getBookmarkId());
        }
}
```

That's all of the changes that we need to do to make the sync run. All that we have to do now is replace the stubs for PushInsert, PushUpdate, and PushDelete with real logic. We'll do this now.

Issuing Server Requests to Insert, Update, and Delete

In the last chapter, we requested XML data from the server that described our server-side entities in OData format. When we send insert and update requests back to the server, we need to create XML documents that adhere to that format. (Delete does not have a payload, so you do not need to send an XML document.)

However, on Android there is a problem. The org.w3c.dom namespace in Android will let you *read* a document, but it will not let you *write* one. Interestingly, you can go through all of the steps of physically creating a document tree, but you can't then actually serialize it to a stream and send it. Android instead provides an implementation of the XML Pull library (www.xmlpull.org/) and we can use its XmlSerializer class to create a document.

■**NOTE** XML Pull is designed to provide a mechanism for reading XML documents that is very fast. I chose not to use it in the last chapter primarily because it's easier to understand what's happening with an object-model based approach used in org.w3c.dom.

The three operations we need to fire can be described thus:

- For **insert** operations, we issue an **HTTP POST** to the base URL of the entity's service and supply XML that describes the initial value of the fields, e.g., http://services. multimobiledevelopment.com/services/Bookmarks.svc/Bookmark.

- For **update** operations, we issue an **HTTP MERGE** to the URL of the item in question and supply XML that describes the changed fields, e.g., http://services. multimobiledevelopment.com/services/Bookmarks.svc/Bookmark(1000).

- For **delete** operations, we issue an **HTTP DELETE** to the URL of the item in question and provide no payload, e.g., `http://services.multimobiledevelopment.com/services/Bookmarks.svc/Bookmark(1001)`.

The OData standard allows us to issue an **HTTP MERGE** or an **HTTP PUT** to send an "update" instruction. **MERGE** is better (in this case at least) because it will update the provided fields but leave the remaining fields. **PUT** requires all of the fields to be sent, as any missing fields are reset to their default values. As a general principle of designing systems that have this kind of intraconnected messaging, it's always a good idea to try and keep things loosely coupled, and **MERGE** feels looser to me.

We've already stubbed in methods for each of the three operations, so let's build them now.

Update via "HTTP MERGE" and Insert via "HTTP POST"

We're going to create one main method for doing updates and tweak its operation so that it also works for inserts.

The "ODataOperation" Enumeration

So that we can keep track of what we're doing when we're running, we need an enumeration that represents the type of operation. Here's the listing:

```
package com.amxMobile.SixBookmarks.Services;

public enum ODataOperation
{
        Insert, Update, Delete
}
```

We'll use that later on.

Marking Fields As Being Available on the Server

We're now going to have to make a change to the application to get around an aspect of the OData protocol, namely, that if we try and update a field on the server that does not exist, we'll get an error back. The LocalModified and LocalDeleted columns that we added do not exist on the server, so any update or insert server operations that mention those will fail. (I'm not a fan of this—it seems wrong. It would seem better to me to ignore this situation much as the old SOAP protocol would. It implies it's possible to keep all of the clients that use the service in sync, or makes deprecation of server-side functionality harder than it should be.)

To do this, we'll add a property to EntityField that indicates whether the property is on the server.

■**NOTE** This is one of these application design aspects that end up in a messy design. It's not brilliant to have a metadata layer and the application have this "special" behavior in it—it would be better if this flag did not exist. But as a corollary, I'm not keen on having two classes do roughly the same thing—e.g., a server representation of a bookmark and a local representation. Essentially, there has to be a compromise somewhere…

First, we'll add an IsOnServer property to EntityField (default true), like so:

```
// Add IsOnServer property and field to EntityField…
public class EntityField extends EntityItem
{
        private DataType _type;
        private int _size;
        private boolean _isKey;
        private int _ordinal;
        private boolean _isOnServer = true;

        public EntityField(String name, String nativeName, DataType type, int size,↵ int
ordinal)
        {
                // code omitted for brevity...
        }

        // code omitted for brevity...

        public boolean getIsOnServer()
        {
                return _isOnServer;
        }

        public void setIsOnServer(boolean value)
        {
                _isOnServer = value;
        }
}
```

And when we come to define the fields on Bookmark in our Start method on SixBookmarksRuntime, we'll set the flag for the two applicable fields:

```
// Modify Start method on SixBookmarksRuntime…
        public static void Start()
        {
                // create the entity type...
                EntityType bookmark = new EntityType(Bookmark.class,↵
BookmarkCollection.class, "Bookmarks");
                bookmark.AddField(Bookmark.BookmarkIdKey, Bookmark.BookmarkIdKey,↵
DataType.Int32, -1).setIsKey(true);
                bookmark.AddField(Bookmark.OrdinalKey, Bookmark.OrdinalKey,↵
DataType.Int32, -1);
                bookmark.AddField(Bookmark.NameKey, Bookmark.NameKey,↵ DataType.String, 128);
                bookmark.AddField(Bookmark.UrlKey, Bookmark.UrlKey,↵
DataType.String, 256);
```

```
                bookmark.AddField(Bookmark.LocalModifiedKey,↵
Bookmark.LocalModifiedKey, DataType.Int32, -1).setIsOnServer(false);
                bookmark.AddField(Bookmark.LocalDeletedKey,↵
Bookmark.LocalDeletedKey, DataType.Int32, -1).setIsOnServer(false);

                // register it...
                EntityType.RegisterEntityType(bookmark);
        }
```

Now we can use this property when building the messages to send to the server.

Building the XML

The documentation on the OData web site gives an example of an insert as the following listing:

```
POST /OData/OData.svc/Categories HTTP/1.1
Host: services.odata.org
DataServiceVersion: 1.0
MaxDataServiceVersion: 2.0
accept: application/atom+xml
content-type: application/atom+xml
Content-Length: 634

<?xml version="1.0" encoding="utf-8"?>
<entry xmlns:d="http://schemas.microsoft.com/ado/2007/08/dataservices"
        xmlns:m="http://schemas.microsoft.com/ado/2007/08/dataservices/metadata"
        xmlns="http://www.w3.org/2005/Atom">
    <title type="text"></title>
    <updated>2010-02-27T21:36:47Z</updated>
    <author>
        <name />
    </author>
    <category term="DataServiceProviderDemo.Category"
        scheme="http://schemas.microsoft.com/ado/2007/08/dataservices/scheme" />
    <content type="application/xml">
        <m:properties>
            <d:ID>10</d:ID>
            <d:Name>Clothing</d:Name>
        </m:properties>
    </content>
</entry>
```

If you refer back to the XML retrieved from the server in the last chapter, you can see that this is basically just a rehash of the data that we provided. Our job, then, is to replicate this request.

▤**NOTE** As of the time of writing, the site at `www.odata.org/` is showing the `entry` elements in the preceding listing as having an uppercase "E", e.g., `Entry`. The interface will not work with `Entry` compared to `entry`; hence I have edited it here, assuming a typo on the OData site.

In our request, we're going to trim it down slightly and omit the `title`, `updated`, `author`, and `category` elements. These are not required to make the request work. We'll also omit the `DataServiceVersion` and `MaxDataServiceVersion` headers, but we'll add in our special `x-amx-apiusername` and `x-amx-token` headers. If we patch in bookmark data rather than the sample data from the OData site, we'll have something like this:

```
POST /services/bookmarks.svc/Bookmark HTTP/1.1
Host: services.multimobiledevelopment.com
accept: application/atom+xml
content-type: application/atom+xml
content-encoding: UTF-8
content-length: 384
x-amx-apiusername: amxmobile
x-amx-token: 961c8c1b9d4ddd5799e7f0a7b4a5ee8b

<entry xmlns:d="http://schemas.microsoft.com/ado/2007/08/dataservices"
       xmlns:m="http://schemas.microsoft.com/ado/2007/08/dataservices/metadata"
       xmlns="http://www.w3.org/2005/Atom">
    <content type="application/xml">
        <m:properties>
            <d:Name>Apress</d:Name>
            <d:Url>http://www.apress.com/</d:Url>
            <d:Ordinal>0</d:Ordinal>
        </m:properties>
    </content>
</entry>
```

The `XmlSerializer` class is easy enough to use. You call a method called `startTag` to start an element within the document and `endTag` to close it. For error checking—because this approach is highly error-prone—the `endTag` method is provided with the same arguments used to open it. This ensures that the resulting XML is well formed. There are also methods to add attributes.

The slight complexity with using the `XmlSerializer` is that it needs to be namespace aware. We set up the namespaces used in the document via `setPrefix` calls. One of the calls—the first one that will specify the ATOM namespace—is set to have no prefix and becomes the default namespace.

Here's the listing for the `ODataServiceProxy` class:

```
// Replace stub method on ODataServiceProxy…
        public void PushUpdate(IContextSource context, Entity entity, int serverId)↵
throws Exception
        {
```

```
// update...
XmlSerializer xml = Xml.newSerializer();
StringWriter writer = new StringWriter();
xml.setOutput(writer);

// start...
xml.startDocument("UTF-8", true);
xml.setPrefix("", AtomNamespace);
xml.setPrefix("m", MsMetadataNamespace);
xml.setPrefix("d", MsDataNamespace);

// start entry and content and properties...
xml.startTag(AtomNamespace, "entry");
xml.startTag(AtomNamespace, "content");
xml.attribute("", "type", "application/xml");
xml.startTag(MsMetadataNamespace, "properties");

// fields...
EntityType et = entity.getEntityType();
for(EntityField field : et.getFields())
{
        if(!(field.getIsKey()) && field.getIsOnServer())
        {
                xml.startTag(MsDataNamespace, field.getName());
                xml.text(entity.GetValue(field).toString());
                xml.endTag(MsDataNamespace, field.getName());
        }
}

// end content and entry...
xml.endTag(MsMetadataNamespace, "properties");
xml.endTag(AtomNamespace, "content");
xml.endTag(AtomNamespace, "entry");

// end...
xml.endDocument();

// run...
String url = null;
ODataOperation op = ODataOperation.Update;
String xmlAsString = writer.toString();
if(serverId != 0)
        url = GetEntityUrlForPush(entity, serverId);
```

```
        else
        {
                url = this.GetServiceUrl(et);
                op = ODataOperation.Insert;
        }

        // run...
        ExecuteODataOperation(op, url, xmlAsString);
    }

    private String GetEntityUrlForPush(Entity entity, int serverId)
    {
            return String.format("%s(%d)", GetServiceUrl↵ (entity.getEntityType()),
serverId);
        }
```

The code at the bottom of the PushUpdate defers to ExecuteODataOperation, which we will build a moment. Notice as well that we have sneaked in a helper method—GetEntityUrlForPush. This builds the URL for the item.

The final argument to PushUpdate is the ID of the item on the server. If this is non-zero, we'll assume that we're updating and format the URL and set the operation as appropriate. Conversely, if it is, we'll use the base service URL and specify a different value in op.

Now that we have our PushUpdate method, we'll quickly add PushInsert and PushDelete so that we have a complete set. Here's the listing:

```
// Replace stub methods on ODataServiceProxy…
    public void PushInsert(IContextSource context, Entity entity) throws Exception
    {
            // an insert is an update but with a different url...
            PushUpdate(context, entity, 0);
    }

    public void PushDelete(IContextSource context, Entity entity, int serverId)↵
throws Exception
    {
            // get the entity URL...
            String url = GetEntityUrlForPush(entity, serverId);
            ExecuteODataOperation(ODataOperation.Delete, url, null);
    }
```

Building "ExecuteODataOperation"

ExecuteODataOperation will take all of that information and build a request to issue to the HTTP Client library.

We've used this library in the last chapter. The way that the library works is that you formulate a request object that gets sent to the server. This object can have an "entity" associated with it, which in our case, when making insert or update calls, will be an XML document. (Note that in this context, the "entity" is a block of data used by the HTTP client. For clarity from here on, I'll use "HTTP entity" to refer to this thing that is separate from the database entities we've been defining via our Entity class.) The server will then send a response back, which may include another HTTP entity. It's, in my opinion, a simple and elegant design that I'm rather keen on.

Recall that we need to issue three HTTP methods to the server—POST, MERGE, and DELETE. POST and DELETE are handled directly in the library via the HttpPost and HttpDelete classes. We're going to have to extend the library to support MERGE, which we'll do first by building an HttpMerge class.

HttpPost extends HttpEntityEnclosingRequestBase, which, as its name implies, is a class that can support transmission of an entity up to the server. We also need to extend this class into HttpMerge. Once we've done that, we have to override the getMethod method to tell it what verb to send to the server. Here's the code:

```
package com.amxMobile.SixBookmarks.Runtime;

import java.net.URI;

import org.apache.http.client.methods.HttpEntityEnclosingRequestBase;

public class HttpMerge extends HttpEntityEnclosingRequestBase
{
        public HttpMerge(String url) throws Exception
        {
                this(new URI(url));
        }

        public HttpMerge(URI uri)
        {
                this.setURI(uri);
        }

        @Override
        public String getMethod()
        {
                return "MERGE";
        }
}
```

The other extension we need to make is a special HTTP entity to package our XML up to the server.

HTTP entities in the Jakarta Commons HTTP Client library are bi-directional—i.e., they can upload data to the server or download data from it. In our code here, we're going to worry only about uploading; hence we will leave a bunch of methods unimplemented.

What we need to do with our ODataEntity is pass in the XML and set its content type to be application/atom+xml and the content encoding to UTF-8. We'll use the regular Java code to get transform the String instance containing the XML into an array of bytes. Here's the code:

```java
package com.amxMobile.SixBookmarks.Services;

import java.io.*;

import org.apache.http.*;
import org.apache.http.message.BasicHeader;

public class ODataEntity implements HttpEntity
{
        private static final String Encoding = "UTF-8";

        private byte[] _bytes;

        public ODataEntity(String xml) throws Exception
        {
                _bytes = xml.getBytes(Encoding);
        }

        public void consumeContent() throws IOException
        {
        }

        public InputStream getContent() throws IOException, IllegalStateException
        {
                return null;
        }

        public Header getContentEncoding()
        {
                return new BasicHeader("content-encoding", Encoding);
        }

        public long getContentLength()
        {
                return _bytes.length;
        }

        public Header getContentType()
        {
                return new BasicHeader("content-type", "application/atom+xml");
        }

        public boolean isChunked()
        {
                return false;
        }
```

```
        public boolean isRepeatable()
        {
                return false;
        }

        public boolean isStreaming()
        {
                return false;
        }

        public void writeTo(OutputStream outstream) throws IOException
        {
                outstream.write(_bytes);
        }
}
```

The magic happens there in the `writeTo` method, and, as you can see, all that we do is pass up the byte array that we created in the constructor.

Now we come to building `ExecuteODataOperation`. Here's what it will do:

- We'll ensure that the API has been set up by calling `EnsureApiAuthenticated`.

- We'll choose the type of HTTP Client operation we want to run dependent on what we're looking to achieve.

- To make the request, we need to pass up our special `x-amx-apiusername` and `x-amx-token` headers. We'll obtain these from the `GetDownloadSettings` method that we built earlier and pass those on.

- If we have anything other than a DELETE request, we'll add the XML to the request.

- We'll then execute the request and test the result. We'll either receive a regular HTTP 200 status or get back an HTTP 204 (no content) or 201 (created). If we get anything other than those codes, we'll grab the data that was sent and formulate an exception.

Here's the code:

```
// Modify stub method in ODataServiceProxy...
        private void ExecuteODataOperation(ODataOperation opType, String url, ↵
String xml) throws Exception
        {
                // make sure we're authenticated...
                EnsureApiAuthenticated();

                // show...
                HttpRequestBase op = null;
                if(opType == ODataOperation.Update)
                        op = new HttpMerge(url);
```

```
                    else if(opType == ODataOperation.Insert)
                            op = new HttpPost(url);
                    else if(opType == ODataOperation.Delete)
                            op = new HttpDelete(url);
                    else
                            throw new Exception(String.format("Cannot handle '%s'.",⏎
opType));

                    // add our headers...
                    Hashtable<String, String> extraHeaders = GetDownloadSettings()⏎
.getExtraHeaders();
                    for(String name : extraHeaders.keySet())
                            op.addHeader(name, extraHeaders.get(name));

                    // create an entity...
                    if(xml != null)
                            ((HttpEntityEnclosingRequestBase)op).setEntity(new⏎
ODataEntity(xml));

                    // request...
                    HttpClient client = new DefaultHttpClient();
                    HttpResponse response = client.execute(op);

                    // what happened...  200 is OK, but 204 also is (which means no content)...
                    int code = response.getStatusLine().getStatusCode();
                    if(code != 200 && code != 204)
                    {
                            // get...
                            String error = HttpHelper.GetHttpEntityContent⏎
(response.getEntity());

                            // throw...
                            throw new Exception(String.format("Download of '%s' via⏎
operation '%s' returned HTTP '%d' (%s).\nResponse: %s\nXML: %s",
                                            url, opType, code, response.getStatusLine()⏎
.getReasonPhrase(), error, xml));
                    }
            }
```

And that's it as far as sending up the data is concerned.

To test the code, you'll need to go in and make changes to the bookmarks on the device. It's worth pulling the database off of the device to have a look. Figure 7-10 illustrates the Sqliteman application showing the database with some local changes.

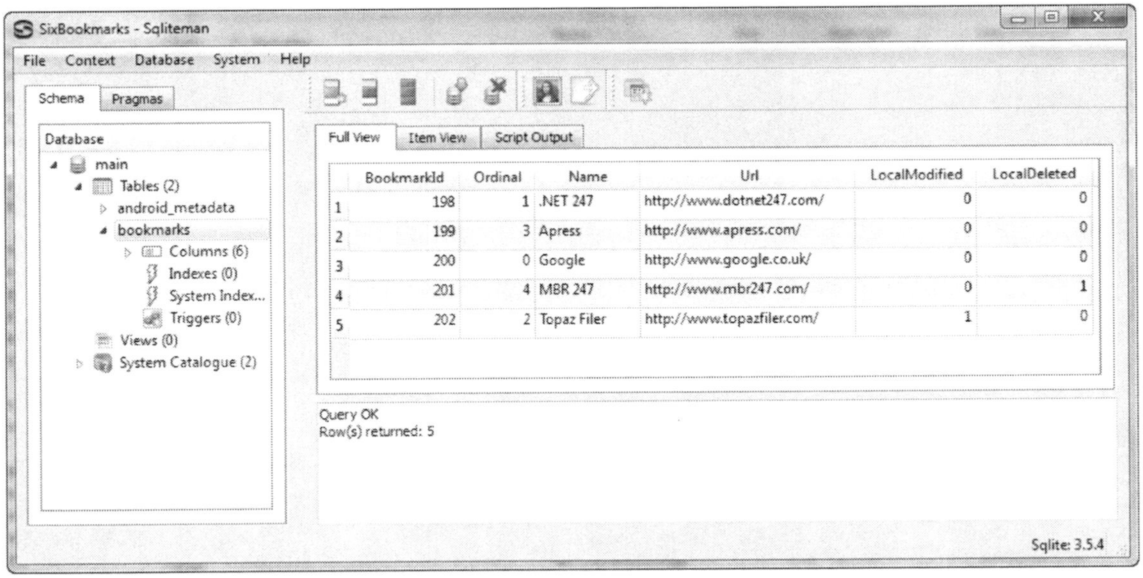

Figure 7-10. *Sqliteman showing the state of the "LocalModified" and "LocalDeleted" flags*

The changes we made to the Sync class earlier will run when the logon operation succeeds, or when the user manually chooses to sync from the configuration screen. When the code runs, the changes will be sent up and new versions downloaded. You can see the results by examining the database directly by managing the appropriate user at `http://services.multimobiledevelopment.com/`.

Conclusion

In this chapter, we have covered a lot of ground. We have looked at how to modify the ORM functionality to bring back selections of data. We have also looked at building a comprehensive user interface for editing the bookmarks, including how to handle standard UI elements such as lists and menus. Finally, we completed our synchronization routine so that we can send back updates to the server using the OData protocol.

CHAPTER 8

■ ■ ■

iOS: Installing the Toolset

In this chapter, we're going to look at getting started with iOS development using Xcode, Objective-C, and Cocoa Touch. This chapter is going to be longer than the other "installing the toolset" chapters. The Objective-C language is very different than other languages that you are likely to have used in the past, and so most of this chapter is given over to a primer to help you get up to speed. You will need a Mac in order to do any iOS development, as the tools run only on iOS.

iPad Development

This book does not include specific information on building applications for iPad. This was a deliberate decision—despite the runaway success of the platform, and the fact that you'd never get mine out of my cold dead hands. As of the time of writing, there are no iPad-class devices on the other platforms.

Everything you learn here also applies to iPad—the language and toolset are the same. You just to have to do the user interface differently to target iPad, plus you get extra bits to make iPad applications iPad-ish.

Installing Xcode

Everything you need to build iPhone, iPod, and iPad applications (and even full-blown OS X applications) can be obtained by installing Xcode, which is available free of charge from Apple's web site. Visit the SDK portal at http://developer.apple.com/iphone/ and download the iOS SDK.

As of the time of writing, Apple is preparing a major overhaul to the Xcode application. This book is based on the **Xcode 4 Developer Preview 2**. This is now sufficiently mature that you will not find many differences between this and the release version, but any "gotchas" between this beta version and the production versions will be covered on this book's web site in the usual way. The code downloads will not work with Xcode 3.

I won't take you through installing the SDK, as it's straightforward and obvious.

An Objective-C Primer for .NET and Java Developers

As you now know, installing Xcode is very straightforward. However, using Objective-C is not very straightforward; therefore, before we have a look at building a "Hello, World" application for the iPhone, I feel it's prudent to try to take a running leap at the Objective-C language and Cocoa Touch framework. Objective-C is so massively different from C++, C#, VB.NET, and Java (all of which the average reader of this book is more likely to have used than Objective-C), it makes the learning curve incredibly steep. (It took me about five solid days of hard work to get my brain able to read and work with Objective-C when I started.)

Objective-C is a set of object-oriented extensions for C, but rather than being based on C++, it is based on Smalltalk. This means that rather than writing code like this:

```
Foo foo = new Foo();
foo.DoMagic(27, "Pickle");
```

…you write code like this:

```
Foo *foo = [[Foo alloc] init];
[foo doMagic:27 aPickle:@"Pickle"];
[foo release];
```

In this section, I'm going to run through the process of working with and manipulating classes in Objective-C. I'm going to write it from the perspective of a C#/Java developer—the code I present that is not Objective-C will be C#/Java-inspired pseudocode.

▪**NOTE** Objective-C was developed by two developers named Brad Cox and Tim Love in the early 1980s and marketed by a company called Stepstone. When Steve Jobs left Apple in 1985 and started NeXT, he needed to use and market a toolset to support the platform and hence licensed Objective-C. NeXTstep lends its name to the Cocoa Touch framework used for developing for Apple hardware (both Mac OS X and the iPhone OS), in that classes and methods are prefixed with "NS", for "NeXTstep."

Problems with Objective-C

Before I go on to talk about the problems with Objective-C and Cocoa Touch, it's worth saying that I do actually like developing applications for the iPhone using this toolset; however, it's worth understanding the limitations.

The biggest problem by far is the memory management. Objective-C on the iPhone does not have automated memory management using garbage collection. (Objective-C for OS X does have this as an option.) This is a horrible problem—you're walking a thin line between missing objects out of the cleanup and having an application that uses all the available memory and crashing, or an application that over-releases memory and crashes because of memory corruption.

The other major problem is that Objective-C and the Cocoa Touch library just have not had the level of interest and hence the level of investment that Java and .NET have had over the past decade or so, and, as a result, it all looks and feels rather arcane. There's an odd juxtaposition between using tools that feel rooted in the 1990s and these wonderful-looking applications that look like they are running on devices delivered from the future. Developing iPhone and iPad applications is simply *difficult* in a way that developing for other platforms isn't.

But there is a major plus. Apple's investment in the platform has been to create a toolset that lets you create fabulous-looking applications with fantastic user experiences. It's possible to do so with less heartache compared to the other platforms. Once you persevere and get through it, you will end up with a faster and more pleasing application than you will on the other platforms. In fact, there are some applications—particularly games—that you just could not make work on Android or the other platforms.

Calling Methods (aka "Sending Messages")

The code example I presented previously looks alien because of the signaling infrastructure built into the Objective-C language. While C++-based OO implementations use dot notation to chain method calls together, Objective-C uses messages. C++-based OO is essentially a call that says "take this, do that," whereas Objective-C's OO is a call that says "send this message to that." One key point to understand when moving to Objective-C is that a message is basically a method call. For example, consider this line:

```
[foo doMagic:27 aPickle:@"Pickle"];
```

All this is actually saying is "send message 'doMagic' to object 'foo' and pass in these parameters."

The parameters are a little fiddly to get your head around. Whereas C++-based OO assumes that you know what each parameter is and you string them together using commas, in Objective-C you can have either zero parameters, one parameter that does not have a name, or one unnamed parameter and a collection of named parameters. In the preceding line, "aPickle" is the name of a parameter, so the complete call is "send message 'doMagic' to object 'foo', passing in '27' as the unnamed parameter and value 'Pickle' into parameter 'aPickle'."

Let's look at building a simple iPhone application to explore these items in more detail. This application will not have a user interface—it will run and log information to the debugging console so that we can see what's happening.

Creating the Project

Unusually for any book or article that attempts to take you through iPhone development, we're not going to look at any UI bits and pieces at all to start with. Instead we're going to have a look around the language and environment in this section, go on to building our traditional "Hello, World" application in the later section, and then start building the Six Bookmarks application proper in the next few chapters.

To start the project, start up Xcode and select **Create a new Xcode project** from the splash window. You'll then see a window like Figure 8-1. You want to create a new view-based application. Although we're not going to have a UI in this application, when we build proper applications, this is the project template that we're going to use.

Click **Next** and you'll be prompted for the name of a project. Xcode will name the classes in the project after the project name, so it's worth choosing a short name here even if you go in and rename it later. I'm going to call my project **ObjectiveCPrimer**. The company identifier that you'll be asked to provide is not super-important. I've set mine to com.amxMobile.iOS.

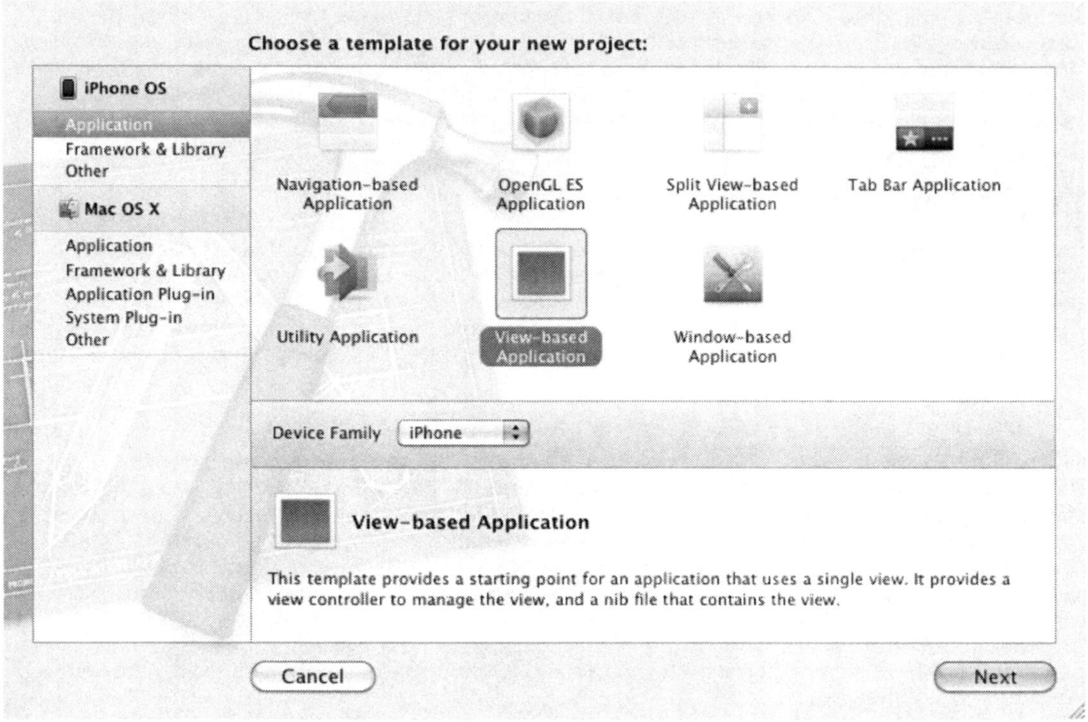

Figure 8-1. *Choosing the template for our new project.*

After the project has been created, you will be presented with the Xcode environment. Although done in an Apple-y way, this is a classic developer's IDE that you'll be used to using with other toolsets. Figure 8-2 illustrates.

We have more files available here than we are interested in—really all we want is some point where we can write a little bit of code and examine the output in the debugger window.

You can run the project at this point, but nothing much will happen. Choose the **Product – Run** option from the menu, and the simulator will start and run your app. (You can also press the giant "play" button in the top-left of the Xcode window.) For your troubles, you'll get a gray window.

■NOTE The iPhone simulator is a *simulator*, not an emulator. The iPhone toolset is unique in that it compiles the application targeted for your host computer's processor, including plenty of code to slow down the application to make it feel like it's running on the phone. The other vendors all use virtual machines to emulate the device. This continues to the extent that your device application running in the simulator writes files to your host computer's disk directly!

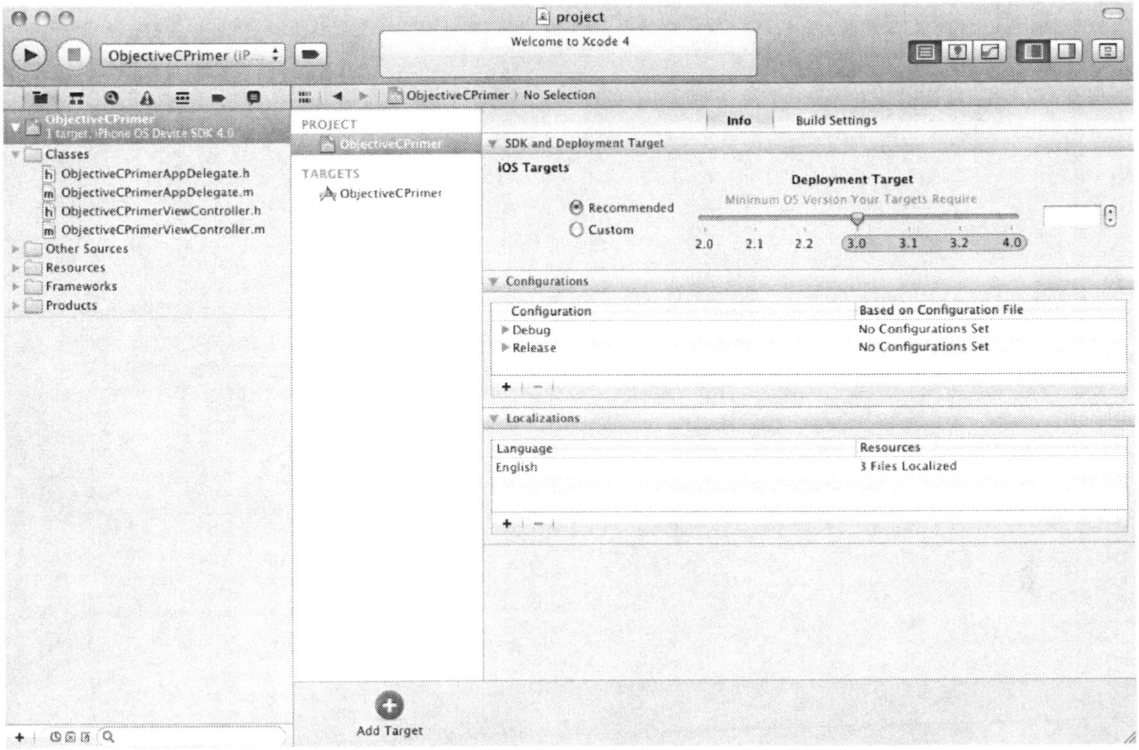

Figure 8-2. *The Xcode development environment.*

Let's start looking at the language.

Properties (and a Little Memory Management)

As discussed, Objective-C is a set of extensions on the traditional C language, which means that you can do everything you ever could do with C in Objective-C, but you can also do some other bits and pieces. The traditional calling C conventions, data types, and constructs are all there. I am going to assume a working knowledge of C and/or C++ development going forward; however, I will try to present this in a way that is gentle to readers who have no experience of this language.

One construct that remains is that it is necessary to create separate header and implementation files (**.h** and **.m** files) for each class. Moreover, you have to forward-define everything that you want to do in the header files and in the implementation. If you're used to .NET and Java, this will feel a little strange, as for those platforms you chuck everything where you fancy putting it and the compiler works it out, such as Java and .NET.

We're going to do everything in the ObjectiveCPrimerAppDelegate.m file. Open this file and locate a method called didFinishLaunchingWithOptions. Change the contents to this:

```
-(BOOL)application:(UIApplication *)application didFinishLaunchingWithOptions:(NSDictionary
*)launchOptions
{
        // log a message...
        NSLog(@"Hello, world.");

        // ok...
        return YES;
}
```

This is the method (in this context, Objective-C refers to this as a "delegate") that will be called when the application boots. The NSLog function is a C-style function that takes a string and writes it to the debugging console. You can find this window by selecting **View** ➤ **Show Debugger Area** from the menu. This will reveal a small area at the bottom of the window. The right-hand side of this is the debug console. Figure 8-3 illustrates.

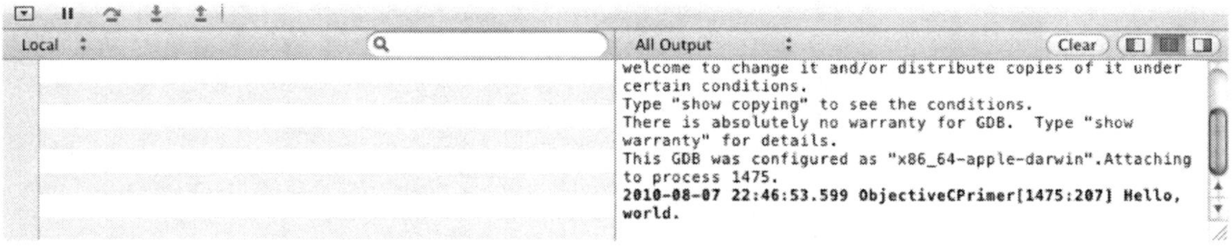

Figure 8-3. *The debug view available at the bottom of the Xcode window.*

■**TIP** You can make the console bigger using the button in the top right of the **All Output** area.

Now that we know we can run the application and get some result onto the screen, let's take a look at working with properties.

Whenever you want to define a property in a class, you have to do four things:

- You have to create an instance variable in which to hold its value.

- You have to define a property in the header that maps to the instance variable.

- You have to create getter and setter methods for the property using the **@synthesize** construct.

- You have to remember to clean up the value when you are finished with it.

We already have some properties defined in our class that are necessary for actually getting the display on the screen. If you open the ObjectiveCPrimerAppDelegate.h file, you will see properties called window and viewController referenced in two places. Here's the existing listing:

```
@interface MyObjectiveCAppDelegate : NSObject <UIApplicationDelegate> {
    UIWindow *window;
    ObjectiveCPrimerViewController *viewController;
}

@property (nonatomic, retain) IBOutlet UIWindow *window;
@property (nonatomic, retain) IBOutlet ObjectiveCPrimerViewController *viewController;

@end
```

The first declaration in this file—@interface ...—is how we declare a class in Objective-C. In this instance, we have extended the NSObject class, which is the base class for all Objective-C classes. The <UIApplicationDelegate> you can ignore for now.

The code within the braces at the top is used to define the instance variables. These are where the values are actually stored, *but it is critically important not to reference these values directly* (for reasons I'll go into later). The @property definitions are Objective-C extensions that declare that someone is going to build an implementation of those properties later.

Note the types of these properties. UIWindow * specifies a pointer to an instance of class UIWindow, which is the class used to hold the application's window. Likewise, ObjectiveCPrimerViewController * specifies a point to an instance of another class that drives an actual view. We are worried about neither of those, but we *are* worried about the pointers. For .NET and Java developers who have never seen C before, pointers may seem a little odd. They simply refer to a location in memory where an object can be found. In .NET and Java, really all object references are pointers, but the language and runtime hide this fact from the developer.

You will notice that all of the property declarations have (nonatomic, retain) set as modifiers against the property. These are hugely important.

nonatomic means that you do not care about thread safety and that you're happy for multiple threads to be getting and setting this value simultaneously; or, rather, you're saying that there is no intention in the code to allow this. There is another option—atomic—that is used to say that access does need to be thread-safe, but that is beyond the scope of this book. Suffice it to say that if you are storing an object reference (i.e., a pointer) in a property, you should say nonatomic and endeavor not to access it from multiple threads.

retain is where we start talking about memory management. I'll back up a little to talk about how memory is managed in Objective-C.

■**NOTE** If you're a COM developer, Objective-C's memory management works on a basis identical to COM.

Objective-C uses a system of "reference counting" to control object lifetimes. What this means is that every object on the system holds an integer value representing how many people are still using the object. When an object is created, its reference count is **1**. During its life, the reference count can be "retained," i.e., increased, or "released," i.e., decreased. When a reference count hits **0**, the object is deleted and its memory returned to the system for other objects.

The headache of working with a referencing counting model is that as simple humans, we are incredibly fallible, and the chances of getting this right 100 percent of the time is either zero or very close to zero, which means that almost every application we ever build is likely to leak or be prone to crashing.

On our property declaration, we have said retain, and what this means is that when we set our property to a given value, Objective-C will automatically increase its reference count from **1** to **2**. Thus when the originator of the object releases it, the count goes from **2** to **1**, the object remains alive, and we can use it. When we ourselves are disposed of (in Objective-C this is called "deallocating"), we go through all of our instance fields and release the objects.

One major trick in managing memory is to remember that this magic retaining behavior happens only if we access the property and not the instance variable directly. You will get in a very big muddle if you access the instance variables directly and bypass the memory management.

We'll create a new object called Foo. Ctrl+Click on the **Classes** folder (right-click if you're using a Windows mouse) on the Xcode project tree and select **New File**. Create a new Objective-C class file and call it Foo.

We'll add a property of type Foo to our class. Modify the ObjectiveCPrimerAppDelegate.h header file so that it looks like this:

```
#import <UIKit/UIKit.h>
#import "Foo.h"

@class ObjectiveCPrimerViewController;

@interface ObjectiveCPrimerAppDelegate : NSObject <UIApplicationDelegate> {
    UIWindow *window;
    ObjectiveCPrimerViewController *viewController;
        Foo *myFoo;
}

@property (nonatomic, retain) IBOutlet UIWindow *window;
@property (nonatomic, retain) IBOutlet ObjectiveCPrimerViewController *viewController;
@property (nonatomic, retain) Foo *myFoo;

@end
```

Note that we have to bring forward the declaration for the class by using the #import "foo.h" declaration.

We didn't discuss this before, but in the header file, all we're doing is saying that we intend to have such-and-such methods. We still need to implement them. In the implementation file, we have to "synthesize" getters and setters for the properties. Find the @synthesize declarations at the top of the ObjectiveCPrimerAppDelegate.m class and add another for myFoo.

```
#import "ObjectiveCPrimerAppDelegate.h"
#import "Foo.h"

@implementation ObjectiveCPrimerAppDelegate

@synthesize viewController;
@synthesize window;
@synthesize myFoo;
```

Again, note how we've had to import the Foo.h file. In the other projects, we'll do this in a more sophisticated way.

In the Foo.m file, add a dealloc method, like this: (dealloc is defined on NSObject, and as we're overriding it, not defining it, we don't have to change the header file.)

```
#import "Foo.h"
```

```
@implementation Foo

-(void)dealloc
{
        NSLog(@"Foo deallocated...");
        [super dealloc]; // call the parent class' dealloc…
}

@end
```

This code will cause a debug message to be written when Foo is deallocated.

By convention, all Objective-C objects have constructors that can be overloaded and overridden in the usual object-orientated way. These constructors are always implemented in methods that begin with the word init. What we're going to do is override the constructor of ObjectiveCPrimerAppDelegate to create an instance of Foo and store it in the myFoo property.

Add this new init method to the ObjectiveCPrimerAppDelegate.m class file:

```
@implementation ObjectiveCPrimerAppDelegate

@synthesize viewController;
@synthesize window;
@synthesize myFoo;

-(id)init
{
        if(self = [super init])
        {
                // create it...
                Foo *theFoo = [[Foo alloc] init];
                NSLog(@"theFoo's retain count: %d", theFoo.retainCount);

                // set it...
                self.myFoo = theFoo;
                NSLog(@"theFoo's retain count: %d", theFoo.retainCount);

                // we've handed it over, release the original...
                [theFoo release];
                NSLog(@"theFoo's retain count: %d", theFoo.retainCount);
        }

        // return...
        return self;
}
```

If you run the project, you'll get a listing like this:

```
2010-08-07 22:54:50.754 ObjectiveCPrimer[1547:207] theFoo's retain count: 1
2010-08-07 22:54:50.756 ObjectiveCPrimer[1547:207] theFoo's retain count: 2
2010-08-07 22:54:50.757 ObjectiveCPrimer[1547:207] theFoo's retain count: 1
2010-08-07 22:54:50.759 ObjectiveCPrimer[1547:207] Hello, world.
```

This listing is perfect—it shows that we know what we're doing. Note that we still have our "Hello, World" message from before.

The first call [[Foo alloc] init] says that we want to call static method alloc on the Foo class to create a new instance of foo. (This construct of [[<Class> alloc] init] is very common in Objective-C.) We then call init, which is the constructor. The object is created with a retain count of 1, which is what we see in the log.

The second call—self.myFoo = theFoo—calls the setter of the myFoo property. The retain declaration on this property causes the reference count to increase. (self is the equivalent of this in C++, Java, and C#.)

The third call—[theFoo release]—releases our original hold on the object, reducing the count to 1. Thus the only reference to the Foo instance created is held by our MyObjectiveCPrimer instance.

The final point to touch on with regards to memory management is deallocations. dealloc is called on your object the moment before its memory is released and it's killed. It's your opportunity to release any objects that you no longer need. Here's a dealloc call for the ObjectiveCPrimerAppDelegate class:

```
- (void)dealloc
{
        [myFoo release];
    [viewController release];
    [window release];
    [super dealloc];
}
```

Note how we're referring to the instance variable and not the property—this is OK in the dealloc call, as we don't want any special magic going on.

A Little More about Memory Management

The last thing we need to discuss with memory management relates to the rules around whether when we get objects we need to release them.

There is a *convention* in the Cocoa Touch documentation that methods with certain names need deallocation, and everything else doesn't. The policy is *not* to document which calls do or don't.

There is a mnemonic called "**NARC**" in Objective-C memory management, which means that if the method refers to new, alloc, retain, or copy, you *do* have to release it. If it does not refer to any of these, you do not.

Most of the classes in Cocoa Touch have helper methods that do not contain any of the NARC words, although under the hood their memory is being managed. Objective-C handles this through a mechanism called autorelease, which is like a quasi-garbage collection. Essentially it puts the object into an autorelease queue, which is like saying "at some point in the future, call release." Thus here's a way of creating new string instances from a concept, one of which refers to a NARC word and needs releasing, and another that does not refer to a NARC word and hence does not need releasing.

```
// this one needs releasing...
```

```
NSString *str = [[NSString alloc] initWithString:@"Hello, world."];
NSLog(str);
[str release];

// this one does not need releasing...
str = [NSString stringWithString:@"Hello, world"];
```

Autoreleasing does imply a performance penalty; however, it's so much easier having the framework deal with memory problems that you should use the non-NARC helper methods wherever possible. The universe balances this out, however, as you may end up with hard-to-find bugs with exceptions happening some distance away from the actual cause of the error. This autorelease functionality is not proper garbage collection.

Methods

Let's look at how we define and call methods.

As discussed previously, methods can have zero or more parameters. The first parameter is special and is unnamed; all other parameters have a name.

To illustrate, we'll add a few methods to Foo. Open the header file for Foo, and add these three method declarations:

```
@interface Foo : NSObject {

}

// parameterless method...
-(NSString *)doMagic;

// method with one parameter...
-(NSString *)doMoreMagic:(NSString *)theName;

// method with two parameters...
-(NSString *)doYetMoreMagic:(NSString *)theName barCount:(int)theBarCount;

@end
```

▓**NOTE** As a hint, you can run into naming collision problems between local variables, properties, and instance variables, so I tend to prefix the names of the parameters with the so that it's clearer when you're in the method what you're doing.

Let's look at the methods.

doMagic will return just a literal string. (The @ prefix is used in Objective-C to differentiate an NSString instance from a classic char * C-style string.) Here's the listing to add to the **Foo.m** implementation file:

```
-(NSString *)doMagic
{
        // return a constant string...
        return @"Hello, world.";
}
```

doMoreMagic will take a string value containing a name and create a new string using the stringWithFormat method on NSString. stringWithFormat is the same operation as string.Format in .NET and String.format in Java, although the format string is based on the C-style and, consequently, the Java style. Note how stringWithFormat is not a NARC word, and hence does not need explicit releasing. Add this method to the Foo.m implementation file:

```
-(NSString *)doMoreMagic:(NSString *)theName
{
        // format a string using placeholders...
        return [NSString stringWithFormat:@"Hello, '%@'.", theName];
}
```

The final doYetMoreMagic takes a name and an integer number and concatenates the result of doMoreMagic the number of times specified in theBarCount. This method uses NSMutableString. This idea of "mutable" occurs a lot in the Objective-C—most classes contain data that cannot be changed and have a companion "mutable" class that is changeable. Add this method to the Foo.m implementation file:

```
-(NSString *)doYetMoreMagic:(NSString *)theName barCount:(int)theBarCount
{
        // take the result of doMoreMagic... and build a long string...
        NSString *magicString = [self doMoreMagic:theName];

        // build a string...
        NSMutableString *builder = [NSMutableString string];
        for(int index = 0; index < theBarCount; index++)
        {
                if(builder.length > 0)
                        [builder appendString:@"..."];
                [builder appendString:magicString];
        }

        // return...
        return builder;
}
```

To test that this works, we'll call doYetMoreMagic from MyObjectiveCPrimer. Here's the code—modify the application:didFinishLaunchingWithOptions method within ObjectiveCPrimerAppDelegate.m:

```
-(BOOL)application:(UIApplication *)application didFinishLaunchingWithOptions:(NSDictionary *)launchOptions
{
        // call doYetMoreMagic...
        NSLog([self.myFoo doYetMoreMagic:@"Ellie" barCount:5]);
```

```
        // ok...
        return YES;
}
```

The output from that looks like this:

```
2010-06-03 22:15:20.692 AmxMobile.IPhone.ObjectiveC[2095:207] Hello,
'Ellie'....Hello, 'Ellie'....Hello, 'Ellie'....Hello, 'Ellie'....Hello, 'Ellie'.
```

Namespaces

There are no namespaces in Objective-C, and hence convention is to start class names with some prefix that tells you which library you are working with. You'll commonly use NS classes (NeXTstep) and UI classes (user interface). In the next chapters, when we're building the Six Bookmarks application, we'll prefix our classes with SB.

The Biggest Gotcha in Objective-C

I've saved the best gotcha for last! In Objective-C, you can send messages to null objects, i.e., this is perfectly valid:

```
Foo *foo = nil;
[foo doMagic];
[foo doSomeMoreMagic];
[foo release];
```

All of those calls are perfectly valid. Whereas in Classic VB, C#, Java, and JavaScript, calling a method on a null object would raise an exception, Objective-C just ignores the call.

The plus side is that this makes cleanup code much easier—you don't have to check that you still have an object before you call release on it, but this is bound to cause you frustration. For example, you may create a dictionary in your class. You can make calls to add objects, and make calls to enumerate over it, but none of these calls will actually *do* anything. It can be very confusing. The easiest way to investigate this in the debugger is to hover your mouse over the offending variable and see whether its value is 0x0.

"Hello, World" for iPhone

We'll now go ahead and build the "Hello, World" application, building on the elements that we've just gone through.

Create a new Xcode view-based application project called HelloWorld. (Remember that the Xcode project wizard will base the name of the classes on the name of your project, and thus having a short name for the project is helpful, even if you ultimately rename the containing folder.)

This will give you a project similar to the one that you had before. Figure 8-4 illustrates.

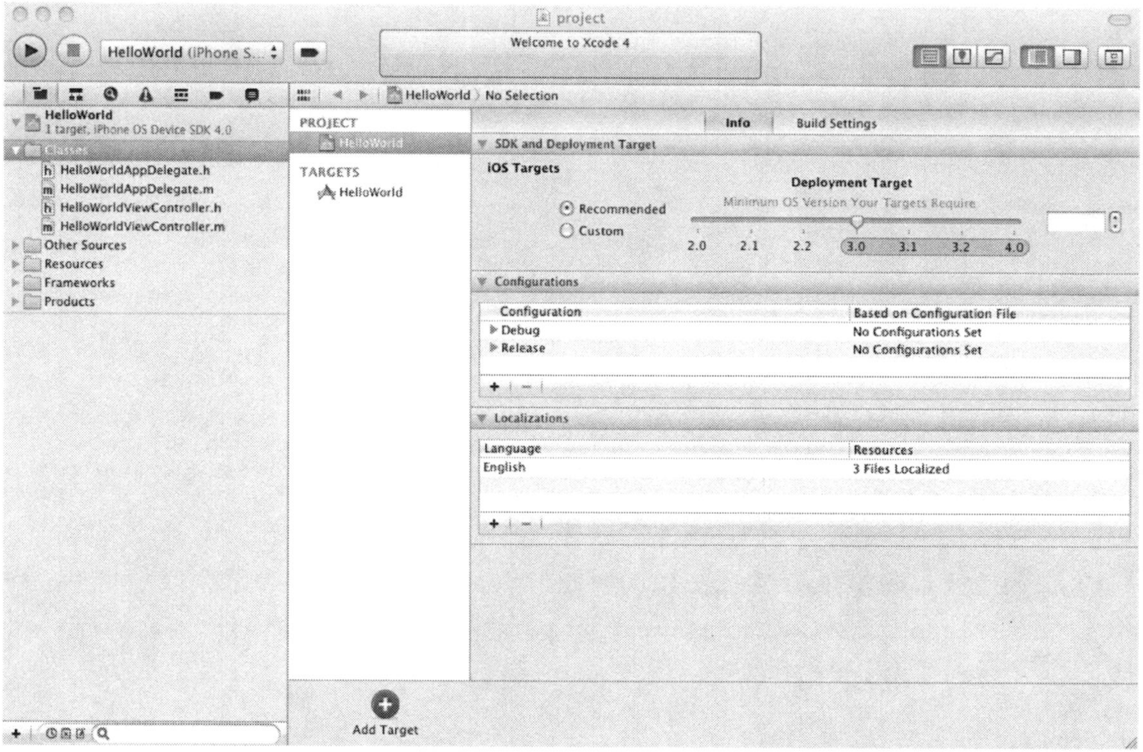

Figure 8-4. *The new "Hello World" project.*

In this project, we're going to start to look at the features in Xcode that allow us to build our user interface. In versions of Xcode prior to version 4, this was achieved using a separate application called Interface Builder. In the new version of Xcode, this is neatly integrated into the main environment.

We're going to build a basic form with a button on it and then have the application display a message box when the user clicks the button.

The way that the user interface designer works is a little weird, so it's worth trying to get your head around this concept before we start.

Recall how Objective-C is based on the idea of messaging—when we want to ask an object to do something, we have to send it a message. This principle extends to the user interface, i.e., when the user interface wants us to tell it that something has happened, it will send us a message. To receive the messages, we will create a **controller** class.

The controller class is any class that extends `UIViewController`. This arrangement is pitched as a model-view-controller (MVC) pattern, but it is more closely aligned to code-behind classes as found in ASP.NET. But then, we're not strictly adhering to MVC in the applications we build in this book, and so we'll stay in line with Apple's recommendations.

The old Interface Builder application works with files of type `.xib`, and opening a `.xib` file in the Xcode results in the interface editor being opened. `.xib` is pronounced "NIB" (as in NeXTstep Interface Builder). NIB files are XML files. They are bound closely to the definition of the class that they work with.

In order to address a user interface element on a view, you need to have a property that maps to that view. We did something similar when we built our views in the Android chapters, and .NET developers will be used to this model in both ASP.NET and Windows Forms. When we define a property, we have to mark it as IBOutlet, like the following example:

```
@property (nonatomic, retain) IBOutlet UIButton *buttonHello;
```

This tells the user interface editor that the property should be presented in the designer for potential binding of user interface elements. Once a property is bound (which we'll do in a moment), when the form starts, the property is assigned to the instance of the relevant user interface control, and you can address the control via the property.

The other markup we'll need is IBAction. This is used to declare an event handler method. Again, once the event handler is bound in Interface Builder, when the control needs to raise the event, it will use this binding to call your property. Here's an example of a method declaration:

```
-(IBAction)handleClick:(id)sender;
```

In this instance, IBAction is used as an alias for void—this method won't actually return anything.

Let's look now at building the interface.

Building the User Interface

We've called out a possible definition of our buttonHelper property and handleClick method. Formalize this by making the HelloWorldViewController.h file look like this:

```
#import <UIKit/UIKit.h>

@interface HelloWorldViewController : UIViewController {
        UIButton *buttonHello;
}

@property (nonatomic, retain) IBOutlet UIButton *buttonHello;

-(IBAction)handleClick:(id)sender;

@end
```

We need to do that first so that Interface Builder has something to bind to.

Xcode has created a .xib file for us, although it has stored it in the **Resources** folder. (Figure 8-5 illustrates.) Double-click on the HelloWorldViewController.xib to open it.

Xcode will load the .xib file, and you'll see a design surface that looks like Figure 8-6.

Figure 8-5. *The location of the "HelloWorldViewController.xib" file in the project tree.*

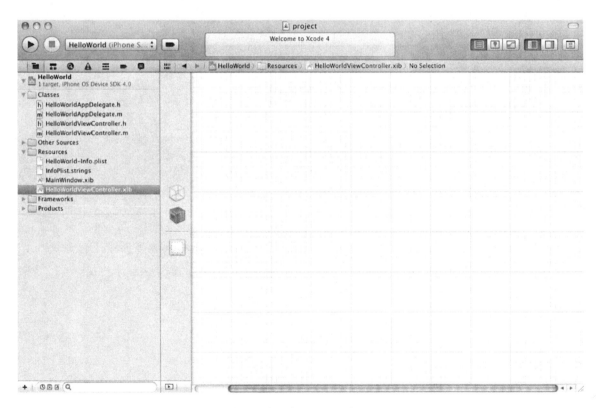

Figure 8-6. *The user interface design surface when first opened.*

At this point, Xcode takes a page out of the book called "How to make an interface really, *really* obscure." Virtually every developer on earth has used some sort of GUI designer, and what virtually every developer will expect here is a representation of the window to draw on and a control palette. What you have here is a design surface that is missing a control palette *and* something to draw the controls onto! It must surely be the case that this is fixed prior to the full release of Xcode 4. So if you can already see a representation of an iPhone display and a control palette, you can miss these next few steps.

To the right of the project tree, you will see three icons: two 3D boxes and one 2D square. The square is actually the view, so if you double-click on this, it will give you a view to draw on. Figure 8-7 illustrates.

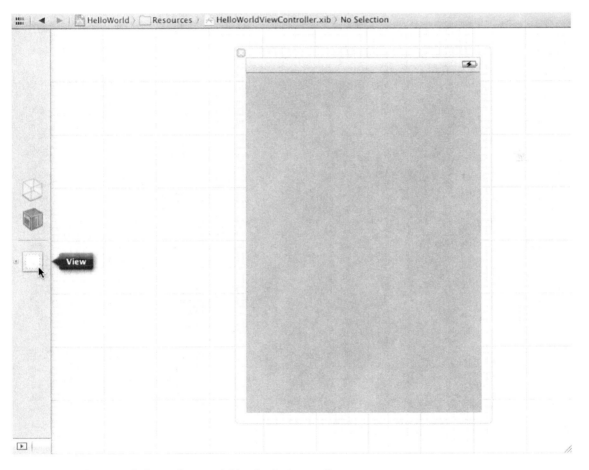

Figure 8-7. *The "View" object shown within the design surface.*

The next thing to find is the control palette. In the top right-hand corner of the window is a button with a tooltip that reads **Hide or Show: Navigator | Utility**. (Figure 8-8 illustrates.) If you click this, a pane will appear to the right of the designer. (Figure 8-9 illustrates.)

Figure 8-8. *The toolbar option for accessing the right-hand pane.*

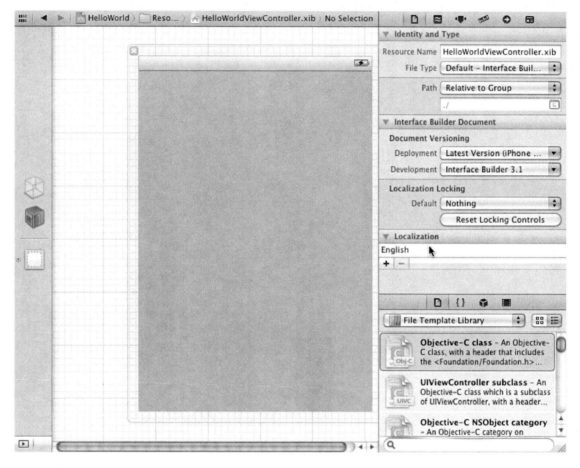

Figure 8-9. *The right-hand pane now visible.*

From the menu, select **View ➤ Utilities ➤ Object Library**. This will change the view in the bottom subpane of the **Navigator** window to show the control palette. Figure 8-10 illustrates.

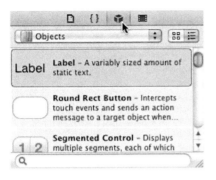

Figure 8-10. *The location of the "Objects" button that allows access to the control palette.*

Once you actually have the control palette and the view available, drawing controls is likely a familiar experience. Locate the **Round Rect Button** control in the **Objects** pane and drag one onto the view. Make it a little wider and center it on the view. Figure 8-11 illustrates.

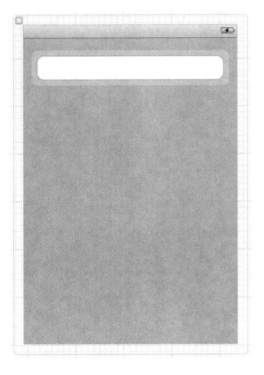

Figure 8-11. *A "Round Rect Button" on the view's design surface.*

You can define the text for the button either by double-clicking the button, or by using the **Object Attributes** subpane at the top of the **Navigator** pane that you opened previously. Set the text to be Say Hello.

This next bit is where things get a little strange, or rather, strange compared to most UI editors on the market. We have to bind up the `buttonHello` property and the `handleClick` methods. In Visual Basic and the tools that came after it, all you'd do is double-click the button, and you'd get a event handler stub created for you—all is good to go.

In Xcode, this is very much a drag-and-drop operation.

■**NOTE** It is important that before you proceed, you have saved the modifications that you made previously to `HelloWorldViewController.h` when you added the `buttonHello` property and `handleClick` methods.

In the **Navigator** pane, one of the subpanes at the top is labeled **Connections**. You can get to this by selecting **View ➤ Utilities ➤ Connections** from the menu. Select the File's Owner object to the left of the design surface, and the **Connections** subpane will show the connection points into the code-behind class. The `helloWorld` property and `handleClick` methods are available. Figure 8-12 illustrates.

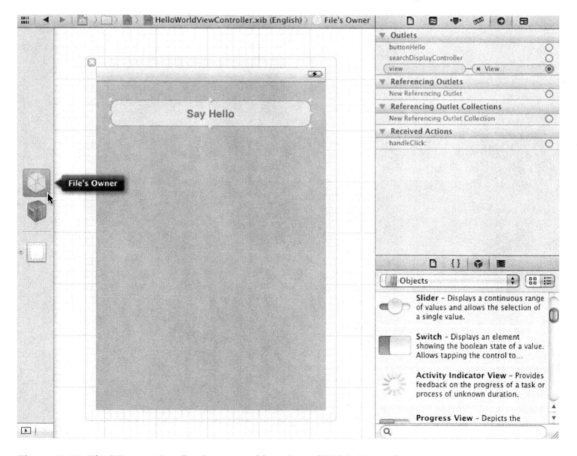

Figure 8-12. *The "Connections" subpane and location of "File's Owner".*

■**NOTE** File's Owner refers to the "owner of the .xib file," which is our HelloWorldController class. This File's Owner object essentially contains the forward-declared IBAction and IBOutlet artifacts within our project code.

We need to do two things—we need to set the button Touch Up Inside event to invoke the handleClick method, and we need the button to store a handle to itself into the buttonHello property.

To start, select the button, and the **Connections** window will change to show a list of events. Click and drag the circle to the right of Touch Up Inside and drop it onto the File's Owner icon on the left-hand side of the design surface. This will pop up a window showing the available methods that can receive this event. Select handleClick to finish the wiring process. Figure 8-13 shows the **Connections** window after the fact.

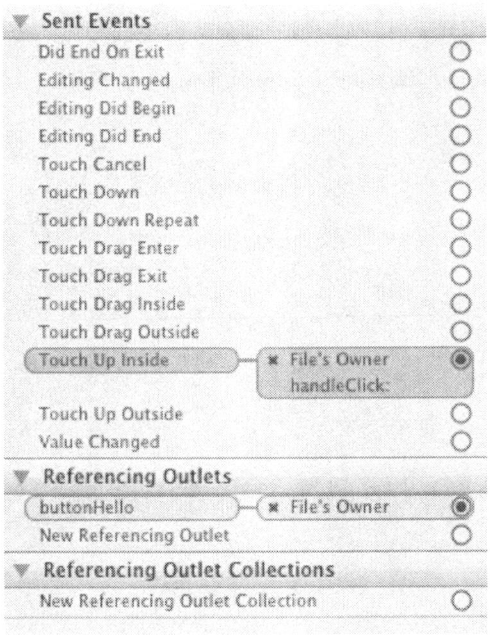

Figure 8-13. *The "Connections" subpane for the button showing the binding to the "handleClick" method.*

The properties work in a similar way, but the other way around. If you select File's Owner and open the **Connections** subpane, you will see the properties marked as IBOutlet. Figure 8-14 shows our buttonHello property.

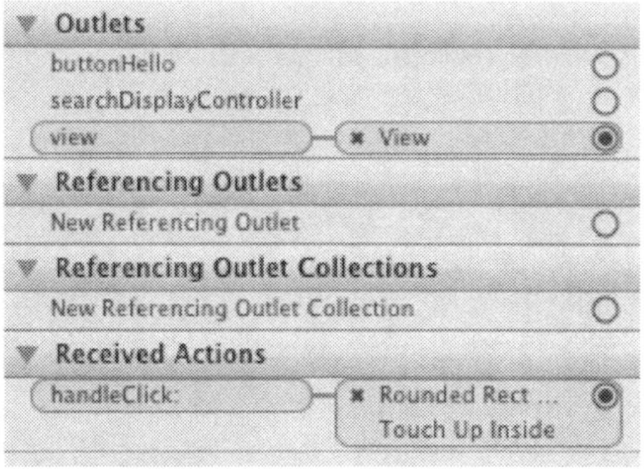

Figure 8-14. *The "Connections" subpane for "File's Owner" prior to the "buttonHello" outlet being wired-up.*

This time, drag from the buttonHello property to the button. The Connections Inspector will be updated to reflect the binding, as shown in Figure 8-15.

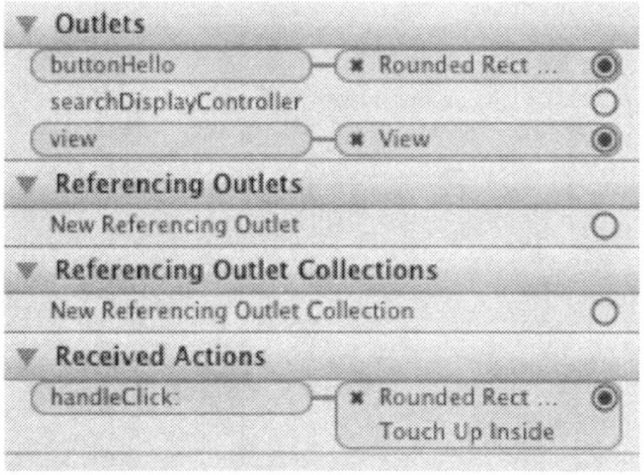

Figure 8-15. *The "Connections" subpane for "File's Owner" post the "buttonHello" outlet being wired-up.*

That's the user interface built—we now just need to run it.

Creating a Windows and Showing the View

We can't run our application until we implement the property and method that we defined in the header file. Open the HelloWorldViewController.m file and add this code:

```
#import "HelloWorldViewController.h"

@implementation HelloWorldViewController
```

```
@synthesize buttonHello;

-(IBAction)handleClick:(id)sender
{
        // we'll do something here...
}
```

Run the project, and the simulator will start and show the button, as shown in Figure 8-16. Clicking the button has no discernable function at the moment.

Figure 8-16. *The "Hello, World" application running in the simulator.*

Displaying the Message Box

We'll build a new class with a method for displaying a message box. We'll reuse this class in the next section, but for now I'm breaking it out into a separate class just to touch on how we define static methods.

You'll note that all methods that we've defined so far have begun with a - sign. This tells Objective-C to create an instance method. We can create static methods by using a + sign instead.

Add a new class to the project called SBMessageBox. In the header file, define a show method, like this:

```
#import <Foundation/Foundation.h>

@interface SBMessageBox : NSObject {
}

+(void)show:(NSString *)message;

@end
```

In the implementation class, we want to create an instance of UIAlertView, which is Cocoa's message box implementation. Here's the implementation of SBMessageBox:

```
#import "SBMessageBox.h"

@implementation SBMessageBox

+(void)show:(NSString *)message
{
        UIAlertView *view = [[UIAlertView alloc] init];
        [view setTitle:@"Hi!"];
        [view setMessage:message];
        [view addButtonWithTitle:@"OK"];
        [view show];

        // we're done with it...
        [view release];
}

@end
```

Note how we release the object at the end because we have used alloc when creating it.

We can now add an implementation to our handleClick method. This requires us to add a reference to SBMessageBox.h to the top of the class. Note how when we're calling a static method, we refer to the class directly, which is what one would expect with static methods. Here are the code changes for HelloWorldViewController.m:

```
#import "HelloWorldViewController.h"
#import "SBMessageBox.h"

@implementation HelloWorldViewController

@synthesize buttonHello;
```

```
-(IBAction)handleClick:(id)sender
{
        // say hello...
        [SBMessageBox show:@"Hello, world."];
}
```

If we run the project now and click the button, the event will get raised, the method will get called, and we'll see the message. Figure 8-17 illustrates.

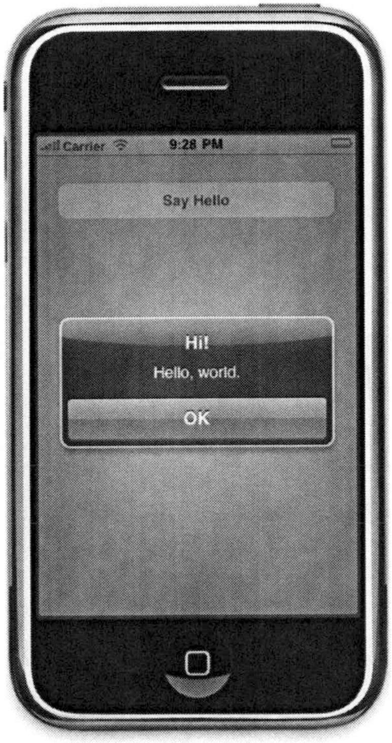

Figure 8-17. *Success! The "Hello, World" message box.*

Conclusion

That brings us to the end of the work to set up and explore the toolset. We looked at installing Xcode (very straightforward) and the Objective-C language (not so straightforward). With any luck, you have gained insight into the potential potholes of using this toolset, but I'm also hopeful that you can see how you can build very compelling applications easily.

■ ■ ■

CHAPTER 9

iOS: Building the Logon Form and Consuming REST Services

In this chapter, we're going to start building our Six Bookmarks application for iPhone. We'll be looking at building the logon form and consuming the REST services from the service.

The approach we take here is going to be a little different. We're still going to need to call the API service to authenticate the API user and then call the Users service to log the user on—but we're going to have to go "round the houses" a little to get the same effect as on Android or on Windows Phone. I'll call these out as we go.

Creating the Project

We'll start by creating the project. As per the instructions in the last chapter, create a new view-based application. When prompted for a name, supply the name **SixBookmarks**. This will give us an "application delegate" called SixBookmarksAppDelegate and a view controller called SixBookmarksViewController.

In the last chapter, we added code to the "application delegate," but we did not describe what it was. The application delegate is the class that is defined as the one that boots the application. This will give us a window into which we can add a view.

In Cocoa Touch, we typically have one window and then add and remove views from that window.

We don't want our SixBookmarksViewController, but we'll look at building the logon user interface now, and as part of that, we'll delete the default controller and add a new one.

Creating the Logon Form

As we work through this and the other chapters, we're going to add four forms—one for logging on, one for navigating bookmarks, one for displaying a list of bookmarks, and one for editing an individual bookmark. Each form will have a layout (i.e., a .xib file) and a controller. We will ultimately need some code that swaps the different forms in and out depending on what we need to do—we'll eventually add that code to SixBookmarksAppDelegate. We will also need a base class that we can derive the controllers from, as there are some common activities that we need to do with all of the forms.

First we'll create our base class for all of the view controllers in our application. Add a new class to the project by right-clicking on **Classes** and choosing **New File**. When prompted, create a new Objective-C class and ensure **Subclass of NSObject** is selected. Click **Next** and you'll be prompted for a name. We're going to prefix all of our classes SB; so provide the name of the new class as SBViewController. Figure 9-1 illustrates.

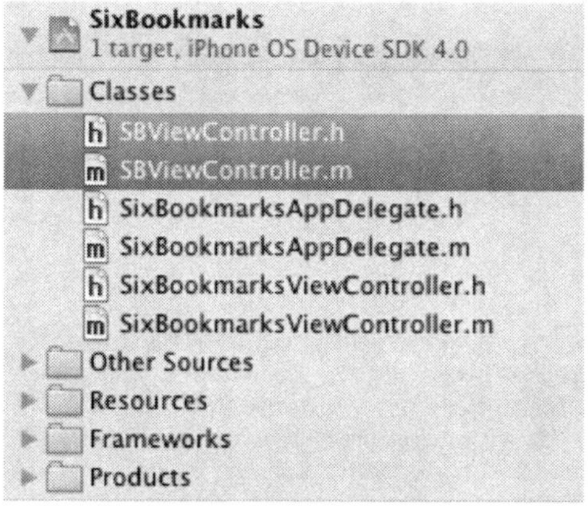

Figure 9-1. *The new "SBViewController" implementation and header file in the project tree.*

The new header file and implementation file will be added to the project tree.

To finish this operation, we need to tell SBViewController to extend UIViewController. In the header file, modify the base class to be **UIViewController** as opposed to NSObject, as per this listing:

```
// SBViewController.h
#import <Foundation/Foundation.h>

@interface SBViewController : UIViewController {

}

@end
```

We now want to create a logon form—aka view. Right-click on **Classes** and choose **New File**, but this time select the option to create a new **UIViewController subclass**. When prompted, enter the name as SBLogonView. Figure 9-2 shows possible results—I've rearranged the files slightly to keep the .xib file with the other .xib files.

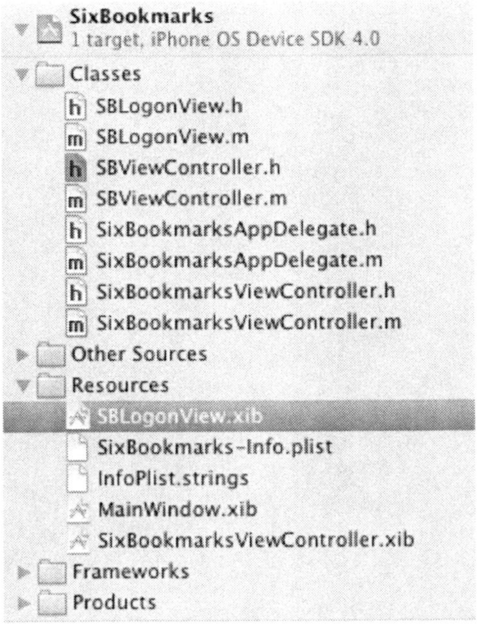

SixBookmarks
1 target, iPhone OS Device SDK 4.0

▼ ☐ Classes
　　h SBLogonView.h
　　m SBLogonView.m
　　h SBViewController.h
　　m SBViewController.m
　　h SixBookmarksAppDelegate.h
　　m SixBookmarksAppDelegate.m
　　h SixBookmarksViewController.h
　　m SixBookmarksViewController.m
▶ ☐ Other Sources
▼ ☐ Resources
　　SBLogonView.xib
　　SixBookmarks-Info.plist
　　InfoPlist.strings
　　MainWindow.xib
　　SixBookmarksViewController.xib
▶ ☐ Frameworks
▶ ☐ Products

Figure 9-2. *The "SBLogonView.xib" file within the project tree.*

Creating the Logon Form User Interface

We'll start on semi-familiar territory by using the user interface editor to create the logon view user interface. Double-click on the SBLogonView.xib file to launch the editor.

To the design surface, start off by adding a **Navigation Bar** control. Virtually every iPhone application has one of these on every form, but (oddly) one is not added by default. You can change the text on it by either selecting it and using the **Attributes** subpane, or double-clicking and editing in place.

Then add two **Text Field** controls, a **Switch** control, a **Label** control, and a Round Rect Button. You're looking to achieve something like Figure 9-3.

Then we'll do the less obvious bits. Select the top-most Text Field control, and use the **Attributes** subpane to change its **Placeholder** value to **Username**. (This will set some grayed-out text on the control to say what the field is intended to do—it's a handy approach with mobile applications, as real estate is so limited.) Do the same for the second field, which is for the **Password**.

For the password field, you also need to set it to be in "password mode"—i.e., to mask characters typed into the screen. Again in the **Attributes** window (with the password field selected), there is a checkbox called **Secure**. Check this to put it into password mode.

You'll now have something like Figure 9-4, which is not vastly different from the last view.

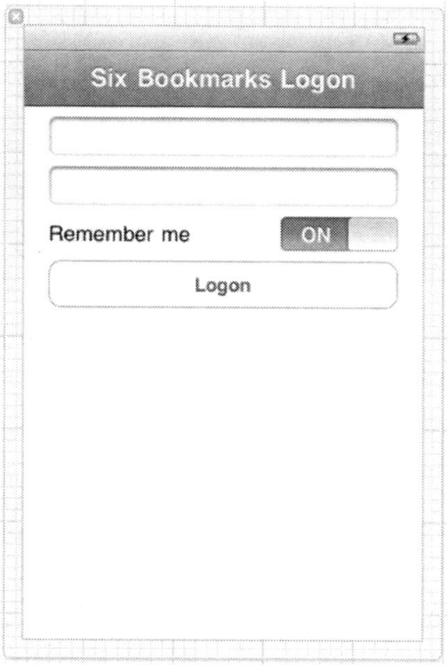

Figure 9-3. *The desired layout for the logon form.*

Figure 9-4. *The logon form now showing the placeholder values on the two text boxes.*

We then need to go on and do the following steps. Here's a summary—we'll detail each one in a moment.

- Change the base class of the form to extend SBViewController.

- Add properties to bind the username and password text fields, the logon button, and the "remember me" checkbox.

- Add a method that will be invoked when the user clicks the **Logon** button.

Save your changes to the user interface editor, and then open the **SBLogonView.h** header file. Add the instance variable and property declarations, and change the header file as per this listing:

```
// SBLogonView.h
#import <UIKit/UIKit.h>
#import "SBViewController.h"

@interface SBLogonView : SBViewController {

        UITextField *textUsername;
        UITextField *textPassword;
        UISwitch *checkRememberMe;
        UIButton *buttonLogon;

}

@property (nonatomic, retain) IBOutlet UITextField *textUsername;
@property (nonatomic, retain) IBOutlet UITextField *textPassword;
@property (nonatomic, retain) IBOutlet UISwitch *checkRememberMe;
@property (nonatomic, retain) IBOutlet UIButton *buttonLogon;

-(IBAction)handleLogonClick:(id)sender;

@end
```

It is very important in the preceding listing that you change the base class of SBLogonView to SBViewController. All of our views will rely on this class, and we're going to change the application delegate to enforce this requirement.

You'll notice that we've had to bring forward the declaration of SBViewController.h via an #import declaration. This is something that's a pain to handle in Objective-C—everything has to be forward-declared. To help with this, we'll create new header file called MyClasses.h that contains the #import declarations for every class in the project. We can add this to the implementation files to bring everything forward easily. We won't use these on the header files, as it's better to be more explicit with the headers rather than using the "catch-all" technique.

Add a **Header file** item to the project (found under the **iPhone OS OSX/C and C++** group). Here's the listing for MyClasses.h.

```
#import "SBViewController.h"
#import "SBLogonView.h"
```

In the implementation file, the properties need to be synthesized, the handleLogonClick method provided with an implementation, and the dealloc method changed to release the control references. Here's the listing:

```
// SBLogonView.m
#import "SBLogonView.h"
#import "MyClasses.h"

@implementation SBLogonView

@synthesize textUsername;
@synthesize textPassword;
@synthesize checkRememberMe;
@synthesize buttonLogon;

-(IBAction)handleLogonClick:(id)sender
{
        // we'll do this in a moment...
}

// code ommitted for brevity…

-(void)dealloc
{
        [textUsername release];
        [textPassword release];
        [checkRememberMe release];
        [buttonLogon release];
    [super dealloc];
}
```

To get the view displayed, we just need to change the application delegate to create our new view and show it. We'll do this next.

Showing the Logon Form

When we created the project, our application delegate was created with a property to SixBookmarksViewController that we want to replace with a reference to our base SBViewController class, which will give us a chance to reuse it later.

Modify the header file of the SixBookmarksAppDelegate class so that it uses the base class, as per this listing:

```
// SixBookmarksAppDelegate.h
#import <UIKit/UIKit.h>
#import "SBViewController.h"

@interface SixBookmarksAppDelegate : NSObject <UIApplicationDelegate> {
    UIWindow *window;
        SBViewController *viewController;
}

@property (nonatomic, retain) IBOutlet UIWindow *window;
@property (nonatomic, retain) IBOutlet SBViewController *viewController;

@end
```

We can then change the application:didFinishLaunchingWithOperations method to create a new instance of SBLogonView, assign it to the property (release it when we're done), and then add the view to window. You must also add an import statement to include MyClasses.h to the top of this file. Here's the listing:

```
// SixBookmarksAppDelegate.m
- (BOOL)application:(UIApplication *)application didFinishLaunchingWithOptions:↵
(NSDictionary *)launchOptions {

        // create and set the view...
        SBLogonView *logon = [[SBLogonView alloc] initWithNibName:@"SBLogonView"↵
 bundle:[NSBundle mainBundle]];
        self.viewController = logon;
        [logon release];

    // Override point for customization after app launch
    [window addSubview:self.viewController.view];
    [window makeKeyAndVisible];

        return YES;
}
```

You can now run the project and view it in the simulator. Figure 9-5 shows the output—and there's a small problem!

Figure 9-5. *The logon form running – however the status bar is overlapping the navigation bar control.*

Although the `.xib` file actually contains a reference indicating that there is a status bar on the form, the layout engine does not make room for this space, and hence we have to do it manually. This is one of the reasons we created SBViewController.

When the view is shown, a method called viewDidAppear will be called. We can override this, and we'll do two things when we do. First we'll call a method called bumpView, which will move the view down by the size of the status bar. Second we'll set the background color of the form so that it has that striped blue color that is so prevalent in iPhone applications (more later). Add this code to SBViewController:

```
// SBViewController.m
#import "SBViewController.h"

@implementation SBViewController

-(void)bumpView
{
        //manually adjust the frame of the main view to prevent it from appearing under↵
    the status bar.
    UIApplication *app = [UIApplication sharedApplication];
```

```
    if(!app.statusBarHidden)
        {
        [self.view setFrame:CGRectMake(0.0,app.statusBarFrame.size.height,↵
self.view.bounds.size.width, self.view.bounds.size.height)];
    }
}

-(void)viewDidAppear:(BOOL)animated
{
        // bump...
        [self bumpView];

        // background...
        self.view.backgroundColor = [UIColor groupTableViewBackgroundColor];

        // do the base's implementation...
        [super viewDidAppear:animated];
}
```

We won't dwell on this code as it's not core to our discussions, but if you run the project again, you will get a more pleasing result, as shown in Figure 9-6.

Figure 9-6. *The logon form now showing correctly.*

Special Note About Grouped Views

Before we go on, it's worth talking about grouped views. It's very common in iPhone applications to have views where you have user interface controls broken up into groups and with a blue striped background. (Figure 9-7 illustrates.) This is done by creating something called a "table view" and creating groups within the view. It's actually reasonably easy to do, but it is very fiddly; so I've decided in these chapters not to do it and to "cheat" by creating a regular view, manually laying out the controls, and fixing the backgrounds. If you want more information, the excellent Apress book *Beginning iPhone 3 Development*, by Dave Mark and Jeff LaMarche, will help.

Figure 9-7. *An illustration of a grouped table view.*

Conventions for Presenting Code in the iPhone Chapters

Now that we've seen a bit of code, let's go through some of the rules I'll be using to present code for the iPhone application.

The split between having to define the intention to build methods in the header file and actually writing the methods in the implementation file makes it difficult to present a narrative in a book form such as this. As such, in code listings I will invite you to define methods in header files within the code listing using the <...> notation in the comments. Where you see this, I have not explicitly asked you to add the definition to the header file.

For example, in the code listing we just did, bumpView was not defined in the header file, and so the convention is the following:

```
// <...> Needs declaration in header...
-(void)bumpView
{
        //manually adjust the frame of the main view to prevent it from appearing under↵
the status bar.
```

```
    UIApplication *app = [UIApplication sharedApplication];
    if(!app.statusBarHidden)
        {
        [self.view setFrame:CGRectMake(0.0,app.statusBarFrame.size.height,↵
self.view.bounds.size.width, self.view.bounds.size.height)];
    }
}
```

The second thing that I will do relates to Objective-C's lack of ability to have private or protected methods. In Objective-C, everything defined in the header is public. Having all methods and properties public is generally regarded as a big problem for object-orientation—it means that anyone can do anything to one of your objects at any time, which is likely to cause all sorts of usage violations. The way that Objective-C developers get around this is to not include definitions in the header. However, when you do this in Objective-C, you have to get the methods in the right order. For example, if our `bumpView` method was not in the header, but declared after the `viewDidAppear` method where it was called, an error would occur. To make life easier when following along, I'm going to declare everything as needing to be in the header, as this is likely to cause less frustration than not being able to compile the code. In a real world application, you would work towards having as few things as possible declared as public.

The final thing that I'll do is assume you know to add new class definitions to the `MyClasses.h` file and that you know that when referring to a class in an instance variable, property, or method declaration, the matching header file must be included using the `#import` declaration.

Calling the Services

Now that we can get the logon view on the screen, we can look at calling our services. First, though, we need to get the data off of the screen.

Capturing the Logon Request

In the Android application, we created an "error bucket" that would capture problems when validating input and report it to the user. We'll do the same thing here via our `SBErrorBucket` class.

This project is going to end up with a lot of classes in it, and we can split up the classes using "groups." Create a new group inside **Classes** called `Runtime`, and then add a new class called `SBErrorBucket` within it. Figure 9-8 illustrates.

Figure 9-8. *The "SBErrorBucket" class and "Runtime" group.*

As before, our error bucket is going to contain a method that lets us add an error, a property to report whether there are any errors, and a method to get back a list of errors for display on the user interface. We'll also require a property that holds the errors.

Objective-C has two classes for holding arrays—one is called NSArray and the other is called NSMutableArray. The first has a fixed set of values and cannot be changed. The second is changeable. NSMutableArray extends NSArray. This pattern is very common in Objective-C—you have one class that has fixed data and another "mutable" class that has changing data. We'll be using a mutable array, as we need to have a list of errors that we can add to.

Here's the definition of the SBErrorBucket class:

```
// SBErrorBucket.h
#import <Foundation/Foundation.h>

@interface SBErrorBucket : NSObject {
        NSMutableArray *errors;
}

@property (nonatomic, retain) NSMutableArray *errors;

-(void)addError:(NSString *)error;
-(BOOL)hasErrors;
-(NSString *)errorsAsString;

@end
```

For the implementation, the first thing we need to do is create a constructor for the class that creates a new mutable array and sets it to be our errors property, and (because it's a good habit to get into) we'll release the property in our dealloc call. Here's the listing:

```
// SBErrorBucket.m
#import "SBErrorBucket.h"
#import "MyClasses.h"

@implementation SBErrorBucket

@synthesize errors;

-(id)init
{
        if(self = [super init])
        {
                self.errors = [NSMutableArray array];
        }

        // return...
        return self;
}
```

```
-(void)dealloc
{
        [errors release];
        [super dealloc];
}
```

Just to recap the memory management, the [NSMutableArray array] call will give an array back with a reference count of 1, but which is set to autorelease. We set our errors property, increasing the count to 2. At some point in the (possibly near) future, the autorelease will fire and our reference count will drop to 1. When we're deallocated, we'll reduce the reference count to 0, and the array will be deleted. NSArray/NSMutableArray itself is also working the reference count of the objects contained within—the reference counts are increased when objects are added and reduced when objects are removed. (From this point, unless there's something we need to talk about that's particularly weird or important, I won't walk you through any more memory management internals now.)

The first method for SBErrorBucket adds an error:

```
// SBErrorBucket.m
-(void)addError:(NSString *)error
{
        [self.errors addObject:error];
}
```

The hasErrors method returns an indication as to whether there are errors "on board":

```
// SBErrorBucket.m
-(BOOL)hasErrors
{
        if(self.errors.count > 0)
                return TRUE;
        else
                return FALSE;
}
```

Finally, the errorsAsString method returns back a concatenated string of errors. Here's the listing:

```
// SBErrorBucket.m
-(NSString *)errorsAsString
{
        NSMutableString * builder = [NSMutableString string];
        for(NSString *error in self.errors)
        {
                if([builder length] > 0)
                        [builder appendString:@"\n"];
                [builder appendString:error];
        }

        // return...
        return builder;
}
```

We met `NSMutableString` in the last section. Its purpose is to manage a string whose contents are built up over some routine.

■**TIP** You should also include an import for `SBErrorBucket.h` into your `MyClasses.h` file.

With `SBErrorBucket` built, we can write the validation routine in our `SBLogonView`.

When we built our form, we didn't hook up the properties and method using the Interface Builder. We'll do this now. Open up `SBLogonView.xib`, link up the four properties to the four controls, and link up the **Touch Up Inside** event to the `handleLogonClick` method. Figure 9-9 and Figure 9-10 illustrate.

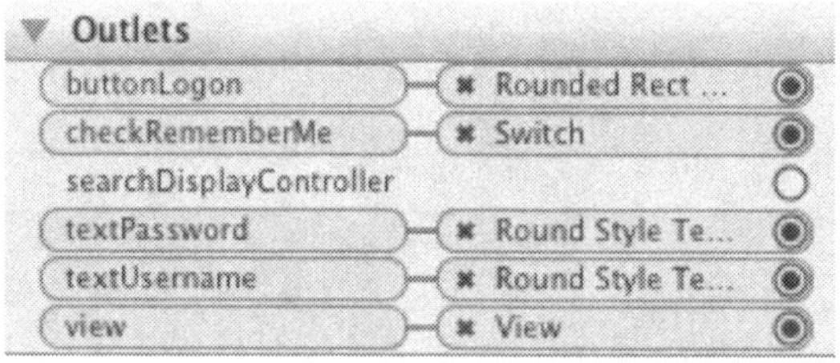

Figure 9-9. *The outlets for the button and the text boxes correctly wired up.*

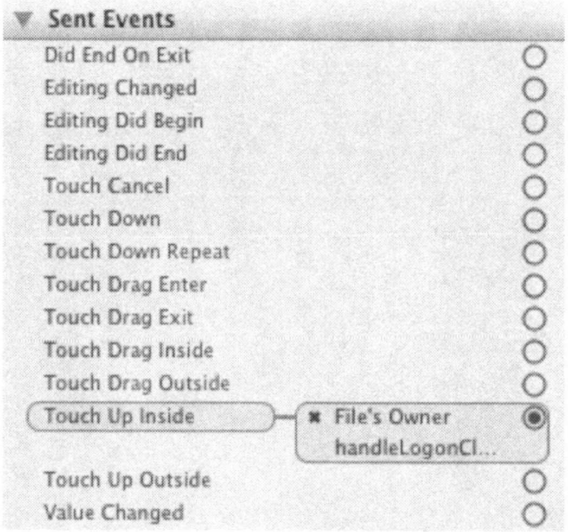

Figure 9-10. *The "Touch Up Inside" event bound to the "handleLogonClick" method.*

Here's the code for `handleLogonClick`—we'll add the code to actually do the logon shortly. The code here is just designed to handle the validation:

```
// SBLogonView.m
-(IBAction)handleLogonClick:(id)sender
{
        // get the values...
        NSString *username = self.textUsername.text;
        NSString *password = self.textPassword.text;

        // valdiate...
        SBErrorBucket *bucket = [[SBErrorBucket alloc] init];
        if(username == nil || username.length == 0)
                [bucket addError:@"Username is required"];
        if(password == nil || password.length == 0)
                [bucket addError:@"Password is required"];

        // now what?
        if(!(bucket.hasErrors))
        {
                // we'll do the logon operation in here...
        }
        else
                [SBMessageBox show:bucket.errorsAsString];

        // cleanup...
        [bucket release];
}
```

Note the reference to SBMessageBox at the end. We built this class in our "Hello, World" application in the last chapter. We now need to bring this forward. Create a new class called SBMessageBox and add this code:

```
// SBMessageBox.m
#import "SBMessageBox.h"

@implementation SBMessageBox

// <…> Needs declaration in header…
+(void)show:(NSString *)message
{
        UIAlertView *alert = [[UIAlertView alloc] init];
        [alert setTitle:@"Six Bookmarks"];
        [alert setMessage:message];
        [alert addButtonWithTitle:@"OK"];
        [alert show];
        // cleanup...
        [alert release];
}

@end
```

■**TIP** You should also add an import for SBMessageBox.h to your MyClasses.h file.

Run the project now, and you'll get some validation. Figure 9-11 shows what happens if you click the logon button without entering a username or password.

Figure 9-11. *The logon form showing a form validation failure.*

Calling the API Service

So far things have been easy—this is where things get a little more complicated!

The HTTP requests to our service will be done using the NSConnection class and related classes. These operations will be asynchronous—i.e., we'll fire off a request, and at some point in the future, we'll get some data back. However, in Objective-C we do not have anonymous methods, which are incredibly helpful when building async code. Also, Objective-C's message infrastructure does have a "function pointer–like" arrangement where it is possible to pass in the address of a method invocation, but a) it's very rarely used and b) it's a low-level function that has all sorts of gotchas in it for different processor types, etc. Function pointers are probably the *right* way to achieve what we want; however, I have a concern that I'll be steering you in the direction of something that will be difficult to get working and might break when new devices are introduced (e.g., today there was a rumor that the next generation of iPad would have a different processor). Therefore we'll use a different method.

The only (practical) way to do the callbacks is to use what in Java and .NET are called "interfaces," i.e., some sort of language construct containing methods that should be invoked on success. In Objective-C, there are two ways to do this. You can create a new class and use multiple inheritance (the informal method), or you can create a protocol (the formal method). We're going to use the informal method, but throughout these chapters we'll refer to these as "interfaces."

However, there is one killer problem with using this interface approach, in that you can have only *one* method that receives a callback of a certain type on a class. For example, imagine you create an interface called MyHttpRequestCallback and put a method called downloadOk. You implement this interface on your class, and now you have a downloadOk method ready to receive a callback from your class that actually makes the HTTP request. That's fine if you want to issue only *one* HTTP sort of request on the class! If you want to reuse the callback for different sorts of requests, your downloadOk method needs to know which request you actually mean. This is going to necessitate passing through some sort of identifier that tells us which request we're referring to. (We'll call this an "operation code," or "op code" for short.)

Moreover, this problem gets doubly worse, as you have to have two levels of indirection. The service calls need to accept interfaces with callbacks on, but then the service-calling methods need to defer processing to the classes that download the HTTP resources, and these also need their own callback interfaces.

We're going to bump right into this problem now, so let's get started.

Building the Proxy Classes

Previously we've built a base service proxy base class, a REST-specific service base class, an API service class, and a Users service class. Repeat this now by building a new group called Services in your project and adding SBServiceProxy, SBRestProxy, SBApiService, and SBUsersService. (Remember to add #import statements for these to MyClasses.h.) Figure 9-12 illustrates.

Figure 9-12. *The various service classes within the project tree.*

We also need to modify the inheritance declarations of these classes as follows:

- SBServiceProxy ➤ NSObject (i.e., no change)

- SBRestServiceProxy ➤ SBServiceProxy

- SBApiService ➤ SBRestServiceProxy

- SBUsersService ➤ SBRestServiceProxy

The SBHttpHelper and SBDownloadBucket Classes

We'll look at the HTTP communication part first. To start, add two new classes—SBHttpHelper and SBDownloadBucket—to the Runtime group. Then add a third class called SBDownloadSettings. This SBDownloadSettings class will be used to hold a list of additional headers to send up to the service. If you recall from previous chapters, our Six Bookmarks service requires us to pass up headers called x-amx-apiusername and x-amx-token to tell the service who we are.

We'll build SBDownloadSettings first. This class needs to take a dictionary of header/value pairs. The Objective-C class used to do this as NSDictionary; but since we need to change the values after instantiation, we'll use NSMutableDictionary. Here's the header listing:

```
// SBDownloadSettings.h
#import <Foundation/Foundation.h>

@interface SBDownloadSettings : NSObject {
        NSMutableDictionary *extraHeaders;
}

@property (nonatomic, retain) NSMutableDictionary *extraHeaders;

-(void)addHeader:(NSString *)value forName:(NSString *)name;

@end
```

And here's the listing for the implementation:

```
// SBDownloadSettings.m
#import "SBDownloadSettings.h"

@implementation SBDownloadSettings

@synthesize extraHeaders;

-(id)init
{
        if(self = [super init])
        {
                extraHeaders = [NSMutableDictionary dictionary];
        }

        // return...
        return self;
}
```

```
-(void)addHeader:(NSString *)value forName:(NSString *)name
{
        [extraHeaders setValue:value forKey:name];
}
-(void)dealloc
{
        [super dealloc];
}

@end
```

SBHttpHelper will have three methods. download will be the one that does our downloading and will take a reference to an interface called SBDownloadCallback. It will also take an "op code," which will be an arbitrary integer value. We're going to use these op codes to track the asynchronous operations as they pass around the code. For example, we could define an op code for the "API logon" operation and use this in the callbacks to reference the meaning of the data that we've been provided. (We'll cover this in more detail later.)

We'll also need two methods for building up a URL from a dictionary of values—these will be called buildQueryString and buildUrl. Here's the header declaration, including the declaration of SBDownloadCallback.

```
// SBHttpHelper.h
#import <Foundation/Foundation.h>
#import "SBDownloadSettings.h"

@class SBDownloadBucket;  // alternative forward declaration c.f. #import

@interface SBDownloadCallback : NSObject
-(void)downloadComplete:(SBDownloadBucket *)data;
@end

@interface SBHttpHelper : NSObject {

}

+(void)download:(NSString *)url settings:(SBDownloadSettings *)theSettings callback:↵
(SBDownloadCallback *)theCallback opCode:(int)theOpCode;

+(NSString *)buildQueryString:(NSDictionary *)theArgs;

+(NSString *)buildUrl:(NSString *)url args:(NSDictionary *)theArgs;

@end
```

We'll look at the easy methods on SBHttpHelper first. buildQueryString will take a dictionary of name/value pairs and build a URL in <name>=<value>&<anotherName>=<anotherValue> format. This will use the NSMutableString class that we've seen a couple of times now.

```
// SBHttpHelper.m
+(NSString *)buildQueryString:(NSDictionary *)theArgs
{
        NSMutableString *builder = [[NSMutableString alloc] init];
        bool first = true;
        for(NSString *name in theArgs)
        {
                if(first)
                        first = false;
                else
                        [builder appendString:@"&"];

                [builder appendString:name];
                [builder appendString:@"="];
                [builder appendString:[theArgs objectForKey:name]];
        }

        // return...
        return builder;
}
```

buildUrl will take a URL, trim off any existing query strings, and then defer to buildQueryString for the rest of the string. Here's the implementation:

```
// SBHttpHelper.m
+(NSString *)buildUrl:(NSString *)url args:(NSDictionary *)theArgs
{
        // trim the query string...
        NSRange range = [url rangeOfString:@"?"];
        if(range.length > 0)
                url = [url substringToIndex:range.location];

        // build...
        url = [NSString stringWithFormat:@"%@?%@", url, [self buildQueryString:theArgs]];

        // return...
        return url;
}
```

The download method will use classes NSConnection and NSMutableRequest. Here's the code—we'll go through it in a moment.

```
// SBHttpHelper.m
+(void)download:(NSString *)url settings:(SBDownloadSettings *)theSettings↵
 callback:(SBDownloadCallback *)theCallback opCode:(int)theOpCode
{
        // create a bucket...
        SBDownloadBucket *bucket = [[SBDownloadBucket alloc] initWithCallback:theCallback↵
 opCode:theOpCode];
```

```
        // run...
        NSMutableURLRequest *request = [NSMutableURLRequest requestWithURL:[NSURL↵
URLWithString:url] cachePolicy:NSURLRequestUseProtocolCachePolicy timeoutInterval:60.0];
        // add the headers...
        for(NSString *name in theSettings.extraHeaders)
        {
                NSString * value = [theSettings.extraHeaders objectForKey:name];
                [request addValue:value forHTTPHeaderField:name];
        }

        // create the connection with the request and start loading the data…
        [NSURLConnection connectionWithRequest:request delegate:bucket];
}
```

The first thing we do in the download method is create a download bucket and pass in the callback and op code. Ultimately it will be the bucket that calls our API service proxy to tell it that the download has been completed.

The second thing we do is create a request. After creation, we'll go through the extra headers provided via our settings instance and add those to the request.

Finally we'll create an NSURLConnection object bound to the request that we made. This object also requires a callback as (although I haven't mentioned it thus far) the class that actually does the downloading needs to call into us to tell us that data is available.

Let's look now at building the SBDownloadBucket class.

Implementing SBDownloadBucket

When we called the connectionWithRequest method on NSURLConnection, we passed in a reference to the download bucket via the delegate parameter. The data type of this parameter is id, which is Objective-C's notation for saying "any object." What happens underneath the hood is that the connection object will test to see whether we implement different methods and, if we do, it will invoke them. For example, we can implement the method connection:didReceiveResponse to be told when a response is received. If we don't invoke that method, the caller won't call it. For those used to other types of OO (e.g., Java, C++, or .NET), this is like a cross between interfaces and inheritance.

We need to implement three methods on the class to receive our callbacks from NSURLConnection. As well as these, we need to support our own bits and pieces for supporting the download operation.

On SBDownloadBucket, we need the following properties:

- A property that holds an NSMutableData instance—this will store the data from the server as it's provided to us.

- A property that holds the reference to our callback

- A property that holds the arbitrary "op code" from the caller

- A property that holds the HTTP status response code

We also want to create two other methods—initWithCallback will be used to initialize our bucket and dataAsString will turn the data held in NSMutableData into an NSString instance.

Here's the listing for the SBDownloadBucket implementation:

```
// SBDownloadBucket.h
#import <Foundation/Foundation.h>

@class SBDownloadCallback;

@interface SBDownloadBucket : NSObject {
        NSMutableData * data;
        SBDownloadCallback *callback;
        int opCode;
        int statusCode;
}

@property (nonatomic, retain) NSMutableData *data;
@property (nonatomic, retain) SBDownloadCallback *callback;
@property (assign) int opCode;
@property (assign) int statusCode;

-(id)initWithCallback:(SBDownloadCallback *)theCallback opCode:(int)theOpCode;

-(NSString *)dataAsString;

@end
```

For the implementation, the first thing we need to do is synthesize the properties and implement the constructor:

```
// SBDownloadBucket.m
#import "SBDownloadBucket.h"
#import "MyClasses.h"

@implementation SBDownloadBucket

@synthesize data;
@synthesize callback;
@synthesize opCode;
@synthesize statusCode;

-(id)initWithCallback:(SBDownloadCallback *)theCallback opCode:(int)theOpCode;
{
        // set...
        if(self = [super init])
        {
                self.callback = theCallback;
                self.opCode = theOpCode;
                self.data = [NSMutableData data];
        }
```

```
        // return...
        return self;
}
```

The three callback methods we need to support have the following signatures, and it's worth having a look at how this is constructed, as the pattern is very common in Objective-C. They are the following:

- -(void)<u>connection</u>:(NSURLConnection *)connection <u>didReceiveResponse</u>: (NSURLResponse *)response

- -(void)<u>connection</u>:(NSURLConnection *)connection <u>didReceiveData</u>:(NSData *)theData

- -(void)<u>connectionDidFinishLoading</u>:(NSURLConnection *)connection

Two things to note here—first, all of the methods take an NSURLConnection instance as their first parameter. This is to get around the problems related to a lack of anonymous methods and difficulties with function pointers that we're going to get around using our op codes—the idea is that callers can de-reference their own internal state based on the identity of the connection instances. The second thing is that the names of these methods are as follows:

- connection:didReceiveResponse

- connection:didReceiveData

- connectionDidFinishLoading

If you look at it like this, you can see that the first two are actually overloads of a method called connection. connectionDidFinishLoading doesn't take a second parameter and hence cannot be overloaded, which is why it has a different name. Once you can identify this pattern, you can more easily identify places in Objective-C where you have to adhere to it.

In any case, the first method we have to implement—connection:didReceiveResponse—needs to do two things. It needs to extract the HTTP status response code from the request and store it in a property, and also it needs to reset the data property back to being empty. You can receive more than one connection:didReceiveResponse call in situations where you have redirects. Here's the code:

```
// SBDownloadBucket.m
-(void)connection:(NSURLConnection *)connection didReceiveResponse:(NSURLResponse *)response
{
        // what did we get?
        if([response isKindOfClass:[NSHTTPURLResponse class]])
                self.statusCode = [(NSHTTPURLResponse *)response statusCode];

        // ensure out bucket is clear...
        [data setLength:0];
}
```

The second method—connection:didReceiveData—will append the received data to the data property:

```
// SBDownloadBucket.m
-(void)connection:(NSURLConnection *)connection didReceiveData:(NSData *)theData
{
    // append the data that we got...
    [data appendData:theData];
}
```

The third and final method—connectionDidFinishLoading—will be called once everything has been downloaded. For debugging, we'll use dataAsString to turn the UTF-8 formatted data to a string. Here's the code:

```
// SBDownloadBucket.m
-(NSString *)dataAsString
{
        return [[[NSString alloc] initWithData:data encoding:NSUTF8StringEncoding]↩
autorelease];
}

-(void)connectionDidFinishLoading:(NSURLConnection *)connection
{
        // log it...
        NSLog(@"%@", self.dataAsString);

        // callback...
        [callback downloadComplete:self];
}
```

Notice how in dataAsString, we call autorelease to put the object into the autorelease pool. It's a good idea to do this here, as callers will not expect to have to release the value of something that looks like a property.

With a little bit more legwork, we can try to use this to download an HTTP resource. We'll take a quick shortcut and get the application to download Google's home page.

The first thing to do is flesh out the implementation of SBServiceProxy. This class needs to hold the service name in a property, return a SBDownloadSettings instance containing the special x-amx-apiusername and x-amx-token HTTP header values up, and also return the URL of the RESTful service. Here's the definition:

```
// SBServiceProxy.h
#import <Foundation/Foundation.h>
#import "SBDownloadSettings.h"

@interface SBServiceProxy : NSObject {
        NSString *serviceName;
}

@property (nonatomic, retain) NSString *serviceName;

-(id)initWithServiceName:(NSString *)theServiceName;

-(NSString *)resolvedServiceUrl;
-(SBDownloadSettings *)getDownloadSettings;

@end
```

And here's the implementation:

```
// SBServiceProxy.m
#import "SBServiceProxy.h"
#import "MyClasses.h"

@implementation SBServiceProxy

@synthesize serviceName;

-(id)initWithServiceName:(NSString *)theServiceName
{
        if(self = [super init])
        {
                self.serviceName = theServiceName;
        }

        // return...
        return self;
}

-(NSString*)resolvedServiceUrl
{
        return [NSString stringWithFormat:@"%@%@", @"http://services.↵
multimobiledevelopment.com/", self.serviceName];
}

-(SBDownloadSettings *)getDownloadSettings
{
        SBDownloadSettings *settings = [[SBDownloadSettings alloc] init];
        return settings;
}

-(void)dealloc
{
        [serviceName release];
        [super dealloc];
}

@end
```

We'll quickly continue the theme with SBRestServiceProxy. This class initially just needs to implement another initWithServiceName method that defers to the base implementation on SBServiceProxy. Here's the definition:

```
#import <Foundation/Foundation.h>
#import "SBServiceProxy.h"
```

```
@interface SBRestServiceProxy : SBServiceProxy
{

}
```

```
-(id)initWithServiceName:(NSString *)theServiceName;
```

And again, here is the implementation:

```
// SBRestServiceProxy.m
#import "SBRestServiceProxy.h"
#import "MyClasses.h"

@implementation SBRestServiceProxy

-(id)initWithServiceName:(NSString *)theServiceName
{
        return [super initWithServiceName:theServiceName];
}
@end
```

We're now in a position within the logon method on SBApiService to call our download method and ask it to go get Google's home page. We'll also provide a callback so that we'll be told when downloading is complete. Here's the code:

```
// SBApiService.m
#import "SBApiService.h"
#import "MyClasses.h"

@implementation SBApiService

// <...> Needs definition in header
-(void)logon:(NSString *)apiPassword
{
        // settings...
        SBDownloadSettings *settings = [self getDownloadSettings];

        // download a fake result for now...
        [SBHttpHelper download:@"http://www.google.co.uk/" settings:settings↵
 callback:(SBDownloadCallback *)self opCode:1000];

        // cleanup...
        [settings release];
}
```

```
-(void)downloadComplete:(SBDownloadBucket *)bucket
{
        [SBMessageBox show:@"Download complete!"];
}
```

@end

We can now make a quick change to the operation of the logon form to run the code, and we can make something happen.

If you run the code, enter any value you like into the username and password fields, and click the Logon button, you'll see a message box, but the more interesting output is in the debugger console. You should see a stream of HTML representing Google's homepage. Figure 9-13 illustrates.

```
GNU gdb 6.3.50-20050815 (Apple version gdb-1502) (Thu Jul  8 12:27:19 UTC 2010)
Copyright 2004 Free Software Foundation, Inc.
GDB is free software, covered by the GNU General Public License, and you are
welcome to change it and/or distribute copies of it under certain conditions.
Type "show copying" to see the conditions.
There is absolutely no warranty for GDB.  Type "show warranty" for details.
This GDB was configured as "x86_64-apple-darwin".Attaching to process 1316.
2010-08-10 19:06:04.047 SixBookmarks[1316:207] ******* Accessibility Status Changed: On
2010-08-10 19:06:04.115 SixBookmarks[1316:207] ********** Loading AX for:
com.amxMobile.iOS.SixBookmarks ************
2010-08-10 19:06:08.010 SixBookmarks[1316:207] <!doctype html><html><head><meta http-
equiv="content-type" content="text/html; charset=ISO-8859-1"><title>Google</
title><script>window.google={kEI:"EJVhTJOWDeiG4gbTx-zABw",kEXPI:"23051",kCSI:
{e:"23051",ei:"EJVhTJOWDeiG4gbTx-zABw",expi:"23051"},ml:function(){},kHL:"en",time:function()
{return(new Date).getTime()},log:function(b,d,c){var a=new
Image,e=google,g=e.lc,f=e.li;a.onerror=(a.onload=(a.onabort=function(){delete g[f]}));g[f]
```

Figure 9-13. *Debug output showing some of the first bytes returned that make up Google's home page HTML.*

Making a Real Call to the API Service and Parsing the XML

Let's look now at making a real call to the API service. This method will return back some XML, and so most of the work in this section will involve parsing and interpreting that XML document.

When we processed received XML in our Android application, we used a DOM approach—i.e., we loaded the entire XML response into an object tree and then walked that tree.

In the Android chapter, I mentioned that it's common to come across a recommendation that using a forward-reading parser is a better approach, especially on memory-constrained devices like a mobile phone. At the time, I said that my preference is typically to take the approach that works but is the most maintainable. Using a DOM is more maintainable than a forward-reading parser in situations where the incoming XML changes or you need to chase down problems.

However, on iPhone there is no XML DOM, and thus we're going to have to use a forward-reading parser. (There is an XML DOM in the full version of Cocoa used on Macs, but it is not included in the iOS subset.) This, at least, does give you as the reader a chance to see how a forward-reading parser is consumed, if you've never done so before.

The general idea of a forward-reading parser is to feed in XML and have it notify you that data is being discovered during the process. To read it, you need to configure some sort of object that will receive the data as it's being read in and track the state of where the "pointer" managed by the reader is.

The class that we need to use in Cocoa Touch is NSXMLParser. We're going to create two classes to support this operation—SBXmlBucketBase and SBFlatXmlBucket. SBFlatXmlBucket will extend SBXmlBucketBase. In the next chapter, we're going to create a class called SBEntityXmlBucket that also extends SBXmlBucketBase, but we don't need to worry about this now.

The purpose of the base class is to store a string builder (NSMutableString) that will capture the contents of the element that is being read. We'll need to do this in both SBFlatXmlBucket and (ultimately) SBEntityXmlBucket. SBFlatXmlBucket is so called because it's designed to read a simple XML file that has only two levels of nodes—the root and one level of children. The XML response that we receive from the RESTful services fits the bill here. (Refer to Chapter 2 for examples of the XML that will be returned.) What will happen with SBFlatXmlBucket is that NSXmlParser will inform it when elements are started and ended. The very first element will always be the root element of the document, and so we'll store the name of that element in a string. Then, for any subsequent elements, we'll create a dictionary of values that store the element name and value contained within each discovered element.

Here's the definition of SBXmlBucketBase:

```
// SBXmlBucketBase.m
#import <Foundation/Foundation.h>

@interface SBXmlBucketBase : NSObject {
        NSMutableString *builder;
}

@property (nonatomic, retain) NSMutableString *builder;

-(void)resetBuilder;
-(NSString *)trimmedBuilder;

@end
```

On this class, the resetBuilder method will be used to clear down the value contained within the builder property—this will happen whenever an element is discovered. The purpose of trimmedBuilder is to trim any whitespace off of the start and end of any discovered text. XML DOM implementations typically do this for you—it's something that we need to explicitly do when using a parser.

The implementation looks like this:

```
// SBXmlBucketBase.m
#import "SBXmlBucketBase.h"

@implementation SBXmlBucketBase

@synthesize builder;

-(id)init
{
        if(self = [super init])
        {
                [self resetBuilder];
        }
```

```
        // return...
        return self;
}

-(void)resetBuilder
{
        [self setBuilder:[NSMutableString string]];
}

-(NSString *)trimmedBuilder
{
        NSString *trimmed = [[self builder] stringByTrimmingCharactersInSet:↵
[NSCharacterSet whitespaceAndNewlineCharacterSet]];
        return trimmed;
}

-(void)dealloc
{
        [builder release];
        [super dealloc];
}

@end
```

The preceding implementation does not include any event handlers that receive notification from the NSXMLParser that we've yet to create. Similar to the work we've already done, this class requires known methods to be available that can be invoked when things happen. We need to add a handler for parser:foundCharacters to SBXmlBucketBase, like so:

```
// Add to SBXmlBucketBase.m
-(void)parser:(NSXMLParser *)parser foundCharacters:(NSString *)buf
{
        // store it...
        [builder appendString:buf];
}
```

Now we can create other classes that extend this and consume the defined functionality that gathers the text inside of elements. We'll now build SBFlatXmlBucket.

This class needs to have properties to store the name of the root element, and the values that are discovered, which we'll hold in an NSMutableDictionary. We'll also require methods that extract strongly-typed values from the dictionary. We'll add handling for strings and Boolean values, as that's what we'll need in this application. (In a real application, you'll likely need wider type support.) Here's the definition:

```
// SBFlatXmlBucket.h
#import <Foundation/Foundation.h>
#import "SBXmlBucketBase.h"
```

```
@interface SBFlatXmlBucket : SBXmlBucketBase {
        NSString *rootName;
        NSMutableDictionary *values;
}

@property (nonatomic, retain) NSString *rootName;
@property (nonatomic, retain) NSMutableDictionary *values;

// extraction...
-(NSString*)getStringValue:(NSString *)name;
-(BOOL)getBooleanValue:(NSString *)name;

@end
```

The implementation is as follows. This class needs methods to support additional callbacks from NSXMLParser, namely parser:didStartElement and parser:didEndElement. The start element handler will set the root name if necessary, and also reset the base class's string builder, whatever the situation. The end element will set the trimmed value contained within the base class's string builder into the dictionary against the element name in question. Here's the code:

```
// SBFlatXmlBucket.m
#import "SBFlatXmlBucket.h"
#import "MyClasses.h"

@implementation SBFlatXmlBucket

@synthesize rootName;
@synthesize values;

-(id)init
{
        if(self = [super init])
        {
                // set...
                self.values = [NSMutableDictionary dictionary];
        }

        // return...
        return self;
}

-(void)parser:(NSXMLParser *)parser didStartElement:(NSString *)elementName
 namespaceURI:(NSString *)namespaceURI qualifiedName:(NSString *)qualifiedName
   attributes:(NSDictionary *)attributeDict
{
        NSLog(@"Processing Element: %@", elementName);
```

```
        // do we have a root?
        if(rootName == nil)
                [self setRootName:elementName];

        // reset the string builder...
        [self resetBuilder];
}

-(void)parser:(NSXMLParser *)parser didEndElement:(NSString *)elementName
 namespaceURI:(NSString *)namespaceURI
qualifiedName:(NSString *)qName
{
        // the value in the string builder needs to be stored...
        [values setValue:[self trimmedBuilder] forKey:elementName];
        [self resetBuilder];
}

-(NSString*)getStringValue:(NSString *)name
{
        return [values objectForKey:name];
}

-(BOOL)getBooleanValue:(NSString *)name
{
        NSString *buf = [self getStringValue:name];
        if(buf == nil || [buf length] == 0 || [buf isEqualToString:@"0"])
                return FALSE;
        else
                return TRUE;
}

-(void)dealloc
{
        [rootName release];
        [values release];
        [super dealloc];
}

@end
```

We are now in a position where we can actually make the call to the API service. That said, this is going to be a bit convoluted, so this is what's going to happen:

- We'll add a method to SBRestServiceProxy called makeRequest. This will accept an SBRestRequestArgs instance and an (arbitrary) op code.

- makeRequest will use SBHttpHelper to download the HTTP resource. This, in turn, will populate an SBDownloadBucket instance with the result, which will get sent to the downloadComplete callback-handling method on SBRestServiceProxy.

- downloadComplete will check the status code to make sure that it's HTTP 200 (i.e., "OK"). If it is, it will create an NSXMLParser instance and ask that to populate one of our new SBFlatXmlBucket instances.

- We'll then take our populated SBFlatXmlBucket instance and check to see if it contains an error message. If no error occurs, a method called processResult also on SBRestServiceProxy will be called. Extended classes will be expected to override this.

- Depending on whether errors occurred during that lot, methods called requestOk or requestFailed will be called on SBRestServiceProxy. The SBApiService class will override these and call its own callback methods to tell the caller what actually happened.

That's quite a lot to absorb—you may find it helpful to get the code that we're about to see working (either by following along or downloading) and stepping through with the debugger.

The first thing to do is build SBRestRequestArgs. This is simply a dictionary that contains the values to patch into the query string of the request. We built a similar class on the generic web application and Android implementations. Here's the definition:

```
// SBRestRequestArgs.h
#import <Foundation/Foundation.h>

@interface SBRestRequestArgs : NSObject {
        NSMutableDictionary *args;
}

@property (nonatomic, retain) NSMutableDictionary *args;

-(id)initWithOperation:(NSString*)theOperation;
-(void) setValue:(id)value forKey:(NSString *)key;

@end
```

The implementation is as follows. The only aspect that makes it different than a regular dictionary is that we force in supply of an operation name. (Again, this is how we did it on the prior implementations.) Here's the implementation code:

```
#import "SBRestRequestArgs.h"

@implementation SBRestRequestArgs

@synthesize args;

-(id)initWithOperation:(NSString*)theOperation
{
        if(self = [super init])
        {
                self.args = [NSMutableDictionary dictionary];
                [self setValue:theOperation forKey:@"operation"];
        }
```

```
        // return...
        return self;
}

-(void)setValue:(id)value forKey:(NSString *)key
{
        [args setValue:value forKey:key];
}

-(void)dealloc
{
        [args release];
        [super dealloc];
}

@end
```

■**NOTE** If you recall on SBHttpHelper we created methods called buildQueryString and buildUrl. These methods will accept values stored in an SBRestRequestArgs instance and create a URL from it.

The actual makeRequest method on SBRestServiceProxy is very straightforward—we'll build the URL and hand it over to SBHttpHelper:

```
// Add to SBRestServiceProxy.m…
// <…> Needs declaration in header
-(void)makeRequest:(SBRestRequestArgs *)args opCode:(int)theOpCode
{
        // get the url...
        NSString *url = [SBHttpHelper buildUrl:[self resolvedServiceUrl] args:[args args]];

        // download...
        SBDownloadSettings *settings = [self getDownloadSettings];
        [SBHttpHelper download:url settings:settings callback:(SBDownloadCallback *)self↵
opCode:theOpCode];
}
```

When the request has been processed and an SBDownloadBucket instance populated, our downloadComplete method will be called. This method contains a little more "meat."

Once we know the bucket is holding the results of a response that returned status HTTP 200 (i.e., "OK"), we can create an NSXMLParser instance and pass in a new instance of an SBFlatXmlBucket instance, which will act as an object that receives the result. When the parser is complete, we can look to see if the root element name is AmxResponse, which it should be if it has come from our services. We can then see if an error was returned.

I've chosen in this project not to use the exception handling, but rather to use a standard Objective-C object called NSError. The exception handling in Objective-C is appalling compared to modern implementations in .NET and Java, and we'll get in a mess if we use exceptions anything more than sparingly. (Your mileage may vary with regards to exception handling, especially as time goes on and the toolset becomes more refined.) SBErrorHelper contains a helper method called error that will package up an error into an NSError instance.

The final important "good path" operation of downloadComplete is to call processResult. We'll look at processResult in a moment.

Here's the implementation of downloadComplete:

```
// Add to SBRestServiceProxy.m…
-(void)downloadComplete:(SBDownloadBucket *)bucket
{
        // did we get a 200?
        NSError *err = nil;
        if(bucket.statusCode == 200)
        {
                // at this point we have a rest response from the server.  what
                // we need to do now is parse it... thus we`ll create a parser
                // and create an SBFlatXmlBucket to collect the data...
                NSXMLParser *parser = [[NSXMLParser alloc] initWithData:[bucket data]];

                // result...
                SBFlatXmlBucket *values = [[SBFlatXmlBucket alloc] init];
                [parser setDelegate:values];

                // run...
                [parser parse];

                // ok - what did we get?
                int result =  [[values rootName] isEqualToString:@"AmxResponse"];
                if([values rootName] == nil || !(result))
                        err = [SBErrorHelper error:self message:[NSString↵
stringWithFormat:@"The REST service `%@` returned a root element with name `%@`, not↵
`AmxResponse`.", [self serviceName], [values rootName]]];
                else
                {
                        // did we get an exception?
                        BOOL hasException = [values getBooleanValue:@"HasException"];
                        if(hasException)
                        {
                                NSString *message = [values getStringValue:@"Error"];
                                err = [SBErrorHelper error:self message:[NSString↵
stringWithFormat:@"The REST service `%@` returned an exception: `%@`.", serviceName,↵
message]];
                        }
```

```
                else
                {
                        // good - now we can do something with it...
                        err = [self processResult:values opCode:[bucket opCode]];
                }
        }

        // cleanup...
        [parser release];
        [values release];
    }
    else
        err = [SBErrorHelper error:self message:[NSString stringWithFormat:↵
@"The server returned HTTP '%d'.", bucket.statusCode]];

    // done that bit - now send a notification...
    if(err == nil)
        [self requestOk:[bucket opCode]];
    else
        [self requestFailed:[bucket opCode] error:err];
}
```

Here are the processResult, requestOk, and requestFailed methods for SBRestServiceProxy:

```
// Add to SBRestServiceProxy.m
// <…> Needs declaration in header
-(NSError *)processResult:(SBFlatXmlBucket *)values opCode:(int)theOpCode
{
        return [SBErrorHelper error:self message:@"processResult handler not implemented."];
}

// <…> Needs declaration in header
-(void)requestOk:(int)theOpCode
{
        // no-op by default...
}

// <…> Needs declaration in header
-(void)requestFailed:(int)theOpCode error:(NSError *)theError
{
        // show an error...
        [SBMessageBox showError:theError];
}
```

We have three more bits to clean up at this point—we need to implement SBErrorHelper, modify SBMessageBox so that it can show errors, and change SBApiService so that the call is actually made.

I won't dwell too much on SBErrorHelper—operationally it's straightforward. Here's the declaration—there are a couple of methods in there that we'll need later on.

271

```
// SBErrorHelper.h
#import <Foundation/Foundation.h>

@interface SBErrorHelper : NSObject {
}

+(NSError *)error:(NSObject *)caller message:(NSString *)theMessage;
+(NSString *)formatError:(NSError *)err;
+(NSError *)wrapError:(NSError *)theError caller:(NSObject *)theCaller message:↵
(NSString *)theMessage;

@end
```

The implementation for SBErrorHelper looks like this:

```
// SBErrorHelper.h
#import "SBErrorHelper.h"

@implementation SBErrorHelper

+(NSError *)error:(NSObject *)caller message:(NSString *)theMessage
{
        NSString *full = [NSString stringWithFormat:@"%@ (%@)", theMessage,↵
 [[caller class] description]];
        return [NSError errorWithDomain:full code:500 userInfo:nil];
}

+(NSString *)formatError:(NSError *)err
{
        NSString *message = [NSString stringWithFormat:@"%@ --> %d", [err domain],↵
 [err code]];
        return message;
}

+(NSError *)wrapError:(NSError *)theError caller:(NSObject *)theCaller message:↵
(NSString *)theMessage
{
        NSString *full = [NSString stringWithFormat:@"%@ (%@) --> %@", theMessage,↵
 [[theCaller class] description],
                                        [self formatError:theError]];
        return [NSError errorWithDomain:full code:500 userInfo:nil];
}

@end
```

We need a way of showing errors, and the easiest thing to do is modify SBMessageBox so that we can pass in an NSError instance and have it display it. You'll notice that we created a method called formatError on SBErrorHelper—SBMessageBox will defer to this to render the error. Here's the method:

```
// Add to SBMessageBox.m…
// <…> Needs declaration in header
+(void)showError:(NSError *)err
{
        NSString *message = [SBErrorHelper formatError:err];
        NSLog(@"%@", message);
        [self show:message];
}
```

We're now at the last phase of getting this working.

When we ask the API to logon, we'll pass in a callback—called SBLogonCallback—that will ultimately be called by SBApiService. However, the most important part of SBApiService will be the processResult method, the purpose of which will be to check the data in the XML and determine whether the logon call succeeded. If it did, it will set a global property called token property on the base SBServiceProxy class, the service access token that the service has granted. If it did not, it will return back an NSError instance.

First of all, let's make two changes to SBServiceProxy. In this class, the first thing we need to do is to create an enumeration that will hold all of the op codes that will be used by all of the methods. At this point, however, we'll just add one of these codes. The second thing we need to do is to add static token, setToken, and hasToken methods that will expose out our global token property. Here's the revised definition for SBServiceProxy:

```
// SBServiceProxy.h
#import <Foundation/Foundation.h>
#import "SBDownloadSettings.h"

typedef enum
{
        OPCODE_APILOGON = 1000

} SBOpCodes;

@interface SBServiceProxy : NSObject {
        NSString *serviceName;
}

@property (nonatomic, retain) NSString *serviceName;

+(NSString *)token;
+(void)setToken:(NSString *)theToken;
+(BOOL)hasToken;

-(id)initWithServiceName:(NSString *)theServiceName;

-(NSString *)resolvedServiceUrl;
-(SBDownloadSettings *)getDownloadSettings;

@end
```

The implementation of the property is a little different. Because it's a static property, we have to roll our own getter and setter implementation. We need to roll our own memory management when we do so. Here's the code:

```
// Add to SBServiceProxy.m...
static NSString *_token;

+(NSString *)token
{
        return _token;
}

+(void)setToken:(NSString *)theToken
{
        [_token release];
        _token = [theToken retain];
}

+(BOOL)hasToken
{
        if(_token != nil && _token.length > 0)
                return TRUE;
        else
                return FALSE;
}
```

When we tested some of the framework by downloading Google's home page, we stubbed out a little of our SBApiService class. We can now build this properly. This class needs to hold the callback as a property, and it also needs a logon method; although we had the logon method earlier, it did not have the callback parameter. Here's the definition—note the inclusion of SBLogonCallback.

```
// SBApiService.h
#import <Foundation/Foundation.h>
#import "SBRestServiceProxy.h"

@interface SBLogonCallback : NSObject
-(void)logonOk;
-(void)logonFailed:(NSError *)theError;
@end

@interface SBApiService : SBRestServiceProxy
{
        SBLogonCallback *callback;
}

@property (nonatomic, retain) SBLogonCallback *callback;
```

```
// Add the "callback" parameter…
-(void)logon:(NSString *)apiPassword callback:(SBLogonCallback *)theCallback;
```

```
@end
```

The implementation SBApiService shouldn't be too surprising at this point. logon needs to get a SBDownloadSettings instance that contains the special headers, build up an SBRestRequestArgs instance, and make the call. processResult needs overriding to actually look at the result from the server and make some decisions. Finally, requestOk and requestFailed need filling out to call back to the caller. Here's the implementation:

```
// SBApiService.m
#import "SBApiService.h"
#import "MyClasses.h"

@implementation SBApiService

@synthesize callback;

-(id)init
{
        return [super initWithServiceName:@"apirest.aspx"];
}

-(void)logon:(NSString *)apiPassword callback:(SBLogonCallback *)theCallback
{
        // store...
        self.callback = theCallback;

        // settings...
        SBDownloadSettings *settings = [self getDownloadSettings];

        // create some args...
        SBRestRequestArgs *args = [[SBRestRequestArgs alloc] initWithOperation:@"logon"];
        [args setValue:apiPassword forKey:@"password"];

        // download...
        [self makeRequest:args opCode:OPCODE_APILOGON];

        // cleanup...
        [args release];
        [settings release];
}

-(NSError *)processResult:(SBFlatXmlBucket *)values opCode:(int)theOpCode
{
        // what happened?
        NSString *result = [values getStringValue:@"Result"];
```

```
        if([result isEqualToString:@"LogonOk"])
        {
                // set the global token...
                NSString *token = [values getStringValue:@"Token"];
                [SBServiceProxy setToken:token];

                // ok...
                return nil;
        }
        else
                return [SBErrorHelper error:self message:[NSString stringWithFormat:↵
@"An error occurred on logon: '%@'.", result]];
}

-(void)requestOk:(int)theOpCode
{
        if(theOpCode == OPCODE_APILOGON)
                [self.callback logonOk];
        else
                [NSException exceptionWithName:[[self class] description] reason:↵
[NSString stringWithFormat:@"Cannot handle '%d'.", theOpCode] userInfo:nil];
}

-(void)requestFailed:(int)theOpCode error:(NSError *)theError
{
        if(theOpCode == OPCODE_APILOGON)
                [self.callback logonFailed:theError];
        else
                [NSException exceptionWithName:[[self class] description] reason:↵
[NSString stringWithFormat:@"Cannot handle '%d'.", theOpCode] userInfo:nil];
}

-(void)dealloc
{
        [callback release];
        [super dealloc];
}

@end
```

Previously, when we tested downloading the Google home page, we referred to an instance of logon on API service that did not have the op code parameter. We'll change this now, as I want to demonstrate the "bad path" handling.

In SBLogonView, we need to implement the logonOk and logonFailed methods that are defined on SBLogonResult. Here's the code:

```
// Add to SBLogonView.m
// <…> Needs declaration in header…
-(void)logonOk
{
    [SBMessageBox show:@"Logon OK."];
}

// <…> Needs declaration in header…
-(void)logonFailed:(NSError *)theError
{
    [SBMessageBox showError:theError];
}
```

Then we need to modify the existing call to pass in a reference to ourselves as the callback. Here's the modification:

```
// SBLogonView.m
-(IBAction)handleLogonClick:(id)sender
{
        // get the values...
        NSString *username = self.textUsername.text;
        NSString *password = self.textPassword.text;

        // valdiate...
        SBErrorBucket *bucket = [[SBErrorBucket alloc] init];
        if(username == nil || username.length == 0)
                [bucket addError:@"Username is required"];
        if(password == nil || password.length == 0)
                [bucket addError:@"Password is required"];

        // now what?
        if(!(bucket.hasErrors))
        {
                // we'll do the logon operation in here...
        SBApiService *api = [[SBApiService alloc] init];
        [api logon:@"Foo" callback:(SBLogonCallback *)self];
        [api release];
        }
        else
                [SBMessageBox show:bucket.errorsAsString];

        // cleanup...
        [bucket release];
}
```

Phew! We have finally arrived at point where we can run the logon operation. However, it won't work just yet—there's a problem in that the special headers are not being passed up. The errors not being passed up give us a chance to test our "bad path" handling, so we'll proceed as is.

Run the application and log on, and you'll see an error like Figure 9-14.

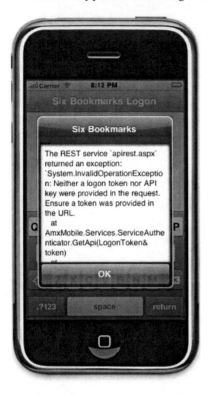

Figure 9-14. *The logon form reporting an error in connecting to the API service.*

The problem that we have is that the getDownloadSettings implementation in SBServiceProxy is not actually setting any headers. We can fix this by passing up the headers.

The first thing to do is modify SBServiceProxy so that the API username and password are hardcoded into the application. Remember that you will need to change this username and password for your own account.

In the definition of SBServiceProxy, define two extern const NSString instances, as per the following.

```
// Modify SBServiceProxy.h…
#import <Foundation/Foundation.h>
#import "SBDownloadSettings.h"
```

```
typedef enum
{
        OPCODE_APILOGON = 1000

} SBOpCodes;

extern const NSString *APIUSERNAME;
extern const NSString *APIPASSWORD;

// code ommitted for brevity…
```

We can then add an implementation of those strings in the main class. Here's the code:

```
// Modify SBServiceProxy.m…
#import "SBServiceProxy.h"
#import "MyClasses.h"

@implementation SBServiceProxy

@synthesize serviceName;

// YOU MUST CHANGE THIS IN ORDER TO USE THE SAMPLE...
const NSString *APIUSERNAME = @"amxmobile";
const NSString *APIPASSWORD = @"password";

// code ommitted for brevity…
```

We also need to make sure we pass the APIPASSWORD value into the logon method. Modify the handleLogonClick method of SBLogonView accordingly:

```
// Modify handleLogonClick on SBLogonView…
-(IBAction)handleLogonClick:(id)sender
{
        // get the values...
        NSString *username = self.textUsername.text;
        NSString *password = self.textPassword.text;

        // valdiate...
        SBErrorBucket *bucket = [[SBErrorBucket alloc] init];
        if(username == nil || username.length == 0)
                [bucket addError:@"Username is required"];
        if(password == nil || password.length == 0)
                [bucket addError:@"Password is required"];
```

```
        // now what?
        if(!(bucket.hasErrors))
        {
                // we'll do the logon operation in here...
        SBApiService *api = [[SBApiService alloc] init];
        [api logon:(NSString *)APIPASSWORD callback:(SBLogonCallback *)self];
        [api release];
        }
        else
                [SBMessageBox show:bucket.errorsAsString];

        // cleanup...
        [bucket release];
}
```

Finally we can change getDownloadSettings to return the username and token back, like this:

```
// Modify getDownloadSettings in SBServiceProxy.m...
-(SBDownloadSettings *)getDownloadSettings
{
        SBDownloadSettings *settings = [[SBDownloadSettings alloc] init];

        // set...
        [settings addHeader:(NSString *)APIUSERNAME forName:@"x-amx-apiusername"];
        NSString *theToken = [SBServiceProxy token];
        if(theToken != nil && theToken.length > 0)
                [settings addHeader:theToken forName:@"x-amx-token"];

        // return...
        return settings;
}
```

Run the project now, and you can test the logon operation. Remember that this is testing the *API* logon, not the users logon. Provided your APIUSERAME and APIPASSWORD constant values are valid, anything you enter into the textboxes will yield a successful result. Figure 9-15 shows an example successful result.

Now that we can call the API service, we can look at calling the Users service. Although we did a ton of work there, calling the other services will now be much easier, as we have a lot of framework code that we can reuse.

Figure 9-15. *The logon form reporting that logging on was OK.*

Calling the Users Service

So far, we've made a manual call to the API service and managed to authenticate against the API. In the Android chapter (and the other platform implementations that you can find on the web site), we did this via a method called EnsureApiAuthenticated that would look at the stored global token and decide whether to authenticate the API. When we come to implement the Users service, we need to do the same thing, but it's going to be a little less different because of the limitations of the Objective-C language.

EnsureApiAuthenticated in the other applications provides a mechanism whereby each service can defer to a base class to make sure the prerequisites to the call are set up correctly. What we're going to do on iPhone is simplify this and make SBUsersService understand how to call SBApiService if it needs to—i.e., make it explicit rather than a "magic" feature of the base class.

The first thing we need to do is change the SBOpCodes enumeration to include OPCODE_USERSLOGON. Here's the modification to the enumeration:

```
// Modify enumeration in SBServiceProxy.h…
typedef enum
{
        OPCODE_APILOGON = 1000,
        OPCODE_USERSLOGON = 2000

} SBOpCodes;
```

281

The next thing to look at is the SBUsersService class. Recall that on the SBApiService class we held a reference to the callback. On SBUsersService we need to hold the callback and the username and password that we want to log on. This is because we're going to run in one of two modes. If the API is authenticated, we will immediately call try and logon. If the API is not authenticated, we need to defer to SBApiService to log it in and once successful, call the Users service. We need to cache the parameters to the Users service in memory while we wait for the API to complete authentication. Here's the definition for SBUsersService:

```
// SBUsersService.h
#import <Foundation/Foundation.h>
#import "SBRestServiceProxy.h"

@class SBLogonCallback;

@interface SBUsersService : SBRestServiceProxy
{
        SBLogonCallback *callback;
        NSString *username;
        NSString *password;
}

@property (nonatomic, retain) SBLogonCallback *callback;
@property (nonatomic, retain) NSString *username;
@property (nonatomic, retain) NSString *password;

-(void)logon:(NSString *)username password:(NSString *)thePassword callback:↵
(SBLogonCallback *)theCallback;
-(void)doLogon;

@end
```

We'll sketch in the simple bits of SBUsersService first—here's the listing:

```
// SBUsersService.m
#import "SBUsersService.h"
#import "MyClasses.h"

@implementation SBUsersService

@synthesize callback;
@synthesize username;
@synthesize password;

-(id)init
{
        return [super initWithServiceName:@"usersrest.aspx"];
}
```

```
-(void)dealloc
{
        [username release];
        [password release];
        [callback release];
        [super dealloc];
}
```

@end

To recap, on SBUsersService, we need to do the following:

- Implement the logon method that will cache the callback, username, and password and either immediately call doLogon, or authenticate the API via SBApiService.

- Implement doLogon to physically make the logon request.

- Implement the SBLogonCallback interface so that the API service can tell us whether we worked.

- Implement processResult to look at the XML coming from the Users service and decide whether the logon worked.

- Call the original callback (i.e., the one issued by the user interface) to say whether we worked.

Taking that in order, here's the implementation of logon:

```
// Add method to SBUsersService.m
-(void)logon:(NSString *)theUsername password:(NSString *)thePassword↵
 callback:(SBLogonCallback *)theCallback
{
        // store...
        self.callback = theCallback;
        self.username = theUsername;
        self.password = thePassword;

        // do we need to logon to the API?
        if([SBServiceProxy hasToken])
                [self doLogon];
        else
        {
                // authenticate the API first...
                SBApiService *api = [[SBApiService alloc] init];
                [api logon:(NSString *)APIPASSWORD callback:(SBLogonCallback *)self];
                [api release];
        }
}
```

The logonOk and logonFailed methods on *this* class are callbacks from the SBApiService call and hence will be invoked only if we need to authenticate the API. If the logon is OK, we run doLogon. If the logon fails, we call the `logonFailed` method on the callback that we were given (i.e., the one provided by the user interface), passing in the same error. Here's the listing:

```
// Add methods to SBUsersService.m…
-(void)logonOk
{
        // we did it - our original logon method will now work...
        [self doLogon];
}

-(void)logonFailed:(NSError *)theError
{
        [self.callback logonFailed:theError];
}
```

Next, the doLogon method itself looks and behaves like the API's logon method. The only concrete difference is that we pass in different arguments because the Users service logon method needs a username and password. Here's the listing:

```
// Add method to SBUsersService.m
-(void)doLogon
{
        // settings...
        SBDownloadSettings *settings = [self getDownloadSettings];

        // create some args...
        SBRestRequestArgs *args = [[SBRestRequestArgs alloc] initWithOperation:@"logon"];
        [args setValue:self.username forKey:@"username"];
        [args setValue:self.password forKey:@"password"];

        // download...
        [self makeRequest:args opCode:OPCODE_USERSLOGON];

        // cleanup...
        [args release];
        [settings release];
}
```

Finally, we need to implement processResult, requestOk, and requestFailed. These work in essentially the same way as the ones that we implemented previously on SBApiService.

```
// Add methods to SBUsersService.m…
-(NSError *)processResult:(SBFlatXmlBucket *)values opCode:(int)theOpCode
{
        // what happened?
        NSString *result = [values getStringValue:@"Result"];
        if([result isEqualToString:@"LogonOk"])
        {
```

```
                // ok...
                return nil;
        }
        else
                return [SBErrorHelper error:self message:[NSString stringWithFormat:↵
@"An error occurred on logon: '%@'.", result]];
}

-(void)requestOk:(int)theOpCode
{
        if(theOpCode == OPCODE_USERSLOGON)
                [callback logonOk];
        else
                [NSException exceptionWithName:[[self class] description] reason:↵
[NSString stringWithFormat:@"Cannot handle '%d'.", theOpCode] userInfo:nil];
}

-(void)requestFailed:(int)theOpCode error:(NSError *)theError
{
        if(theOpCode == OPCODE_USERSLOGON)
                [callback logonFailed:theError];
        else
                [NSException exceptionWithName:[[self class] description] reason:↵
[NSString stringWithFormat:@"Cannot handle '%d'.", theOpCode] userInfo:nil];
}
```

That is everything that we need to do to get the logon method on the Users service working—it really is much easier once the groundwork has been done for calling the services.

Before running the application, we need to make a small tweak to the handleLogonClick method on SBLogonView to change it to call the Users service rather than the API service. Here's the listing:

```
// Change method in SBLogonView.m...
-(IBAction)handleLogonClick:(id)sender
{
        // get the values...
        NSString *username = self.textUsername.text;
        NSString *password = self.textPassword.text;

        // valdiate...
        SBErrorBucket *bucket = [[SBErrorBucket alloc] init];
        if(username == nil || username.length == 0)
                [bucket addError:@"Username is required"];
        if(password == nil || password.length == 0)
                [bucket addError:@"Password is required"];
```

```
        // now what?
        if(!(bucket.hasErrors))
        {
                // we'll do the logon operation in here...
                SBUsersService *users = [[SBUsersService alloc] init];
                [users logon:username password:password callback:(SBLogonCallback *)self];
                [users release];
        }
        else

                [SBMessageBox show:bucket.errorsAsString];

        // cleanup...
        [bucket release];
}
```

You can now run the project and try to log on. Figure 9-16 shows a successful result, and Figure 9-17 shows a result when invalid information is passed.

Figure 9-16. *Another successful logon, but this time we have authenticated to both the API service and the Users service.*

Figure 9-17. *The logon form reporting an error returned by the Users service.*

Notifying That Work Is in Progress

The final thing we'll do in this chapter is have a look at tweaking the user interface. You may have seen that when you click the logon button, the application appears to do nothing—we need to give the user some feedback to say that something is happening.

The standard way to do this on an iPhone is to display a spinning wheel on the status bar. In Objective-C, there is a singleton instance of type UIApplication that provides access to global application-level bits and pieces. One of these is a property called networkActivityIndicatorVisible. In the first instance, we'll show this whenever we process a REST request.

We'll add startSpinning and stopSpinning methods to the SBServiceProxy class. We'll need to access these later on from another class, so we'll make them static. Here's the implementation:

```
// Add to SBServiceProxy.m
// <…> Needs declaration in header
+(void)startSpinning
{
        // start spinning...
        [UIApplication sharedApplication].networkActivityIndicatorVisible = TRUE;
}

// <…> Needs declaration in header
+(void)stopSpinning
{
        // stop spinning...
        [UIApplication sharedApplication].networkActivityIndicatorVisible = FALSE;
}
```

We'll then call these two methods from within the SBRestServiceProxy base class. We'll call the start method when we receive a call to makeRequest, and we'll call the stop method in downloadComplete.

Here's the modification to the makeRequest method:

```
// Modify method in SBRestServiceProxy.m…
-(void)makeRequest:(SBRestRequestArgs *)args opCode:(int)theOpCode
{
        // get the url...
        NSString *url = [SBHttpHelper buildUrl:[self resolvedServiceUrl] args:[args args]];

        // download...
        SBDownloadSettings *settings = [self getDownloadSettings];
        [SBHttpHelper download:url settings:settings callback:(SBDownloadCallback *)self⏎
 opCode:theOpCode];

        // start the wheel spinning...
        [SBServiceProxy startSpinning];
}
```

And here's the modification to the downloadComplete method. I've removed some of the code for brevity:

```
// Modify method in in SBRestServiceProxy.m-(void)downloadComplete:(SBDownloadBucket *)bucket
{
        // did we get a 200?
        NSError *err = nil;
        if(bucket.statusCode == 200)
        {
                // code removed for brevity…
        }
        else
                err = [SBErrorHelper error:self message:[NSString stringWithFormat:↵
@"The server returned HTTP '%d'.", bucket.statusCode]];

        // stop  the wheel spinning...
        [SBServiceProxy stopSpinning];

        // done that bit - now send a notification...
        if(err == nil)
                [self requestOk:bucket.opCode];
        else
                [self requestFailed:bucket.opCode error:err];
}
```

Figure 9-18 shows the results of adding the spinning wheel.

Figure 9-18. *The spinning wheel on the status bar shows that network activity is taking place.*

Conclusion

In this chapter, we have started looking at the first real code for our Six Bookmarks application on iPhone. The lack of features with the language has made some of this less elegant than on other platforms; however, it's important to realize that the application itself is as functional as the other applications despite this. We looked at how to issue HTTP requests and how to process returned data, including parsing the XML via a forward-reading XML parser. In the next chapter, we'll look at using the SQLite implementation on iPhone to store a local copy of the bookmarks.

CHAPTER 10

iOS: An ORM Layer on SQLite

In this chapter, we're going to look at downloading the bookmarks from the server and storing them in the database. iOS comes with a copy of the SQLite database as standard, and so we'll use this as our storage mechanism.

NOTE iOS comes with an object-persistence mechanism called Core Data. We won't be using this in this chapter, mostly because the implementation of the other platforms is based on a relational database, but also because of personal preference.

In the last two chapters, we've been working with Objective-C and Cocoa Touch features, which, as you know, are implemented as class libraries. SQLite is implemented using a flat C API, which means we need to take a slightly different approach. Those of you who are familiar with C/C++ won't see anything odd here at all—in fact, when I use it I get quite nostalgic! However, I will go through the calling conventions of this different style of API in case it's new to you.

We'll structure this chapter in a similar way to the Android chapter—we'll have a look at building an object-relational mapping (ORM) layer on SQLite and then connect to the Bookmarks OData service to retrieve a list of bookmarks for local caching. We'll build a UI that reflects against that local cache for presentation. We'll look at how to post changes back to the server in the next section.

A Note About Content That Has Already Been Covered

One of the challenges with this book is knowing how much content to repeat from previous chapters. On the one hand, you have readers who will go through the book from start to finish and will have pre-knowledge of—in this case—how we did this on Android. On the other hand, you have people who will dip into areas that are of particular interest. In the last chapter, the difference in the code between Android and iPhone was so large this didn't come up; however, in this chapter, the work is very similar.

What I shall try to do with this chapter is form a happy balance between the two.

Entities

In Chapter 3, we discussed some of the building blocks of object-relational mapping (ORM) systems based on my preferred way of building such things. To me, one of the most important things about ORM is creating a strong metadata system—i.e., a set of classes that allow the application to have access to a great deal of knowledge about what the underlying store looks like. That knowledge makes it easier to write "magic" code, i.e., code that's able to adapt its behavior depending on the known metadata.

In this section, we're going to look at building the entity metadata subsystem, and implementing the base entity. The base currency of the metadata system will be a class called SBEntityType. Similarly, the base currency of the actual entities that store data will be called SBEntity. We'll look at SBEntityType first.

The SBEntityType Class

The SBEntityType class has two functions. In the first instance, it will store information about the base database class, and in the second instance, it will maintain a list of all available entity types on the system in static memory. In particular, SBEntityType will store a list of fields against each type by maintaining a list of SBEntityField instances.

To build SBEntityType and SBEntityField, we'll create a base class called SBEntityItem. Each item in our metadata system will maintain two names—the "programmatic name" will be how we want to refer to the item in code. The "native name" will be what the name of the item actually is in the underlying store. Although we won't get much mileage out of this approach here, it pays dividends when you have a situation where you want to fix problems with naming in the underlying store. For example, you may have a table called TBL_CUST that you want to call Customer in code.

SBEntityItem will maintain these two values and implement a constructor that allows them to be set of instantiation. Here is the definition:

```
// SBEntityItem.h
#import <Foundation/Foundation.h>
#import "SBEntityType.h"
#import "SBEntitySetReason.h"
#import "SBEntityFieldFlags.h"

@interface SBEntityItem : NSObject {

        NSString *name;
        NSString *nativeName;

}

@property (nonatomic, retain) NSString *name;
@property (nonatomic, retain) NSString *nativeName;

-(id)initWithNameAndNativeName:(NSString *)theName nativeName:(NSString *)theNativeName;

@end
```

The implementation looks like this:

```
// SBEntityItem.m
#import "SBEntityItem.h"
```

```objc
@implementation SBEntityItem

@synthesize name;
@synthesize nativeName;

-(id)initWithNameAndNativeName:(NSString *)theName nativeName:(NSString *)theNativeName
{
        if(self = [super init])
        {
                [self setName:theName];
                [self setNativeName:theNativeName];
        }

        // return...
        return self;
}

-(void)dealloc
{
        [name release];
        [nativeName release];
        [super dealloc];
}

@end
```

We'll look at the fields first. Each field will store the following information:

- A native name and programmatic name

- A data type

- A size

- In this chapter we're going to have only one, which indicates whether the field is a key field. In a full-on implementation, another example of a flag would be indicating whether the field could be nullable.

In this example, we're going to support just two data types—in a more full-on implementation, we'd obviously need to support all of the data types that the underlying database supports. (If we implement all of them now, half the book will be taken up with methods exposing out all of the data types.) Our server-side service used only strings and 32-bit integers, so these are the two that we will use.

▓**NOTE** We will use Boolean data types on the entity, but we'll store these as integers in the SQLite database. SQLite's data type support is a little strange—you can store any value in any column in SQLite regardless of the definition, and it just tries to "work it out" when it retrieves data. For this and other reasons, we're going to handle Boolean data in our data access layer rather than natively in SQLite.

Here's the SBDataType enumeration that we need to support those two types. (You don't need to add a class for this item—instead you should create a single header file called SBDataType.h.)

```
// SBDataType.h
typedef enum
{
        SBDT_STRING = 0,
        SBDT_INT32 = 1

} SBDataType;
```

Now that we have the enumeration, we can build EntityField. As well as supporting native name, name, data type, size, and an indication as to whether the field is a key, we'll have another property holding the ordinal of the field within the type. Here's the definition:

```
// SBEntityField.h
#import <Foundation/Foundation.h>
#import "SBDataType.h"
#import "SBEntityItem.h"

@interface SBEntityField : SBEntityItem {

        SBDataType type;
        int size;
        BOOL isKey;
        BOOL isOnServer;
        int ordinal;

}

@property (assign) SBDataType type;
@property (assign) int size;
@property (assign) BOOL isKey;
@property (assign) BOOL isOnServer;
@property (assign) int ordinal;

-(id)initWithDetails:(NSString *)theName nativeName:(NSString *)theNativeName↵
 type:(SBDataType)theType size:(int)theSize ordinal:(int)theOrdinal;

@end
```

Notice that because all of the properties are primitive types, the assign keyword has been used on the properties, as no memory management is required.

The implementation of SBEntityField is easy enough. Here it is:

```
// SBEntityField.m
#import "SBEntityField.h"

@implementation SBEntityField

@synthesize type;
@synthesize size;
@synthesize ordinal;
@synthesize isKey;
@synthesize isOnServer;

-(id)initWithDetails:(NSString *)theName nativeName:(NSString *)theNativeName↩
type:(SBDataType)theType size:(int)theSize ordinal:(int)theOrdinal
{
        if(self = [super initWithNameAndNativeName:theName nativeName:theNativeName])
        {
                [self setType:theType];
                [self setSize:theSize];
                [self setOrdinal:theOrdinal];
                self.isOnServer = TRUE;
        }

        // return...
        return self;
}

@end
```

SBEntityType is going to have a reasonable number of methods on it. We'll add them in chunks to make the discourse easier to follow.

So that we can effectively work with entities, we need SBEntityType to be able to instantiate instances of individual entities and collections of entities. In this example, we're going to have only one entity—SBBookmark. In any real world application, you're likely to have many entitity types. This will be done by holding references to the relevant Objective-C types. Our motivation for doing this is that we can say to framework code "give me a list of bookmarks," and the framework code itself will be able to create an appropriate collection type and individual entities.

In addition, we're going to add a method to SBEntityType called addField. This will be used to programmatically define the fields available on an entity type. Here's the definition of SBEntityType:

```
// SBEntityType.h
#import <Foundation/Foundation.h>
#import "SBEntityItem.h"
#import "SBEntityField.h"

@class SBEntity;
```

```
@interface SBEntityType : SBEntityItem {
        Class instanceType;
        NSMutableArray *fields;
}

@property (assign) Class instanceType;
@property (nonatomic, retain) NSMutableArray *fields;

-(id)initWithInstanceTypeNativeName:(Class)theInstanceType nativeName:(NSString↵
*)theNativeName;

-(SBEntityField *)addField:(NSString *)name nativeName:(NSString *)theNativeName↵
type:(SBDataType)theType size:(int)theSize;

-(SBEntity *)createInstance;

@end
```

That listing has a forward reference to a class called SBEntity. This is a class that's used to represent individual database objects. We'll get to this shortly.

Here's the implementation of the methods that we just declared on SBEntityType:

```
// SBEntityType.m
#import "SBEntityType.h"
#import "MyClasses.h"

@implementation SBEntityType

@synthesize instanceType;
@synthesize fields;

-(id)initWithInstanceTypeNativeName:(Class)theInstanceType nativeName:↵
(NSString *)theNativeName;
{
        if(self = [super initWithNameAndNativeName:[theInstanceType description]↵
nativeName:theNativeName])
        {
                // set...
                [self setInstanceType:theInstanceType];
                [self setFields:[NSMutableArray array]];
        }

        // return...
        return self;
}
```

```
-(SBEntityField *)addField:(NSString *)theName nativeName:↵
(NSString *)theNativeName type:(SBDataType)theType size:(int)theSize
{
        // create a field...
        SBEntityField *field = [[SBEntityField alloc]initWithDetails:theName↵
nativeName:theNativeName type:theType size:theSize ordinal:[fields count]];

        // store it...
        [fields addObject:field];

        // return it...
        return field;
}

-(SBEntity *)createInstance
{
        // create it using a generic method and then manually call init...
        SBEntity *newEntity = (SBEntity *)class_createInstance(self.instanceType);
        [newEntity init];

        // return...
        return newEntity;
}

-(void)dealloc
{
        [instanceType release];
        [fields release];
        [super dealloc];
}

@end
```

An important part of the code there is that when we add a field using the addField method, we need to assign each field a unique ordinal. By passing in the length of the array as the ordinal, we effectively do that.

Next we can look some of the other methods on SBEntityType. We're going to need to be able to find a field with a specific name, find the key fields, or determine whether a field with a specified name actually exists. (This latter one is used for populating entities from data received over XML where the XML may reference fields that we don't know about.) Here are the three methods that also need to be added to SBEntityType:

```
// Add methods to SBEntityType.m…
// <…> Needs declaration in header
-(SBEntityField *)getField:(NSString *)theName
{
        for(SBEntityField *field in [self fields])
```

```objc
        {
                NSComparisonResult result = [[field name] compare:theName↵
        options:NSCaseInsensitiveSearch];
                if(result == NSOrderedSame)
                        return field;
        }

        // nope...
        @throw [NSException exceptionWithName:[[self class] description] reason:[NSString↵
stringWithFormat:@"A field with name '%@' was not found on '%@'.", theName, [self name]]↵
userInfo:nil];
}

// <...> Needs declaration in header
-(SBEntityField *)getKeyField
{
        for(SBEntityField *field in [self fields])
        {
                if([field isKey])
                        return field;
        }

        // nope...
        @throw [NSException exceptionWithName:[[self class] description] reason:↵
[NSString stringWithFormat:@"A key field was not found on '%@'.", [self name]]↵
userInfo:nil];
}

// <...> Needs declaration in header
-(BOOL)isField:(NSString *)theName
{
        for(SBEntityField *field in [self fields])
        {
                NSComparisonResult result = [[field name] compare:theName↵
options:NSCaseInsensitiveSearch];
                if(result == NSOrderedSame)
                        return TRUE;
        }

        // nope...
        return FALSE;
}
```

One wrinkle is that we have to use the `compare` method on `NSString` when we're matching the name of the field. This will return a result from the `NSComparisonResult` enumeration. In this case, we want to look for `NSOrderedSame`.

Recall that the other function `SBEntityType` needs is the ability to hold a register of the available entity types. We'll do this by creating a static hashtable on `SBEntityType` and methods called `registerEntityType` and `getEntityType`.

This is a little tricky because we need to add some static methods, and so I'll call out the definition again (with code omitted). Here's the definition of `SBEntityType`:

```
// Add methods to SBEntityType.h…
#import <Foundation/Foundation.h>
#import "SBEntityItem.h"
#import "SBEntityField.h"

@class SBEntity;

@interface SBEntityType : SBEntityItem {
        Class instanceType;
        NSMutableArray *fields;
}

@property (assign) Class instanceType;
@property (nonatomic, retain) NSMutableArray *fields;

+(NSMutableDictionary *)entityTypes;

// code ommitted for brevity…

+(void)registerEntityType:(SBEntityType *)et;
+(SBEntityType *)getEntityType:(Class)theClass;

@end
```

The implementation looks like this:

```
// Add static field and methods to SBEntityType.m…
static NSMutableDictionary *theEntityTypes = nil;

+(NSMutableDictionary *)entityTypes
{
        if(theEntityTypes == nil)
                theEntityTypes = [[NSMutableDictionary dictionary] retain];
        return theEntityTypes;
}
```

```
+(void)registerEntityType:(SBEntityType *)et
{
        [[self entityTypes] setValue:et forKey:[[et instanceType] description]];
}

+(SBEntityType *)getEntityType:(Class)theClass
{
        SBEntityType *et = [[self entityTypes] objectForKey:[theClass description]];
        if(et != nil)
                return et;
        else
                @throw [NSException exceptionWithName:[[SBEntityType class] description]↵
reason:[NSString stringWithFormat:@"Failed to get entity type for '%@'.", [theClass↵
description]] userInfo:nil];
}
```

We can now use this class to create and store entity types. Let's look now at building the SBEntity base class.

The SBEntity Class

The basic functionality of an entity is to store a dynamic list of data that represents the columns in the underlying database table. An entity will be created either manually by the developer or by framework code that retrieves the data from some source. (In our application, the source of data is going to be either the local SQLite database or the Bookmarks data service at http://services.multimobiledevelopment.com/.) At some point during the entity's life, the data stored within will either be read for display on a screen, or be used to issue some sort of change requests to the underlying store.

In our entity, we are going to hold three sets of values. First, we're going to store a reference to our related EntityType instance. Second, we're going to store an array of values that map 1:1 with the data in the underlying store. Third and finally, we're going to store a bunch of flags that help the entity keep track of its internal state.

Storage of data within the entity will be done in "slots." You will notice on our EntityField instance, we have a property called Ordinal. This ordinal value is the index of the slot in the entity. Thus if we have five fields, we'll have five slots numbered from zero to four inclusive.

■**NOTE** Recall in Chapter 3, we spoke about the BootFX application framework and its ORM functionality. Internally within BootFX, this functionality is known as "storage."

To manage the lifetimes of values stored within the new SBEntity class, we need to create an enumeration that indicates the status of the slots. We'll call this enumeration SBEntityFieldFlags, and it needs to be defined prior to building SBEntity. Here's the listing:

```
// SBEntityFieldFlags.h
typedef enum
{
        SBEFFNone = 0,
        SBEFFLoaded = 1,
        SBEFFModified = 2

} SBEntityFieldFlags;
```

Next we'll look at the definition for the basic "storage" capability of SBEntity. Here's the listing:

```
// SBEntity.h
#import <Foundation/Foundation.h>

@interface SBEntity : NSObject {
        SBEntityType *entityType;
        NSMutableArray *values;
        NSMutableArray *flags;
}

@property (nonatomic, retain) SBEntityType *entityType;
@property (nonatomic, retain) NSMutableArray *values;
@property (nonatomic, retain) NSMutableArray *flags;

@end
```

The implementation for those methods looks like this:

```
// SBEntity.h
#import "SBEntity.h"
#import "MyClasses.h"

@implementation SBEntity

@synthesize entityType;
@synthesize values;
@synthesize flags;

static NSObject *theNullValue;
```

```objc
+(NSObject *)nullValue
{
        if(theNullValue == nil)
        {
                theNullValue = [NSObject alloc];
                [theNullValue retain];
        }
        return theNullValue;
}

-(id)init
{
        if(self = [super init])
        {
                // get...
                SBEntityType *et = [SBEntityType getEntityType:self.class];
                self.entityType = et;

                // setup...
                NSMutableArray *theValues = [NSMutableArray array];
                NSMutableArray *theFlags = [NSMutableArray array];
                for(int index = 0; index < entityType.fields.count; index++)
                {
                        [theValues addObject:[SBEntity nullValue]];
                        [theFlags addObject:[NSNumber numberWithInt:SBEFFNone]];
                }

                // set...
                self.values = theValues;
                self.flags = theFlags;
        }

        // return...
        return self;
}

-(void)dealloc
{
        [entityType release];
        [values release];
        [flags release];
        [super dealloc];
}

@end
```

The operation of note there is the constructor. The first thing we do is capture the entity type. We'll need this later so that methods on the base class can reflect against the metadata. The second thing that we do is create two arrays—one to hold the values of the slots, the other to hold the flags. The value has an interesting wrinkle in that we set it to be equal to [SBEntity nullValue]. What we've done here is create a static property on SBEntity called nullValue that returns back a singleton instance of NSObject. We're using this object to represent database null. (For those of you familiar with .NET, what I've done here is analogous to System.DBNull.Value.) I've done this because adding nil to arrays and working with them can get a little non-obvious. This explicit method makes it easier to keep track of what is happening.

Setting Values in an Entity

Whenever we set a value within an entity, we'll be doing one of two things—either we'll be plugging in a value that the user has provided through some form of input, or we'll be plugging in a value that we have retrieved from a database or service. It's important that we can distinguish between these two operations—if the user has changed something, we may need to update the underlying store with that value. Conversely, if the user has not changed something, we do not want to be issuing unnecessary update requests back to the underlying store.

To keep track of which operation we intend when we set a value, we'll create an enumeration called SBEntitySetReason. Here's the listing:

```
// SBEntitySetReason.h
typedef enum
{
        SBESRUserSet = 0,
        SBESRLoad = 1

} SBEntitySetReason;
```

As we add methods to the entity, we'll find that oftentimes we need to add overloads for each of the methods that take either the name of a field as a string or an actual instance of an SBEntityField. This is going to create additional code, but there is a substantially higher level of utility in not requiring the caller to dig out an SBEntityField instance every time he or she wishes to access field data. Whenever one of the string-based "name" overloads is used, we'll defer to the SBEntityType for the field name. Here's a collection of methods that allow values to be set:

```
// Add methods to SBEntity.m
// <...> Needs declaration in header
-(void)setValueByName:(NSString *)name value:(NSObject *)theValue↵
 reason:(SBEntitySetReason)theReason
{
        SBEntityField *field = [self.entityType getField:name];
        [self setValue:field value:theValue reason:theReason];
}
```

```
// <…> Needs declaration in header
-(void)setValue:(SBEntityField *)field value:(NSObject *)theValue↵
 reason:(SBEntitySetReason)theReason
{
        [self.values replaceObjectAtIndex:field.ordinal withObject:theValue];

        // flag...
        [self setFieldFlags:field flags:SBEFFLoaded setOn:TRUE];
        if(theReason == SBESRUserSet)
                [self setFieldFlags:field flags:SBEFFModified setOn:TRUE];
}

// <…> Needs declaration in header
-(void)setFieldFlags:(SBEntityField *)field flags:(SBEntityFieldFlags)theFlags↵
setOn:(BOOL)doSetOn
{
        // get...
        int existing = [(NSNumber *)[self.flags objectAtIndex:field.ordinal] intValue];
        existing |= theFlags;
        if(!(doSetOn))
                existing ^= theFlags;

        // set...
        [self.flags replaceObjectAtIndex:field.ordinal withObject:[NSNumber↵
numberWithInt:existing]];
}
```

The function of setValueByName is to grab a real SBEntityField instance and defer to setValue. The function of setValue is twofold. First, it sets the value in the values array to be the value passed in. Second, it sets the value in the flags to indicate the state of the field. Regardless of the value of the reason parameter, it will indicate that the field has been loaded. If the value of reason indicates that the user changed a value, the field is marked as having been modified.

Retrieving the values is—oddly—a little trickier. In the first instance, we need to be able to behave differently depending on the state of the data. For example, if we're trying to retrieve the value for a field and we have not loaded it, we need to throw an error indicating that the value is not available. (Some implementations, including BootFX, will demand load data in this situation. However, for simplicity, we're not doing this here.)

Before we do that, we'll add a few methods that will help us understand whether fields have been loaded or modified. We'll need these later on. Here's the implementation:

```
// Add methods to SBEntity.m
// <…> Needs declaration in header
-(BOOL)isFieldLoaded:(SBEntityField *)field
{
        return [self getFieldFlags:field flags:SBEFFLoaded];
}
```

```
// <...> Needs declaration in header
-(BOOL)isFieldModified:(SBEntityField *)field
{
        return [self getFieldFlags:field flags:SBEFFModified];
}

// <...> Needs declaration in header
-(BOOL)getFieldFlags:(SBEntityField *)field flags:(SBEntityFieldFlags)theFlags
{
        int existing = [(NSNumber *)[self.flags objectAtIndex:field.ordinal] intValue];
        if((int)(existing & theFlags) != 0)
                return TRUE;
        else
                return FALSE;
}
```

The next few methods help us to tell whether the entity is new or has been modified. The rules here are that in order to tell if the entity is new, if we have a key value, it's not new. Also, if we have modified any field, the whole entity has been modified. Here's the implementation:

```
// Add methods to SBEntity.m
// <...> Needs declaration in header
-(BOOL)isNew
{
        SBEntityField *keyField = [entityType getKeyField];

        // if...
        if([self getFieldFlags:keyField flags:SBEFFLoaded])
                return FALSE;
        else
                return TRUE;
}

// <...> Needs declaration in header
-(BOOL)isModified
{
        for(SBEntityField *field in [entityType fields])
        {
                if([self isFieldModified:field])
                        return TRUE;
        }

        // nope...
        return FALSE;
}
```

```
// <...> Needs declaration in header
-(BOOL)isDeleted
{
    // just say "no" for now - we'll sort this later...
        return FALSE;
}
```

We'll implement the isDeleted property when we come to change our bookmarks in the next chapter.

Those methods lay the groundwork for the getValue and getValueByName methods that we implied must exist when we created our setValue and setValueByName methods earlier. One implementation point is that we have to add a rule whereby if we're not new and we don't have it, we have to throw an error, as we can't demand-load the value. This is called "demand loading." It's common enough in ORM tools, but to keep things simple, I have chosen not to implement it here.

We've touched a few times on this idea that we have deliberately limited data type support in this application to keep the code simple. We're about to see an example—there's quite a lot of code here to support just the few data types that we do support.

One thing of note in these "get value" methods is that we have handling there to deal with the "database null" values. We have to be quite careful of this in Objective-C, as the coercion capability in the language is quite limited. Here's the implementation:

```
// Add methods to SBEntity.m...
// <...> Needs declaration in header
-(NSObject *)getValue:(SBEntityField *)field
{
        return [self.values objectAtIndex:field.ordinal];
}


// <...> Needs declaration in header
-(NSObject *)getValueByName:(NSString *)name
{
        SBEntityField *field = [self.entityType getField:name];
        return [self getValue:field];
}


// <...> Needs declaration in header
-(int)getInt32Value:(SBEntityField *)field
{
        NSObject *obj = [self.values objectAtIndex:field.ordinal];
        if(obj == nil || obj == [SBEntity nullValue])
                return 0;
        else if([obj isKindOfClass:[NSNumber class]])
        {
                NSNumber *num = (NSNumber *)obj;
                return [num intValue];
        }
```

```objc
        else
                @throw [NSException exceptionWithName:[[self class] description]↵
reason:[NSString stringWithFormat:@"An instance of '%@' could not be converted to↵
a Boolean value.", [[obj class] description]] userInfo:nil];
}

// <...> Needs declaration in header
-(int)getInt32ValueByName:(NSString *)name
{
        SBEntityField *field = [self.entityType getField:name];
        return [self getInt32Value:field];
}

// <...> Needs declaration in header
-(BOOL)getBooleanValue:(SBEntityField *)field
{
        NSObject *obj = [self.values objectAtIndex:field.ordinal];
        if(obj == nil || obj == [SBEntity nullValue])
                return FALSE;
        else if([obj isKindOfClass:[NSNumber class]])
        {
                NSNumber *num = (NSNumber *)obj;
                return [num boolValue];
        }
        else
                @throw [NSException exceptionWithName:[[self class] description]↵
reason:[NSString stringWithFormat:@"An instance of '%@' could not be converted to↵
a Boolean value.", [[obj class] description]] userInfo:nil];
}

// <...> Needs declaration in header
-(BOOL)getBooleanValueByName:(NSString *)name
{
        SBEntityField *field = [self.entityType getField:name];
        return [self getBooleanValue:field];
}

// <...> Needs declaration in header
-(NSString *)getStringValue:(SBEntityField *)field
{
        NSObject *obj = [self.values objectAtIndex:field.ordinal];
        if(obj == nil || obj == [SBEntity nullValue])
                return nil;
```

```
        else if([obj isKindOfClass:[NSString class]])
        {
                NSString *buf = (NSString *)obj;
                return buf;
        }
        else

                @throw [NSException exceptionWithName:[[self class] description]↩
reason:[NSString stringWithFormat:@"An instance of '%@' could not be converted to↩
a Boolean value.", [[obj class] description]] userInfo:nil];
}

// <…> Needs declaration in header
-(NSString *)getStringValueByName:(NSString *)name
{
        SBEntityField *field = [self.entityType getField:name];
        return [self getStringValue:field];
}
```

Now that we can get data into and out of our base entity, let's look at creating a strongly typed SBBookmark class.

Building SBBookmark

The point of ORM is that you're looking to get the entity layer to do most of the hard work of managing the data for you—e.g., it's easier to call a property called name and know you're getting a string value back, than it is to request an item with name "name" out of a bucket of values returned over a SQL interface. Thus we need to add a bunch of properties to SBBookmark that abstract calls to getValue and setValue.

Before we do that, though, there's one thing to consider. As discussed in Chapter 2, the database stores against each bookmark an internal ID, the user ID, the name, the URL, and ordinal values. In our database, in order to support the synchronization functionality that we'll build in the next chapter, we also need to store flags to indicate whether the item has been modified or deleted locally. We'll add localModified and localDeleted to achieve this.

Here's the definition of SBBookmark.

```
// SBBookmark.h
#import <Foundation/Foundation.h>
#import "SBEntity.h"

extern NSString * const BOOKMARK_IDKEY;
extern NSString * const BOOKMARK_ORDINALKEY;
extern NSString * const BOOKMARK_NAMEKEY;
extern NSString * const BOOKMARK_URLKEY;
extern NSString * const BOOKMARK_LOCALMODIFIEDKEY;
extern NSString * const BOOKMARK_LOCALDELETEDKEY;
```

```
@interface SBBookmark : SBEntity {

}

-(int)bookmarkId;
-(void)setBookmarkId:(int)theBookmarkId;

-(int)ordinal;
-(void)setOrdinal:(int)theOrdinal;

-(NSString *)name;
-(void)setName:(NSString *)theName;

-(NSString *)url;
-(void)setUrl:(NSString *)theUrl;

-(BOOL)localModified;
-(void)setLocalModified:(BOOL)theLocalModified;

-(BOOL)localDeleted;
-(void)setLocalDeleted:(BOOL)theLocalDeleted;

@end
```

Note how on that class there are no properties in their own rights. What we've done is build methods that look like getters and setters but which will, in fact, defer to the methods on SBEntity that we built earlier. Another point of note is the constants that we have declared—we'll give these real values when we come to build the implementation.

Here's the implementation of SBEntity:

```
#import "SBBookmark.h"
#import "MyClasses.h"

@implementation SBBookmark

NSString *const BOOKMARK_IDKEY = @"BookmarkId";
NSString *const BOOKMARK_ORDINALKEY = @"Ordinal";
NSString *const BOOKMARK_NAMEKEY = @"Name";
NSString *const BOOKMARK_URLKEY = @"Url";
NSString *const BOOKMARK_LOCALMODIFIEDKEY = @"LocalModified";
NSString *const BOOKMARK_LOCALDELETEDKEY = @"LocalDeleted";

-(int)bookmarkId
{
        return [self getInt32ValueByName:BOOKMARK_IDKEY];
}
```

```objc
-(void)setBookmarkId:(int)theBookmarkId
{
        [self setValueByName:BOOKMARK_IDKEY value:[NSNumber numberWithInt:theBookmarkId]↵
reason:SBESRUserSet];
}

-(int)ordinal
{
        return [self getInt32ValueByName:BOOKMARK_ORDINALKEY];
}

-(void)setOrdinal:(int)theOrdinal
{
        [self setValueByName:BOOKMARK_ORDINALKEY value:[NSNumber numberWithInt:theOrdinal]↵
reason:SBESRUserSet];
}

-(NSString *)name
{
        return [self getStringValueByName:BOOKMARK_NAMEKEY];
}

-(void)setName:(NSString *)theName
{
        [self setValueByName:BOOKMARK_NAMEKEY value:theName reason:SBESRUserSet];
}

-(NSString *)url
{
        return [self getStringValueByName:BOOKMARK_URLKEY];
}

-(void)setUrl:(NSString *)theUrl
{
        [self setValueByName:BOOKMARK_URLKEY value:theUrl reason:SBESRUserSet];
}

-(BOOL)localModified
{
        return [self getBooleanValueByName:BOOKMARK_LOCALMODIFIEDKEY];
}

-(void)setLocalModified:(BOOL)theLocalModified
{
        [self setValueByName:BOOKMARK_LOCALMODIFIEDKEY value:[NSNumber↵
numberWithBool:theLocalModified] reason:SBESRUserSet];
}
```

```
-(BOOL)localDeleted
{
        return [self getBooleanValueByName:BOOKMARK_LOCALDELETEDKEY];
}

-(void)setLocalDeleted:(BOOL)theLocalDeleted
{
        [self setValueByName:BOOKMARK_LOCALDELETEDKEY value:[NSNumber↩
numberWithBool:theLocalDeleted] reason:SBESRUserSet];
}
```

@end

Note how the implementation does not need an explicit declaration of init and dealloc. Because we've inherited from SBEntity, the base implementation will handle the setup and cleanup for you.

Another thing to look at there is that we've had to explicitly turn primitive integer and Boolean values into objects—specifically into instances of NSNumber. Arguably another approach that you could take to make this easier would be to create strongly typed "set value" methods in the base class that would handle this boxing for us. However, it's commonplace for this sort of entity wrapping code to be generated for you by a tool, and as such, there are relatively thin arguments for one way over and above another.

Creating SBEntityType Instances

Before we can create instances of SBBookmark and use them, we need to be able to create an instance of SBEntityType that supports it. In more sophisticated ORM layers, it is commonplace to build the metadata up from some sort of decoration in the code (e.g., attributes in .NET). In this implementation, we're going to build a class called SBRuntime and have it register the entity type on start. Here's the definition:

```
// SBRuntime.h
#import <Foundation/Foundation.h>

@interface SBRuntime : NSObject {
}

+(SBRuntime *)current;

+(void)start;
```

@end

The implementation SBRuntime creates a new singleton instance of the runtime class, stores it in static memory and then defines the new entity type. This last operation primarily consists of defining the fields. Here's the implementation:

```objc
// SBRuntime.m
#import "SBRuntime.h"
#import "MyClasses.h"

@implementation SBRuntime

static SBRuntime *theCurrent = nil;

+(SBRuntime *)current
{
        return theCurrent;
}

+(void)setCurrent:(SBRuntime *)rt
{
        theCurrent = rt;
        [theCurrent retain];
}

+(void)start
{
        // create...
        SBRuntime *rt = [[SBRuntime alloc] init];
        [SBRuntime setCurrent:rt];

        // type...
        SBEntityType *et = [[SBEntityType alloc] initWithInstanceTypeNativeName:↵
[SBBookmark class] nativeName:@"Bookmark"];
        [[et addField:BOOKMARK_IDKEY nativeName:BOOKMARK_IDKEY type:SBDT_INT32 size:-1]↵
setIsKey:TRUE];
        [et addField:BOOKMARK_ORDINALKEY nativeName:BOOKMARK_ORDINALKEY type:SBDT_INT32↵
size:-1];
        [et addField:BOOKMARK_NAMEKEY nativeName:BOOKMARK_NAMEKEY type:SBDT_STRING↵
size:128];
        [et addField:BOOKMARK_URLKEY nativeName:BOOKMARK_URLKEY type:SBDT_STRING size:256];
        [et addField:BOOKMARK_LOCALMODIFIEDKEY nativeName:BOOKMARK_LOCALMODIFIEDKEY↵
type:SBDT_INT32 size:-1];
        [et addField:BOOKMARK_LOCALDELETEDKEY nativeName:BOOKMARK_LOCALDELETEDKEY↵
type:SBDT_INT32 size:-1];
        [SBEntityType registerEntityType:et];
        [et release];
}

@end
```

We're essentially done here—we can now move on to creating some fake bookmarks and showing them on the device.

Displaying Some Fake Bookmarks

We've still got a long way to go until we can get some data out of the database and onto the screen, so we'll take a little diversion here and display some fake bookmarks so that we have some confidence in the work done thus far. This will involve us creating the form that will be used to show the bookmarks, and then we'll manually create some SBBookmark objects to show on them.

This section is going to involve creating the view in the same simple way that we've done before—i.e., adding six buttons to a page. We'll then go on to look at how we display the view, which is the more complicated aspect of the operation.

Creating the View

To create the view, instruct Xcode to add a new UIViewController Subclass item called SBNavigatorView. (Make sure you select the option to create a .xib file at the same time.) In the first instance, change the base class of the controller to be of type SBViewController, as follows:

```
// SBNavigatorView.h
#import <UIKit/UIKit.h>
#import "SBViewController.h"


@interface SBNavigatorView : SBViewController {
}


@end
```

For our form, we're going to add six buttons to the main window (as we have done before), but for the other options—**configure**, **about**, and **logoff**—we're going to use other iPhone user interface elements on the navigation bar and toolbar.

Also on the form, we're going to need events to handle clicks of one of the six navigation buttons, a handler for **configure**, a handler for **logoff**, and a handler for **about**. Finally, we're going to want to store the bookmarks in a property called bookmarks of type NSMutableArray. Here's the definition:

```
// Add properties and methods to SBNavigatorView.h…
#import <UIKit/UIKit.h>
#import "SBViewController.h"


@interface SBNavigatorView : SBViewController {
        UIButton *buttonNavigate1;
        UIButton *buttonNavigate2;
        UIButton *buttonNavigate3;
        UIButton *buttonNavigate4;
        UIButton *buttonNavigate5;
        UIButton *buttonNavigate6;
        NSMutableArray *bookmarks;
}
```

```
@property (nonatomic, retain) IBOutlet UIButton *buttonNavigate1;
@property (nonatomic, retain) IBOutlet UIButton *buttonNavigate2;
@property (nonatomic, retain) IBOutlet UIButton *buttonNavigate3;
@property (nonatomic, retain) IBOutlet UIButton *buttonNavigate4;
@property (nonatomic, retain) IBOutlet UIButton *buttonNavigate5;
@property (nonatomic, retain) IBOutlet UIButton *buttonNavigate6;
@property (nonatomic, retain) NSMutableArray *bookmarks;

-(IBAction)handleLogoff:(id)sender;
-(IBAction)handleConfigure:(id)sender;
-(IBAction)handleNavigate:(id)sender;
-(IBAction)handleAbout:(id)sender;

@end
```

For the view implementation, we'll add in the properties and cleanup code and build the implementation proper as we work through the chapter. Here's the implementation:

```
// SBNavigatorView.m
#import "SBNavigatorView.h"
#import "MyClasses.h"

@implementation SBNavigatorView

@synthesize buttonNavigate1;
@synthesize buttonNavigate2;
@synthesize buttonNavigate3;
@synthesize buttonNavigate4;
@synthesize buttonNavigate5;
@synthesize buttonNavigate6;
@synthesize bookmarks;

-(IBAction)handleLogoff:(id)sender
{
        [SBMessageBox show:@"TBD"];
}

-(IBAction)handleConfigure:(id)sender
{
        [SBMessageBox show:@"TBD"];
}

-(IBAction)handleNavigate:(id)sender
{
        [SBMessageBox show:@"TBD"];
}
```

```
-(IBAction)handleAbout:(id)sender
{
        [SBMessageBox show:@"TBD"];
}

// designer-generated code ommitted for clarity…

// replace existing dealloc…
-(void)dealloc
{
        [buttonNavigate1 release];
        [buttonNavigate2 release];
        [buttonNavigate3 release];
        [buttonNavigate4 release];
        [buttonNavigate5 release];
        [buttonNavigate6 release];
        [bookmarks release];
    [super dealloc];
}

@end
```

We can now design the view. Double-click the SBNavigatorView.xib file to launch the user interface designer. You'll see the view surface appear. Add a **Navigation Bar**, **Toolbar**, and six **Round Rect Buttons** controls until you see something like Figure 10-1.

Figure 10-1. *The basics of our* SBNavigatorView *form*

First, change the title of the navigation bar to **Six Bookmarks**. Next, the toolbar comes with a button by default. Change the text of this button to **Logoff**. Add two new **Bar Button Item** controls and label them **Configure** and **About**. You'll notice that these push themselves towards the left of the view—Figure 10-2 illustrates.

Figure 10-2. *Showing the default positions of the toolbar buttons*

What we want is the **Logoff** button on the left and the other two on the right. To do this, add a **Flexible Space Bar Button Item** control between the **Logoff** and **Configure** buttons. You'll then end up with something like Figure 10-3.

The final tweak to make to the UI is to wire up the buttons and controls. Here's what you need to do:

- Associate the six navigation buttonNavigateN properties on **File's Owner** with the six buttons.

- Associate the **Touch Up Inside** event of the six navigation buttons with the same, single handleNavigate method. (We'll de-reference the button that was clicked in the handler method itself, so we need only a single method reused by each button.)

- Associate the **selector** event of the Logoff button with handleLogoff method.

- Associate the **selector** event of the Configure button with handleConfigure method.

- Associate the **selector** event of the About button with handleAbout method.

Figure 10-3. *The "Flexible Space Bar Button" shifts objects to the far side of the form.*

You can then save the file—your work here is done.

We have to do a decent amount of work to get the view on the screen, so we'll look at that first and then look at how to display our fake bookmarks.

Building the View Engine

Structurally, the way we're supposed to build iOS applications is to create a single window and then swap views in and out of that window depending on what we want to do. To support this, we're going to have to create our own "view engine."

The design of the view engine that we'll build here is one that retains a pool of views in memory. When the application requires a view, it'll request one from the pool, creating one if one does not exist or recycling an existing view if it does. This sort of pattern is memory-efficient and hence lends itself to memory-constrained devices like phones.

To support the recycling, we need to define a common method for view initialization that we will use across all of our SBViewController-based views. Specifically, we'll add a method called refreshView to SBViewController that we can override in our specific implementations. In addition to this, we want each view to be given a reference back to its owner, which in this case is the SixBookmarksAppDelegate instance.

Add the refreshView method to SBViewController:

```
// Add to SBViewController.m…
// <…> Needs declaration in header
-(void)refreshView
{
        // we'll override this on each view...
}
```

SBViewController also needs to keep track of the thing that opened it—i.e., its "owner." We need to create a property on SBViewController that does this. Follow these steps to add the property:

- Create an instance variable called owner of type SixBookmarksAppDelegate.

- Add a @property declaration in the header.

- Add a @synthesize declaration in the implementation file.

- Add the cleanup code to dealloc.

For our view engine, we already have our application delegate class called SixBookmarksAppDelegate. We might as well repurpose this for our view engine.

The first thing we need to do is add a property to controllers to the SixBoomarksAppDelegate class. This involves the following steps:

- Create an instance variable called controllers of type NSMutableDictionary.

- Add a @property declaration in the header.

- Add a @synthesize declaration in the implementation file.

- Add the cleanup code to dealloc.

- Because we no longer need it, remove the viewController property from the class entirely.

Next we need to override the default constructor and set up the controllers property. Here's the implementation:

```
// Add method to SixBookmarksAppDelegate.m…
-(id)init
{
        if(self = [super init])
        {
                self.controllers = [NSMutableDictionary dictionary];
        }

        // return...
        return self;
}
```

Once this is done, we can build three methods that support swapping views in and out. currentController will return the currently active controller. getController will return the controller instance for a given class, and showView will put a view on the screen.

currentController and getController are the easy ones. For currentController, we can check to see if a view is visible by asking the view to de-reference its "superview"—i.e., its window. For getController, we used a dictionary keyed off of the name of the associated class to look up an existing view (if there is one). Here's the implementation:

```
// Add methods to SixBookmarksAppDelegate.m…
// <…> Needs declaration in header
-(SBViewController *)currentController
{
        // find the current view - this is the one that has a superview...
        for(NSString *key in self.controllers)
        {
                SBViewController *controller = [self.controllers objectForKey:key];
                if(controller.view != nil && controller.view.superview != nil)
                        return controller;
        }

        // none...
        return nil;
}


// <…> Needs declaration in header
-(SBViewController *)getController:(Class)theClass
{
        return (SBViewController *)[self.controllers objectForKey:[theClass description]];
}
```

The showView method is more complicated, which is why I have left it until last. This method will load the current controller out of the instance memory of the app delegate instance for later use. It will then set the owner of the to-be-shown controller to be the app delegate instance and look to see if the controller is stored in the pool—adding it if it's not. Finally it will add the view to the window, and if the current controller is null (i.e., it's the first view that we've shown), we'll make the view visible. If the current controller is not null, we'll remove its view from the window. Finally we'll call refreshView so that the controller has a chance to update its state. Here's the implementation:

```
// Add method to SixBookmarksAppDelegate…
// <…> Needs declaration in header
-(void)showView:(SBViewController *)theController
{
        // is this first?
        SBViewController *current = self.currentController;

        // set the owner to be us...
        [theController setOwner:self];
```

```
        // do we have it in the collection?
        NSString *key = [theController.class description];
        if([self.controllers objectForKey:key] == nil)
                [self.controllers setValue:theController forKey:key];

        // add...
        [window addSubview:theController.view];

        // do we have a view?
        if(current == nil)
                [window makeKeyAndVisible];
        else
        {
                // remove...
                [current.view removeFromSuperview];
        }

        // update it...
        [theController refreshView];
}
```

Whenever we want to show a view, we need to call a method that specializes in showing that view. Each of these methods will look in the pool to see if a controller of the appropriate type is available. If not, it will create one. In either case, the controller is passed to showView for display.

Here's a listing for openLogon, which, as the name suggests, opens the logon view:

```
// Add to SixBookmarksAppDelegate.m…
// <…> Needs definition in header
-(void)openLogon
{
        // find a preexisting view...
        SBViewController *view = [self getController:[SBLogonView class]];
        if(view == nil)
                view = [[SBLogonView alloc] initWithNibName:@"SBLogonView" bundle:↵
[NSBundle mainBundle]];

        // show the view...
        [self showView:view];
}
```

In order to make this work, we need to change the existing implementation of
application:didFinishLaunchingWithOptions that we had earlier, so that rather than manually creating
an instance of SBLogonView, it defers to openLogon. This is also a good time to call our start method on
the SBRuntime class that we built earlier but so far have not used. Here's the modified implementation:

```
// Replace existing method in SixBookmarksAppDelegate.m…
-(BOOL)application:(UIApplication *)application didFinishLaunchingWithOptions:↵
(NSDictionary *)launchOptions
{
        // start the runtime…
        [SBRuntime start];

        // show the form…
        [self openLogon];
        return YES;
}
```

If you run the application at this point, the logon form will show as it has done before. To complete
this part, we need to create an openNavigator method on the app delegate and get the logon controller to
call it.

First, add openNavigator. This method is similarly structured to openLogon:

```
// Add method to SixBookmarksAppDelegate.m…
// <…> Needs declaration in header…
-(void)openNavigator
{
        // find a preexisting view...
        SBViewController *view = [self getController:[SBNavigatorView class]];
        if(view == nil)
                view = [[SBNavigatorView alloc] initWithNibName:↵
@"SBNavigatorView" bundle:[NSBundle mainBundle]];

        // show the view...
        [self showView:view];
}
```

If you recall, the logonOk method on SBLogonView was rigged to display a message box on successful
logon. All we have to do now is change this to call the openNavigator method. Here's the
implementation:

```
// Replace method in SBLogonView…
-(void)logonOk
{
        [self.owner openNavigator];
}
```

Now you can run the application and log on. If your logon is successful, you'll see our navigator view. Figure 10-4 illustrates.

Figure 10-4. *The* SBNavigatorView *successfully displayed via our view engine*

Displaying Bookmarks

Given that we can show the navigator form, it's time to rig it up to show some fake buttons. Recall that previously we added a refreshView method to our base SBViewController class. We can now use this by overriding it on SBNavigatorView. Within the new implementation, we'll create an NSMutableArray, put two bookmarks in it and then defer to showBookmarks, which we'll build in a moment. Here's the implementation:

```
// Add method to SBNavigatorView.m…
-(void)refreshView
{
        // create some fake bookmarks...
        NSMutableArray *theBookmarks = [NSMutableArray array];
```

```
        // first one...
        SBBookmark *bookmark = [[SBBookmark alloc] init];
        bookmark.ordinal = 0;
        bookmark.name = @".NET 247";
        bookmark.url = @"http://www.dotnet247.com/";
        [theBookmarks addObject:bookmark];
        [bookmark release];

        // second one...
        bookmark = [[SBBookmark alloc] init];
        bookmark.ordinal = 1;
        bookmark.name = @"Apress";
        bookmark.url = @"http://www.apress.com/";
        [theBookmarks addObject:bookmark];
        [bookmark release];

        // show...
        [self showBookmarks:theBookmarks];
}
```

showBookmarks will operate in the same way as the previous implementations. We'll reset all of the buttons first, and then we'll go through the buttons that we were given and configure them on an ordinal-by-ordinal basis. Here's the implementation:

```
// Add to SBNavigatorView.m…
// <…> Needs declaration in header
-(UIButton *)getButton:(int)ordinal
{
        if(ordinal == 0)
                return self.buttonNavigate1;
        else if(ordinal == 1)
                return self.buttonNavigate2;
        else if(ordinal == 2)
                return self.buttonNavigate3;
        else if(ordinal == 3)
                return self.buttonNavigate4;
        else if(ordinal == 4)
                return self.buttonNavigate5;
        else if(ordinal == 5)
                return self.buttonNavigate6;
        else
                return nil;
}
```

```
// <...> Needs declaration in header
-(void)resetButton:(int)ordinal
{
        // get...
        UIButton *button = [self getButton:ordinal];
        [button setTitle:@"..." forState:UIControlStateNormal];
}


// <...> Needs declaration in header
-(void)setupButton:(SBBookmark *)bookmark
{
        // get...
        UIButton *button = [self getButton:[bookmark ordinal]];
        [button setTitle:[bookmark name] forState:UIControlStateNormal];
}


// <...> Needs declaration in header
-(void)showBookmarks:(NSMutableArray *)theBookmarks
{
        // reset all buttons...
        for(int index = 0; index < 6; index++)
                [self resetButton:index];

        // show the buttons...
        for(SBBookmark *bookmark in theBookmarks)
                [self setupButton:bookmark];

        // store the bookmarks...
        self.bookmarks = theBookmarks;
}
```

Note how at the end of the showBookmarks method, we store the supplied bookmarks in the bookmarks property. We'll need this later when we come to handle the navigation.

Run the project and log on, and you'll see the configured view. Figure 10-5 illustrates:

Figure 10-5. *Fake bookmarks now shown on the navigator form.*

Handling Navigation

At the moment, the buttons do not do anything. We'll do this now by replacing our stub implementation of handleNavigate.

First of all, we need to actually show the URL. There are two ways to do this on iPhone—we can either shell out to Safari and ask it to show the URL, or host it internally. We'll use the method to shell out in this application, as this offers the user the greater utility. The implementation is very simple—here it is:

```
// Add method to SBRuntime.m…
// <…> Needs declaration in header
-(void)showUrl:(NSString *)theUrl
{
        [[UIApplication sharedApplication] openURL:[NSURL URLWithString:theUrl]];
}
```

To handle the button click, we have to go round the houses a little. We will receive event notification via our handleNavigate method. We then will defer to a method called doNavigate, passing in the ordinal that corresponds to the button that we clicked. We'll then find an SBBookmark instance for that ordinal. If we find one, we'll call the `showUrl` method on `SBRuntime`. If we don't find one, we'll call `handleConfigure` and deal with it in the next chapter. Here's the implementation:

```
// Add methods to SBNavigatorView…
// Replace existing handleNavigate method…
-(IBAction)handleNavigate:(id)sender
{
        if(sender == self.buttonNavigate1)
                [self doNavigate:0];
        else if(sender == self.buttonNavigate2)
                [self doNavigate:1];
        else if(sender == self.buttonNavigate3)
                [self doNavigate:2];
        else if(sender == self.buttonNavigate4)
                [self doNavigate:3];
        else if(sender == self.buttonNavigate5)
                [self doNavigate:4];
        else if(sender == self.buttonNavigate6)
                [self doNavigate:5];
}


// <…> Needs declaration in header
-(SBBookmark *)getBookmarkByOrdinal:(int)ordinal
{
        for(SBBookmark *bookmark in self.bookmarks)
        {
                if([bookmark ordinal] == ordinal)
                        return bookmark;
        }

        // nope...
        return nil;
}


// <…> Needs declaration in header
-(void)doNavigate:(int)ordinal
{
        SBBookmark *bookmark = [self getBookmarkByOrdinal:ordinal];
        if(bookmark != nil)
                [[SBRuntime current] showUrl:bookmark.url];
        else
                [self handleConfigure:self];
}
```

Apart from the fact that we don't have real bookmarks, we're ready to go. Figure 10-6 illustrates what happens when we click on the **Apress** button.

Figure 10-6. *The Apress site rendered by the iPhone's browser*

Building the Sync Class

We now have the infrastructure in place to log users on and show them their bookmarks. All we have to do now is download the bookmarks from the server, store them locally, and when the time comes, retrieve them again. In the next chapter, we're going to look at how we can push changes back up to the server.

Calling the Server's Bookmarks OData Service

In the last chapter, we created a few classes, including SBServiceProxy, SBApiService, and SBUsersService, to communicate with the restful services at http://services.multimobiledevelopment.com/. In this section, we're going to look at building SBBookmarksService, which is able to communicate with the Bookmarks OData service.

■ **NOTE** Although in Microsoft's toolset for targeting Windows Phone 7 and ASP.NET applications, there is a library we can use for accessing OData, on Android and iOS there isn't such a library, and hence we need to roll our own. A lot of this chapter will therefore be given over to this work. As of the time of writing, there isn't a dominant OData library that can be used on iPhone, and hence this section and the next section describe how we can do this manually. If you are reading this book in Summer 2011 or later, there is a good chance there will be a dominant library to use. The web site at `www.odata.org/` will tell you if there are any iOS libraries available.

As we know, the OData service returns XML, and by default the format of this XML is ATOM. All we have to do then is issue the requests and interpret the results. We can take the ATOM-formatted list of bookmarks and turn them into SBBookmark entities for later use.

The URL is the easy part—we need to issue a request to the following URL, passing up the special x-amx-apiusername and x-amx-token HTTP headers. Here's the URL:

```
http://services.multimobiledevelopment.com/services/bookmarks.svc/Bookmark
```

Let's use the test tool presented in Chapter 2 to get the XML so that we know what we need to parse. Here's an XML response containing a single bookmark:

```
<feed xml:base="http://services.amxmobile.com/services/Bookmarks.svc/"↵
xmlns:d="http://schemas.microsoft.com/ado/2007/08/dataservices"↵
xmlns:m="http://schemas.microsoft.com/ado/2007/08/dataservices/metadata"↵
xmlns="http://www.w3.org/2005/Atom">
  <title type="text">Bookmark</title>
  <id>http://services.amxmobile.com/services/bookmarks.svc/Bookmark</id>
  <updated>2010-05-15T06:22:09Z</updated>
  <link rel="self" title="Bookmark" href="Bookmark" />
  <entry>
    <id>http://services.amxmobile.com/services/Bookmarks.svc/Bookmark(1002)</id>
    <title type="text">
    </title>
    <updated>2010-05-15T06:22:09Z</updated>
    <author>
      <name />
    </author>
    <link rel="edit" title="Bookmark" href="Bookmark(1002)" />
    <category term="AmxMobile.Services.Bookmark" scheme=↵
"http://schemas.microsoft.com/ado/2007/08/dataservices/scheme" />
    <content type="application/xml">
      <m:properties>
        <d:BookmarkId m:type="Edm.Int32">1002</d:BookmarkId>
        <d:UserId m:type="Edm.Int32">1001</d:UserId>
```

```
        <d:Name>.NET 247</d:Name>
        <d:Url>http://www.dotnet247.com/</d:Url>
        <d:Ordinal m:type="Edm.Int32">1</d:Ordinal>
      </m:properties>
    </content>
  </entry>
</feed>
```

The thing that I like about XML is that with a bit of common sense—providing the developer has not created horrendously bad XML—it's normally easy to understand what you need to do. There, we can clearly see that the entry element contains the bookmark data and that the content/m:properties element contains the fields we want. All we have to do now is walk the document, creating new SBBookmark instances for each entry, and use the metadata of the entity to populate the fields.

Namespaces

If you are not familiar with XML namespaces, please read the discussion in Chapter 6 before continuing. It will orient you to what we're going to need to do with the XML parsing to make sense of the data.

Querying the Feed

Let's look now at parsing the XML we get back from the server. First of all, let's stub out our SBBookmarksService class. This is going to extend a new class called SBODataServiceProxy and reuse the SBHttpHelper class to physically get the XML document from the server.

This operation is going to be a little complicated, again because of the way that Objective-C forces you to deal with asynchronous code. What's going to happen is that we're going to create a callback interface called SBODataFetchCallback that will implement odataFetchOk and odataFetchFailed methods. We'll create a getAll method that will take one of these callbacks and call the download method on SBHttpHelper. The download method will call back to us, giving us an instance of an SBDownloadBucket object. We'll then pass the XML using a new class that we'll build called SBEntityXmlBucket. SBEntityXmlBucket will work in a similar fashion to SBFlatXmlBucket, except that it will be specialized to work with OData results.

Without further ado, we'll start by building out our SBODataServiceProxy. Here's the definition:

```
// SBODataServiceProxy.h
#import <Foundation/Foundation.h>
#import "SBServiceProxy.h"
#import "SBEntityType.h"

@class SBEntityXmlBucket;

@interface SBODataFetchCallback : NSObject
-(void)odataFetchOk:(SBEntityXmlBucket *)bucket opCode:(int)theOpCode;
-(void)odataFetchFailed:(NSError *)err opCode:(int)theOpCode;
@end
```

```
@interface SBODataServiceProxy : SBServiceProxy {
        SBEntityType *entityType;
        SBODataFetchCallback *callback;
}

@property (nonatomic, retain) SBEntityType *entityType;
@property (nonatomic, retain) SBODataFetchCallback *callback;

-(id)initWithTypeAndServiceName:(Class)theType serviceName:(NSString *)theServiceName;

-(NSString *)getServiceUrl:(SBEntityType *)et;
-(void)getAll:(SBODataFetchCallback *)theCallback;

@end
```

We'll break out the methods in a moment, but we'll quickly look at the non-method bits. Here's the definition:

```
// SBODataServiceProxy.m
#import "SBODataServiceProxy.h"
#import "MyClasses.h"

@implementation SBODataServiceProxy

@synthesize entityType;
@synthesize callback;

-(id)initWithTypeAndServiceName:(Class)theType serviceName:(NSString *)theServiceName;
{
        if(self = [super initWithServiceName:theServiceName])
        {
                [self setEntityType:[SBEntityType getEntityType:theType]];
        }

        // return...
        return self;
}

-(void)dealloc
{
        [callback release];
        [entityType release];
        [super dealloc];
}

@end
```

Recall that when we issue calls to our services, we need to have an op code defined so that we can reference back to the original operation on callbacks. We need to create an OPCODE_ODATAFETCHALL op code for this next part.

In SBServiceProxy.h, add the new entry to the enumeration:

```
typedef enum
{
        OPCODE_APILOGON = 1000,
        OPCODE_USERSLOGON = 2000,
        OPCODE_ODATAFETCHALL = 3000
} SBOpCodes;
```

Because we're running asynchronously, the getAll method is pretty straightforward. We have to get the URL of the service, get the download settings (containing our special headers), and call download on SBHttpHelper. Eventually we'll get a callback call to downloadComplete with the bucket. In this implementation, we'll simply write out the response XML to the debugging log. Here's the implementation:

```
// Add methods to SBODataServiceProxy.m…
-(NSString *)getServiceUrl:(SBEntityType *)et
{
        return [NSString stringWithFormat:@"%@/%@", [self resolvedServiceUrl], et.name];
}


-(void)getAll:(SBODataFetchCallback *)theCallback
{
        // store the callback...
        self.callback = theCallback;

        // get the url...
        NSString *url = [self getServiceUrl:self.entityType];

        // run...
        SBDownloadSettings *settings = [self getDownloadSettings];
        [SBHttpHelper download:url settings:settings callback:↵
(SBDownloadCallback *)self opCode:OPCODE_ODATAFETCHALL];
}


-(void)downloadComplete:(SBDownloadBucket *)bucket
{
        // log it...
        NSLog([bucket dataAsString]);
}
```

Before we go on, we said we need to create our SBBookmarksService class, and we haven't yet done so. For the moment, we don't need to add too much to this—all you need to do is create a new class, have it extend SBODataServiceProxy, and implement a constructor. Here's the definition:

```
#import <Foundation/Foundation.h>
#import "SBODataServiceProxy.h"

@interface SBBookmarksService : SBODataServiceProxy {

}

@end
```

...and here's the implementation:

```
#import "SBBookmarksService.h"
#import "MyClasses.h"

@implementation SBBookmarksService

-(id)init
{
        return [super initWithTypeAndServiceName:[SBBookmark class]
serviceName:@"Bookmarks.svc"];
}

@end
```

We've got a lot of mileage to cover to get this working, so we'll build out our SBSync class now so that we can prove we can get some data back.

Stubbing SBSync

SBSync will handle our synchronization for us. In this chapter, we're going to download bookmarks. In the next chapter, we're going to send them up to the server again. We'll also need a callback interface, which we'll call SBSyncCallback, and we'll also need an enumeration that allows us to keep track of whether we're getting the latest or saving changes. We'll use this enumeration in the next chapter, but we'll add it now to make life easier later on.

Here's the definition:

```
// SBSync.h
#import <Foundation/Foundation.h>

@interface SBSyncCallback : NSObject
-(void)syncOk;
-(void)syncFailed:(NSError *)err;
@end
```

```
typedef enum
{
        SBSMGetLatest,
} SBSyncMode;

@interface SBSync : NSObject {
        SBSyncCallback *callback;
        SBSyncMode mode;
}

@property (nonatomic, retain) SBSyncCallback *callback;
@property (assign) SBSyncMode mode;

-(void)doSync:(SBSyncCallback *)theCallback;
-(void)getLatest;

@end
```

The declaration needs to create a SBBookmarksService instance and call getAll. This will ripple through until we get to our downloadComplete callback. Here's the implementation:

```
// SBSync.m
#import "SBSync.h"
#import "MyClasses.h"

@implementation SBSync

@synthesize callback;
@synthesize mode;

-(void)doSync:(SBSyncCallback *)theCallback
{
        self.callback = theCallback;

        // run...
        [self getLatest];
}

-(void)getLatest
{
        // connect to the service and get them all...
        self.mode = SBSMGetLatest;
        SBBookmarksService *service = [[SBBookmarksService alloc] init];
        [service getAll:(SBODataFetchCallback *)self];
        [service release];
}
```

```
-(void)dealloc
{
        [callback release];
        [super dealloc];
}
```

@end

The sync operation has to run after the user has logged on. Therefore we need to go back and modify our logonOk callback handler on SBLogonView method on call doSync. doSync will then callback into SBLogonView to indicate whether the sync completed or failed. If it failed, we'll show an error, otherwise we'll proceed to the navigator. Here are the changes:

```
// Change logonOk method on SBLogonView and add new methods…
-(void)logonOk
{
        // do a sync...
        SBSync *sync = [[[SBSync alloc] init] autorelease];
        [sync doSync:(SBSyncCallback *)self];
}

-(void)syncOk
{
        [self.owner openNavigator];
}

-(void)syncFailed:(NSError *)error
{
        [SBMessageBox showError:error];
}

// This method is unchanged - included for clarity…
-(void)logonFailed:(NSError *)theError
{
        [SBMessageBox showError:theError];
}
```

Now run the application and log on. The application will stop on the logon screen. What's happened here is that our downloadComplete handler on SBODataServiceProxy has output the XML to the debugging window, but it has not called our callback to say what happened.

If you look in the debugging window, you will see a statement like the one shown in Figure 10-7.

```
2010-08-11 17:33:46.485 SixBookmarks[10053:207] <?xml version="1.0" encoding="utf-8" standalone="yes"?>
<error xmlns="http://schemas.microsoft.com/ado/2007/08/dataservices/metadata">
  <code></code>
  <message xml:lang="en-GB">Resource not found for the segment 'SBBookmark'.</message>
</error>
```

Figure 10-7. *An error message from the OData service*

What's happened here is that the URL used has been this:

http://services.multimobiledevelopment.com/services/bookmarks.svc/SBBookmark

This URL is not the correct URL to use—it should read just Bookmark at the end. What's happened here is because we have changed the name of the class from Bookmark to SBBookmark to accommodate Objective-C's lack of namespaces, we've ended up with the wrong name. I've left this problem in until now to illustrate how tricky it can be to manage the same codebase on these very different platforms. This is an example of where we need to vary the code just because of a difference in the approach of the toolset.

The SBODataServiceProxy class is using the programmatic name of the entity to build the URL. What we need to do is change it to use the native name. (When we built SBRuntime, the code listing showed the native name of the entity type as "Bookmark".) Here's the modified method:

```
// Modify the getServiceUrl method in SBODataServiceProxy…
-(NSString *)getServiceUrl:(SBEntityType *)et
{
        return [NSString stringWithFormat:@"%@/%@", [self resolvedServiceUrl],↵
et.nativeName];
}
```

Run the project now and you'll still get stuck on the logon screen; however, the output in the debugger output will be different. Figure 10-8 illustrates.

```
2010-08-11 17:36:59.517 SixBookmarks[10110:207] <?xml version="1.0" encoding="utf-8" standalone="yes"?>
<feed xml:base="http://services.multimobiledevelopment.com/Bookmarks.svc/" xmlns:d="http://schemas.microsoft.com/ado/2007/08/dataservices"
xmlns:m="http://schemas.microsoft.com/ado/2007/08/dataservices/metadata" xmlns="http://www.w3.org/2005/Atom">
  <title type="text">Bookmark</title>
  <id>http://services.multimobiledevelopment.com/Bookmarks.svc/Bookmark</id>
  <updated>2010-08-11T16:36:30Z</updated>
  <link rel="self" title="Bookmark" href="Bookmark" />
  <entry>
    <id>http://services.multimobiledevelopment.com/Bookmarks.svc/Bookmark(1027)</id>
    <title type="text"></title>
    <updated>2010-08-11T16:36:30Z</updated>
    <author>
      <name />
    </author>
    <link rel="edit" title="Bookmark" href="Bookmark(1027)" />
    <category term="AmxMobile.Services.Bookmark" scheme="http://schemas.microsoft.com/ado/2007/08/dataservices/scheme" />
    <content type="application/xml">
      <m:properties>
        <d:BookmarkId m:type="Edm.Int32">1027</d:BookmarkId>
        <d:UserId m:type="Edm.Int32">1001</d:UserId>
        <d:Name>.NET 247</d:Name>
        <d:Url>http://www.dotnet247.com/</d:Url>
        <d:Ordinal m:type="Edm.Int32">1</d:Ordinal>
      </m:properties>
    </content>
  </entry>
  <entry>
    <id>http://services.multimobiledevelopment.com/Bookmarks.svc/Bookmark(1018)</id>
```

Figure 10-8. *A successful OData fetch result from the server*

Now that we know that we're getting XML back, we just need to make sense of it and turn it into entities.

Parsing the XML

In the last chapter, we said how in order to parse XML, we needed to use the NSXMLParser class. We created a SBFlatXmlBucket class as a companion to this for reading the results from our RESTful services. In this section, we're going to create SBEntityXmlBucket and use that with NSXMLParser.

The operation of SBEntityXmlBucket will be to look for entry elements in the XML. When it finds one, it will initialize an array of values and wait until it picks up elements that it determines are in the namespace http://schemas.microsoft.com/ado/2007/08/dataservices. Elements that represent fields on an entity are in this namespace. When it finds the end of the entry element, it'll create a new entity and transfer the values it collected into it. It will maintain a property called mode of type SBEntityReadMode to help keep track of where it is in the document. We'll also need to create constant strings that hold the namespace URLs.

Here's the definition:

```
// SBEntityXmlBucket.h
#import <Foundation/Foundation.h>
#import "SBEntityType.h"
#import "SBXmlBucketBase.h"

typedef enum
{
        SBERMNone = 0,
        SBERMEntry = 1

} SBEntityReadMode;

@interface SBEntityXmlBucket : SBXmlBucketBase {
        SBEntityType *entityType;
        NSMutableDictionary *values;
        NSMutableArray *entities;
        SBEntityReadMode mode;
}

@property (nonatomic, retain) SBEntityType *entityType;
@property (nonatomic, retain) NSMutableDictionary *values;
@property (nonatomic, retain) NSMutableArray *entities;
@property (assign) SBEntityReadMode mode;

// namespaces...
+(NSString *)atomNamespace;
+(NSString *)msMetadataNamespace;
+(NSString *)msDataNamespace;
```

```
// constructor...
-(id)initWithEntityType:(SBEntityType *)et;

// parser...
-(void)parser:(NSXMLParser *)parser didStartElement:(NSString *)elementName
 namespaceURI:(NSString *)namespaceURI qualifiedName:(NSString *)qualifiedName
   attributes:(NSDictionary *)attributeDict;
-(void)parser:(NSXMLParser *)parser didEndElement:(NSString *)elementName↵
 namespaceURI:(NSString *)namespaceURI
qualifiedName:(NSString *)qName;

@end
```

As before, we'll look at the basic structure of the implementation and then drill into more detail of the methods. Here's the implementation stub:

```
// SBEntityXmlBucket.m
#import "SBEntityXmlBucket.h"
#import "MyClasses.h"

@implementation SBEntityXmlBucket

@synthesize entityType;
@synthesize values;
@synthesize mode;
@synthesize entities;

NSString * const AtomNamespace = @"http://www.w3.org/2005/Atom";
NSString * const MsMetadataNamespace = ↵
@"http://schemas.microsoft.com/ado/2007/08/dataservices/metadata";
NSString * const MsDataNamespace = @"http://schemas.microsoft.com/ado/2007/08/dataservices";

-(id)initWithEntityType:(SBEntityType *)et
{
        if(self = [super init])
        {
                self.entityType = et;
                self.entities = [NSMutableArray array];
        }

        // return...
        return self;
}
```

```
-(void)dealloc
{
        [values release];
        [entities release];
        [entityType release];
        [super dealloc];
}


@end
```

Note that on this class, we've extended `SBXmlBucketBase`. The main function of this base class is to collect the text that appears within each element.

We'll look at the implementation of `parser:didStartElement` first. What we need to do in the handler for this is to see if our mode is `SBERMNone` (i.e., we're not currently tracking an entity), and if our mode is that, we'll listen out for the start of an entry element that is also in the regular ATOM namespace. If it is, we'll initialize a bucket of values and set our mode to indicate that we are currently listening for entity values. Here's the implementation:

```
// Add method to SBEntityXmlBucket.m…
-(void)parser:(NSXMLParser *)parser didStartElement:(NSString *)elementName
 namespaceURI:(NSString *)namespaceURI qualifiedName:(NSString *)qualifiedName
   attributes:(NSDictionary *)attributeDict
{
        // what's our read mode?
        if(self.mode == SBERMNone)
        {
                // do we have an entity?
                if([namespaceURI isEqualToString:AtomNamespace] && [elementName⏎
 isEqualToString:@"entry"])
                {
                        // we're in an entry...
                        if(values == nil)
                        {
                                self.values = [NSMutableDictionary dictionary];
                                self.mode = SBERMEntry;
                        }
                }
        }

        // reset the builder...
        [self resetBuilder];
}
```

The handler for parser:didEndElement has two functions. If we end the entry element, we have to create an entity and pack the values into it. (This is done using a method called populateFromValues on SBEntity, which we'll build later.) Alternatively, if we get anything in the Microsoft data namespace, we'll treat that as a value and store it. We could make this operation a little more sophisticated and only capture values that we know are on the entity, but we'll actually do this in populateFromValues. Here's the implementation:

```
// Add method to SBEntityXmlBucket.m…
-(void)parser:(NSXMLParser *)parser didEndElement:(NSString *)elementName↵
 namespaceURI:(NSString *)namespaceURI
qualifiedName:(NSString *)qName
{
        // did we get to the end of an entity...
        if(self.mode == SBERMEntry)
        {
                // is this the end of an entity?
                if([namespaceURI isEqualToString:AtomNamespace] && [elementName↵
isEqualToString:@"entry"])
                {
                        // patch it in...
                        SBEntity *theEntity = [self.entityType createInstance];
                        [theEntity populateFromValues:self.values];
                        [self.entities addObject:theEntity];

                        // clear it...
                        [values removeAllObjects];
                        self.values = nil;

                        // none...
                        self.mode = SBERMNone;
                }
                else if([namespaceURI isEqualToString:MsDataNamespace])
                {
                        // add...
                        [self.values setObject:self.trimmedBuilder forKey:elementName];
                        [self resetBuilder];
                }
        }
}
```

If we implement populateFromValues on SBEntity, we'll have completed this part of the process end to end.

The function of this method will be to go through each value in the dictionary and see if a corresponding field can be found. If it is, we'll set the value on the field using the SBESRLoad so that the modified flag on the entity is not changed.

A wrinkle on this method is that we have to convert the string value in the dictionary to either a string or an integer field, depending on the type. Here's the implementation:

```
// Add method to SBEntity.m…
// <…> Needs declaration in header
-(void)populateFromValues:(NSMutableDictionary *)theValues
{
        SBEntityType *et = [self entityType];
        for(NSString *name in theValues)
        {
                // do we support this field?
                if([et isField:name])
                {
                        // find the field...
                        SBEntityField *field = [et getField:name];

                        // get...
                        NSString *value = [theValues valueForKey:name];
                        NSLog(@"Value: '%@'", value);

                        // what to do...
                        SBDataType type = [field type];
                        if(type == SBDT_STRING)
                                [self setValue:field value:value reason:SBESRLoad];
                        else if(type == SBDT_INT32)
                        {
                                NSNumberFormatter *formatter = [[NSNumberFormatter alloc]↩
init];

                                NSNumber *theNumber = [formatter numberFromString:value];
                                [formatter release];
                                [self setValue:field value:theNumber reason:SBESRLoad];
                        }
                        else
                                @throw [NSException exceptionWithName:[[self class]↩
description] reason:[NSString stringWithFormat:@"Cannot handle '%d'.", type] userInfo:nil];
                }
        }
}
```

The next step in this process is to wire up downloadComplete method so that it actually calls through to the parser and hydrates a collection of bookmarks.

When downloadComplete is called, we need to check whether the request worked. We can do this by looking at the HTTP status code returned in the statusCode property of the SBDownloadBucket instance. In our case, successful codes are **200** and **204**. **200** is the regular "OK" response. **204** is a special response that means that the request was OK but that there is now data to return. If we get an HTTP status code other than **200** or **204**, we need to raise an error via the callback's odataFetchFailed method.

If the request is OK, we need to look at the op code and then defer to a specialized method to handle the result. This specialized method—handleFetchAllComplete—will parse the results and call the odataFetchOk method of the callback. Here's the implementation:

```
// Replace method in SBODataServiceProxy.m…
-(void)downloadComplete:(SBDownloadBucket *)bucket
{
        // did we fail - i.e. not 200 and not 204 (OK, but nothing to say)...
        if(bucket.statusCode != 200 && bucket.statusCode != 204)
        {
                // create an error...
                NSString *message = [NSString stringWithFormat:@"An OData request↵
returned HTTP status '%d'.", bucket.statusCode];
                NSString *html = bucket.dataAsString;
                NSLog(@"%@ --> %@", message, html);
                [html release];
                NSError *err = [SBErrorHelper error:self message:message];

                // flip back...
                [self.callback odataFetchFailed:err opCode:bucket.opCode];
        }
        else
        {
                // ok...
                if(bucket.opCode == OPCODE_ODATAFETCHALL)
                        [self handleFetchAllComplete:bucket];
                else
                        @throw [NSException exceptionWithName:[[self class] description]↵
reason:[NSString stringWithFormat:@"An op code of '%d' was not recognised.", [bucket↵
opCode]] userInfo:nil];
        }
}
```

```
// Add method to SBODataServiceProxy.m
// <…> Needs declaration in header
-(void)handleFetchAllComplete:(SBDownloadBucket *)bucket
{
        // parse it...
        NSXMLParser *parser = [[[NSXMLParser alloc] initWithData:[bucket data]]↩
 autorelease];
        [parser setShouldProcessNamespaces:TRUE];

        // new...
        SBEntityXmlBucket *entities = [[[SBEntityXmlBucket alloc] initWithEntityType:↩
[self entityType]] autorelease];
        [parser setDelegate:entities];
        [parser parse];

        // at this point we have a populated bucket, so send it back to the caller...
        [self.callback odataFetchOk:entities opCode:[bucket opCode]];
}
```

To complete this chunk of work, we need to implement the callback methods on SBSync. Here are the methods:

```
// Add methods to SBSync.m
-(void)odataFetchOk:(SBEntityXmlBucket *)bucket opCode:(int)theOpCode
{
        [SBMessageBox show:@"Got some entities."];
}

-(void)odataFetchFailed:(NSError *)err opCode:(int)theOpCode
{
        [SBMessageBox showError:err];
}
```

If you run the project now and log on, the sync process will run and (we hope) odataFetchOk will be called. Figure 10-9 illustrates the results.

Figure 10-9. *The application tells us that some entities were downloaded.*

Spinning the Progress Wheel

You may have noticed that when you are connecting to the OData service, the wheel is not spinning in the status bar. Frankly, I'm never sure where to put the code to start and stop the spinning wheel on iOS applications. It makes sense to do them in the "business tier," but it is a user interface element and should properly be done from the user interface. However, locating the code in the business tier often offers an easier and more reliable implementation. Thus on balance, we'll add the spinning wheel into the sync operation.

Here's a modified implementation that includes the spin operations.

```
// Modify doSync method in SBSync.m…
-(void)doSync:(SBSyncCallback *)theCallback
{
        self.callback = theCallback;

        // start spinning...
        [SBServiceProxy startSpinning];
```

```
        // run...
        [self getLatest];
}

// Modify odataFetchOk method in SBSync.m…
-(void)odataFetchOk:(SBEntityXmlBucket *)bucket opCode:(int)theOpCode
{
        // stop spinning...
        [SBServiceProxy stopSpinning];

        // show...
        [SBMessageBox show:@"Got some entities."];
}

// Modify odataFetchFailed method in SBSync.m…
-(void)odataFetchFailed:(NSError *)err opCode:(int)theOpCode
{
        // stop spinning...
        [SBServiceProxy stopSpinning];

        // show...
        [SBMessageBox showError:err];
}
```

Now when you run the application, the spinning wheel will operate as desired.

Database Operations

We now know that we can communicate with the OData service. The next trick is to store the retrieved entities in a local database.

As discussed at the top of the chapter, iPhone has a built-in implementation of SQLite that is accessed through a flat C-style API. We'll continue building our object-relational mapping layer so that it can create and access a SQLite database.

Including SQLite

Our initial work involves configuring our Xcode project with references to the SQLite library. The first step is to add a new "framework" to the project.

■**NOTE** This process is quite complicated in the Xcode 4 beta that I'm using—it's possible that this will be made slightly easier in the production version. Refer to the web site if these steps seem to bear no relation to your edition of Xcode.

In the Project Navigator, click on the project entry at the top of the tree. This is the blue box titled **SixBookmarks**. You will see a view like the one in Figure 10-10.

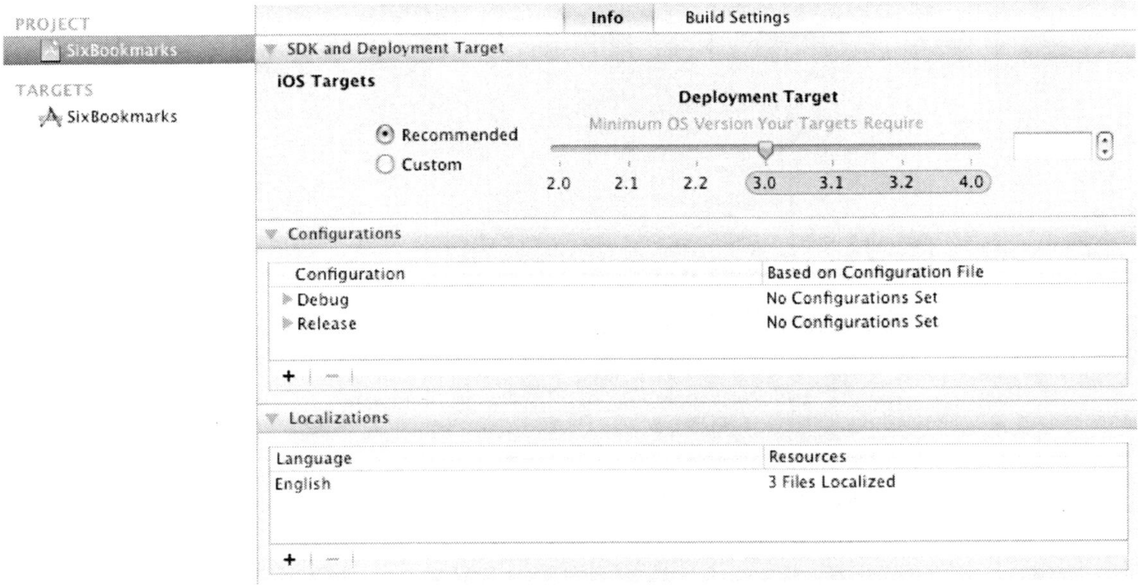

Figure 10-10. *The project settings view*

On the left, select the **SixBookmarks** entry under **Targets**. You will see something like Figure 10-11.

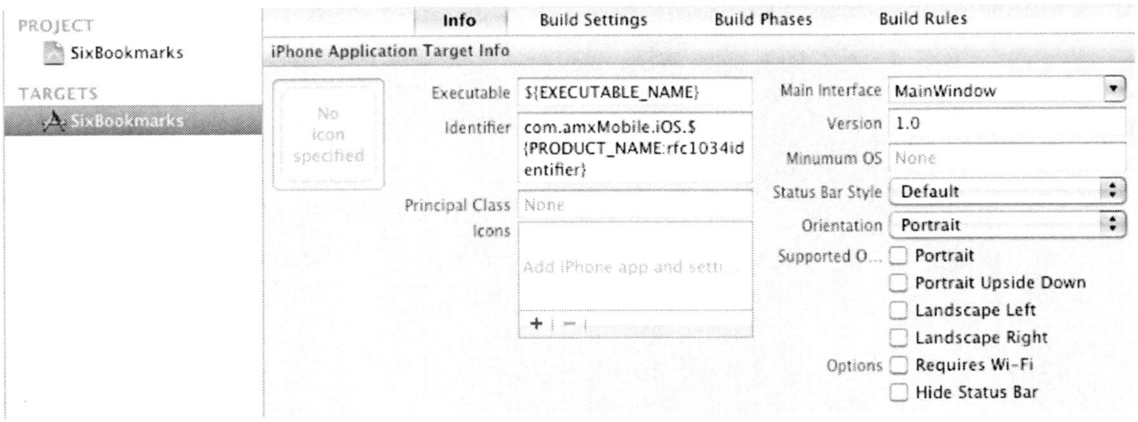

Figure 10-11. *The target details view for "SixBookmarks"*

At the top of the right-hand pane, select **Build Phases**. You can then expand an entry called **Link Binary With Libraries**. It's this entry that specifies the frameworks that you wish to include in your project. Figure 10-12 illustrates.

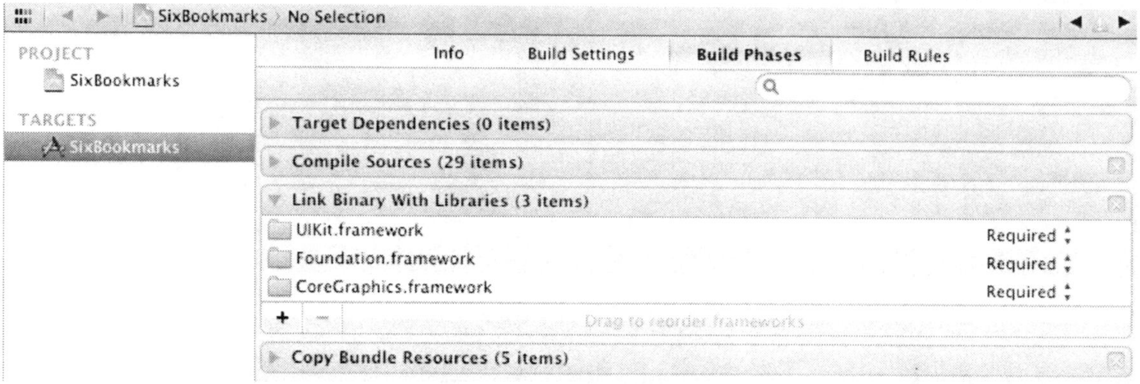

Figure 10-12. *The current packages related to the "SixBookmarks" target*

Click the **Add** button and add a reference to libsqlite3.dylib. Figure 10-13 illustrates.

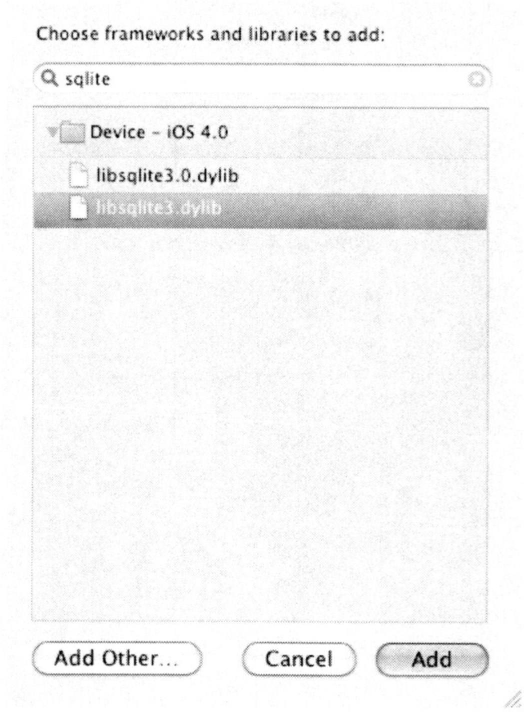

Figure 10-13. *Searching for the SQLite framework*

When you click **Add** you'll be shown a confirmation window. Click **Finish** and the framework will be added. You're now ready to use SQLite in the project.

Building SBDBHelper and Implementing Error Handling

We're going to funnel our database operations through a new class called SBDBHelper. This class will wrap an instance of a database and provide a "managed" interface over the flat C-style API of SQLite.

One problem we're going to need to solve with this library is that the error handling is very old-fashioned. Each SQLite method returns back an integer that represents the state of the call. If this value is SQLITE_OK (i.e., **0**), we know the call succeeded. If the value is anything else, we know that the call failed. If the call does fail, we need to retrieve the error text and store it with SBDBHelper. (By implication, if the call succeeds, we need to clear any previously held error text.) The caller will be able to call getLastError to return back an NSError instance—i.e., we'll build our implementation so that it is in line with the remainder of error handling in the application.

Another wrinkle is that in our constructor, we will attempt to connect to a database. We cannot fail within the constructor, so there's a chance that the caller could end up with an instance of SBDBHelper that looks like it's working but is not bound to a database. Therefore we also have to keep track of whether an error occurred on initialization.

We're not going to store the "last error" value in a property. Instead we're going to create an instance variable called theLastError and set it using methods called setLastError and setLastErrorWithMessage. Errors will be retrieved through the getLastError method, but this will return an NSError instance.

All of this means that the error handling, oddly, takes up the majority of the code! Here's the definition:

```
// SBDBHelper.h
#import <Foundation/Foundation.h>
#import <sqlite3.h>

#import "SBEntityType.h"

@interface SBDBHelper : NSObject {
        sqlite3 *db;
        int theLastError;
        int initError;
        NSString *lastErrorMessage;
}

@property (assign) sqlite3 *db;
@property (assign) int initError;
@property (assign) int theLastError;
@property (nonatomic, retain) NSString *lastErrorMessage;

-(id)initWithDatabaseName:(NSString *)dbName;

-(void)setLastError:(int)theError;
-(void)setLastErrorWithMessage:(int)error message:(NSString *)theMessage;
-(NSError *)getLastError;

@end
```

Here's the implementation. The important part is the constructor that initializes the database.

```objc
// SBSBHelper.m
#import "SBDBHelper.h"
#import "MyClasses.h"

@implementation SBDBHelper

@synthesize db;
@synthesize initError;
@synthesize theLastError;
@synthesize lastErrorMessage;

-(id)initWithDatabaseName:(NSString *)dbName
{
        if(self = [super init])
        {
                // create the database...
                sqlite3 *theDb = nil;
                int result = sqlite3_open([dbName UTF8String], &theDb);
                if(result == SQLITE_OK)
                        self.db = theDb;

                // clear...
                [self setLastError:result];
                self.initError = result;
        }

        // return...
        return self;
}

-(void)setLastError:(int)theError
{
        [self setLastErrorWithMessage:theError message:nil];
}

-(void)setLastErrorWithMessage:(int)error message:(NSString *)theMessage
{
        self.theLastError = error;
        self.lastErrorMessage = theMessage;
}
```

```
-(NSError *)getLastError
{
        // do we have a database?
        if(db == nil)
                return [SBErrorHelper error:self message:[NSString↵
 stringWithFormat:@"Database creation failed with code '%d'.", self.initError]];
        else if(theLastError != SQLITE_OK)
        {
                if([self lastErrorMessage] != nil)
                        return [SBErrorHelper error:self message:[NSString↵
stringWithFormat:@"Last error was '%d', with message '%@'.", theLastError,↵
self.lastErrorMessage]];
                else
                        return [SBErrorHelper error:self message:[NSString↵
stringWithFormat:@"Last error '%d'.  (No error provided.)", theLastError]];
        }
        else
                return nil;
}

-(void)disposeDb
{
        // do we have one?
        if(self.db != nil)
        {
                sqlite3_close(self.db);
                self.db = nil;
        }
}

-(void)dealloc
{
        [self disposeDb];
        [super dealloc];
}

@end
```

The first thing we need to prove is that we can issue statements and create tables, and so we'll look at this first.

Defining SQL Statements

You may recall from Chapter 9 that one of the things that I find most helpful when building an ORM layer is creating a class that holds SQL statements and then passing instances of that class around, as opposed to passing dynamic SQL strings or stored procedure names. I typically do this by creating a class that holds a statement and then an interface that provides access to a statement at runtime. This lets us create a rich data access layer where we're passing around not only objects that are statements, but also objects that can become statements.

On the iPhone, this abstraction with the interfaces is not straightforward; hence I'm proposing not to do this here. However, we do need a class that holds a SQL statement, and so we will build SBSqlStatement. Initially this class will simply hold some text and an array of parameters. We'll need to flesh this out more later as we go. Here's the definition:

```
// SBSqlStatement.h
#import <Foundation/Foundation.h>

@interface SBSqlStatement : NSObject {
        NSString *commandText;
        NSMutableArray *params;
}

@property (nonatomic, retain) NSString *commandText;
@property (nonatomic, retain) NSMutableArray *params;

-(id)initWithCommandText:(NSString *)theCommandText;

-(void)addParameter:(NSObject *)value;

@end
```

For the definition, you can see that we have defined a constructor called initWithCommandText. Later on, we're going to create another constructor, and so on the implementation we're going to override the default constructor and initialize the params property. Here's the implementation:

```
#import "SBSqlStatement.h"

@implementation SBSqlStatement

@synthesize commandText;
@synthesize params;

-(id)init
{
        if(self = [super init])
        {
                self.params = [NSMutableArray array];
        }

        // return...
        return self;
}
```

```
-(id)initWithCommandText:(NSString *)theCommandText
{
        if(self = [self init])
        {
                self.commandText = theCommandText;
        }

        // return...
        return self;
}

-(void)addParameter:(NSObject *)value
{
        [self.params addObject:value];
}

-(void)dealloc
{
        [params release];
        [commandText release];
        [super dealloc];
}

@end
```

That's all we need to do for now. Let's move on to looking at how we create tables.

Creating Tables

Job one with regards to our new database is to create new tables to store data in. We're going to do this by examining at runtime the structure of the entity that we need to create a table for, and we'll do this by walking the fields defined against the entity type.

As we know, SQLite uses a regular ANSI-92 SQL syntax; therefore we want to issue a statement that looks something like this:

```
CREATE TABLE IF NOT EXISTS Bookmarks
        (BookmarkId integer primary key autoincrement,
        Ordinal integer,
        Name varchar(128),
        Url varchar(256))
```

We're going to add two methods to SBDBHelper. One is called getCreateScript, and this method will be responsible for returning a script like the one shown previously. This will defer during processing to a method called appendCreateSnippet. This second method's job will be to write into the SQL string the snippet that defines the field, e.g., Ordinal integer or Name varchar(128). Here's the implementation:

```objc
// Add methods to SBDBHelper.m…
// <…> Needs declaration in header
-(SBSqlStatement *)getCreateScript:(SBEntityType *)et
{
        // builder...
        NSMutableString *builder = [NSMutableString string];
        [builder appendString:@"CREATE TABLE IF NOT EXISTS "];
        [builder appendString:[et nativeName]];
        [builder appendString:@" ("];

        // walk the fields...
        BOOL first = TRUE;
        for(SBEntityField *field in [et fields])
        {
                if(first)
                        first = FALSE;
                else
                        [builder appendString:@", "];

                // snippet...
                [self appendCreateSnippet:builder field:field];
        }

        // end...
        [builder appendString:@")"];

        // return...
        SBSqlStatement *sql = [[SBSqlStatement alloc] initWithCommandText:builder];
        return sql;
}

// <…> Needs declaration in header
-(void)appendCreateSnippet:(NSMutableString *)builder field:(SBEntityField *)theField
{
        [builder appendString:[theField nativeName]];
        [builder appendString:@" "];

        // type...
        SBDataType type = theField.type;
        if(type == SBDT_STRING)
```

```
        {
                [builder appendString:@"varchar("];
                [builder appendFormat:@"%d", theField.size];
                [builder appendString:@")"];
        }
        else if(type == SBDT_INT32)
        {
                [builder appendString:@"integer"];

                // key?
                if(theField.isKey)
                        [builder appendString:@" primary key autoincrement"];
        }
        else
                @throw [NSException exceptionWithName:[[self class] description]↵
reason:[NSString stringWithFormat:@"Cannot handle '%d'.", type, nil] userInfo:nil];
}
```

▨**NOTE** Recall that we support only two datatypes in this implementation—strings and 32-bit integers. Here's another reason I've chosen that for this book—the appendCreateSnippet method would be huge if we supported all available data types.

We obviously need to call that method somehow. One way to do this is to create a method that ensures the table for a given entity type exists prior to use. In fact, this is exactly what we'll do by adding a method called ensureTableExists to the SBDBHelper class.

You'll notice in our create script that we're using the special SQLite IF TABLE EXISTS directive to tell SQLite to ignore the create call if the table is already there. It would be acceptable, therefore, to issue a call to create the table every time we received a call into ensureTableExists. However, for efficiency—especially important as we're on a low-horsepower device—we'll make ensureTableExists keep track of whether a create call has been called in the running session. We'll do this by adding a static property to the SBDBHelper class that keeps a list of the names of the entities that have been "ensured." If we get asked to ensure the table for an entity that we think we've already done, we'll quit the method early and save processor cycles. Here's the code, which uses execNonQuery, which is a method that we will build shortly.

```
// Add member and methods to SBDBHelper.m…
static NSMutableArray * loadMap;

// <…> Needs declaration in header;
+(NSMutableArray *)loadMap
{
        if(loadMap == nil)
        {
```

```
                // create one, and manage the memory…
                loadMap = [NSMutableArray array];
                [loadMap retain];
        }
        return loadMap;
}


// <…> Needs declaration in header;
-(void)ensureTableExists:(SBEntityType *)et
{
        // have we already done this one?
        if([[SBDBHelper loadMap] containsObject:et])
                return;

        // get create script...
        SBSqlStatement *sql = [self getCreateScript:et];
         [self execNonQuery:sql];
        [sql release];

        // set...
        [[SBDBHelper loadMap] addObject:et];
}
```

We can now build the "meaty" execNonQuery method. This method has a few associated parts, which we'll also need to build.

We need a method called handleResult that will take the last result from a SQLite API call and update the internal lastError and lastErrorMessage properties accordingly. The SQLite sqlite3_errmsg function will retrieve some meaningful text related from the error code. Here's the implementation:

```
// Add method to SBDBHelper.m….
// <…> Needs declaration in header
-(void)handleResult:(int)result
{
        self.theLastError = result;
        if(result != SQLITE_OK)
        {
                const char *cError = sqlite3_errmsg(self.db);
                if(cError != nil)
                {
                        NSString *buf = [NSString stringWithCString:cError⏎
encoding:NSUTF8StringEncoding];
                        self.lastErrorMessage = buf;
                }
```

```
            else
                    self.lastErrorMessage = nil;
    }
    else
            self.lastErrorMessage = nil;
}
```

When we come to run a statement using SQLite, we need to create a statement (known as "preparing") and bind any parameters that we've been given. (In the first few statements that we create in this book, there are no parameters.) If binding goes OK, we need to "step" through the query. This is the process that physically runs the query. If we issue a statement that has no return value, we'll get back a status code of SQLITE_DONE. The approach I have taken with this is that if we receive a "done" message, we'll assume that it is "OK." (Otherwise we need to maintain a set of values that mean "OK.") The final thing that we need to do is clear up the statement, known as "finalizing."

Here's the execNonQuery method. We will implement bindParams in a moment.

```
// Add method to SBDBHelper.m…
// <…> Needs declaration in header
-(BOOL)execNonQuery:(SBSqlStatement *)sql
{
        // check that we have a database...
        if(self.db == nil)
                return FALSE;

        // expand the statement...
        const char *sqlString = [sql.commandText UTF8String];

        // prep...
        sqlite3_stmt *statement = nil;
        int result = sqlite3_prepare_v2(self.db, sqlString, -1, &statement, nil);
        if(result == SQLITE_OK)
        {
                // bind...
                result = [self bindParams:statement statement:sql];
                if(result == SQLITE_OK)
                {
                        // actually run it...
                        result = sqlite3_step(statement);

                        // did we do ok?  fudge it so that we don't have to worry about↵
it in the next bit...
                        if(result == SQLITE_DONE)
                                result = SQLITE_OK;
                }
        }
```

```
            // set the last error...
            [self handleResult:result];

            // release...
            if(statement != nil)
                    sqlite3_finalize(statement);

            // return...
            if(result == SQLITE_OK)
                    return TRUE;
            else
                    return FALSE;
}
```

By convention, our methods will return a Boolean value indicating success or failure. If the caller detects a failure, he can call getLastError to return back a full NSError instance.

For our bindParams implementation, we use runtime reflection to get the type of value and then call the appropriate strongly-typed method on the SQLite API. One wrinkle with this is that when we walk our parameters, the array is not zero-based but 1-based. This isn't actually the case for other arrays that SQLite works with (which we'll see later), so some caution is needed.

Here's the implementation:

```
// Add method to SBDBHelper…
// <…> Needs declaration in header
-(int)bindParams:(sqlite3_stmt *)statement statement:(SBSqlStatement *)sql
{
        int result = SQLITE_OK;

        // args...
        int index = 1; // param bindings are 1-based, not 0-based...
        for(NSObject *param in sql.params)
        {
                if([param isKindOfClass:[NSString class]])
                        result = sqlite3_bind_text(statement, index, [((NSString*)param)↵
 UTF8String], -1, nil);
                else if([param isKindOfClass:[NSNumber class]])
                {
                        int theInt = [((NSNumber*)param) intValue];
                        result = sqlite3_bind_int(statement, index, theInt);
                }
                else
                        @throw [NSException exceptionWithName:[[self class] description]↵
reason:[NSString stringWithFormat:@"Cannot handle '%@'.", [[param class] description],↵
nil] userInfo:nil];
```

```
            // did something go wrong?
            if(result != SQLITE_OK)
                    break;

            // next...
            index++;
      }

      // handle the result...
      [self handleResult:result];

      // return...
      return result;
}
```

Note as well that we call handleResult before returning from this method. This isn't strictly necessary, but it is a good habit to get into when wrapping up this old-style form of error handling to try to keep your internal state consistent.

Now we need to get to a position where we can call ensureTableCreated for our SBBookmark class.

In the Android chapter, we named the database using the name of the logged-on user. We'll continue this on iPhone, as this allows multiple users to be able to log onto the device (which we've implied will happen by virtue of creating a logon form). Therefore we need to store the username in the application. We'll do this by storing it in instance memory on the singleton SBRuntime. As well as storing the username, we'll create a method on SBRuntime called getDatabase that will return us back a configured SBDBHelper instance. Here's the implementation:

```
// Add property so SBRuntime.m…
// <…> Needs matching instance variable and @property declaration in header
@synthesize username;

// <…> Needs declaration in header
-(SBDBHelper *)getDatabase
{
        // name...
        NSString *name = [NSString stringWithFormat:@"SixBookmarks-%@", self.username];
        SBDBHelper *db = [[SBDBHelper alloc] initWithDatabaseName:name];

        // return...
        return db;
}
```

```
// Override dealloc…
-(void)dealloc
{
        [username release];
        [super dealloc];
}
```

On SBLogonView, we need to set the logged-on user. This includes a little wrinkle in that we are logging on asynchronously and the callback does not tell us the name of the user that was logged on. To get around this, we'll store the logged-on user in a property called loggingOnUser before we make the call to the service and use this when we have logged on. Here's the implementation:

```
// Add property and modify methods on SBLogonView…
// <…> Needs instance varaible and @property declaration in header, plus and cleanup⏎
 code in dealloc)
@synthesize loggingOnUser;

// Modify this method…
-(IBAction)handleLogonClick:(id)sender
{
        // get the values...
        NSString *username = self.textUsername.text;
        NSString *password = self.textPassword.text;

        // valdiate...
        SBErrorBucket *bucket = [[SBErrorBucket alloc] init];
        if(username == nil || username.length == 0)
                [bucket addError:@"Username is required"];
        if(password == nil || password.length == 0)
                [bucket addError:@"Password is required"];

        // now what?
        if(!(bucket.hasErrors))
        {
                // store for future use...
                self.loggingOnUser = username;

                // we'll do the logon operation in here...
                SBUsersService *users = [[SBUsersService alloc] init];
                [users logon:username password:password callback:(SBLogonCallback *)self];
                [users release];
        }
```

```
            else
                    [SBMessageBox show:bucket.errorsAsString];

            // cleanup...
            [bucket release];
}


// Modify this method...
-(void)logonOk
{
            // store the username...
            [[SBRuntime current] setUsername:self.loggingOnUser];
            self.loggingOnUser = nil;

            // do a sync...
            SBSync *sync = [[[SBSync alloc] init] autorelease];
            [sync doSync:(SBSyncCallback *)self];
}
```

At this point, we're storing the username in SBRuntime, and we're able to create a SBDBHelper instance that points at the correct database.

In SBSync, we'll get the database, call ensureTableExists, and close it again. This usage pattern of keeping the SBDBHelper instance around for as short a time as possible is really important. The SQLite API is, as I've implied, an old-fashioned API, and it's designed for an old-style "open the database and keep it open" usage. The world we live in now is not one that rewards holding databases open, and as such we need to be careful to minimize its lifetime.

Here's the implementation:

```
// Modify doSync method in SBSync.m...
-(void)doSync:(SBSyncCallback *)theCallback
{
            self.callback = theCallback;

            // start spinning...
            [SBServiceProxy startSpinning];

            // check the database...
            SBDBHelper *db = [[SBRuntime current] getDatabase];
            [db ensureTableExists:[SBEntityType getEntityType:[SBBookmark class]]];
            [db release];

            // run...
            [self getLatest];
}
```

If you run the project and log on, the database will be created, and you'll be presented with the message that we saw before in Figure 10-9.

I'll be honest with you here—when I first started iOS development and created my first SQLite database, I spent *ages* trying to find out where it was! Most emulators work using a virtual machine, and I assumed the file had been written to a virtual device. As mentioned before, the iPhone simulator runs directly on the host machine; hence the file system that the simulator uses *is* the file system of the host. You can therefore find the database file in the root of your Mac's file system. Figure 10-14 illustrates.

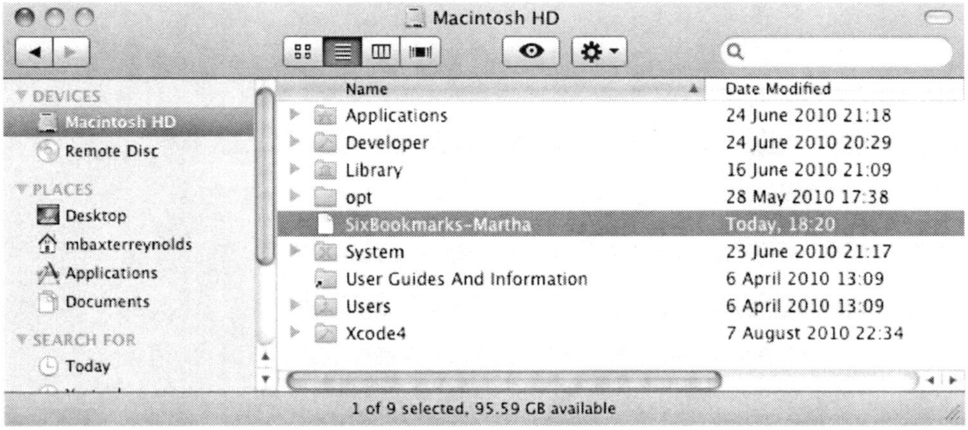

Figure 10-14. *The Six Bookmarks database on the root of the "host" machine*

Storing the Database in the Correct Location

Storing the file anywhere we like on disk works only on the simulator and not on the actual device. There are strict rules surrounding where we can store files—as we know from the PC era, giving applications *carte blanche* to do whatever they want with root/administrative permissions causes major problems.

We can use the NSSearchPathForDirectoriesInDomains method to find the correct path. Here's a modified version of initWithDatabaseName that puts the database file in the correct location. Don't forget to change the sqlite3_open call to use the value in filePath rather than dbName.

```
// Modify method in SBDBHelper.m…
-(id)initWithDatabaseName:(NSString *)dbName
{
        if(self = [super init])
        {
                // find the path...
                NSArray* paths = NSSearchPathForDirectoriesInDomains(NSDocumentDirectory,↵
NSUserDomainMask, YES);
                NSString* documentsFolder = [paths objectAtIndex:0];
                NSString* filePath = [documentsFolder↵
stringByAppendingPathComponent:dbName];
                NSLog(@"Database path: %@", filePath);
```

```
            // create the database...
            sqlite3 *theDb = nil;
            int result = sqlite3_open([filePath UTF8String], &theDb);
            if(result == SQLITE_OK)
                    self.db = theDb;

            // clear...
            [self setLastError:result];
            self.initError = result;
    }

    // return...
    return self;
}
```

If you run the code, the file will be created in the proper location; however, it's not easy to know what that location is. In the preceding code, I have added an NSLog call to render the location to the debug log. Figure 10-15 illustrates.

```
2010-08-11 18:23:55.181 SixBookmarks[11416:207] Database path: /Users/mbaxterreynolds/Library/Application Support/iPhone
Simulator/4.0.1/Applications/99EC336C-C8E1-4CA4-B86D-4D9C85F738A8/Documents/SixBookmarks-Martha
```

Figure 10-15. *A debug message showing the chosen path of the database file based on the package that the application is owned by*

Writing Bookmarks to the Database

At this point the SBSync is able to request a collection of SBBookmark entities. The next step is to write the entities to the database.

When using an ORM layer, what we want to be able to do is ask the entity itself to commit in-memory changes to the database. Further, we want to be able to use the metadata system to build the query that we wish to use. We're going to use a unit of work pattern to do this by implementing a class called SBEntityChangeProcessor, giving this an entity to work with, having the processor work out whether it's to do nothing or it needs to issue an insert, update, or delete operation.

On the SBEntity class, we have already defined methods called isNew, isModified, and isDeleted. isNew and isModified have been implemented to work already, whereas isDeleted is a stub implementation that just returns false. In this chapter, we're going to make the processor understand insert operations *only* and look at update and delete in the next chapter.

Building the Change Processor

First off, let's add a saveChanges method to SBEntity. All this will do is create a processor based on the entity type and defer to the processor. Here's the implementation:

```
// Add method to SBEntity…
// <…> Needs declaration in header
-(void)saveChanges
```

```
{
        SBEntityChangeProcessor *processor = [[SBEntityChangeProcessor alloc]↵
initWithEntityType:[self entityType]];
        [processor saveChanges:self];
        [processor release];
}
```

As we've done a few times now already, we'll look at the structure of SBEntityChangeProcessor and then start filling in the detail. Here's the definition:

```
// SBEntityChangeProcessor.h
#import <Foundation/Foundation.h>
#import "SBEntity.h"

@interface SBEntityChangeProcessor : NSObject {
        SBEntityType *entityType;
}

@property (nonatomic, retain) SBEntityType *entityType;

-(id)initWithEntityType:(SBEntityType *)et;

-(void)saveChanges:(SBEntity *)entity;

-(void)insert:(SBEntity *)entity;
-(void)update:(SBEntity *)entity;
-(void)delete:(SBEntity *)entity;

@end
```

Here's the basic implementation. As we're not going to be handling updates or deletes until the next section, we'll stub their implementation. We'll look at insert shortly.

```
#import "SBEntityChangeProcessor.h"
#import "MyClasses.h"

@implementation SBEntityChangeProcessor

@synthesize entityType;

-(id)initWithEntityType:(SBEntityType *)et
{
        if(self = [super init])
        {
                [self setEntityType:et];
        }
```

```
        // return...
        return self;
}

-(void)saveChanges:(SBEntity *)entity
{
        if([entity isNew])
                [self insert:entity];
        else if([entity isModified])
                [self update:entity];
        else if([entity isDeleted])
                [self delete:entity];
}

-(void)update:(SBEntity *)entity
{
        @throw [NSException exceptionWithName:[[self class] description]↩
 reason:@"Not implemented." userInfo:nil];
}

-(void)delete:(SBEntity *)entity
{
        @throw [NSException exceptionWithName:[[self class] description] reason:↩
@"Not implemented." userInfo:nil];
}

-(void)dealloc
{
        [entityType release];
        [super dealloc];
}
```

@end

The insert method simply has to build a SQL statement that can insert the entity and then execute it against the database.

The SQL statement that we wish to issue looks like this. Note how in this statement we're not specifying a value for BookmarkId—this will be allocated for us by the database. Also, just a reminder that the ? characters in the statement are placeholders for parameters.

```
INSERT INTO Bookmarks (Ordinal, Name, Url) VALUES (?, ?, ?)
```

■**NOTE** For simplicity, the implementation here does not select back from the database the ID that was allocated as part of the statement. If you need to do this, issuing the select last_insert_rowid() statement on the same connection will return back the ID.

Here's the implementation of insert:

```
// Add method to SBEntityChangeProcessor…
-(void)insert:(SBEntity *)entity
{
        SBEntityType *et = self.entityType;

        // do we have a table?
        SBDBHelper *db = nil;
        SBSqlStatement *sql = nil;
        @try
        {
                db = [[SBRuntime current] getDatabase];
                [db ensureTableExists:et];

                // create a statement...
                NSMutableString *builder = [NSMutableString string];
                sql = [[SBSqlStatement alloc] init];

                // header...
                [builder appendString:@"INSERT INTO "];
                [builder appendString:et.nativeName];
                [builder appendString:@" ("];
                BOOL first = TRUE;
                for(SBEntityField *field in et.fields)
                {
                        if([entity isFieldModified:field])
                        {
                                if(first)
                                        first = FALSE;
                                else
                                        [builder appendString:@", "];

                                // name...
                                [builder appendString:field.nativeName];
                        }
                }

                // values...
                [builder appendString:@") VALUES ("];
                first = TRUE;
                for(SBEntityField *field in et.fields)
                {
```

```
                        if([entity isFieldModified:field])
                        {
                                if(first)
                                        first = FALSE;
                                else
                                        [builder appendString:@", "];

                                // name...
                                [builder appendString:@"?"];
                                [sql addParameter:[entity getValue:field]];
                        }
                }
                [builder appendString:@")"];

                // attach...
                sql.commandText = builder;

                // run...
                BOOL ok = [db execNonQuery:sql];
                if(!(ok))
                {
                        NSError *err = [db getLastError];
                        @throw [NSException exceptionWithName:[[self class] description]↵
    reason:[SBErrorHelper formatError:err] userInfo:nil];
                }
        }
        @finally
        {
                // release...
                [sql release];
                [db release];
        }
}
```

The only slightly odd part of that method is the error handling. As you know by now, I'm not a huge fan of the way Objective-C deals with exceptions, and I try not to use them where possible. However, in this situation, we really do need to be looking at throwing exceptions if we can't manage to get through the operation nicely. Because we are likely to throw an exception, we can use a @try...@finally to ensure that the resources that we create—particularly the database—are cleaned up.

We can now call saveChanges on an entity. We need to go back into the SBSync class and complete the getLatest operation to do so.

Completing getLatest

The first job to do to complete the getLatest operation is that inside the odataFetchOk callback we have to make a decision about what we're doing. Recall that we're having to reuse this method for multiple operations—although you won't see this in action until the next chapter. What we'll do is modify the odataFetchOk method to look at the op code and look at the mode property, and defer to a method called processServerItemsForGetAll. (We'll build this method in a moment.) Here's the revised implementation:

```
// Replace odataFetchOk method in SBSync.m….
-(void)odataFetchOk:(SBEntityXmlBucket *)bucket opCode:(int)theOpCode
{
        // what's our mode?
        if(theOpCode == OPCODE_ODATAFETCHALL)
        {
                if(self.mode == SBSMGetLatest)
                        [self processServerItemsForGetAll:bucket];
                else
                        @throw [NSException exceptionWithName:[[self class]↵
description] reason:@"Cannot handle mode." userInfo:nil];
        }
        else
                @throw [NSException exceptionWithName:[[self class]↵
description] reason:@"Cannot handle op code." userInfo:nil];

        // stop spinning...
        [SBServiceProxy stopSpinning];
}
```

Before we look at inserting the entity, we have to be able to clear out all existing entities. We'll do this with a static method on SBBookmark called deleteAll. Here's the implementation:

```
// Add method to SBBookmark.m…
// <…> Needs declaration in header
+(void)deleteAll
{
        SBDBHelper *db = [[SBRuntime current] getDatabase];

        // check...
        SBEntityType *et = [SBEntityType getEntityType:[SBBookmark class]];
        [db ensureTableExists:et];

        // run...
        SBSqlStatement *sql = [[SBSqlStatement alloc] initWithCommandText:@"delete↵
from bookmark"];
```

```
        [db execNonQuery:sql];
        [sql release];
        [db release];

}
```

When we created the OData service proxy method to return all the bookmarks, we made this return SBBookmark entities. I chose to do that because I felt it was unnecessarily complicated to have a separate set of classes representing bookmarks that go over the wire compared to bookmarks that live in the local database. It's not unusual to have this separation, and in many cases it is desirable.

Where this gets a little strange is that the OData service returns back the entities with the bookmarkId property populated with values that represent the internal, private IDs in the *server's* database. Our change processor is configured to treat entities that do not have a loaded ID as new and entities that do have a loaded ID as potentially modified and deleted. Thus if we pass our change processor an entity that we have downloaded, it will look at it and assume it has been modified. It will attempt to issue an UPDATE rather than an INSERT statement, and the process will create incorrect results.

What we therefore have to do is walk each downloaded bookmark and create a new SBBookmark instance for each. We'll walk the fields described in the metadata and patch all of the fields that are not *key* fields into the new entity. We can then pass this entity over to the change processor. It will detect an unloaded ID value and assume it is to be inserted. Thus the operation will work properly. Finally, when we create our new entity, we have to set the localModified and localDeleted properties. As the server does not know about these, they won't be loaded, and the database will try to insert them as null. We want these explicitly to be FALSE, which will get translated into **0** in the database by the SBEntityChangeProcessor. Here's the implementation:

```
// Add method to SBSync.m…
// <…> Needs declaration in header
-(void)processServerItemsForGetAll:(SBEntityXmlBucket *)entities
{
        // we have them - so clear down the database and insert them...
        [SBBookmark deleteAll];

        // walk...
        SBEntityType *et = [SBEntityType getEntityType:[SBBookmark class]];
        for(SBBookmark *server in entities.entities)
        {
                // create a new one, skipping the key...
                SBBookmark *local = [[SBBookmark alloc] init];
                for(SBEntityField *field in et.fields)
                {
                        // only do this if we've been set and we're a key...
                        if(!([field isKey]) && [server isFieldLoaded:field])
                        {
                                NSObject *value = [server getValue:field];
                                [local setValue:field value:value reason:SBESRUserSet];
                        }
                }
```

```
                // force the special fields...
                local.localModified = FALSE;
                local.localDeleted = FALSE;

                // save...
                [local saveChanges];

                // release...
                [local release];
        }

        // great - we're done...
        [self.callback syncOk];
}
```

That should be it! You can now run the application and log on, and it will download the bookmarks to your local database. However, you won't see any different results because at this point, our project is still rigged to display the fake bookmarks that we created much earlier in the chapter.

Reading Bookmarks and Displaying Them on the Navigator

Now that we have bookmarks in our local database, we can replace the code that displays the fake bookmarks with code that retrieves the entities from the database. The code we've written to display the bookmarks on the screen remains unchanged—we only need to modify the retrieval code.

We already have a database method that will execute a query without expecting a result (executeNonQuery). We now need to write a method that will return a collection of entities— executeEntityCollection. To do this, we're going to create a class called SBSqlFilter.

The purpose of SBSqlFilter is to retrieve values from the database based on the principle of constraining data down from the maximum possible set (all rows in a given table) to the set that you want. It could be that the set you want is the maximum possible set ("get all"), a single row represented by a key value ("get by ID"), or some other set.

So that we can tell SBSqlFilter what constraints we want to work with, we'll create a base SBSqlConstraint class and a specialized SBSqlFieldConstraint class. The filter will ask the constraints to contribute their own snippets of SQL to the main SQL query that it will build.

■NOTE If you've looked at the other "SQL filter" implementations for the other platforms, you'll note that there was a companion interface called ISqlStatementSource. Although I'm a big fan of the approach of having this separate layer of abstraction, limitations in Objective-C remove the advantage of using such an interface. As such, we won't be repeating ISqlStatementSource in this chapter.

First, here's the definition of the base SBSqlConstraint class:

```
// SBSqlConstraint.h
#import <Foundation/Foundation.h>
```

```
#import "SBSqlStatement.h"

@interface SBSqlConstraint : NSObject {
}

-(void)append:(NSMutableString *)builder statement:(SBSqlStatement *)theStatement;

@end
```

and the implementation:

```
// SBSqlConstraint.m
#import "SBSqlConstraint.h"

@implementation SBSqlConstraint

-(void)append:(NSMutableString *)builder statement:(SBSqlStatement *)theStatement
{
        @throw [NSException exceptionWithName:[[self class] description] reason:↵
@"Not implemented." userInfo:nil];
}

@end
```

Here's the definition of the specialized SBSqlFieldConstraint class:

```
// SBSqlFieldConstraint.h
#import <Foundation/Foundation.h>
#import "SBSqlConstraint.h"
#import "SBEntityField.h"

@interface SBSqlFieldConstraint : SBSqlConstraint {

        SBEntityField *field;
        NSObject *value;

}

@property (nonatomic, retain) SBEntityField *field;
@property (nonatomic, retain) NSObject *value;

-(id)initWithFieldAndValue:(SBEntityField *)theField value:(NSObject *)theValue;

@end
```

And here's its implementation:

```
// SBSqlFieldConstraint.m
#import "SBSqlFieldConstraint.h"
#import "MyClasses.h"

@implementation SBSqlFieldConstraint

@synthesize field;
@synthesize value;

-(id)initWithFieldAndValue:(SBEntityField *)theField value:(NSObject *)theValue
{
        if(self = [super init])
        {
                self.field = theField;
                self.value = theValue;
        }

        // return...
        return self;
}

-(void)append:(NSMutableString *)builder statement:(SBSqlStatement *)theStatement
{
        [builder appendString:[[self field] nativeName]];
        [builder appendString:@"=?"];

        // arg...
        [theStatement addParameter:[self value]];
}

-(void)dealloc
{
        [value release];
        [field release];
        [super dealloc];
}

@end
```

Now that we can define constraints, we'll look at using them. The job of SBSqlFilter is to create a SQL statement that can be used with a to-be-built method on SBDBHelper called executeEntityCollection. It will maintain a list of constraints and will have two constructors—one that can be used with a SBEntityType instance, and once that can be used with a class. (This latter one will de-reference the relevant SBEntityType instance and is included for ease of use.)

Here's the definition:

```
// SBSqlFilter.h
#import <Foundation/Foundation.h>
#import "SBSqlStatement.h"
#import "SBEntityType.h"
#import "SBEntity.h"

@interface SBSqlFilter : NSObject {

        SBEntityType *entityType;
        NSMutableArray *constraints;

}

@property (nonatomic, retain) SBEntityType *entityType;
@property (nonatomic, retain) NSMutableArray *constraints;

-(id)initWithType:(Class)typeToDereference;
-(id)initWithEntityType:(SBEntityType *)et;

-(SBSqlStatement *)getSqlStatement;

-(NSError *)executeEntityCollection:(NSMutableArray **)theResults;

@end
```

The basic implementation is shown here. We'll build getSqlStatement, executeEntityCollection, and executeEntity shortly.

```
// SBSqlFilter.m
#import "SBSqlFilter.h"
#import "MyClasses.h"

@implementation SBSqlFilter

@synthesize entityType;
@synthesize constraints;

-(id)initWithEntityType:(SBEntityType *)et
{
        if(self = [super init])
        {
                self.entityType = et;
                self.constraints = [NSMutableArray array];
        }
```

```
        // return...
        return self;
}

-(id)initWithType:(Class)typeToDereference
{
        SBEntityType *et = [SBEntityType getEntityType:typeToDereference];
        return [self initWithEntityType:et];
}

-(void)dealloc
{
        [constraints release];
        [entityType release];
        [super dealloc];
}

@end
```

As mentioned previously, the purpose of SBSqlFilter is to create a SQL statement that can be executed against the database. This statement will obviously be a SELECT statement.

We have to overcome a limitation of the SQLite API in this next part because we need to use a strongly-typed method on the API to extract values from the column. (Specifically, we'll be using sqlite3_column_text and sqlite3_column_int.) However, when we run the statement, we don't know the types of the columns. What we need to do to fix this is create a "select map." We'll add this to SBSqlStatement. It'll be structured as an array of SBEntityField instances, the idea being that when we come to extract the values from the rows returned via SQLite, we can look at the column and determine the type, as the entity field is associated with exactly one data type. Here are the changes:

```
// Add property, modify init method and add initWithEntityType on SBSqlStatement
// Code has been omitted - do NOT remove or change other methods!
// <…> Needs instance variables and @property statements in header
@synthesize selectMap;  // type NSMutableArray…
@synthesize entityType; // type SBEntityType…

-(id)init
{
        if(self = [super init])
        {
                self.params = [NSMutableArray array];
                self.selectMap = [NSMutableArray array];
        }

        // return...
        return self;
}
```

```
// <…> Needs declaration in header…
-(id)initWithEntityType:(SBEntityType *)theEntityType
{
        if(self = [self init])
        {
                self.entityType = theEntityType;
        }

        // return...
        return self;
}
```

In addition, dealloc needs to change:

```
// Modify dealloc method in SBSqlStatement…
-(void)dealloc
{
        [entityType release];
        [selectMap release];
        [params release];
        [commandText release];
        [super dealloc];
}
```

And finally we need to add an addToSelectMapMethod:

```
// Add method to SBSqlStatement…
// <…> Needs declaration in header…
-(void)addToSelectMap:(SBEntityField *)field
{
        [self.selectMap addObject:field];
}
```

We can now go back and look at the getSqlStatement method on SBSqlFilter. The purpose of this method is to build a SQL statement, adding to the select map as it goes and also asking any available constraints to contribute towards any WHERE class. Here's the implementation:

```
// Add to SBSqlFilter.m…
-(SBSqlStatement *)getSqlStatement
{
        SBEntityType *et = [self entityType];

        // create...
        NSMutableString *builder = [NSMutableString string];
        SBSqlStatement *sql = [[SBSqlStatement alloc] initWithEntityType:et];
```

```
        // walk...
        [builder appendString:@"SELECT "];
        BOOL first = true;
        for(SBEntityField *field in et.fields)
        {
                if(first)
                        first = FALSE;
                else
                        [builder appendString:@", "];

                // name...
                [builder appendString:field.nativeName];
                [sql addToSelectMap:field];
        }

        // table...
        [builder appendString:@" FROM "];
        [builder appendString:et.nativeName];

        // constraints...
        NSMutableArray *items = self.constraints;
        if(items.count > 0)
        {
                [builder appendString:@" WHERE "];
                first = TRUE;
                for(SBSqlConstraint *constraint in items)
                {
                        if(first)
                                first = FALSE;
                        else
                                [builder appendString:@" AND "];
                        [constraint append:builder statement:sql];
                }
        }

        // return...
        sql.commandText = builder;
        return sql;
}
```

The implementation of executeEntityCollection is going to happen in two ways. We're going to add a helper method to SBSqlFilter, but do the main work in SBDBHelper. Here's the helper implementation on SBSqlFilter:

```
// Add method to SBSqlFilter…
-(NSError *)executeEntityCollection:(NSMutableArray **)theResults;
{
        SBSqlStatement *sql = [self getSqlStatement];

        // run...
        SBDBHelper *db = [[SBRuntime current] getDatabase];
        NSError *err = nil;
        BOOL ok = [db executeEntityCollection:sql results:theResults];
        if(!(ok))
                err = [db getLastError];

        // cleanup...
        [sql release];
        [db release];

        // return...
        return err;
}
```

This is the first time we've seen a "pointer to a pointer" on one of our method declarations. What we're doing here is allowing executeEntityCollection to set the value of a variable that we pass in. This allows us to return both an error and a result set back from this method without having to build a special "return result" class.

Now that we can call it, we can look at the executeEntityCollection method on SBDBHelper. This method is pretty complicated—easily the single largest method that we've built in this chapter. We'll go through it in sections.

The first job is to check that the SBSqlStatement has an associated entity type. We need to know this because we need to know if the select map is valid.

```
// Add method to SBDBHelper…
// <…> Needs declaration in header
-(BOOL)executeEntityCollection:(SBSqlStatement *)sql results:(NSMutableArray **)theResults
{
        // reset...
        *theResults = nil;

        // check that we have a database...
        if(db == nil)
                return FALSE;
```

```
        // set the entity type...
        SBEntityType *et = [sql entityType];
        if(et == nil)
                @throw [NSException exceptionWithName:[[self class] description] reason:@"The
provided SQL statement did not have an entity type." userInfo:nil];
```

We can then check that the table exists, get a C-style string out of the NSString-typed commandText property, and then create an array to store the results.

```
        // ensure...
        [self ensureTableExists:et];

        // expand the statement...
        const char *sqlString = [[sql commandText] UTF8String];
        NSLog(@"Executing: %s", sqlString);

        // create somewhere to put the results...
        NSMutableArray *results = [NSMutableArray array];
```

Next we prepare the statement. This is similar to how we did executeNonQuery.

```
        // prep...
        sqlite3_stmt *statement = nil;
        int result = sqlite3_prepare_v2(db, sqlString, -1, &statement, nil);
        if(result == SQLITE_OK)
        {
                result = [self bindParams:statement statement:sql];
                if(result == SQLITE_OK)
                {
```

As opposed to executeNonQuery, we need to walk through a set of rows that come back from the database. When we call the sqlite3_step statement, this will return SQLITE_ROW if our cursor is pointing at a row.

```
                        while(TRUE)
                        {
                                // step...
                                result = sqlite3_step(statement);
                                if(result == SQLITE_ROW)
                                {
```

Once we know we have a row, we can create an instance. We then use the map to de-reference each field in turn and use the type value contained within the field to call a specialized SQLite API function to get a value out.

```
                              // create an instance...
                              SBEntity *entity = [et createInstance];

                              // load the values out...
                              NSArray *map = [sql selectMap];
                              for(int index = 0; index < [map count]; index++)
                              {
                                      SBEntityField *field = (SBEntityField *)↵
[map objectAtIndex:index];

                                      int columnIndex = index;

                                      // get the value...
                                      NSObject *value = nil;
                                      SBDataType type = [field type];
                                      if(type == SBDT_STRING)
                                      {
                                              const char *cString =↵
(const char *)sqlite3_column_text(statement, columnIndex);
                                              value = [NSString↵
stringWithCString:cString encoding:NSUTF8StringEncoding];
                                      }
                                      else if(type == SBDT_INT32)
                                              value = [NSNumber↵
numberWithInt:sqlite3_column_int(statement, columnIndex)];
                                      else
                                              @throw [NSException↵
exceptionWithName:[[self class] description] reason:[NSString stringWithFormat:v
@"Cannot handle '%d'.", type, nil] userInfo:nil];
```

Once we have the value, we set the value on the entity and add it to the collection.

```
                                      // set (with a 'load' set reason)...
                                      [entity setValue:field value:value↵
reason:SBESRLoad];
                              }

                              // add...
                              [results addObject:entity];
                      }
```

```
                              else if(result == SQLITE_DONE)
                              {
                                      // reset and stop...
                                      result = SQLITE_OK;
                                      break;
                              }
                              else
                                      break;
                      }
              }
      }
```

At the end of the loop, the operation is essentially the same as executeNonQuery. The only real difference is that if we executed OK, we set the results so that they can be seen by the caller, otherwise we release them.

```
      // set the last error...
      [self handleResult:result];

      // release...
      if(statement != nil)
              sqlite3_finalize(statement);

      // return...
      if(result == SQLITE_OK)
      {
              *theResults = results;
              return TRUE;
      }
      else
      {
              // trash the results and return nil...
              [results release];
              return FALSE;
      }
}
```

All that remains now is creating the method that will get the bookmarks for display. We'll add a method called getBookmarksForDisplay to SBBookmark. This will create a filter but constrain the results so that only those that have not been locally deleted are included. Here's the implementation:

```
// Add method to SBBookmark.m…
// <…> Needs declaration in header
+(NSError *)getBookmarksForDisplay:(NSMutableArray **)theBookmarks
{
        SBSqlFilter *filter = [[SBSqlFilter alloc] initWithType:[SBBookmark class]];
        [filter.constraints addObject:[[SBSqlFieldConstraint alloc]↲
initWithFieldAndValue:[filter.entityType getField:@"localdeleted"]
                        value:[NSNumber numberWithBool:FALSE]]];

        // return...
        NSError *err = [filter executeEntityCollection:theBookmarks];
        [filter release];
        return err;
}
```

All that remains now is to replace the fake bookmark creation with code that calls getBookmarksForDisplay. Here it is:

```
// Replace method in SBNavigatorView.m…
-(void)refreshView
{
        // get them...
        NSMutableArray *theBookmarks = nil;
        NSError *err = [SBBookmark getBookmarksForDisplay:&theBookmarks];
        if(err != nil)
        {
                [SBMessageBox showError:err];
        return;
        }

        // show...
        [self showBookmarks:theBookmarks];
}
```

You can now run the application and have the satisfaction of seeing your bookmarks downloaded and visible. Figure 10-16 illustrates.

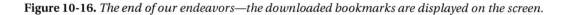

Figure 10-16. *The end of our endeavors—the downloaded bookmarks are displayed on the screen.*

Conclusion

In this chapter we have gone deep into the functionality of Six Bookmarks on iPhone. We've built two user interface forms and an entire object-relational mapping data access layer. We've communicated with our OData bookmarks service and updated a local SQLite database. In the next chapter, we'll look at how to configure our bookmarks and send changes back to the server.

CHAPTER 11

iOS : Pushing Changes Back to the Server

In this chapter, we're going to continue the work of the Six Bookmarks application by implementing the code that allows the user to modify the bookmarks and then push them back to the server. We'll start by looking at the user interface.

Configuring Bookmarks

We're going to base the user interface for our configuration window on a **Table View** control. The Table View control is perhaps the most common user interface metaphor on iOS devices—it seems to me that every application I ever download and use on iPhone or iPad is based on tables!

We'll jump right in and start designing the user interface. Similar to the Android application, what we're going to do is build a form that shows the current bookmarks. Selecting a bookmark will take us into a "singleton edit" page. We'll also be able to add new bookmarks, edit (i.e., delete) bookmarks, and manually initiate a sync routine.

Add a new **UIViewController Subclass** item to the project called SBConfigureView. When the view is created, double-click on the SBConfigureView.xib file to start editing the UI. Once there, add the following elements:

- Add a **Navigation Bar** control, changing its text to **Configure**.

- Add a **Toolbar** control. Change the default button text to **Done**, and add two new buttons. When you add the buttons, use the **Attributes Inspector** to change the **Identifier** of one to be **Edit** and the other to be **Refresh**. The **Refresh** button will automatically adopt a built-in image. Also add a **Flexible Space Bar Button Item** to push the **Edit** and **Refresh** buttons to the right of the bar.

- To the navigation bar, add a button and set its **Identifier** button to be **Add**. This, too, will adopt a built-in image.

- Finally, add a **Table View** control to the main area of the form.

You should end up with something like Figure 11-1.

In terms of the code, we need to maintain a property for referencing the table, and a property for holding a list of bookmarks in memory. We also need event handlers to receive notifications of the done, edit, sync/refresh, and add buttons. (We can implement handleClose straightaway, as we know what we're doing with this—we just need to go back to the navigator form.) We also need to change the base class to be our special SBViewController class and also implement the UITableViewDelegate and UITableViewDataSource protocols.

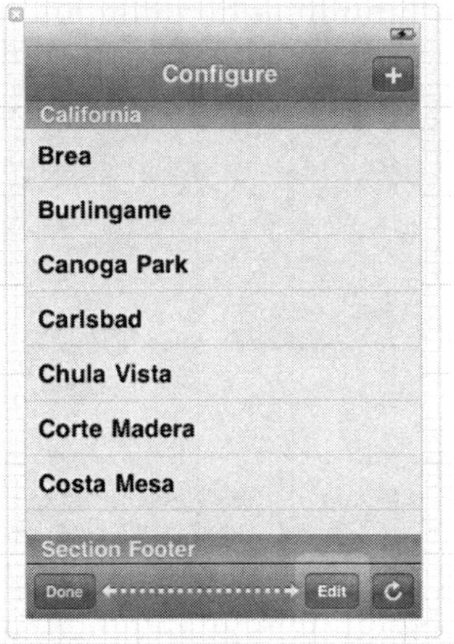

Figure 11-1. *The design of the configuration form*

Here's the definition:

```
// SBConfigureView.h
#import <UIKit/UIKit.h>
#import "SBViewController.h"
#import "SBSync.h"

@interface SBConfigureView : SBViewController <UITableViewDelegate, UITableViewDataSource> {

        NSMutableArray *bookmarks;
        UITableView *table;
        SBSync *syncEngine;

}

@property (nonatomic, retain) NSMutableArray *bookmarks;
@property (nonatomic, retain) IBOutlet UITableView *table;
@property (nonatomic, retain) SBSync *syncEngine;

-(IBAction)handleClose:(id)sender;
-(IBAction)handleSync:(id)sender;
-(IBAction)handleEdit:(id)sender;
-(IBAction)handleAdd:(id)sender;

@end
```

And here's the implementation:

```objc
// SBConfigureView.m
#import "SBConfigureView.h"
#import "MyClasses.h"

@implementation SBConfigureView

@synthesize bookmarks;
@synthesize table;
@synthesize syncEngine;

-(IBAction)handleClose:(id)sender
{
        // go back to the navigator…
        [self.owner openNavigator];
}

-(IBAction)handleSync:(id)sender
{
        [SBMessageBox show:@"TBD"];
}

-(IBAction)handleEdit:(id)sender
{
        [SBMessageBox show:@"TBD"];
}

-(IBAction)handleAdd:(id)sender
{
        [SBMessageBox show:@"TBD"];
}

// Some wizard-generated code has been ommitted for brevity

-(void)dealloc
{
        [syncEngine release];
        [bookmarks release];
        [table release];
    [super dealloc];
}

@end
```

When we put together the view in the user interface editor, we didn't wire up the controls and events using the **Connections Inspector**. We can do this now to wire up the following:

- **selector** event of **Add** button goes to handleAdd method.

- **selector** event of **Done** button goes to handleClose method.

- **selector** event of **Edit** button goes to handleEdit method.

- **selector** event of **Sync/Refresh** button goes to handleSync method.

- **table** property on **File's Owner** goes to the **Table View** control.

- *Very important*, the **dataSource** member of the **Table View** control has to be bound back to **File's Owner**. This is the mechanism through which the view discovers its data.

- *Also very important*, the **delegate** member of the **Table View** control also has to be bound back to **File's Owner**. This is the mechanism through which the view raises user interaction events.

That's essentially it for the user interface basics—we'll look now at how to put data onto the table.

Putting Data on the Table

The approach that Cocoa Touch takes with the table view is that we wire up the **dataSource** member of the Table View control and then wait for events to be called. The minimum two events that we need to support are tableView:numberOfRowsInSection and tableView:cellForRowAtIndexPath. We'll look at those methods in a moment—our immediate concern is implementing refreshView so that our bookmarks property gets populated with the visible bookmarks from the SQLite database.

We've already seen how we can use the getBookmarksForDisplay method on the navigator. We'll reuse this method here, but we'll capture the results in a property for later use.

The listing follows—one thing to mention beforehand is that if we happen to load a new list of bookmarks, we need to tell the table to reload. We'll keep track of this state in a local variable called doReload and call reloadData as needed.

```
// Add method to SBConfigureView.m
-(void)refreshView
{
        // do we have bookmarks?
        BOOL doReload = FALSE;
        if(self.bookmarks != nil)
                doReload = TRUE;

        // get our bookmarks...
        NSMutableArray *theBookmarks = nil;
        NSError *err = [SBBookmark getBookmarksForDisplay:&theBookmarks];
        if(err != nil)
                [SBMessageBox showError:err];
        else
        {
                // keep track...
                self.bookmarks = theBookmarks;
        }
```

```
        // reload...
        if(doReload)
                [self.table reloadData];
}
```

tableView:numberOfRowsInSection simply needs to return the number of bookmarks for display. tableView:cellForRowAtIndexPath is more interesting—this method requires us to return back a cell for it to show on the view. The way it does this is quite interesting. It assumes that memory on the device is limited (which it is), and so if you have a long list of items (many tens up to many thousands and beyond), it will attempt to recycle and reuse cells that have become no-longer-visible—for example, when the user scrolls the view. To do this, each cell is given a key, which is a classifier of type rather than instance—it's very common to find Table View instances in applications that use a single table but multiple types of cells. When we are asked for a cell at a given path (which in our case will be a row ordinal), we can ask the Table View control to recycle one of those cells for us. If it can't, we'll create one and return it. Either way, we'll update the text on the cell that we either got given or created and hand it back. The recycling process works by providing an arbitrary string to the type of cell. (It's common in iOS applications to have multiple types of cell on a table.) Our arbitrary string will be stored in a constant variable called cellId and will have value BookmarkKey.

Here's the implementation:

```
// Add methods to SBConfigureView.m…
-(NSInteger)tableView:(UITableView *)tableView numberOfRowsInSection:(NSInteger)section
{
        return [self.bookmarks count];
}


-(UITableViewCell *)tableView:(UITableView *)tableView cellForRowAtIndexPath:↵
(NSIndexPath *)indexPath
{
        static NSString *cellId = @"BookmarkKey";

        // find one...
        UITableViewCell *cell = [tableView dequeueReusableCellWithIdentifier:cellId];
        if(cell == nil)
                cell = [[[UITableViewCell alloc] initWithStyle:UITableViewCellStyleDefault↵
 reuseIdentifier:cellId] autorelease];

        // set...
        NSUInteger row = [indexPath row];
        cell.textLabel.text = [[self.bookmarks objectAtIndex:row] name];
        return cell;
}
```

We are very nearly at a point where we can run this and get some data on the screen, which is a good indicator as to how simple working with lists is in iOS. To get it working, we first need to add a method called openConfiguration to our SixBookmarksAppDelegate class, which is patterned on the openLogon and openNavigator methods that we built earlier. Here's the code:

```
// Add method to SixBookmarksAppDelegate…
// <…> Needs declaration in header
```

385

```
-(void)openConfiguration
{
        // find a preexisting view...
        SBViewController *view = [self getController:[SBConfigureView class]];
        if(view == nil)
                view = [[SBConfigureView alloc] initWithNibName:@"SBConfigureView"↵
bundle:[NSBundle mainBundle]];

        // show the view...
        [self showView:view];
}
```

Previously, our method on SBNavigatorView for handling the **Configure** button click simply displayed a message box. We can change this now to physically open the form:

```
// Modify method in SBNavigatorView…
-(IBAction)handleConfigure:(id)sender
{
        [self.owner openConfiguration];
}
```

Run the application and you will be able to click through, open the new form, and see the bookmarks. Figure 11-2 illustrates.

Figure 11-2. *The configuration form*

Sorting the Bookmarks

If you recall from the Android chapter, when we displayed the bookmarks in its Table View equivalent, we ended up with bookmarks sorted by name rather than by ordinal. This would undoubtedly lead to user confusion, and so we sorted the bookmarks before display. We need to do the same thing.

The way you do a sort in Objective-C is functional, but a little odd. What we have to do is provide a "function pointer" of sorts through to the sort routine. When the sort routine chugs along sorting, it will call this function pointer to compare two items. We're going to sort by ordinal, and so we need to add a method called ordinalComparer to SBBookmark. Here's the code:

```
// Add method to SBBookmark.m
-(NSComparisonResult)ordinalComparer:(id)otherObject
{
        SBBookmark *other = (SBBookmark *)otherObject;
        if(self.ordinal < other.ordinal)
                return NSOrderedAscending;
        else if(self.ordinal > other.ordinal)
                return NSOrderedDescending;
        else
                return NSOrderedSame;

}
```

As you can see, this works by giving the method another bookmark instance to compare.

To call this method, we use the special Objective-C syntax of @selector to create a "function pointer" (a "method pointer," really) to the ordinalComparer method which we can then pass into the sortUsingSelector method of the NSMutableArray. Here's the implementation:

```
// Modify method in SBConfigureView.m…
-(void)refreshView
{
        // do we have bookmarks?
        BOOL doReload = FALSE;
        if(self.bookmarks != nil)
                doReload = TRUE;

        // get our bookmarks...
        NSMutableArray *theBookmarks = nil;
        NSError *err = [Bookmark getBookmarksForDisplay:&theBookmarks];
        if(err != nil)
                [SBMessageBox showError:err];
        else
        {
                // keep track...
                self.bookmarks = theBookmarks;

                // sort by ordinal...
                [theBookmarks sortUsingSelector:@selector(ordinalComparer:)];
        }
```

```
        // reload...
        if(doReload)
                [self.table reloadData];
}
```

Now if you run the code again, you will end up with a list sorted in ordinal order. Figure 11-3 illustrates.

Figure 11-3. *The configuration view, now with items correctly ordered*

Singleton View

We now need a singleton view for editing single bookmarks. To the project, add a new **UIViewController Subclass** item called **SBConfigureSingletonView**. Once added, open the SBConfigureSingletonView.xib file in the usual way.

To the form, add the following:

- A **Navigation Bar** control, with the title changed to **Configure**

- A **Bar Button** Item control on the left of the navigation bar with its **Identifier** set to **Cancel**

- Another **Bar Button** Item control on the right of the navigation bar with its **Identifier** set to **Save**

- Two **Text Field** controls—set the **Placeholder** to **Name** and **URL** respectively.

Figure 11-4 illustrates.

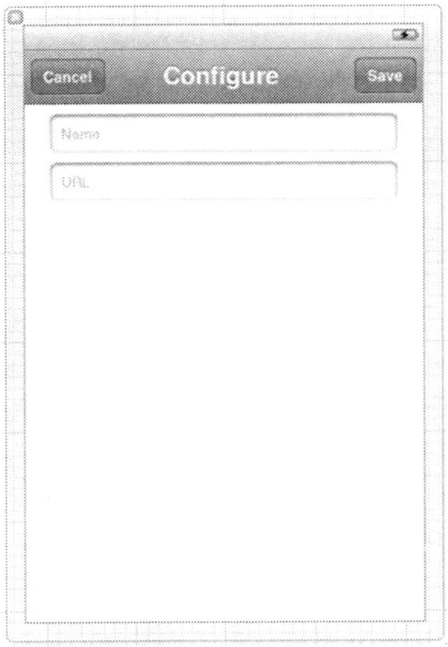

Figure 11-4. *The designer view for "configure singleton"*

Again in the usual way, we need to go back into the code to add properties for the text boxes and methods to receive event notifications for the buttons. In addition, the form will also need to hold a reference to the current SBBookmark instance and also have a method called setOrdinal. This setOrdinal method will be used to initialize the view.

Here's the definition:

```
// SBConfigureSingletonView.h
#import <UIKit/UIKit.h>
#import "SBViewController.h"
#import "SBBookmark.h"

@interface SBConfigureSingletonView : SBViewController {

        SBBookmark *bookmark;
        UITextField *textName;
        UITextField *textUrl;

}

@property (nonatomic, retain) SBBookmark *bookmark;
@property (nonatomic, retain) IBOutlet UITextField *textName;
@property (nonatomic, retain) IBOutlet UITextField *textUrl;
```

```objc
-(void)setOrdinal:(int)theOrdinal;

-(IBAction)handleCancel:(int)sender;
-(IBAction)handleSave:(int)sender;

@end
```

And then the implementation:

```objc
// SBConfigureSingletonView.m
#import "SBConfigureSingletonView.h"
#import "MyClasses.h"

@implementation SBConfigureSingletonView

@synthesize bookmark;
@synthesize textName;
@synthesize textUrl;

-(void)setOrdinal:(int)theOrdinal
{
        // we'll do this later…
}

-(IBAction)handleCancel:(int)sender
{
        [self.owner openConfiguration];
}

-(IBAction)handleSave:(int)sender
{
        [SBMessageBox show:@"TBD"];
}

// Some wizard-generated code has been omitted.

-(void)dealloc
{
        [bookmark release];
        [textName release];
        [textUrl release];
    [super dealloc];
}

@end
```

With the class stubbed out in the way, we can go back into the user interface editor and bind up the methods and properties, specifically:

- **selector** event of **Cancel** button goes to handleCancel method.

- **selector** event of **Save** button goes to handleSave method.

- **textName** property of **File's Owner** goes to the **Name** text box.

- **textUrl** property of **File's Owner** goes to the **URL** text box.

Next we can add an openBookmarkSingleton method to the SixBookmarksAppDelegate class that will open the view and call the setOrdinal method. (We haven't implemented setOrdinal properly yet, so all this will do is show a message box.)

Here's the implementation:

```
// Add method to SixBookmarksAppDelegate.m
// <...> Needs declaration in header
-(void)openBookmarkSingleton:(int)theOrdinal
{
        // find a preexisting view...
        SBViewController *view = [self getController:[SBConfigureSingletonView class]];
        if(view == nil)
                view = [[SBConfigureSingletonView alloc] initWithNibName:↲
@"SBConfigureSingletonView" bundle:[NSBundle mainBundle]];

        // set...
        [((SBConfigureSingletonView *)view) setOrdinal:theOrdinal];

        // show the view...
        [self showView:view];
}
```

OK, so at this point, we can view the view and show it, but how do we configure the table so that we can click on it and make all this happen?

Each cell on the table can be configured with a "disclosure indicator." You will have undoubtedly seen this used in iOS applications before—it is a small arrow to the right of each item that tells you that you can "drill into" the item for more information. (There is a variation on this called a "disclosure button," which we're not going to use. A disclosure button lets you do something with an item, e.g., make a phone call or start an email, but it isn't designed to indicate that an item can be drilled into.)

This is very easy to do—all we have to do when we configure our table cell is set the **cellAccessory** property. Here's the code:

```
// Modify method in SBConfigureView.m...
-(UITableViewCell *)tableView:(UITableView *)tableView cellForRowAtIndexPath:↲
(NSIndexPath *)indexPath
{
        static NSString *cellId = @"BookmarkKey";

        // find one...
        UITableViewCell *cell = [tableView dequeueReusableCellWithIdentifier:cellId];
        if(cell == nil)
                cell = [[[UITableViewCell alloc] initWithStyle:UITableViewCellStyleDefault↲
 reuseIdentifier:cellId] autorelease];
```

```
    // set...
    NSUInteger row = [indexPath row];
    cell.textLabel.text = [[self.bookmarks objectAtIndex:row] name];

    // set the disclosure indicator...
    cell.accessoryType = UITableViewCellAccessoryDisclosureIndicator;

    // return...
    return cell;
}
```

If you run the code now, you can see the disclosure indicators. Figure 11-5 illustrates.

Figure 11-5. *The configuration view, now with disclosure indicators against each item*

We can now implement the tableView:didSelectRowAtIndexPath method and open the singleton editor. Here's the implementation:

```
// Add method to SBConfigureView.m…
-(void)tableView:(UITableView *)tableView didSelectRowAtIndexPath:(NSIndexPath *)indexPath
{
```

```
        // find it...
        SBBookmark *bookmark = [self.bookmarks objectAtIndex:[indexPath row]];
        [self.owner openBookmarkSingleton:[bookmark ordinal]];
}
```

Run the project again, and you can now click on the cells in the table to bring up the singleton editing UI. (The name and URL fields will not be populated—we're going to do this shortly.) Figure 11-6 illustrates.

Figure 11-6. *The "configure singleton" view being displayed, but with no data*

Editing a Bookmark

The code to edit a bookmark is reasonably straightforward. We have to implement setOrdinal so that it will either load a bookmark from disk or create a new one for us, implement refreshView so that the text boxes are updated, handle validation of the text contained within when the user clicks the **Save** button, and if saving is OK, commit the changes to the database.

Looking at setOrdinal first, the approach here needs to be that we'll create a SBSqlFilter instance to try to load a bookmark from disk. (This filter will exclude deleted bookmarks with the given ordinal.) If there isn't a bookmark on disk, we'll create one and set its ordinal so that it goes into the correct location when we do come to save it.

Here's the implementation (we'll build getByOrdinal in a moment):

```
// Replace setOrdinal method in SBConfigureSingletonView…
-(void)setOrdinal:(int)theOrdinal
{
        // try and load it...
        SBBookmark *theBookmark = nil;
        NSError *err = [SBBookmark getByOrdinal:theOrdinal bookmark:&theBookmark];
        if(err != nil)
                [SBMessageBox showError:err];
        else
        {
                // create...
                if(theBookmark == nil)
                {
                        theBookmark = [[[SBBookmark alloc] init] autorelease];

                        // set the ordinal (so that we save into the right place)...
                        theBookmark.ordinal = theOrdinal;
                }

                // set...
                self.bookmark = theBookmark;
        }

        // update...
        self.refreshView;
}
```

The getByOrdinal method on SBBookmark is going to need a new method to be added to SBSqlFilter, namely a method that returns a single entity back as opposed to a collection. The logic is that it will fetch a collection and return back the topmost item. (Although this is a bit hacky—it should check that exactly one or exactly zero items are returned and return the solo item if one is found—I know from experience this approach tends to be fine from a practical perspective.)

```
// Add method to SBSqlFilter.m…
// <…> Needs declaration in header
-(NSError *)executeEntity:(SBEntity **)theEntity
{
        // reset...
        *theEntity = nil;

        // run...
        NSMutableArray *entities = nil;
        NSError *err = [self executeEntityCollection:&entities];
```

```
        // get...
        if([entities count] > 0)
                *theEntity = [entities objectAtIndex:0];

        // return...
        return err;
}
```

getByOrdinal on SBBookmark can then configure a filter and use this method to return back a single bookmark from the database. The filter will be configured to select back the item that has a given ordinal, but that is not marked as locally deleted. Here's the implementation:

```
// Add method to SBBookmark.m…
// <…> Needs declaration in header
+(NSError *)getByOrdinal:(int)theOrdinal bookmark:(SBBookmark **)theBookmark
{
        SBSqlFilter *filter = [[SBSqlFilter alloc] initWithType:[SBBookmark class]];
        [filter.constraints addObject:[[SBSqlFieldConstraint alloc]
initWithFieldAndValue:[filter.entityType getField:@"ordinal"]

value:[NSNumber numberWithInt:theOrdinal]]];
        [filter.constraints addObject:[[SBSqlFieldConstraint alloc]↵
 initWithFieldAndValue:[filter.entityType getField:@"localdeleted"]

value:[NSNumber numberWithBool:FALSE]]];

        // return...
        NSError *err = [filter executeEntity:theBookmark];
        [filter release];
        return err;
}
```

Finally for this section, if we implement refreshView, we can see the data on the screen. Here's the implementation:

```
// Add method to SBConfigureSingletonView.m…
-(void)refreshView
{
        // set...
        if(self.bookmark != nil)
        {
                [self.textName setText:[self.bookmark name]];
                [self.textUrl setText:[self.bookmark url]];
        }
```

```
        else
        {
                [self.textName setText:nil];
                [self.textUrl setText:nil];
        }
}
```

Figure 11-7 illustrates a successful result.

Figure 11-7. *The "configure singleton" view, now with data*

Capturing and Committing Changes

The next step is to implement the singleton view so that we can enter a new name and URL and commit it to the database. As part of this work, we'll have to modify the SBEntityChangeProcessor so that it is able to handle updates—if you recall, when we built this in the last chapter, it could only handle inserts.

The actual code to handle the save operation is very straightforward. Here's the implementation to add to SBConfigureSingletonView:

```objc
// Modigy handleSave method in SBConfigureSingletonView…
-(IBAction)handleSave:(int)sender
{
        // get the values...
        NSString *name = self.textName.text;
        NSString *url = self.textUrl.text;

        // can we?
        SBErrorBucket *errors = [[SBErrorBucket alloc] init];
        if(name == nil || [name length] == 0)
                [errors addError:@"Name is required."];
        if(url == nil || [url length] == 0)
                [errors addError:@"URL is required."];

        // ok...
        if(!([errors hasErrors]))
        {
                // save the regular bits...
                [self.bookmark setName:name];
                [self.bookmark setUrl:url];

                // set the flags...
                [self.bookmark setLocalModified:TRUE];
                [self.bookmark setLocalDeleted:FALSE];

                // save...
                [self.bookmark saveChanges];

                // ok...
                [self.owner openConfiguration];
        }
        else

                [SBMessageBox show:[errors errorsAsString]];

        // release...
        [errors release];

}
```

You can see from the code that we are reusing the SBErrorBucket class that we built before. Also note how when we have a successful validation, we set the localModified property to TRUE and the localDeleted property to FALSE. We'll need this when we complete the synchronization routine and commit the changes back to the server.

If you run the application and attempt to modify a bookmark, the application will crash, as we have not yet added the capability to run UPDATE queries against the database. (You can discover the cause of the crash by using the debugger's output console.) Let's build the update capability now.

What we're looking to do is build an UPDATE query like this one:

```
UPDATE Bookmark SET Name=?, Url=?, LocalModified=?, LocalDeleted=? WHERE BookmarkId=?
```

Recall that the entity is able to tell us which columns have been modified. We'll use this capability in the handleUpdate method of SBEntityChangeProcessor to build up a SQL query. We'll also use the SBEntityType class's ability to return back to us the key field, as we obviously need to constrain the update query to operate only against the bookmark that we wish to update. Here's the implementation:

```objc
// Replace method in SBEntityChangeProcessor…
-(void)update:(SBEntity *)entity
{
        // create...
        SBEntityType *et = self.entityType;

        // do we have a table?
        SBDBHelper *db = [[SBRuntime current] getDatabase];
        [db ensureTableExists:et];

        // create a statement...
        NSMutableString *builder = [NSMutableString string];
        SBSqlStatement *sql = [[SBSqlStatement alloc] init];

        // header...
        [builder appendString:@"UPDATE "];
        [builder appendString:et.nativeName];
        [builder appendString:@" SET "];
        BOOL first = TRUE;
        for(SBEntityField *field in et.fields)
        {
                if([entity isFieldModified:field])
                {
                        if(first)
                                first = FALSE;
                        else
                                [builder appendString:@", "];

                        // name...
                        [builder appendString:field.nativeName];
                        [builder appendString:@"=?"];

                        // param...
                        [sql addParameter:[entity getValue:field]];
                }
        }

        // constrain by the key field...
        SBEntityField *keyField = [et getKeyField];
        [builder appendString:@" WHERE "];
        [builder appendString:keyField.nativeName];
        [builder appendString:@"=?"];
        [sql addParameter:[entity getValue:keyField]];
```

```
    // attach...
    [sql setCommandText:builder];

    // run...
    @try
    {
            BOOL ok = [db execNonQuery:sql];
            if(!(ok))
            {
                    NSError *err = [db getLastError];
                    @throw [NSException exceptionWithName:[[self class] description]↵
reason:[SBErrorHelper formatError:err] userInfo:nil];
            }
    }
    @finally
    {
            // release...
            [sql release];
    }
}
```

Now if you run the application, you will be able to update a bookmark. Figure 11-8 and Figure 11-9 illustrate.

Figure 11-8. *Editing a bookmark*

Figure 11-9. *The configuration screen showing the changed data*

Implementing the Delete Method

We're not going to be issuing DELETE statements against individual bookmarks in this project, but we can delete from the UI. This simply issues an UPDATE operation to mark the entity as deleted. However, for completeness, here's the delete implementation:

```
// Replace method in SBEntityChangeProcessor.m…
-(void)delete:(SBEntity *)entity
{
        // create...
        SBEntityType *et = [self entityType];

        // do we have a table?
        SBDBHelper *db = [[SBRuntime current] getDatabase];
        [db ensureTableExists:et];

        // create a statement...
        NSMutableString *builder = [NSMutableString string];
        SBSqlStatement *sql = [[SBSqlStatement alloc] init];
```

```
        // create a statement...
        SBEntityField *keyField = [et getKeyField];
        [builder appendString:@"DELETE FROM "];
        [builder appendString:et.nativeName];
        [builder appendString:@" WHERE "];
        [builder appendString:keyField.nativeName];
        [builder appendString:@"=?"];
        [sql addParameter:[entity getValue:keyField]];

        // attach...
        [sql setCommandText:builder];

        // run...
        @try
        {
                BOOL ok = [db execNonQuery:sql];
                if(!(ok))
                {
                        NSError *err = [db getLastError];
                        @throw [NSException exceptionWithName:[[self class] description]⮠
reason:[SBErrorHelper formatError:err] userInfo:nil];
                }
        }
        @finally
        {
                // release...
                [sql release];
        }
}
```

Adding a Bookmark

Now that we can change bookmarks, we need to be able to add or delete them. We'll look at add first.

The "add" operation shouldn't require us to do too much work. When we built the singleton view, the setOrdinal method would create a new SBBookmark instance if a bookmark with the given ordinal did not exist. When we have a new bookmark and call saveChanges on it, the existing functionality of the SBEntityChangeProcessor should issue an INSERT statement. In fact, the only tricky bit is finding a blank ordinal to set. We'll add a method called getOrdinalToAdd, which will create an array of six BOOL values, set them all to FALSE, and then walk the bookmarks setting values into the array to TRUE based on ordinal value. The routine then looks back through the array for the first FALSE value, indicating an empty slot. (Personally, this routine is why I'm not mad keen on Objective-C as a language—this is some pretty complicated code for doing something very easy.) If we get an ordinal, we can defer to SBConfigureSingletonView to edit it, otherwise we'll display an error. Here's the implementation:

```objc
// Add and change methods in SBConfigureView.m…
// <…> Needs declaration in header
-(int)getOrdinalToAdd
{
        NSMutableArray *array = [NSMutableArray array];
        for(int index = 0; index < 6; index++)
                [array addObject:[NSNumber numberWithBool:FALSE]];
        for(SBBookmark *bookmark in self.bookmarks)
                [array replaceObjectAtIndex:[bookmark ordinal] withObject:[NSNumber↵
 numberWithBool:TRUE]];

        // walk...
        for(int index = 0; index < 6; index++)
        {
                NSNumber *value = [array objectAtIndex:index];
                if([value boolValue] == FALSE)
                        return index;
        }

        // return...
        return -1;
}

-(IBAction)handleAdd:(id)sender
{
        int ordinal = [self getOrdinalToAdd];
        if(ordinal != -1)
                [self.owner openBookmarkSingleton:ordinal];
        else
                [SBMessageBox show:@"No more bookmarks can be added."];
}
```

You can now run the application and add a new bookmark. Figure 11-10 illustrates.

Figure 11-10. *The configuration screen, having added a new bookmark*

Deleting Bookmarks

To round off the operations, we'll implement the delete functionality. This is going to take advantage of functionality already in the Table View control. You will most likely already have seen this functionality in other iPhone applications—you can put the table in edit mode and see little red "wheels" to the left of each item that allow you to access a delete button. To be truly iOS standards compliant, we need to be able to do more "edit mode," such as reordering the items. However, I'm calling this as "out of scope," and we'll just look at handling the delete operations.

Turning the grid into "edit" mode is easy—all we have to do is call the setEditing method. Here's the implementation:

```
// Replace handleEdit method on SBConfigureView.m
-(IBAction)handleEdit:(id)sender
{
        [self.table setEditing:TRUE animated:TRUE];
}
```

If you run the project now, you can access "edit" mode and from there access a **Delete** button by turning the wheel. Figure 11-11 illustrates.

Figure 11-11. *The configuration screen in "edit" mode*

One question that occurs is how do we exit edit mode? iOS applications tend towards having a minimal set of buttons; hence my proposal is that we rework the **Done** button so that if we're in "edit" mode, we'll return to "normal" mode, whereas if we're in "normal" mode, we'll quit. Here's the implementation:

```
// Replace handleClose method in SBConfigureView.m and add stopEditing method…
-(IBAction)handleClose:(id)sender
{
        // are we editing?
        if(self.table.editing)
                [self stopEditing];
    else
                [self.owner openNavigator];
}

// <…> Needs declaration in header…
-(void)stopEditing
{
        [self.table setEditing:FALSE animated:TRUE];
}
```

Now if you run the project you can enter and exit "edit" mode at will.

When the user clicks a **Delete** button, the tableView:commitEditingStyle method will be called. When we detect this has happened, all we have to do is set the localDeleted property of the entity to TRUE and commit the change to the database. When we next retrieve bookmarks from the view, the filter will exclude ones that are marked as locally deleted, and it will appear as having been deleted. Remember that we cannot physically delete the bookmark because we need to keep track of the fact that it has to be deleted from the server.

Here's the implementation of tableView:commitEditingStyle:

```
// Add method to SBConfigureView.m…
-(void)tableView:(UITableView *)tableView commitEditingStyle:(UITableViewCellEditingStyle)↵
style forRowAtIndexPath:(NSIndexPath *)indexPath
{
        // great - get rid of it...
        SBBookmark *bookmark = [self.bookmarks objectAtIndex:[indexPath row]];
        [bookmark setLocalDeleted:TRUE];
        [bookmark saveChanges];

        // update...
        [self stopEditing];
        [self refreshView];
}
```

If you run the project at this point, you can delete the bookmarks from the local database. Figure 11-12 and Figure 11-13 illustrate.

Figure 11-12. *The configuration view with a deleted bookmark*

Figure 11-13. *The navigator view showing the deleted bookmark*

Manually Syncing

We've almost finished the section covering the user interface—in the next section, we'll move onto physically pushing the changes back up to the server. Before we finish the section, we'll wire up the manual sync operation. All this will do is call the doSync method on the SBSync class. This will call back to us via syncOk and syncFailed, which we also need to add. Here's the implementation:

```
// Replace method in SBConfigureView.m and add syncOk and syncFailed methods…
-(IBAction)handleSync:(id)sender
{
        if(self.syncEngine == nil)
                self.syncEngine = [[SBSync alloc] init];
        [self.syncEngine doSync:(SBSyncCallback *)self];
}

-(void)syncOk
{
        [self refreshView];
        [SBMessageBox show:@"Sync OK."];
}
```

```
-(void)syncFailed:(NSError *)err
{
        // nope...
        [SBMessageBox showError:err];
}
```

One thing to note on that operation is that we demand-initialize the syncEngine property when we need it.

If we run the project and click the **Sync/Refresh** button, the doSync operation will run. As we haven't implemented the code to push changes up the server, when we do this, it will restore the local database to be in-sync with the set of bookmarks on the server—any local changes will be scrapped. Figure 11-14 illustrates a successful sync.

Figure 11-14. *Message box indicating the the sync operation ran*

Pushing Changes to the Server

We can now move onto looking at the code to push changes to the server. This operation essentially involves getting the bookmarks from the server, comparing it to the local set, and working out a set of changes to push.

When we built this operation for the generic web application for Android, we were lucky in that we could get the bookmarks back from the server as a synchronous method. However, on iPhone we have to retrieve the bookmarks back asynchronously through our callback, *and* we have to deal with the fact that our callback is already being used by the getLatest operation. Recall that when we built our SBSync class, initially we added an enumeration called SBSyncMode with a single member SBSMGetLatest. We now need to add a second member—SBSMPushChanges—to this. Here's the definition:

```
// Modify enumeration in SBSync.h…
typedef enum
{
        SBSMGetLatest = 0,
        SBSMPushChanges = 1

} SBSyncMode;
```

The second thing we need to do is add two properties of type NSMutableArray. One will hold the list of bookmarks that are flagged as locally modified, and a second will hold the list of bookmarks that are flagged as locally deleted. Here are the @property definitions:

```
// Add @property definitions to SBSync.h, also add instance variables, @synthesize↵
declaration and cleanup code in dealloc…
@property (nonatomic, retain) NSMutableArray *updates;
@property (nonatomic, retain) NSMutableArray *deletes;
```

We've alluded to the fact a few times now that we need to be able to get the locally modified and locally deleted methods from the database. Here are the methods to add to SBBookmark that will issue these requests:

```
// Add method to SBBookmark.m…
// <…> Needs declaration in header
+(NSError *)getBookmarksForServerUpdate:(NSMutableArray **)theBookmarks
{
        SBSqlFilter *filter = [[SBSqlFilter alloc] initWithType:[SBBookmark class]];
        [filter.constraints addObject:[[SBSqlFieldConstraint alloc]↵
initWithFieldAndValue:[filter.entityType getField:@"localmodified"]

value:[NSNumber numberWithBool:TRUE]]];
        [filter.constraints addObject:[[SBSqlFieldConstraint alloc]↵
initWithFieldAndValue:[filter.entityType getField:@"localdeleted"]

value:[NSNumber numberWithBool:FALSE]]];
        // return...
        NSError *err = [filter executeEntityCollection:theBookmarks];
        [filter release];
        return err;
}
```

```
// <...> Needs declaration in header
+(NSError *)getBookmarksForServerDelete:(NSMutableArray **)theBookmarks
{
        SBSqlFilter *filter = [[SBSqlFilter alloc] initWithType:[SBBookmark class]];
        [filter.constraints addObject:[[SBSqlFieldConstraint alloc]↵
initWithFieldAndValue:[filter.entityType getField:@"localdeleted"]

value:[NSNumber numberWithBool:TRUE]]];
        // return...
        NSError *err = [filter executeEntityCollection:theBookmarks];
        [filter release];
        return err;
}
```

The sendChanges method is the first "meaty" method to add to SBSync. This will be called first, ahead of getLatest (as we need to update the server prior to getting the canonical set from the server). Its job will be to get the locally modified and locally deleted bookmarks and store them in the updates and deletes properties. If no changes are detected, it will defer immediately to getLatest. If changes are detected, a request to get the bookmark set from the server will be called, and we'll wait until this returns. Here's the implementation:

```
// Add method to SBSync.m...
// <...> Needs declaration in header
-(void)sendChanges
{
        // do we have anything to send?
        NSMutableArray *updates = nil;
        NSMutableArray *deletes = nil;
        NSError *err = [SBBookmark getBookmarksForServerUpdate:&updates];
        if(err != nil)
        {
                [self.callback syncFailed:err];
                return;
        }
        err = [SBBookmark getBookmarksForServerDelete:&deletes];
        if(err != nil)
        {
                [self.callback syncFailed:err];
                return;
        }

        // do we have anything to do?
        if(updates.count == 0 && deletes.count == 0)
        {
                [self getLatest];
        }
        else
        {
```

```
                        // store the updates - we're going to come back async later...
                        self.updates = updates;
                        self.deletes = deletes;

                        // ok - we have to create a delta, get the server items...
                        self.mode = SBSMPushChanges;
                        SBBookmarksService *service = [[SBBookmarksService alloc] init];
                        [service getAll:(SBODataFetchCallback *)self];
                        [service release];
               }
      }
```

One more piece of housekeeping here is that we need to modify the doSync method to call sendChanges as opposed to getLatest. Here's the implementation:

```
// Modify doSync method in SBSync.m…
-(void)doSync:(SBSyncCallback *)theCallback
{
        self.callback = theCallback;

        // start spinning...
        [SBServiceProxy startSpinning];

        // check the database...
        SBDBHelper *db = [[SBRuntime current] getDatabase];
        [db ensureTableExists:[SBEntityType getEntityType:[SBBookmark class]]];
        [db release];

        // run...
        [self sendChanges];
}
```

We can now move on and look at detecting the actual changes and pushing them up.

Work Items

Detecting the changes is straightforward—we have done this already in our Android application. The problem for our iOS implementation is that our OData change requests will be issued asynchronously, which means we need to maintain a queue of items, progressing each one in turn until all have been sent.

To handle this, we will create a class called SBSyncWorkItem, which will hold a reference to an entity, the ID of the entity on the server, and the mode of operation (i.e., insert, update, or delete). We can maintain a queue of those in SBSync and, like the preceding example, work through the queue in turn until they have all been sent.

Before we can build SBSyncWorkItem, we need to create an enumeration that holds the operation type. This can be added anywhere in the project (even in a new file); however, my one will be added to the SBODataServiceProxy.h file. Here's the definition:

```
// Add enumeration to SBODataServiceProxy.h…
typedef enum
{
        SBODOInsert = 0,
        SBODOUpdate = 1,
        SBODODelete = 2

} SBODataOperation;
```

As I alluded to previously, SBSyncWorkItem is a simple class that holds a set of properties. Here's the definition:

```
// SBSyncWorkItem.h
#import <Foundation/Foundation.h>
#import "SBEntity.h"
#import "SBODataServiceProxy.h"

@interface SBSyncWorkItem : NSObject {
        SBEntity *entity;
        int serverId;
        SBODataOperation mode;
}

@property (nonatomic, retain) SBEntity *entity;
@property (assign) int serverId;
@property (assign) SBODataOperation mode;

-(id)initWithData:(SBEntity *)theEntity serverId:(int)theServerId↵
mode:(SBODataOperation)theMode;

@end
```

And here's the implementation:

```
// SBSyncWorkItem.m
#import "SBSyncWorkItem.h"
#import "MyClasses.h"

@implementation SBSyncWorkItem

        @synthesize entity;
        @synthesize serverId;
        @synthesize mode;

        -(id)initWithData:(SBEntity *)theEntity serverId:(int)theServerId↵
mode:(SBODataOperation)theMode
        {
                if(self = [super init])
```

```
        {
                self.entity = theEntity;
                self.serverId = theServerId;
                self.mode = theMode;
        }

        // return...
        return self;
}

-(void)dealloc
{
        [entity release];
        [super dealloc];
}
```

@end

The next job is to build up a list of work items.

The odataFetchOk method will be called on SBSync when entities have been loaded from the server. At the moment, this is being used to service the getLatest method. The mode property allows us to vary its function depending on how it is being called. In this case, we now need to make this call a method called receiveServerItemsForPushChanges when we have the appropriate mode. Here's the code—we'll build receiveServerItemsForPushChanges in a moment.

```
// Modify method in SBSync.m…
-(void)odataFetchOk:(SBEntityXmlBucket *)entities opCode:(int)theOpCode
{
        if(theOpCode == OPCODE_ODATAFETCHALL)
        {
                // mode?
                if(self.mode == SBSMGetLatest)
                        [self receiveServerItemsForGetLatest:bucket];
                else if(self.mode == SBSMPushChanges)
                        [self receiveServerItemsForPushChanges:bucket];
                else
                        @throw [NSException exceptionWithName:[[self class] description]↵
reason:@"Mode was unhandled" userInfo:nil];
        }
        else
                @throw [NSException exceptionWithName:[[self class] description]↵
reason:@"Operation code was unhandled" userInfo:nil];

        // stop spinning...
        [SBServiceProxy stopSpinning];
}
```

We've seen the code for calculating the change delta a few times now. Let's recap the logic:

- We start by walking a list of locally modified entities, and for each we look in the server's set to find a match by ordinal.

- If we find one that matches, this is an UPDATE. We override the fields in the in-memory copy of the server's bookmark with the local data and queue an update. We create a work unit based on the server's bookmark.

- If we have one locally that is not referenced on the server, this is an INSERT. We create a work unit based on the local bookmark.

- If we have one in our deleted set that is matched by one in the server set, this is a DELETE. We create a work unit accordingly.

The receiveServerItemsForPushChanges does that logic, plus a little bit more. On SBSync we will hold two properties—workItems (an NSMutableArray instance) and workItemIndex (an integer). We'll add these now so that we don't forget.

```
// Add properties to SBSync.h…
// <…> Needs instance variable, @synthesize declaration and cleanup code in dealloc↩
 for workItems.
@property (nonatomic, retain) NSMutableArray *workItems;
@property (assign) int workItemIndex;
```

Next here's the implementation of receiveServerItemsForPushChanges that implements the algorithm that we just discussed:

```
// Add method to SBSync.m…
// <…> Needs declaration in header
-(void)receiveServerItemsForPushChanges:(SBEntityXmlBucket *)entities
{
        SBEntityType *et = [SBEntityType getEntityType:[SBBookmark class]];

        // good - we got this far... build a set of work to do...
        NSMutableArray *theWorkItems = [NSMutableArray array];
        for(SBBookmark *local in self.updates)
        {
                // find it in our set...
                SBBookmark *toUpdate = nil;
                for(SBBookmark *server in entities.entities)
                {
                        if(local.ordinal == server.ordinal)
                        {
                                toUpdate = server;
                                break;
                        }
                }
```

```objc
                    // did we have one to change?
                    if(toUpdate != nil)
                    {
                            // walk the fields...
                            int serverId = 0;
                            for(SBEntityField *field in et.fields)
                            {
                                    if(!(field.isKey))
                                            [toUpdate setValue:field value:[local↵
getValue:field] reason:SBESRUserSet];
                                    else
                                            serverId = toUpdate.bookmarkId;
                            }

                            // send that up...
                            [theWorkItems addObject:[[SBSyncWorkItem alloc]↵
initWithData:toUpdate serverId:serverId mode:SBODOUpdate]];
                    }
                    else
                    {
                            // we need to insert it...
                            [theWorkItems addObject:[[SBSyncWorkItem alloc] initWithData:local↵
serverId:0 mode:SBODOInsert]];
                    }
            }

    // what about ones to delete?
    for(SBBookmark *local in self.deletes)
    {
            // find a matching ordinal on the server...
            for(SBBookmark *server in entities.entities)
            {
                    if(local.ordinal ==  server.ordinal)
                    {
                            int serverId = server.bookmarkId;
                            [theWorkItems addObject:[[SBSyncWorkItem alloc]↵
initWithData:server serverId:serverId mode:SBODODelete]];
                    }
            }
    }

    // now we have a list of work, we have to process it... asynchronously...
    self.workItems = theWorkItems;
    self.workItemIndex = 0;
    [self processWorkItems];
}
```

At the bottom of the method, we set the workItems property and also set the workItemIndex to be 0. workItemIndex will act as a pointer into the queue. Once workItemIndex reaches the length of the workItems array, we know that we are finished.

So that we know we're on the right track, I'm going to propose that we display a message box that shows the number of discovered work items. Here's the code:

```
// Add to SBSync.m
// <…> Needs declaration in header
-(void)processWorkItems
{
        [SBMessageBox show:[NSString stringWithFormat:@"We have %d work item(s) to do.",↵
 self.workItems.count]];
}
```

If you run the project, go into the configuration screen and change the bookmarks, and then run a manual sync, you will see something like Figure 11-15.

Figure 11-15. *The sync operation reporting that we have two items to sync*

Now that we know our work items are being populated, we can turn our attention to actually issuing the OData requests to the server.

415

Issuing OData Change Requests

When we needed to create XML documents on Android, we used the XML Pull Library and its XmlSerializer class to manually create the document. You may also recall that my preferred method for building XML documents is to use a DOM approach, such as the XmlDocument class in .NET. However, just as Android does not give us a DOM-style API for creating documents, neither does iOS. Instead we have to use the **Libxml2** library, which is an open-source library that is part of Gnome. It essentially works in the same way as the XmlSerializer on Android, apart from the fact that the API is a flat, C-style API (like SQLite) rather than an object-orientated API.

To access Libxml2 in our project, we need to add a reference to it. Follow the steps that you undertook to add the SQLite library to the project, but this time add libxml2.dylib. Figure 11-16 illustrates.

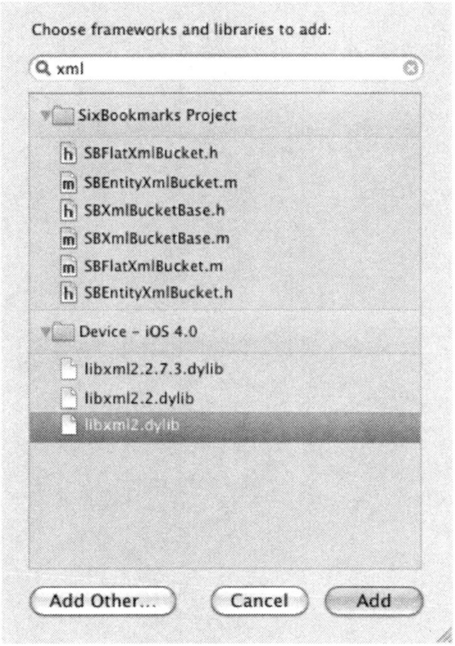

Figure 11-16. *Adding the* libxml2.dylib *library*

The other thing you need to do when adding the library is change the search path of the project to include the header files for Libxml2. Specifically, these are libxml/encoding.h and libxml/xmlwriter.h.

To do this, bring up the project settings and select the **SixBookmarks** *project* (not the target). At the top of the window, select **Build Settings**. This will offer you a *lot* of options. Into the little search box, enter **search**—this will limit the options to those that relate to headers and will show you an option called **Header Search Paths**.

To this **Header Search Paths** value, add a reference to this path:

```
/Developer/Platforms/iPhoneOS.platform/Developer/SDKs/iPhoneOS4.0.sdk/usr/include/libxml2
```

Figure 11-17 illustrates.

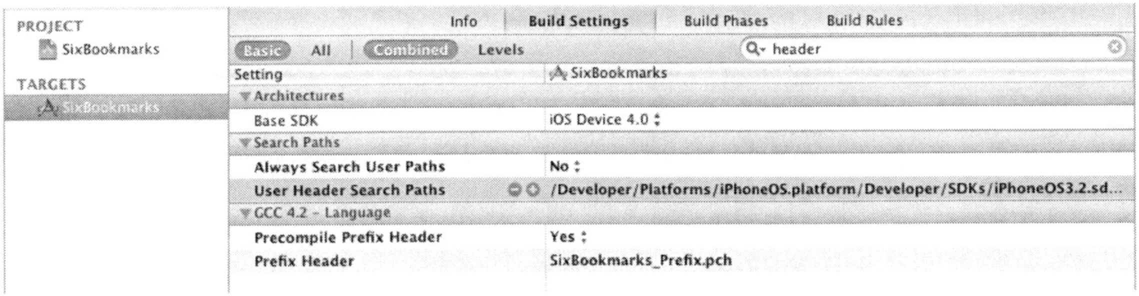

Figure 11-17. *Project settings showing the "Header Search Paths" option*

■**NOTE** Your mileage may vary on that path if you are using a later version of the SDK. One option is to use Spotlight to find the file on disk and add a reference to that. Check the support forums at `http://forums.multimobiledevelopment.com/` for updated information if you are stuck.

Once you've added the path, accept the various dialogs we have opened and return to the project.

Flagging Fields As "Not on Server"

Recall that when we built the sync operation in Android, we had to indicate that certain fields were not available on the server, otherwise the OData operation would crash. We need to repeat this now, and it's easily enough done—in fact, we added an isOnServer property when we built SBEntityField in the last chapter. Thus all that remains is when we declare the entity type in SBRuntime, we need to set the isOnServer property to FALSE for the localModified and localDeleted fields. Here's the implementation:

```
// Modify start method on SBRuntime.m…
+(void)start
{
        // create...
        SBRuntime *rt = [[SBRuntime alloc] init];
        [SBRuntime setCurrent:rt];

        // type...
        SBEntityType *et = [[SBEntityType alloc] initWithInstanceTypeNativeName:↵
[SBBookmark class] nativeName:@"Bookmark"];
        [[et addField:BOOKMARK_IDKEY nativeName:BOOKMARK_IDKEY type:SBDT_INT32 size:-1]↵
setIsKey:TRUE];
        [et addField:BOOKMARK_ORDINALKEY nativeName:BOOKMARK_ORDINALKEY type:SBDT_INT32↵
size:-1];
```

```
        [et addField:BOOKMARK_NAMEKEY nativeName:BOOKMARK_NAMEKEY type:SBDT_STRING↵
size:128];
        [et addField:BOOKMARK_URLKEY nativeName:BOOKMARK_URLKEY type:SBDT_STRING size:256];
        [[et addField:BOOKMARK_LOCALMODIFIEDKEY nativeName:BOOKMARK_LOCALMODIFIEDKEY↵
type:SBDT_INT32 size:-1] setIsOnServer:FALSE];
        [[et addField:BOOKMARK_LOCALDELETEDKEY nativeName:BOOKMARK_LOCALDELETEDKEY↵
type:SBDT_INT32 size:-1] setIsOnServer:FALSE];
        [SBEntityType registerEntityType:et];
        [et release];
}
```

Issuing Requests

I won't repeat the discussion from the Android chapter that has a quick look at the OData protocol, but I will repeat the presentation of the XML that we need to issue. This is an example of an OData XML document used to create a bookmark on the server:

```
POST /services/bookmarks.svc/Bookmark HTTP/1.1
Host: services.multimobiledevelopment.com
accept: application/atom+xml
content-type: application/atom+xml
content-encoding: UTF-8
content-length: 384
x-amx-apiusername: amxmobile
x-amx-token: 961c8c1b9d4ddd5799e7f0a7b4a5ee8b

<entry xmlns:d="http://schemas.microsoft.com/ado/2007/08/dataservices"
        xmlns:m="http://schemas.microsoft.com/ado/2007/08/dataservices/metadata"
        xmlns="http://www.w3.org/2005/Atom">
    <content type="application/xml">
        <m:properties>
            <d:Name>Apress</d:Name>
            <d:Url>http://www.apress.com/</d:Url>
            <d:Ordinal>0</d:Ordinal>
        </m:properties>
    </content>
</entry>
```

We might as well jump straight in and build the methods to issue the insert, update, and delete instructions to the server.

We're going to add the calls that require Libxml2 to SBODataServiceProxy, and so we need to add the header files that we mentioned previously to this project. Add these to the top of the implementation, like so:

```
// Add header files to SBODataServiceProxy.m…
#import <libxml/encoding.h>
#import <libxml/xmlwriter.h>
```

```
#import "SBODataServiceProxy.h"
#import "MyClasses.h"

@implementation SBODataServiceProxy

// reminder of implementation ommitted for brevity…
```

pushUpdate is the complicated one to do, so we'll look at this first. pushUpdate is going to do a lot for us—it's going to build the XML document and then call a method called executeODataOperation, passing in the URL and the XML. (We'll build the executeODataOperation method and its companion getEntityUrlForPush method in a moment.) Here is the implementation of pushUpdate:

```
// Add method to SBODataServiceProxy…
// <…> Needs declaration in header
-(void)pushUpdate:(SBEntity *)entity serverId:(int)theServerId↵
callback:(SBODataFetchCallback *)theCallback
{
        // create...
        xmlBufferPtr buffer = xmlBufferCreate();
    xmlTextWriterPtr writer = xmlNewTextWriterMemory(buffer, 0);

        // start the document...
        xmlTextWriterStartDocument(writer, "1.0", "UTF-8", NULL);

        // bring forward...
        const char *atomUri = [[SBEntityXmlBucket atomNamespace]↵
cStringUsingEncoding:NSUTF8StringEncoding];
        const char *atomPrefix = nil;
        const char *metadataUri = [[SBEntityXmlBucket msMetadataNamespace]↵
cStringUsingEncoding:NSUTF8StringEncoding];
        const char *metadataPrefix = "m";
        const char *dataUri = [[SBEntityXmlBucket msDataNamespace]↵
cStringUsingEncoding:NSUTF8StringEncoding];
        const char *dataPrefix = "d";

        // start entry and content and properties...
        xmlTextWriterStartElementNS(writer, BAD_CAST atomPrefix, BAD_CAST "entry",↵
BAD_CAST atomUri);
        xmlTextWriterStartElementNS(writer, BAD_CAST atomPrefix, BAD_CAST "content",↵
BAD_CAST atomUri);
        xmlTextWriterWriteAttribute(writer, BAD_CAST "type", BAD_CAST "application/xml");
        xmlTextWriterStartElementNS(writer, BAD_CAST metadataPrefix, BAD_CAST↵
"properties", BAD_CAST metadataUri);

        // fields...
        SBEntityType *et = entity.entityType;
        for(SBEntityField *field in et.fields)
        {
```

```
                        if(!(field.isKey) && field.isOnServer)
                        {
                                xmlTextWriterStartElementNS(writer, BAD_CAST dataPrefix,↵
BAD_CAST [field.nativeName cStringUsingEncoding:NSUTF8StringEncoding], BAD_CAST dataUri);
                                NSObject *value = [entity getValue:field];
                                if(field.type == SBDT_STRING)
                                        xmlTextWriterWriteString(writer, BAD_CAST↵
[(NSString *)value cStringUsingEncoding:NSUTF8StringEncoding]);
                                else if(field.type == SBDT_INT32)
                                        xmlTextWriterWriteString(writer, BAD_CAST↵
[[NSString stringWithFormat:@"%d", [(NSNumber *)value intValue]]↵
cStringUsingEncoding:NSUTF8StringEncoding]);
                                else
                                        @throw [NSException exceptionWithName:[[self class]↵
description] reason:@"Unhandled data type." userInfo:nil];
                                xmlTextWriterEndElement(writer);
                        }
                }

        // end content and entry...
        xmlTextWriterEndElement(writer);
        xmlTextWriterEndElement(writer);
        xmlTextWriterEndElement(writer);

        // end the document...
        xmlTextWriterEndDocument(writer);

        // get the data out...
    xmlFreeTextWriter(writer);
    NSData *xmlData = [NSData dataWithBytes:(buffer->content) length:(buffer->use)];
    xmlBufferFree(buffer);
        NSString *xml = [[NSString alloc] initWithData:xmlData↵
encoding:NSUTF8StringEncoding];

        // dump the data...
        NSLog(@"%@", xml);

        // now we can send it...
        NSString *url = nil;
        SBODataOperation opType;
        if(theServerId == 0)
        {
                url = [self getServiceUrl:et];
                opType = SBODOInsert;
        }
```

```
        else
        {
                url = [self getEntityUrlForPush:entity serverId:theServerId];
                opType = SBODOUpdate;
        }

        // call...
        [self executeODataOperation:opType url:url xml:xml callback:theCallback];
}
```

Although that method is quite long, I personally think that it is reasonably straightforward. A lot of the code relates to marshalling data from the "managed" Objective-C world to the flat, C-style API of Libxml2. When we call the method, we pass in an SBODataFetchCallback instance. We've already used this to retrieve items—we're going to reuse it with a different op code. Ultimately within SBSync, when our odataFetchOk method is called, we'll look at this op code and know that the callback relates to an OData change operation.

However, it's worth mentioning the BAD_CAST calls. This is a macro defined in the Libxml2 headers that is needed to cast strings. I'm not entirely sure why it's called a "bad cast"—seems to me that anything that makes it work is a "good cast"!

When we issue an OData change request to the server, the URL will refer either to a specific entity (for updates and deletes) or to the class (for inserts). We already have a method called getServiceUrl, which returns back a URL to the class based on an entity type. We can now extend this to return a URL for a specific entity. Here's the implementation:

```
// Add method to SBODataServiceProxy.m…
// <…> Needs declaration in header
-(NSString *)getEntityUrlForPush:(SBEntity *)theEntity serverId:(int)theServerId
{
        return [NSString stringWithFormat:@"%@(%d)", [self⏎
getServiceUrl:theEntity.entityType], theServerId];
}
```

Before we look at the executeODataOperation implementation, we'll add pushInsert and pushDelete, as these are easy. pushInsert defers to pushUpdate, but uses a different URL. pushDelete just defers to executeODataOperation. Here they are:

```
// Add methods to SBODataServiceProxy.m…
// <…> Needs declaration in header
-(void)pushDelete:(SBEntity *)entity serverId:(int)theServerId⏎
callback:(SBODataFetchCallback *)theCallback
{
        // get...
        NSString *url = [self getEntityUrlForPush:entity serverId:theServerId];
        [self executeODataOperation:SBODODelete url:url xml:nil callback:theCallback];
}
```

```
// <…> Needs declaration in header
-(void)pushInsert:(SBEntity *)entity callback:(SBODataFetchCallback *)theCallback
{
        // an insert is an update but with a different url...
        [self pushUpdate:entity serverId:0 callback:theCallback];
}
```

Implementing executeODataOperation

In the Android application, when we looked at the equivalent method, we learned that each of the three options requires different HTTP methods. Specifically, we learned that insert requires a POST, update requires a MERGE, and delete requires a DELETE. We already know that all of the HTTP requests to the service require our special x-amx-apiusername and x-amx-token headers provided through our getDownloadSettings method. Hence all we have to do is package up an appropriate request and send it.

The only wrinkle in this process is that the request will run in an asynchronous fashion, and hence we have to handle the callback. The callback gets passed into the pushInsert, pushUpdate, and pushDelete methods—we pass this all the way through to executeODataOperation and store it in the callback property that we built before. However, when the request is done, we want to capture the result and then decide whether we want to call the method that indicates success or the method that indicates failure on callback. Hence the callback that we pass into the SBDownloadBucket that we prepare to hold the result of the HTTP download is a reference to self.

Before we build executeODataOperation, we need to change the SBOpCodes enumeration to include OPCODE_ODATACHANGE. Here's the revised definition:

```
// Modify SBOpCodes in SBServiceProxy.h…
typedef enum
{
        OPCODE_APILOGON = 1000,
        OPCODE_USERSLOGON = 2000,
        OPCODE_ODATAFETCHALL = 3000,
        OPCODE_ODATACHANGE = 3001

} SBOpCodes;
```

Here's the implementation of executeODataOperation:

```
// Add method to SBODataServiceProxy.m
// <…> Needs declaration in header
-(void)executeODataOperation:(SBODataOperation)opType url:(NSString*)theUrl xml:↵
(NSString *)theXml callback:(SBODataFetchCallback *)theCallback
{
        // store the callback...
        self.callback = theCallback;

        // create a request...
        NSMutableURLRequest * request = [NSMutableURLRequest requestWithURL:↵
[NSURL URLWithString:theUrl]];
        [request setValue:@"application/atom+xml" forHTTPHeaderField:@"Content-type"];
```

```
        // what method?
        if(opType == SBODOInsert)
                [request setHTTPMethod:@"POST"];
        else if(opType == SBODOUpdate)
                [request setHTTPMethod:@"MERGE"];
        else if(opType == SBODODelete)
                [request setHTTPMethod:@"DELETE"];
        else
                @throw [NSException exceptionWithName:[[self class]↵
 description] reason:@"Unhandled operation type." userInfo:nil];

        // get the settings...
        SBDownloadSettings *settings = [self getDownloadSettings];
        for(NSString *name in settings.extraHeaders)
        {
                NSString * value = [settings.extraHeaders objectForKey:name];
                [request addValue:value forHTTPHeaderField:name];
        }
        [settings release];

        // set the body...
        if(theXml != nil && theXml.length > 0)
                [request setHTTPBody:[theXml dataUsingEncoding:NSUTF8StringEncoding]];

        // create the connection with the request and start loading the data
        SBDownloadBucket *bucket = [[SBDownloadBucket alloc]↵
initWithCallback:(SBDownloadCallback *)self opCode:OPCODE_ODATACHANGE];
        NSURLConnection *connection = [[NSURLConnection alloc] initWithRequest:↵
request delegate:bucket];
        if(connection != nil)
                NSLog(@"Connection started...");
}
```

Once the HTTP operation has completed, we'll receive notification into our downloadComplete method. This is currently coded up to understand OPCODE_ODATAFETCHALL. We need to modify this so that it additionally understands OPCODE_ODATACHANGE and defer to a new method called handleODataChangeComplete. Here is the revised implementation of downloadComplete:

```
// Modify downloadComplete method in SBODataServiceProxy...
-(void)downloadComplete:(SBDownloadBucket *)bucket
{
        // did we fail - i.e. not 200, not 204 (OK, but nothing to say) and not 201
("created")...
        if(bucket.statusCode != 200 && bucket.statusCode != 204 && bucket.statusCode != 201)
        {
                // create an error...
                NSString *message = [NSString stringWithFormat:@"An OData request↵
returned HTTP status '%d'.", bucket.statusCode];
```

```
                    NSString *html = bucket.dataAsString;
                    NSLog(@"%@ --> %@", message, html);
                    NSError *err = [SBErrorHelper error:self message:message];

                    // flip back...
                    [self.callback odataFetchFailed:err opCode:bucket.opCode];
          }
          else
          {
                    // ok...
                    if(bucket.opCode == OPCODE_ODATAFETCHALL)
                            [self handleFetchAllComplete:bucket];
                    else if(bucket.opCode == OPCODE_ODATACHANGE)
                            [self handleODataChangeComplete:bucket];
                    else
                            @throw [NSException exceptionWithName:[[self class]⏎
description] reason:[NSString stringWithFormat:@"An op code of '%d' was not⏎
recognised.", [bucket opCode]] userInfo:nil];
          }
}
```

As previously, we haven't implemented handleODataChangeComplete, but it's very easy—it simply defers to our callback. Here's the implementation:

```
// Add method to SBODataServiceProxy.m…
// <…> Needs declaration in header
-(void)handleODataChangeComplete:(SBDownloadBucket *)bucket
{
          // good, tell the callback that we did it...
          [self.callback odataFetchOk:nil opCode:bucket.opCode];
}
```

We're now at a point where once we kick off an OData request, we can send it to the server, receive a callback into the proxy and then hand that callback back to the originator of the request. The next stage is to modify the processWorkItems method that we stubbed earlier so that it does something meaningful.

Modifying processWorkItems

Recall that we have an array of work items stored in our workItems property and that processWorkItems is called as soon as the queue has been initialized. The first operation that processWorkItems will undertake will be to look at the current workItemIndex in relation to the list of work items. If workItemIndex is the same as the length of workItems, there is no more work to be done and getLatest can be called. If there is work to be done, the bookmark referenced from workItemIndex can be handed over the service proxy. Here's the implementation:

```
// Replace method in SBSync.m…
-(void)processWorkItems
{
```

```
        // are we at the end of the list?  if so... time to get latest...
        if(self.workItemIndex == [self.workItems count])
        {
                // return...
                [self getLatest];
                return;
        }

        // get the work item...
        SBSyncWorkItem *item = [self.workItems objectAtIndex:self.workItemIndex];
        NSLog(@"Syncing: %d, %d, %@", item.mode, item.serverId, [[item.entity class]↵
description]);

        // call the service...
        SBBookmarksService *service = [[SBBookmarksService alloc] init];
        if(item.mode == SBODOInsert)
                [service pushInsert:item.entity callback:(SBODataFetchCallback *)self];
        else if(item.mode == SBODOUpdate)
                [service pushUpdate:item.entity serverId:item.serverId↵
callback:(SBODataFetchCallback *)self];
        else if(item.mode == SBODODelete)
                [service pushDelete:item.entity serverId:item.serverId↵
callback:(SBODataFetchCallback *)self];

        // we now need to wait for something to happen...
}
```

When an OData change operation succeeds, the odataFetchOk method will be called on SBSync. We need to do something similar now in the callback depending on the op code as we did in SBODataServiceProxy—specifically, if we receive an OPCODE_ODATACHANGE notification, we need to increment the workItemIndex and call processWorkItems. The logic of processWorkItems dictates whether to run getLatest or do the next in the queue. Here's the revised implementation of odataFetchOk:

```
// Modify odataFetchOk method in SBSync.m…
-(void)odataFetchOk:(SBEntityXmlBucket *)entities opCode:(int)theOpCode
{
        if(theOpCode == OPCODE_ODATAFETCHALL)
        {
                // mode?
                if(self.mode == SBSMPushChanges)
                        [self receiveServerItemsForPushChanges:entities];
                else if(self.mode == SBSMGetLatest)
                        [self receiveServerItemsForGetLatest:entities];
                else
                        @throw [NSException exceptionWithName:[[self class]↵
description] reason:@"Mode was unhandled" userInfo:nil];
        }
```

```
        else if(theOpCode == OPCODE_ODATACHANGE)
        {
                // fire the next one in the queue...
                self.workItemIndex++;
                [self processWorkItems];
        }
        else

                @throw [NSException exceptionWithName:[[self class] description]↵
reason:@"Operation code was unhandled" userInfo:nil];
}
```

We're now at a point where we can run the application and successfully synchronize some changes up to the server. Figure 11-18 illustrates a change to the text of my **Topaz Filer** bookmark example being propagated all the way up to the server and back down again into the generic web application, the source code to which can be downloaded from the web site.

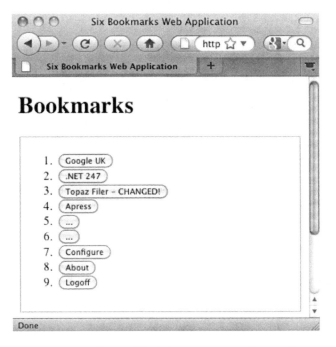

Figure 11-18: *The modified data represented on the Web application.*

Conclusion

In this chapter, we have completed the work to make our Six Bookmarks application fully functional. We can now synchronize our bookmarks with the server and present a user interface for modification.

CHAPTER 12

■ ■ ■

iOS: MonoTouch

In this "bonus" iOS chapter, we're going to take a quick look at MonoTouch. Mono is an open-source project led by Novell to—put simplistically—port the .NET Framework and toolset over to other platforms. MonoTouch is an extension of Mono that essentially ".NET-ifies" Cocoa Touch. You get all of the Cocoa Touch classes exposed as .NET managed classes. You get garbage collection and you get the C# language. It makes developing iOS applications a lot easier.

There are two reasons MonoTouch is an "also-ran" in this book, rather than a main feature. In the first instance, this book is about achieving common tasks natively and directly on the platform of choice. MonoTouch is a third-party, commercial extension and hence does not fit this bill of what I was trying to do with the book. The second instance is that Apple's iOS development ecosystem is a tightly closed and constrained one, and, as of the time of writing, there are many question marks over whether, if you built a solution on MonoTouch today, the resulting stack of source code would have long term viability. Apple have in the past exercised their rights to change the terms and conditions for App Store publications and have a philosophy that the only guaranteed OK way of building applications for the App Store is via Xcode and Cocoa Touch directly. . As of the time of writing, Apple is having a very public spat with Adobe about Flash and the language that they are using in their terms and conditions to control that what goes onto and stays on the App Store excludes third-party frameworks. Although MonoTouch is currently safe (the code it generates is compiled down to native Objective-C, and as such MonoTouch is not an intermediate layer), there's no reason it will remain safe. The only guaranteed safe way to maintain a source code stack that will always compile with Apple's terms for the App Store is to develop natively in Objective-C using Xcode.

■**NOTE** MonoTouch is a slightly strange beast This FAQ contains useful information: `http://monotouch.net/` FAQ.

All that said, if I were to wake up tomorrow and learn that Apple had decided to junk Objective-C and adopt MonoTouch as the preferred way of building applications for iOS, I would be a very happy man. Perhaps even one day, Apple will buy Novell in order to better control the toolset.

Mono in the Big Picture

As of the time of writing, MonoDroid is currently in beta. As its name implies, this is MonoTouch's counterpart on Android.

One of the problems this book is trying to address is how you have a single stack of source code that supports applications running on devices with no common ground. As of the time of writing, it's this author's opinion that the "Coke and Pepsi" of this market will end up being iOS and Android, especially when strong iPad-class devices start coming along from the Android camp. But, in terms of development, iOS and Android could not be more dissimilar if you tried.

If we assume that Apple remains friendly to Novell and Mono in their efforts to bring Mono to the iPhone (and that's an "if" of reasonable size), one interesting solution is to build your business logic in Mono and individual device-specific code for the user interface. This would allow you to simplify the stack of code that you had to develop.

If, in the future, Windows Phone 7 does become a dominant platform, the C# nature of Mono will allow you to continue that strategy over on that camp, too.

(One thing to note about MonoTouch is that you cannot just "dynamically link" to an assembly from a non-MonoTouch world—you have to recompile the code natively on the iOS platform. It's this "recompilation" step that is currently keeping MonoTouch acceptable to those who police the App Store. If it used MSIL and JIT compilation like .NET does, MonoTouch applications would not be allowed.)

Lots of "ifs," but one really important point here is that Mono is really easy to work with and very natural if you're a Java or .NET developer; hence I would say it's definitely worth exploring.

Chapter Structure

In the other sections of this book, the first chapter on each platform has contained instructions on how to install the toolset and create a "Hello, World" application. In this chapter, we'll also follow this format. I'll also run through a quick example of how we can make a call over to our API service; however, we won't be recreating the Six Bookmarks application.

Installing MonoTouch

MonoTouch is a commercial product, and as such you can either download an evaluation version or install a full version. (Mono itself is open-source.) MonoTouch runs only on Mac, which is understandable, seeing as you still need the Interface Builder component of Xcode 3 to build the UI and also need the execution environment and libraries that Xcode itself needs to build and run iOS applications.

■**NOTE** For those that have come to iOS development fresh on Xcode v4, in previous versions the user interface development was done in a separate application called Interface Builder. Starting with v4 of Xcode, Apple rolled the Interface Builder functionality directly into the environment. Thus as of the time of writing, my development box has a production copy of Xcode 3 with Interface Builder and MonoTouch, plus a beta version of Xcode 4.

There are a number of prerequisites that you need in order to install MonoTouch. This chapter is based on MonoTouch version 3.0.9, and the steps here are correct for that version. That said, you should review the prerequisites and the steps required for the version of MonoTouch that is current as of the time you are undertaking this work.

MonoTouch can be downloaded from http://monotouch.net/. The prerequisites for 3.0.9 are the following:

- iPhone SDK (including Xcode)

- Mono for OS X

- MonoDevelop for OS X (the IDE that you use for developing the code)

Once those are installed, you can then install the MonoTouch SDK.

"Hello, World"

I'm going to assume in this chapter that you have already worked through Chapters 11 to 14 and are familiar with building iOS applications in Objective-C.

To get started, open up MonoDevelop—the IDE for Mono applications. (Visual Studio users will notice that MonoDevelop is structured and laid out similarly to Visual Studio.) Create a new project, and from the list select **C# - iPhone and iPad - Universal Window-based Project** and enter the project name.

▦**NOTE** In the version of MonoTouch that I was using, if I created solutions with periods in the name (e.g., "AmxMobile.Something"), the resulting project would not run. If I created solutions with no dots, it would. In addition, I could not get the iPhone Window-based Project working either and hence chose to create a "universal" project.

Figure 12-1 illustrates.

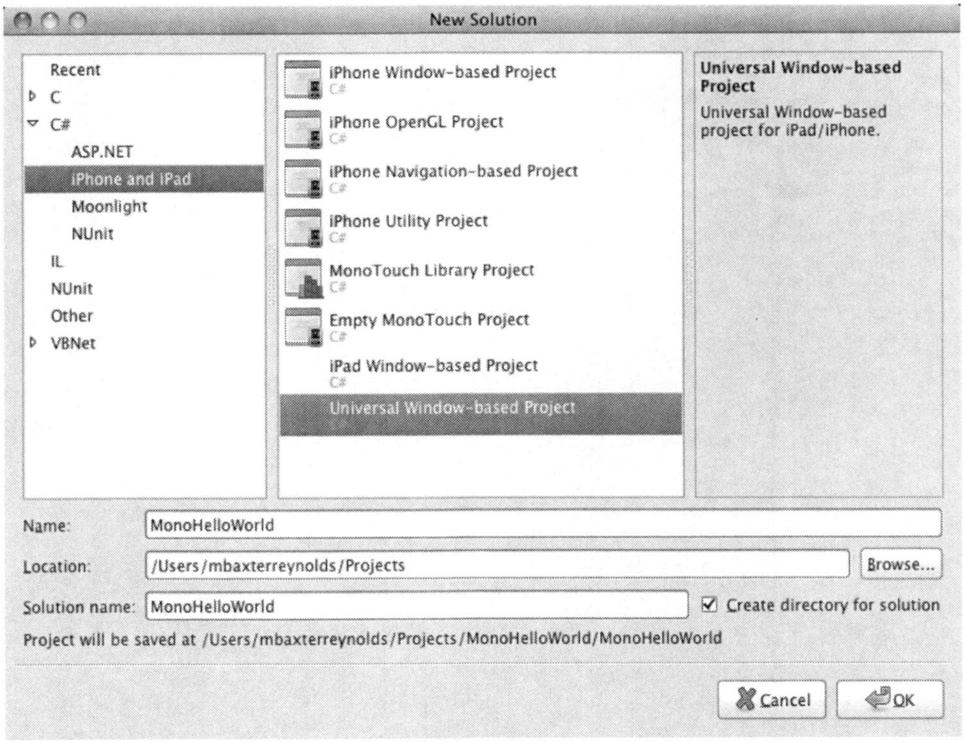

Figure 12-1. *The MonoTouch **New Solution** window*

The project will be created, and you will be presented with a **Solution** explorer view and some code. In the solution tree, you will notice two app delegate classes—one for iPhone and one for iPad. You will also notice two .xib files, again one for iPhone and another for iPad. Figure 12-2 illustrates.

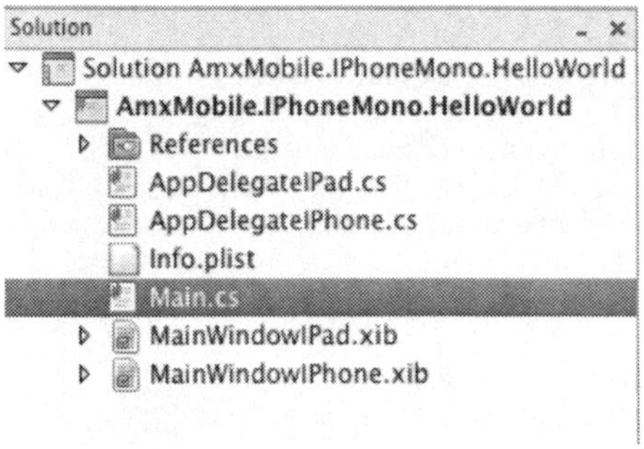

Figure 12-2. *The Solution tree showing iPad and iPhone-specific class and* .xib *files*

Double-click on the MainWindowIPhone.xib file and Interface Builder will start.

You've obviously seen the new "Xcode 4" way of doing this in previous chapters. Interface Builder is essentially the same animal and works in the same way. When the file opens, you'll be presented with a user interface that's comprised of separate windows, as opposed to the Xcode 4 way of doing things, which is to display the items in panes. The functionality is the same, however—you have a control palette, a way of accessing File's Owner, and a separate inspector window for setting attributes and viewing connections.

To get started, onto the design surface add a button and change the text. Figure 12-3 illustrates.

Figure 12-3. *The Interface Builder design surface showing a button*

When we're using MonoTouch, we can take advantage of using .NET events as opposed to the IBAction-marked methods in code. What we need to do is expose the button out to the C# MonoTouch code and at runtime wire up an event.

Before, when we've needed to attach buttons up to code, we've created a property marked with IBOutlet in the Objective-C header file, and made the connection using the **Connections** pane. We need to do this a little bit differently when working with MonoTouch.

We can instruct Interface Builder to create the outlets for us. On the **Library** window, select the **Classes** option from the top. Towards the top of the window, you will see an option for **AppDelegateIPhone**. This option represents the class in our solution. Figure 12-4 illustrates.

Figure 12-4. *The **Classes** view in the **Library** window*

In the bottom panel, there is a list that currently has **Inheritance** selected. Choose **Outlets** from this list. You can now click the **plus** button at the bottom of the window to add a new outlet. Call it **buttonHello** and change its type to **UIButton**. (Changing the type is non-obvious—use the Tab key to move from the name to the type field.) Figure 12-5 illustrates.

Figure 12-5. *Adding an outlet*

We'll see what this does to the code-behind in a moment. For now, we need to wire up the button. This is a little different than how we did it in Objective-C/Xcode.

In the documents window (the one that displays a list of "File's Owner", etc.), select the **App Delegate** object. (This is different in MonoTouch—in Objective-C/Xcode we would have selected **File's Owner**.) In the **Connections** pane you will see **buttonHello**. Drag a connection between this item and the button.

That's all that we need to do in Interface Builder. Quit Interface Builder to save your work and return to MonoDevelop.

■**NOTE** Quitting Interface Builder when you're done tends to be a little more reliable than just saving your work.

Inspecting the Code-Behind

Back in MonoDevelop, it's possible to expand out the MainWindowIPhone.xib file to find a MainWindowIPhone.xib.designer.cs file nestling within. (Visual Studio developers will find this idea of a code-behind file familiar.) Figure 12-6 illustrates.

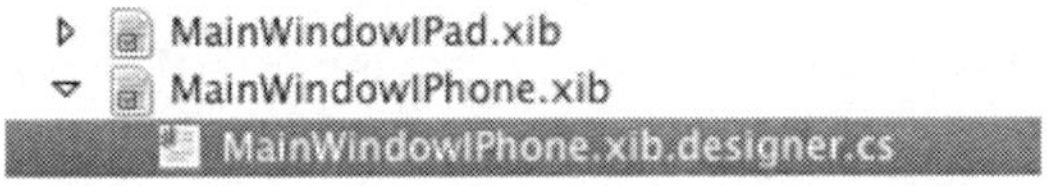

▷ 🗔 MainWindowIPad.xib
▽ 🗔 MainWindowIPhone.xib
    🗎 MainWindowIPhone.xib.designer.cs

Figure 12-6. *The location of the* `.designer.cs` *file behind the* `.xib` *file*

Double-click on the `.designer.cs` file to open in the editor and you will see code like this:

```
namespace MonoHelloWorld {


        // Base type probably should be MonoTouch.Foundation.NSObject or subclass
        [MonoTouch.Foundation.Register("AppDelegateIPhone")]
        public partial class AppDelegateIPhone {

                private MonoTouch.UIKit.UIWindow __mt_window;

                private MonoTouch.UIKit.UIButton __mt_buttonHello;

                #pragma warning disable 0169
                [MonoTouch.Foundation.Connect("window")]
                private MonoTouch.UIKit.UIWindow window {
                        get {
                                this.__mt_window =↩
((MonoTouch.UIKit.UIWindow)(this.GetNativeField("window")));
                                return this.__mt_window;
                        }
                        set {
                                this.__mt_window = value;
                                this.SetNativeField("window", value);
                        }
                }

                [MonoTouch.Foundation.Connect("buttonHello")]
                private MonoTouch.UIKit.UIButton buttonHello {
                        get {
                                this.__mt_buttonHello =↩
((MonoTouch.UIKit.UIButton)(this.GetNativeField("buttonHello")));
                                return this.__mt_buttonHello;
                        }
                        set {
                                this.__mt_buttonHello = value;
                                this.SetNativeField("buttonHello", value);
                        }
                }
        }
}
```

I've highlighted the important code there—what MonoDevelop has done is created for us a read/write property and associated field for holding an instance of `MonoTouch.UIKit.UIButton`. This class is a .NET managed wrapper class over the standard Cocoa Touch UIButton class. Let's look at how we use it.

Wiring Up the Button

To wire up the button, open the `AppDelegateIPhone.cs` class. Within it you will find a method called `FinishedLaunching`. (You may remember a method with the same name in the Objective-C/Xcode world.) What we need to do is wire up a handler.

I'll take you through this step-by-step—although you're already hugely familiar with how Intellisense-like autocompletion works, I want to illustrate how much like working with C# in Visual Studio this is.

With your cursor inside the `FinishedLaunching` method, type `button,` and you will be presented with a code-completion popup. Figure 12-7 illustrates.

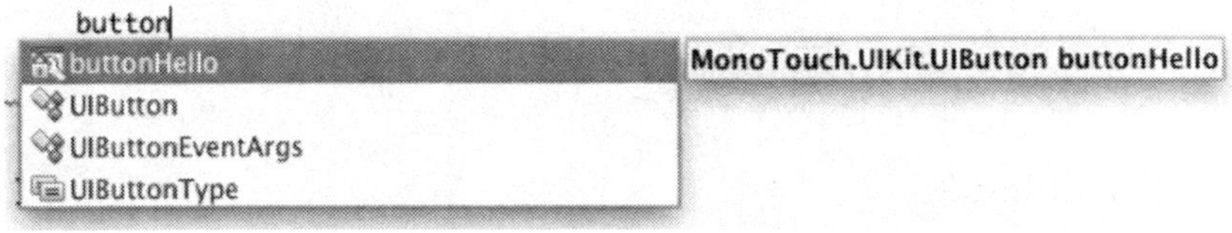

Figure 12-7. *Starting to show the autocomplete feature in MonoDevelop*

Press Tab to complete `buttonHello`, then press "." to pop up the next set of members. Type **touch** and you will be presented with more options. The `TouchUpInside` event is now available. Figure 12-8 illustrates.

Figure 12-8. *Available events on the button that start with the text "touchup"*

Press Tab to autocomplete and then enter "+=" to indicate that you want to add a handler. You'll be given two options to create an anonymous method to use as a handle, and one option to create a stubbed-out full/regular method handler. Figure 12-9 illustrates.

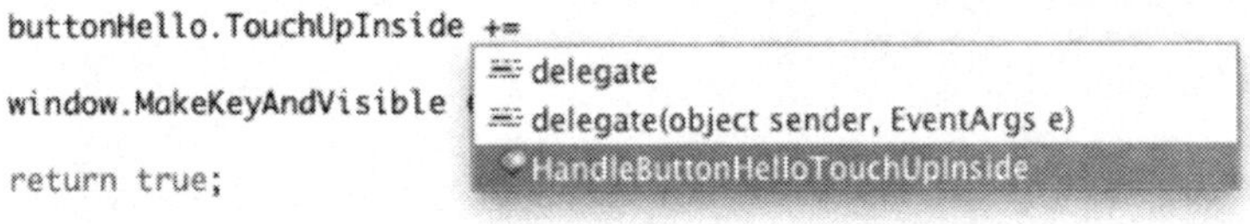

Figure 12-9. *Autocomplete offers to create a method stub or anonymous method handlers.*

Press Tab and the new method will be created. Our FinishedLaunching code now looks like this:

```
        public override bool FinishedLaunching (UIApplication app, NSDictionary↵
options)
        {
                // If you have defined a view, add it here:
                // window.AddSubview (navigationController.View);

                window.MakeKeyAndVisible ();

                buttonHello.TouchUpInside += HandleButtonHelloTouchUpInside;

                return true;
        }
```

In the method handler, we can use the regular UIAlertView class, although what we're actually using is a MonoTouch wrapper class over the underlying Cocoa Touch class. Here's the code:

```
// Implement method in AppDelegateIPhone.cs…
void HandleButtonHelloTouchUpInside (object sender, EventArgs e)
{
        UIAlertView view = new UIAlertView();
        view.Title = "Say Hello!";
        view.Message = "Hello, World!";
        view.AddButton("OK");
        view.Show();
}
```

A quick thing to note about memory management—we don't need to call release on the UIAlertView instance. MonoTouch's garbage collection implementation is going to deal with this for us. Fabulous!

Running the Project

Running the project is just a matter of compiling and asking the iPhone Simulator to run it for us—exactly the same as we would do in Xcode.

The only thing we need to do before we can run it is to configure MonoDevelop to use the simulator and not a physical device. From the menu, select **Project ➤ iPhone Simulator Target ➤ iPhone Simulator 4.0**. Then run the project by selecting **Run ➤ Run** from the menu. The project will start and you can click the button. Figure 12-10 illustrates.

Figure 12-10. *MonoTouch says "Hello"!*

Calling the Six Bookmarks API RESTful Service

We now know that we can do something trivial (and familiar) with MonoTouch. Let's look now at how we can do something a little more meaningful.

As I said before, one option we have for Mono is to build our business tier in Mono and device-specific UIs in the native API. What we'll do in this section is put together some really basic code that calls up to our API Six Bookmarks service, grabs a token, and puts it on the screen.

We'll recreate some of the relevant classes from the previous Android and iPhone sections (the code will be more similar to the Android code, as Java is closer to .NET than Objective-C), but certainly not all of the classes and methods will be created. I'm not going to go through the code in any detail—we've seen these classes in one form or another already. My objective here is to give you a sense of how you can create a .NET/Java-like structure in an iOS world.

Creating the Project

To start, create a new **C# - Universal Window-based Project** in MonoDevelop called **MonoApiLogon** or something similar.

Building ServiceProxy Et Al.

Recall that in the Android application, we had ServiceProxy, RestServiceProxy, and ApiService classes, all with varying specializations. We also had sister classes to those in the iOS application. These classes need some support classes—specifically RestRequestArgs, which holds a list of arguments to go up to the RESTful service, HttpDownloadSettings, which holds a list of special HTTP headers (specifically we're going to need **x-amx-apiusername**), and HttpHelper, which in this case will have a sole activity of creating the URL to the RESTful service based on settings in RestRequestArgs.

First, here's RestRequestArgs. Whenever we create a class in this chapter, just right-click on the file and select **Add ➤ New File**. Create a regular **Empty Class** from the **General** group.

■**NOTE** If you're using a Mac Mini with a Windows two-button mouse, you may find that MonoDevelop's context menus do not work properly when opened with a right-click. Hold down the Ctrl key and left-click instead.

```
using System;
using System.Collections.Generic;

namespace MonoApiLogon
{
        public class RestRequestArgs : Dictionary<string, string>
        {
                public RestRequestArgs (string operation)
                {
                        this["operation"] = operation;
                }
        }
}
```

Of note here is that we have generics in MonoTouch, which we do not have in Objective-C.

Second, here's HttpDownloadSettings:

```
using System;
using System.Collections.Generic;

namespace MonoApiLogon
{
        public class HttpDownloadSettings
        {
                public Dictionary<string, string>  ExtraHeaders { get; private set; }

                public HttpDownloadSettings ()
                {
                        this.ExtraHeaders = new Dictionary<string, string>();
                }
        }
}
```

And finally for the helper methods, here's `HttpHelper`:

```
using System;
using System.Text;
using System.Collections;

namespace MonoApiLogon
{
        public static class HttpHelper
        {
                public static string BuildUrl(string url, IDictionary values)
                {
                        StringBuilder builder = new StringBuilder();

                        // existing?
                        int index = url.IndexOf("?");
                        if(index == -1)
                                builder.Append(url);
                        else
                                builder.Append(url.Substring(0, index));

                        // add...
                        bool first = true;
                        foreach(string name in values.Keys)
                        {
                                if(first)
                                {
                                        builder.Append("?");
                                        first = false;
                                }
                                else
                                        builder.Append("&");

                                // value...
                                builder.Append(name);
                                builder.Append("=");
                                builder.Append(values[name]);
                        }

                        // return...
                        return builder.ToString();
                }
        }
}
```

Our ServiceProxy implementation needs to hold the service name, return the resolved URL of the service, and provide access to our download settings. (As this implementation is incomplete, GetDownloadSettings will not return the x-api-token value.) Here's the code:

```
using System;

namespace MonoApiLogon
{
        public abstract class ServiceProxy
        {
                // YOU MUST CHANGE THESE IN ORDER TO USE THIS SAMPLE...
                public const string ApiUsername = "amxmobile";
                public const string ApiPassword = "password";

                private string ServiceName { get; set; }

                protected ServiceProxy (string serviceName)
                {
                        // set...
                        this.ServiceName = serviceName;
                }

                public string ResolvedServiceUrl
                {
                        get
                        {
                                return "http://services.multimobiledevelopment.com/" +↩
this.ServiceName;
                        }
                }

                internal HttpDownloadSettings GetDownloadSettings()
                {
                        HttpDownloadSettings settings = new HttpDownloadSettings();
                        settings.ExtraHeaders["x-amx-apiusername"] =↩
ServiceProxy.ApiUsername;

                        // return...
                        return settings;
                }
        }
}
```

RestServiceProxy is the method that contains the "meat." This will use the regular .NET System.Net.HttpWebRequest to make the call up to the server. (We saw this in use in the generic web application.) This is a synchronous call, and hence the thread will block until we return. When we have a return result, we can load it into a System.Xml.XmlDocument instance and parse it. Here's the code:

```
using System;
using System.IO;
using System.Net;
```

```csharp
using System.Xml;
using System.Text;

namespace MonoApiLogon
{
        public abstract class RestServiceProxy : ServiceProxy
        {
                public RestServiceProxy (string serviceName)
                        : base(serviceName)
                {
                }

                protected XmlElement SendRequest(RestRequestArgs args)
                {
                        // build a url...
                        string url = HttpHelper.BuildUrl(this.ResolvedServiceUrl, args);

                        // make a request...
                        HttpWebRequest request = (HttpWebRequest)WebRequest.Create(url);

                        // headers...
                        HttpDownloadSettings settings = this.GetDownloadSettings();
                        foreach(string header in settings.ExtraHeaders.Keys)
                                request.Headers.Add(header, settings.ExtraHeaders[header]);

                        // get a response...
                        HttpWebResponse response = (HttpWebResponse)request.GetResponse();
                        if(response == null)
                                throw new InvalidOperationException("'response' is null.");
                        using(response)
                        {
                                // load the response into xml...
                                XmlDocument doc = new XmlDocument();
                                using(Stream stream = response.GetResponseStream())
                                        doc.Load(stream);

                                // did we get an AmxResponse?
                                XmlElement amxElement =↵
(XmlElement)doc.SelectSingleNode("AmxResponse");
                                if(amxElement == null)
                                        throw new InvalidOperationException↵
("The response did not include an AmxResponse element.");

                                // find the error element...
                                XmlElement hasExceptionElement =↵
(XmlElement)amxElement.SelectSingleNode("HasException");
```

```
                              if(hasExceptionElement == null)
                                      throw new InvalidOperationException↵
("The response did not include a HasException element.");

                              // did we?
                              if(hasExceptionElement.Value == "1" ||↵
string.Compare(hasExceptionElement.Value, "true", true) == 0)
                              {
                                      // error...
                                      XmlElement errorElement =↵
(XmlElement)amxElement.SelectSingleNode("Error");
                                      if(errorElement == null)
                                              throw new InvalidOperationException↵
("The error has not found.");
                                      else
                                              throw new InvalidOperationException↵
(string.Format("The server returned an exception: {0}", errorElement.Value));
                              }
                              else
                                      return amxElement;

                      }
                  }
              }
}
```

Finally, we can build the ApiService. I've made the Logon method very simple—it does not check that the result passed to the service was OK. Here's the code:

```
using System;
using System.Xml;

namespace MonoApiLogon
{
        public class ApiService : RestServiceProxy
        {
                public ApiService ()
                        : base("apirest.aspx")
                {
                }

                public string Logon(string apiPassword)
                {
                        // package a request...
                        RestRequestArgs args = new RestRequestArgs("logon");
                        args["password"] = apiPassword;
```

```
                    // send it...
                    XmlElement element = SendRequest(args);
                    if(element == null)
                            throw new InvalidOperationException("'element' was null.");

                    // find it...  in a real implementation we'd need to look
                    // for logon result, but for now we'll just get the element
                    // out.  see the other implementations for how this is done
                    // properly...
                    XmlElement tokenElement =↵
(XmlElement)element.SelectSingleNode("Token");
                    if(tokenElement == null)
                            throw new InvalidOperationException("A token element was↵
not found.");

                    // return...
                    return tokenElement.InnerText;
            }
        }
}
```

That's all of the business-tier code that we need to build. If you're of a mind to, on the web site you can download the code for the Windows Phone 7 and an ASP.NET-based generic web application, both of which are from the sister book to this one. In those other projects, you will find classes that are very similarly presented to the ones we've just built, illustrating how powerful Mono can be at building cross-platform business-tier code.

Calling the Service Method

When we call the service method, we'll need a way of putting the results on the screen. We'll use the perennial MessageBox class to do this. Here's the code that has two methods—one to display a given piece of text, and another to show an exception.

```
using System;
using MonoTouch.Foundation;
using MonoTouch.UIKit;

namespace MonoApiLogon
{
        public static class MessageBox
        {
                public static void Show(string message)
                {
                        UIAlertView view = new UIAlertView();
                        view.Title = "API Service";
                        view.Message = message;
                        view.AddButton("OK");
```

```
                // show...
                view.Show();
        }

        public static void Show(Exception ex)
        {
                // defer...
                Show(ex.ToString());
        }
    }
}
```

■**NOTE** Although .NET has a System.Windows.Forms.MessageBox class, you don't get this with MonoTouch.

We now need a user interface! This is just going to have a button on it called buttonGo, which the user can click. I won't go through the process of creating the user interface, as apart from the text on the button and the name of the property that maps to the control, it is exactly the same. Figure 12-11 illustrates what the form in MainWindowIPhone.xib looks like.

Figure 12-11. *Another simple form design with a button*

The code for AppDelegateIPhone then has to subscribe to the TouchUpInside event on the button and run the Logon method. Here's the code:

```
// AppDelegateIPhone.cs
using System;
using System.Collections.Generic;
using System.Linq;
using MonoTouch.Foundation;
using MonoTouch.UIKit;

namespace MonoApiLogon
{

    // The name AppDelegateIPhone is referenced in the MainWindowIPhone.xib file.
    public partial class AppDelegateIPhone : UIApplicationDelegate
    {
        // This method is invoked when the application has loaded its UI and
its ready to run
        public override bool FinishedLaunching (UIApplication app, NSDictionary
options)
        {
            // If you have defined a view, add it here:
            // window.AddSubview (navigationController.View);

            // sub...
            this.buttonGo.TouchUpInside += HandleButtonGohandleTouchUpInside;

            window.MakeKeyAndVisible ();

            return true;
        }

        void HandleButtonGohandleTouchUpInside (object sender, EventArgs e)
        {
            // create the API service and make the call...
            try
            {
                ApiService service = new ApiService();
                string token = service.Logon(ServiceProxy.ApiPassword);

                // did we get one?
                if(!(string.IsNullOrEmpty(token)))
                    MessageBox.Show("The token: " + token);
```

```
                    else
                            throw new InvalidOperationException("A token was↵
not returned.");
                    }
                    catch(Exception ex)
                    {
                            MessageBox.Show(ex);
                    }
            }
       }
}
```

If you run the project and click the button, you'll be logged on. Figure 12-12 illustrates a successful result.

■**NOTE** Don't forget to set the target to your iPhone simulator before running the project.

Figure 12-12. *The result! The Mono-based business-tier is able to call the service.*

You may have noticed with that application that when you click the button, the application will hang while the call is made. In addition, the "busy wheel" on the status bar does not spin. This is because we've used a synchronous HTTP call up to the server—as we know it's better on mobile apps to make an asynchronous call. We can accommodate this using the `BeginGetResponse` call on the `HttpWebRequest` instance and then building a delegate-based callback method as we typically would on .NET or Java. However, in terms of our example, I believe we've made the point.

Conclusion

In this chapter, we've looked at MonoTouch, a C#/.NET Framework implementation that runs on iOS and provides some important features, such as garbage collection and anonymous methods to iOS developers. The "fly in the ointment" of MonoTouch is that because it's not 100 percent Apple ratified, there's a chance that Apple may, without notice, turn around and block all MonoTouch applications from the App Store. (If you are building in-house applications with no intention of distribution through the App Store, there's no problem here.) Personally I really like MonoTouch—it makes developing for iOS a hundred times easier than developing in Objective-C and Xcode, plus it goes a long way to solving the problem of having to support applications on Android and iPhone by allowing a common business tier to be based on Mono and custom UIs built for each platform.

Index

▪▪▪

You Need the Companion eBook

Your purchase of this book entitles you to buy the companion PDF-version eBook for only $10. Take the weightless companion with you anywhere.

We believe this Apress title will prove so indispensable that you'll want to carry it with you everywhere, which is why we are offering the companion eBook (in PDF format) for $10 to customers who purchase this book now. Convenient and fully searchable, the PDF version of any content-rich, page-heavy Apress book makes a valuable addition to your programming library. You can easily find and copy code—or perform examples by quickly toggling between instructions and the application. Even simultaneously tackling a donut, diet soda, and complex code becomes simplified with hands-free eBooks!

Once you purchase your book, getting the $10 companion eBook is simple:

❶ Visit **www.apress.com/promo/tendollars/**.

❷ Complete a basic registration form to receive a randomly generated question about this title.

❸ Answer the question correctly in 60 seconds, and you will receive a promotional code to redeem for the $10.00 eBook.

THE EXPERT'S VOICE™

233 Spring Street, New York, NY 10013

Offer valid through 3/11.

Breinigsville, PA USA
24 September 2010
245991BV00004B/1/P

9 781430 231981